# MADAM SPEAKER

ALSO BY SUSAN PAGE

*The Matriarch:*
*Barbara Bush and the Making of an American Dynasty*

# MADAM SPEAKER

## NANCY PELOSI AND THE LESSONS OF POWER

## SUSAN PAGE

TWELVE

NEW YORK   BOSTON

Twelve
Hachette Book Group
1290 Avenue of the Americas, New York, NY 10104
twelvebooks.com
twitter.com/twelvebooks

First Edition: April 2021

Twelve is an imprint of Grand Central Publishing. The Twelve name and logo are trademarks of Hachette Book Group, Inc.

The publisher is not responsible for websites (or their content) that are not owned by the publisher.

The Hachette Speakers Bureau provides a wide range of authors for speaking events. To find out more, go to www.hachettespeakersbureau.com or call (866) 376-6591.

Library of Congress Control Number: 2020948678

ISBNs: 978-1-5387-5069-8 (hardcover), 978-1-5387-5071-1 (ebook)

Printed in the United States of America

LSC-C

Printing 1, 2021

*To Carl*

# Contents

# A CHANGE OF PLANS

*November 8, 2016—Washington, D.C.*

Nancy Pelosi dressed that morning in the colors of the suffragettes, in a white pantsuit and purple top. By the end of the day, she was certain that Hillary Clinton would make history by winning the White House, nearly a century after women had won the right to vote.

As the polls were beginning to close, the House Democratic leader headed to the set of *PBS NewsHour* in suburban Virginia for an interview. When she arrived, she got distressing news, but it wasn't about the election. Sharon Percy Rockefeller, the CEO of public TV station WETA, took her aside to let her know that Gwen Ifill, the program's groundbreaking anchor, was on her deathbed. "She said, 'It's coming to the end for Gwen,'" Pelosi told me, her voice emotional at the memory even four years later. It was public knowledge that Ifill was battling cancer, but only a handful knew that she had gone into hospice care. She would pass away a week later. "It was a very tearful thing—so saddening, so personal for all of us. The night didn't start out well."

On the air, though, Pelosi projected nothing but positivity about what was going to happen when the polls closed. "We will, of course, retain the White House, with the election of Hillary Clinton," she declared flatly. Her self-confidence had been honed by an aptitude for political warfare and a history of election nights. "It will be close, but we will regain the United States Senate. And we will pick up many seats in the House of Representatives."

"Why are you so confident about the White House?" anchor Judy Woodruff asked.

"Because I'm confident in the American people," Pelosi answered. Her certainty was being echoed by the entire Washington political class, an ecosystem that she had maneuvered through and thrived in for decades—and one that was about to get an epic comeuppance.

When Woodruff opened the interview by noting that Pelosi was the highest-ranking female politician in American history, she replied with a smile, "I'm counting the minutes to relinquish that title." At the end, when the journalist repeated that distinction, Pelosi looked theatrically at her watch and replied, "For the moment! For the moment!"

To the astonishment of Pelosi and just about everyone else in American politics, of course, her moment wasn't over. When the returns were counted, the new president would be real estate magnate and reality-TV star Donald Trump. Like it or not, Pelosi would keep her standing as the most powerful woman in American political history for a while longer, and one whose personal plans, known only to her confidantes, had just been upended. She had intended to step back from elective office once Hillary was in the White House. That idea was instantly shelved.

She was crushed that Hillary Clinton had lost. The two women had known each other since they met at the Democratic National Convention in 1984, when Pelosi was chair of the San Francisco host committee and Clinton was the wife of the up-and-coming governor of Arkansas. After Bill Clinton was elected president, they had occasionally clashed, notably over Hillary Clinton's decision to address the United Nations Conference on Women in Beijing in 1995. "She was really against my going," Clinton told me; Pelosi argued it sent the wrong signal at a time when Chinese American human rights activist Harry Wu had been arrested. But over the years they had worked in concert on Democratic politics and policy, and Pelosi had long been an advocate for more women in public office. They shared a certain kinship. Both women were trailblazers who had been attacked and caricatured by their critics.

In 2016, Nancy Pelosi was delighted by the prospect of turning over the most-powerful-woman mantle to a President Hillary Clinton.

At the time, few knew that Pelosi was making plans for the 2016 election to be her valedictory. (To be fair, some of those close to her questioned whether she actually would have followed through if Clinton had won.) After three decades as a congresswoman from California, nearly half of that time as the leader of the House Democrats, Pelosi said she was getting ready to take a breath, dote on her nine grandchildren, perhaps write her memoirs. At seventy-six years old, she was well past the retirement age for almost every workplace except Congress. Some friends thought she might cap her career with an appointment as the U.S. ambassador to Italy or the Vatican. With Hillary Clinton in the White House, Pelosi could be confident that the causes she had fought for would be protected, especially the Affordable Care Act that she had pushed through Congress against all odds.

"I have things to do," she would muse. "Books to write; places to go; grandchildren, first and foremost, to love."

After Nancy Pelosi left the PBS studio, she dropped by the headquarters of the Democratic Congressional Campaign Committee (or DCCC, dubbed "the D-Triple-C") on Capitol Hill, then joined a poll-watching party for big donors at Maryland representative John Delaney's town house nearby. She was on her cell phone, tracking key House races, when she began to get an inkling about what was happening.

She checked in with Pennsylvania congressman Bob Brady, a big-city pol in the mold of Pelosi's father, who had been a three-term mayor of Baltimore. Brady had led the Philadelphia Democratic organization for decades; he knew how to read elections. "My dear friend and confidant," she called him. In their first conversation that night, he was upbeat. Democrats always needed a big edge from the Philadelphia vote to carry the state, and he assured her they would deliver it. In their second conversation, he struck a note of caution. "We're going to get our vote," he told her, but "there's a lot coming in for the rest of the state [that was] not so good." He still thought the city vote could offset it, though.

"Then he called and said, 'It's not going to happen here,'" Pelosi recalled, a conversation that took her breath away. She told me she wasn't ready to inform those around her that, in her judgment, the loss of the swing state of Pennsylvania meant the presidential election was over. But she did stop offering reassurances. "I didn't deflect their concern by saying, 'Don't worry; it's going to be okay,' because it wasn't going to be okay."

The blunt-spoken, gravelly-voiced Brady recalled the conversation for me, too.

"I told her in the city of Philadelphia, we turned out maybe the most we ever did, a 470,000 majority," he told me. "But she was kind of pissed off at a couple other people" in the state who hadn't delivered, including in the area around Pittsburgh. "The ones in Allegheny County, they usually do 150, 130"—meaning a Democratic advantage of 150,000 or 130,000 votes, needed to offset Republican areas of the state. "They did like 80 or 90. She was pretty disturbed about that."

Trump would carry Pennsylvania by less than a single percentage point, driven by turnout in small towns and rural areas and unexpected strength around industrial centers like Pittsburgh. His narrow victories in a trio of manufacturing states that Democrats had counted on—Michigan, Wisconsin, and Pennsylvania—would give him a majority in the Electoral College, though he lost the national popular vote.

Even more than being disappointed that Hillary Clinton had lost, Nancy Pelosi was horrified over the candidate who had won. The shock and pain she felt that night when she realized Donald Trump would win the presidency "was physical; it was actually physical," she told me. "Like a mule kicking you in the back over and over again." Trump's improbable victory changed his life and the country's trajectory. It changed her life as well.

Republicans had won the White House and maintained majorities, albeit smaller ones, in the Senate and the House of Representatives. Their unified control of the executive and legislative branches could make it possible for them to deliver on their campaign promises to unravel the landmark health care legislation and to reverse the course President Barack Obama, with her crucial support, had set during the previous eight years on health care, climate change, nuclear proliferation, and more.

"I was like, 'How could it be that person is going to be president of the United States?'" Pelosi told me. It wasn't just that the glass ceiling for women in American politics had been left intact. "That was saddening, but the election of Donald Trump was stunningly scary, and it was justified to be scared. How could they elect such a person—who talked that way about women, who was so crude and...to me, creepy. And now he's going to be president of the United States?"

She saw him as unfit for the White House. Now she would emerge as his most persistent Democratic foil on Capitol Hill and across the country. By midnight Tuesday, Nancy Pelosi knew that she wasn't going anywhere. The election she thought would be the end of her career became instead the beginning of its most consequential chapter.

———

Early Wednesday morning, when the six-year-old daughter of Nadeam Elshami, Pelosi's chief of staff, woke up, she asked her father expectantly, "Did the girl win?"

"No," he told her.

She burst into tears.

Elshami relayed his daughter's reaction to Hillary Clinton's defeat when Pelosi's staff gathered later that morning. That was how a lot of them felt, he said. "Everybody can cry," he said. "You can let it out now." But get over it fast, he went on, because they needed to get back to work. "Look, this is where we are. We have a new president. We have a job to do. The leader has a job to do."

Pelosi reached out to Hillary Clinton the day after the election. "It was a somber and sad conversation," Clinton told me, "because it wasn't what either of us expected."

She also reached out to the president-elect. Pelosi called him at Trump Tower in New York; he was the one who picked up the phone at the other end. He was clearly surprised. How did she get the number? he asked. She thanked him for taking the call and offered her congratulations. She told him she looked forward to working with him, especially where they shared common ground, including the idea of a major federal investment in infrastructure projects.

"Nancy, me too," he replied. "We'll get some good things done." The president-elect praised her as someone who could deliver, "better than anybody." When Pelosi suggested that the president-elect schedule a session soon with the bipartisan Congressional Caucus for Women's Issues, Trump replied, "Talk to my daughter about it," then passed the phone to Ivanka Trump. Now it was Pelosi's turn to be surprised. The House Democratic leader found herself listening to Trump's thirty-five-year-old daughter, whose résumé mostly involved working on enterprises named Trump, relay her thoughts on childcare policy.

It was an early sign of how old norms were going to be disrupted.

"Don't forget, I was a supporter of yours," Trump said at the end of their conversation, a reference to a contribution she had once gotten from him for the Democratic Congressional Campaign Committee, before he was a Republican. "I think you're terrific."

Over time, his view of her would change, and radically. Pelosi would become the unyielding counterpart to Trump, consistently able to get under his skin. She had the power to stand up to him and the aplomb to stare him down, the singular figure who would decide whether and when he would be impeached. The photographs of her in action would become iconic: Striding out of the West Wing in a brick-red coat after she had rebutted the president in their first Oval Office meeting in the wake of the 2018 midterm elections, when Democrats won back the House. Delivering an exaggerated, sardonic clap at his State of the Union address two months later. Standing up at the table in the Cabinet

Room that fall, jabbing her finger at him before she led a Democratic walkout from a meeting where he had derided her as "a third-rate politician." Tearing up the text of the 2020 State of the Union he had just delivered as he stood with his back to her, basking in applause from the Republican side of the chamber.

Her choice of apparel in each of these encounters seemed to telegraph a message, a declaration of intent in red, white, and blue. She wore that memorable red coat talking to reporters in the White House driveway, a white pantsuit at the joint session of Congress, a blue suit in the Cabinet Room session. When she opened the House debate on the articles of impeachment in 2019, she wore a somber black sheath. On her shoulder was a gold brooch that depicted the mace of the House of Representatives, a symbol of authority.

The *New Yorker*'s annual Christmas poem by Ian Frazier, a compendium of couplets about the year's famous, took note of her role.

*And Ms. Pelosi, you are great,*
*The keelson of our ship of state.*

Even after former vice president Joe Biden became the party's presumptive presidential nominee in 2020, Nancy Pelosi would continue to be the most prevalent face of the Democratic Party during a perilous time. While the COVID-19 pandemic forced Biden to conduct a virtual campaign for months from his home in Delaware, Pelosi was on Capitol Hill week after week negotiating trillions of dollars in relief aid and stimulus spending. She became a ubiquitous presence on cable TV, arguing the Democrats' case, negotiating with Treasury Secretary Steven Mnuchin, doing her best to ignore or dismiss the president's tweets. Holding the Democratic Party together.

————

Nancy Pelosi is a tough interview. She is disciplined and precise. She is unapologetic about repeating the same talking points. More than once, she recites favored historic quotes, from Thomas Paine (on the times finding us) to Abraham Lincoln (on the power of public sentiment), from John Kennedy (on world leadership) to Ronald Reagan (on the strength of an immigrant nation). She isn't inclined to indulge in speculation, to discuss the what-ifs. She is rarely willing to dish, although she became more open with me the more often I saw her and the more research I completed. Over time, she became more willing to discuss her thoughts about this triumph or that setback.

In our third interview for this book, I ventured gingerly to ask if she would give me permission to see her high school and college transcripts. I already had interviewed classmates at the Institute of Notre Dame in Baltimore and at Trinity Washington University, and I had spent time on both campuses. At her alma maters, officials expressed pride in their most famous alumna, and they assured me that she had been a perfect student in every way. But because of federal rules and their own policies, they wouldn't let me see her records without her approval. I didn't expect to uncover some explosive revelation—a fourth-grade essay on her secret strategy to become the first female Speaker of the House, say—but I thought her choice of activities or a teacher's notation might be interesting, even illuminating.

When I made the same request of former First Lady Barbara Bush while I had been working on a biography of her, she sent a bemused note to the authorities at the College of Charleston, which had charge of the archives from her former boarding school. "Although I fear she will be unimpressed," she wrote, "I am giving my permission for Susan Page to have access to my academic records at Ashley Hall."

That was not Pelosi's reaction. She looked appalled, as though I had asked to rifle through her closet. She did give me the courtesy of an explanation for turning me down flat.

"I'm a very private person," she told me. That is not the typical attitude of elected officials; some of them pursue political careers precisely because they revel in the spotlight. "That's the thing, when people talk about me in public, I'm like—if I go someplace and I don't have to speak, I'm in my glory. I'm not looking for an audience. I'm as private a person as there is, and a shy one. I've had to be in this role—but I don't intend to go into personal, personal aspects." In case I had somehow missed the point, she added firmly: "No."

That said, as I researched and wrote this biography, she did occasionally go into "personal, personal aspects," although not always intentionally. I am grateful that she agreed to a series of interviews for the book. In the Speaker's office, she would sit so I had the majestic view of the National Mall, and of her four TVs, screens on but sound off. (I wasn't sure she would invite me back after the first interview, when I took a bite into the Dove ice cream bar she had offered and sent tiny shards of the dark chocolate shell flying onto her pristine cream-colored carpet.) The second interview, sans treats, was on the summer afternoon in July 2019 when her dispute with the Squad had exploded; her anger at the four new progressive congresswomen was palpable. The fourth interview fell on the autumn day in November that Trump's impeachment hearings began in the House. Then, she was almost preternaturally calm. I interviewed her the following spring during the coronavirus pandemic that had all but closed the Capitol, on the day after the House passed a historic $484 billion relief package, and again in the summer. By then, in July 2020, the Capitol had been shut down because of COVID-19; besides a handful of aides and Capitol police officers, she and I seemed to be just about the only people in the building. My footsteps echoed through the empty hallways.

Occasionally, I would bring artifacts that my research had uncovered, some of them new to her. There were the precise drawings her mother had submitted to the U.S. Patent Office for a device she had invented in the 1940s to give steam facials. A formal portrait of her father as a young man with his parents, uncovered in a dusty cardboard box of mayoral memorabilia stored at the University of Baltimore. A tiny "D'Alesandro for Mayor" campaign button, found by one of my sons on eBay. Handwritten memos dictated by Pennsylvania congressman John Murtha, the crusty Marine veteran who had run her first campaign for the leadership. Discovered in a file in his archives at the University of Pittsburgh, the notes were preparation for a memoir he never got around to writing before he died.

Pelosi, openly moved when she read those notes, asked to keep a copy.

"Some of the old guys were very hesitant to have a woman as Speaker," Murtha had said, dictating to an aide who wrote in red ink across a white legal pad. Elected eighteen times to represent Pennsylvania's 12th Congressional District, Murtha had been a crucial voice in reassuring "the old guys" about her. He listed lessons he had learned from her, about playing the long game and sharing the credit. "Good a political mind as I have ever seen," he said.

———————

While she is a devout Catholic, Nancy Pelosi is not generally given to the mystical. Still, she relayed one hard-to-explain moment at her first meeting with a president at the White House as a member of the congressional leadership. She had just won election as Democratic whip in 2001, making her the highest-ranking woman in the 213-year history of Congress.

She suddenly realized that never before in the nation's history had a woman attended one of these sessions. As President George W. Bush began to speak, "I suddenly felt crowded in my chair," Pelosi recalled. "It was truly an astonishing experience, as if Susan B. Anthony, Elizabeth Cady Stanton, Lucretia Mott, Alice Paul, and all the other suffragettes and activists who had worked hard to advance women in government and in life were right there with me. I was enthralled by their presence, and then I could clearly hear them say: *At last we have a seat at the table.*' After a moment, they were gone."

She insisted that the moment seemed concrete to her, not metaphorical. It was as physical as the kick of a mule she felt on Election Night 2016.

A year later, when Representative Dick Gephardt of Missouri

resigned as Democratic leader after disappointing midterm elections, Pelosi broke a new barrier, becoming the first woman to lead a party in either house of Congress. In 2007, she made the biggest break in what she called the "marble ceiling," a reference to Congress's stately chambers. Democrats had won the House majority and she was elected Speaker, second to the vice president in the line of succession to the presidency. No woman in American history had ever held such a high office.

One of those applauding her rise was Madeleine Albright, the woman who had previously held that distinction. As secretary of state in the Clinton administration, she had been fourth in line. "When I was named secretary of state, I was always introduced as the highest-ranking woman in the American government, in American history at that time," Albright told me. "And I was very glad to give that title up to her."

By then, the relationship between Bush and Pelosi was strained. Pelosi had admired and liked his parents; she kept a photograph of herself with the elder George Bush and Barbara Bush and their families on the mantel in her office. She and George W. Bush shared a certain political heritage; both were members of big political families. But they battled over the war he had launched and she had opposed from the start. She was increasingly frustrated over his refusal to change course in Iraq. Indeed, it was growing public disapproval of the war that had helped Democrats win back the House and install her as Speaker.

Even so, when he arrived in the House chamber to deliver the State of the Union address, on January 23, 2007, Bush struck a gracious note. She introduced him with the traditional words of welcome for the annual speech. "Members of Congress, I have the high privilege and distinct honor of presenting to you the president of the United States," Pelosi said.

When the applause subsided, President Bush replied, "And tonight, I have a high privilege and distinct honor of my own—as the first president to begin the State of the Union message with these words: Madam

Speaker." The chamber erupted in a new wave of applause; Pelosi rose to acknowledge it and broke into a wide smile.

Bush mentioned Pelosi's father, elected five times to Congress and present for State of the Union addresses himself in the 1930s and 1940s. In 1987, at age eighty-three and ailing, he summoned the strength to return to the House floor one last time to watch his daughter's first swearing-in. From his wheelchair, he didn't miss the opportunity to lobby House Speaker Jim Wright to give her a prized spot on the Appropriations Committee, a panel on which he had served. He would die two months later. "In his day, the late Congressman Thomas D'Alesandro Jr., from Baltimore, Maryland, saw Presidents Roosevelt and Truman at this rostrum," Bush said. "But nothing could compare with the sight of his only daughter, Nancy, presiding tonight as Speaker of the House of Representatives."

Her gender was groundbreaking. Her legislative achievements would be as well. In 2008, during a financial meltdown that threatened to ignite another Great Depression, Pelosi pushed through an unpopular Wall Street bailout—rescuing Bush, a Republican president, and the nation's economy—even though the GOP didn't deliver the votes promised from its side of the aisle. Two years later, with Democrat Barack Obama in the White House, she muscled through the Affordable Care Act after almost everyone else doubted it could be done.

Yet Nancy Pelosi was regularly demonized and routinely underestimated.

Sexism was part of it, the sort of reflexive brush-off faced by many women breaking into more powerful roles in business and the military, in arts and academia. There had never been another politician at her level who wore Armani suits and four-inch Manolos. In a slight she never forgot, *Time* magazine didn't put her on its cover through her entire first tenure as Speaker, despite the history she had made. Two weeks after the 2010 midterms gave back the House majority to Republicans, the magazine's cover featured a flattering photo of John Boehner and the headline "Mr. Speaker."

Some of it also reflected her own particular combination of strengths and weaknesses. She was a master of the inside game of politics. "One of the very best inside political players that I've ever seen," Hillary Clinton told me. But even after decades in office, Nancy Pelosi wasn't particularly skilled at the outside game. She was never a compelling orator. "A rhetorical clunkiness—heavy on the alliteration—that makes her sound now and then like a compendium of bumper stickers," a friendly commentator observed. In a television age, she wasn't as comfortable as former Speaker Newt Gingrich in the back-and-forth combat of the Sunday morning shows. She didn't project the reassuring, old-shoe mien of former Speaker Tip O'Neill.

Nancy Pelosi typically came across as determined, focused, even fierce—all qualities that helped her rise in a man's world. Only occasionally would she display flashes of the warmth and humor that her friends described. She was so disciplined that she could seem robotic. She had to work to slow down her breathless staccato. She would sometimes stumble over words, prompting detractors to falsely accuse her of being drunk, although in fact she rarely had a drink beyond a sip of champagne on celebratory occasions. (That included the time Janet Yellen rather than Larry Summers was named to chair the Federal Reserve.) Republicans caricatured her as a loony left-winger, a "San Francisco liberal."

Her reputation became sufficiently toxic among conservative voters that GOP groups used the prospect of having her in power as a reason to defeat Democratic candidates generally. During her leadership race in 2016, the National Republican Congressional Committee hung a sarcastic "Hire Pelosi" banner across the front of GOP headquarters, within sight of the Capitol grounds. The House Republicans' campaign arm expressed delight when she prevailed. "Congrats Nancy!" a new banner declared.

Unknown to most, she had been seriously contemplating retirement that year when the unexpected election of Trump changed her mind. Now, whatever her shortcomings, she seemed to be precisely the right person at the right time. Tim Ryan, the Ohio congressman who challenged her for the Democratic leadership in 2016, acknowledged that to me in 2020. "Her political instincts—nobody I ever worked with had any better instincts," he told me. She eventually would command the solid backing of Democrats. Even those who had questioned her leadership in the past came to view her as indispensable in the era of Trump.

President Trump rattled her publicly only once—during a State of the Union address that included the presentation of the Presidential Medal of Freedom to Rush Limbaugh—but Pelosi regularly rattled him. When he stomped out of a White House meeting after a confrontation over funding a wall along the Mexican border, she was dismissive. "It's a temper tantrum by the president," she said.

Here's how she described her job: "Every day I'm like, 'Don a suit of armor, put on your brass knuckles, eat nails for breakfast, and go out there and stop them from taking children out of the arms of their parents, food out of the mouths of babies." She didn't see all that as particularly remarkable. "I mean, it's just the way it is."

Her attitude of politics-as-war fueled the capital's hyperpartisanship. The Republican Speaker who succeeded her, John Boehner, told me that she didn't moderate her rhetoric even when he tried to do so. President George W. Bush privately complained to aides that she was unwilling to respond to his outstretched hand. Even Democrat Barack Obama told a senior White House aide that he felt at times as though she was hectoring him. Pelosi only had one gear—full steam ahead—even when the occasion might have welcomed a lighter touch.

That said, it was a trait her allies came to appreciate.

"The one thing that I understood about Nancy fairly quickly was the fact that she was as tough or tougher than anybody in the world," Obama told me, declaring himself "a booster" of Pelosi. "There are times that I think we underestimate just that kind of being able to grind and grit it out, and she has that kind of capacity." He called her "as effective as any legislative leader I've seen in managing a diverse and often contentious group of folks with a lot of different points of view."

Boehner told me she was "one of the top leaders that I've worked with over my career, no question." But he added that her unyielding liberal ideology opened the door for the GOP to win back control and make him her successor as Speaker in 2011.

The long and unexpected course of Pelosi's life prepared her to face down a disruptive president during a critical time. The youngest child and only daughter in a family with five brothers, she had figured out from an early age how to assert herself in a male-dominated world. "With all those older brothers, I did have to find ways to hold my own," she said. She grew up comfortable with competition and appreciative of sports; she would later be an avid fan and season-ticket holder for the San Francisco Giants and the San Francisco 49ers. She had been trained in politics by her larger-than-life father, the mayor known to all in Baltimore as Tommy the Elder. She had learned about the art of granting favors and organizing the grass roots from her ambitious, restless mother, known as Big Nancy. She had risen in the Democratic Party as a formidable fund-raiser from the opposite coast, where the Democratic base was shifting. She understood how Congress worked after spending decades there, taking the lead on issues ranging from HIV/AIDS to human rights in China. She had confronted a string of presidents on a variety of issues.

From her first meeting in the White House with Trump, just three days after his inauguration, she would be the figure in the room willing and able to push back at his provocative declarations, the ones she saw as at odds with reality and, eventually, as dangerous to democracy. It was her ability to stand up to President Donald Trump that finally meant Nancy D'Alesandro Pelosi would be underestimated no more.

CHAPTER ONE

# TOMMY THE ELDER AND BIG NANCY

*1916—St. Leo's School, Baltimore*

Thomas Ludwig John D'Alesandro Jr., who in time would become the father of Nancy D'Alesandro Pelosi, was thirteen years old when Sister Pauline informed him that St. Leo's School would not be the place for him to complete his education.

It had begun, as some catastrophes do, with what seemed like good news.

Weeks before his eighth-grade graduation ceremony was planned at Little Italy's parochial school, Tommy D'Alesandro won a spelling bee and was awarded a medal of the Blessed Virgin, which the nun pinned to his shirt. "At recess time one of the boys in my class gave me the razz-berry as a sissy for wearing the medal," Tommy would recall toward the end of his long and eventful life. What's a boy to do? "I picked up a rock and threw it at him, cutting his head."

That started a downward spiral. Sister Pauline, both the teacher of his class of five students and the head of the school, told him she wanted to see his father the next morning. Wary of a whipping, Tommy was reluctant to tell his dad about the day's developments. When he returned to school the next morning, no parent in sight, he told her that his father couldn't be there because he was suffering from pleurisy, a painful inflammation of the chest and an ailment so particular that surely no child would have made it up. A day later, Sister Pauline saw Tommy's mother at morning Mass—Mrs. D'Alesandro attended every day—and told her that she was praying for her husband in his (imaginary) battle with pleurisy.

With that, the jig was up, the lie revealed. It was not the first mischief by Tommy, and it was the last straw for Sister Pauline. He was expelled. For good measure, so were the three other boys in his class. The sole eighth grader who managed to graduate from St. Leo's that spring was the only girl in the class, Catherine Clark. (In that small-world way of things, she would become the matriarch of one of Baltimore's most prominent political families.)

To be clear, Tommy D'Alesandro wasn't exactly devastated by the abrupt end of his formal education. He was smart but not serious about his studies, ambitious but not persuaded that the classroom was going to provide the essential skills for the adventurous if ill-defined life he saw ahead for himself. Barely a teenager, he already was remarkably self-confident, a master storyteller in the making who could charm just about anyone—a notable exception being Sister Pauline, who warned him that he would never amount to much in life. While he was no longer welcome at St. Leo's School, he could have enrolled in the local public school, of course, although the families in his neighborhood favored St. Leo's. In Baltimore, St. Leo the Great Roman Catholic Church was the place where the babies of Little Italy were baptized, the children educated, the couples married, the dead mourned.

Tommy's sprawling family sat squarely in the middle of it all.

He was born at the start of an optimistic new American century, on August 1, 1903, the son of Tommaso D'Alesandro Sr. and Marie Antoinette Foppiano. He was one of thirteen children. His mother could not have been happy about the news of her son's expulsion from her alma mater, though the demands of rearing her brood and keeping boarders in the basement—among them the occasional organ grinder and his monkey—meant that she had no shortage of other things to worry about as well.

Years later, after he had been elected mayor of Baltimore, Tommy D'Alesandro Jr. kept in an office drawer a formal photograph of himself as a young man, standing behind his parents; they are seated on small chairs set up on a sidewalk. Father and son are wearing three-piece suits, starched white shirts, four-in-hand ties. White handkerchiefs peek from the pockets of their jackets. A watch chain loops across the front of the elder man's vest; his shoes are polished to a shine. Tommy's mother, a sturdy woman in a simple dark dress, has pulled up her hair into a frazzled bun, her lined face betraying just a hint of bemusement.

Their errant son would go far, although he never went far. He grew up in a crowded row house at 235 Albemarle Street; he would die eighty-four years later while living in another small row house down the block, at 245 Albemarle Street. He never moved out of the neighborhood, not even after he had the money and stature to choose fancier precincts. "I'm a *paisano*," he would explain—a peasant, a countryman. "These are my people. This is where I belong." He would be elected to Congress and to City Hall. He would drink bourbon with Harry Truman and call Franklin D. Roosevelt "boss." He would live to see one son inaugurated as mayor and his only daughter launch an unexpected career that would make her the most powerful woman in American history.

All that was down the road, though. At the moment, Tommy needed a toehold. He had been earning pocket change by selling newspapers on the street and peddling chewing gum to the prostitutes who leaned out the windows of the brothels along Caroline Street. He was paid seven or eight cents a week—"enough to go to the movies and buy an apple on the stick"—for serving as a *Shabbos goy*, performing small household tasks for Orthodox Jews during the Sabbath. He got a job at the Union Box Factory for $6.60 a week, building ammunition boxes for French and British troops fighting in World War I. He worked briefly, and unhappily, at the McCormick & Company spice plant, then an institution in downtown Baltimore, assigned to the powdered mustard department.

Finally, he landed a job as an office boy for the Harry T. Poor Insurance Agency, even though he was on the lam from the city's truant officers and working in violation of the state's child labor laws. When he turned fourteen years old, he demanded a raise. His boss offered him $5 a week. "No, I got to have $7," Tommy said. Why? "A dollar a day for working and a dollar for Sunday," he replied. Fine, his boss agreed, giving him an early lesson in the rewards of asserting himself, of chutzpah.

Finally, Tommy had found an education he saw as valuable. Sent out to collect fees from insurance clients, he learned to speak Italian dialects other than his father's Abruzzese. He ventured beyond Little Italy's boundaries into other ethnic enclaves, making friends and connections with the Irish and the Poles and the Jews. He spoke a little Yiddish and picked up a bit of Chinese. When he turned twenty-one, Tommy was old enough to get a license to sell insurance policies for the firm, by then called Poor and Alexander. The insurance business proved to be an apt and lucrative fit for his powers of persuasion, and a lifetime vocation. For a time, he attended Calvert Business College at night, though he never received a degree. That seemed an unnecessary formality.

He had settled on a new course: politics.

Even Sister Pauline eventually came around. "Many years later, when I was a congressman, the good sisters of St. Leo's set up a ceremony in the school yard," Tommy D'Alesandro recalled, "and presented me with my diploma, at last."

———

Eight years old and perched on his mother's shoulders, Tommy D'Alesandro was introduced to the drama of politics courtesy of William Jennings Bryan and Woodrow Wilson.

Baltimore was hosting the 1912 Democratic National Convention, gaveled to order in the Fifth Regiment Armory, an imposing brick fortress in midtown. A small temporary stage and rows of folding chairs had been set up in the cavernous main hall and draped with red–white–and-blue bunting. "The way I've heard the story is that when he was a little boy, his mother took him to the convention that was held in Baltimore," Nancy Pelosi said of her father years later. "She carried him on her shoulders, and he felt the spark and then it just continued."

There were plenty of sparks in the armory; choosing the nominee would require the most ballots cast at any convention since the Civil War. As it happened, the Speaker of the House, Champ Clark of Missouri, was the early front-runner. On the ninth ballot, he seemed poised to prevail when Tammany Hall threw its support behind him. But William Jennings Bryan, the Nebraska populist, roared in objection. His voice carried: Democrats had nominated Bryan for president three times in the past, though he had lost the general election each time. He had stayed neutral in the 1912 nomination battle until then.

Denouncing New York's political machine as corrupt and Clark as the candidate of Wall Street, Bryan endorsed New Jersey governor Woodrow Wilson, a former president of Princeton University who had been elected to office just two years earlier. Bryan revived Wilson's presidential prospects, by then so faded that he was preparing a concession statement. Not until the forty-sixth ballot was the nomination settled, and in Wilson's favor. That fall, he would become the first Democratic president to win the White House in two decades. He was helped by the divisions in the GOP between incumbent William Howard Taft and Teddy Roosevelt, a former Republican president running as the Progressive Party nominee.

Soon after he was old enough to vote, at twenty-one, Tommy D'Alesandro was ready to run for office himself. He was a popular young man, active in church carnivals and neighborhood dramatic productions, a natty dresser and a ballroom dancer so dexterous that he entered regional competitions. He groomed a pencil mustache that would become his signature. He already had been ringing doorbells and passing out flyers for local candidates. He wanted to run for the

Maryland House of Delegates, so he sought the blessing of the Third Ward Democratic Club, which included Little Italy. The local bosses could be found playing pinochle and smoking cigars in the grand Rennert Hotel, famed for its oysters and the watering hole for journalist H. L. Mencken, among others.

They told the cocky young man to come back when he had a petition of support signed by five hundred local voters.

That was no problem. He had been working the neighborhood since Sister Pauline expelled him from the eighth grade. He returned with a petition signed by five hundred people and a few extra. A half century later, long retired from politics, he could still recite the petition, word by word, from memory: "We the undersigned registered Democratic voters of the Third Ward of the First Legislative District recommend for your favorable consideration the candidacy of Thomas D'Alesandro, Jr. for the House of Delegates. He was born and raised in the District, knows the people and their needs and would be a credit to both City and State if elected."

Not everyone was charmed. Vincent Palmisano, a Democratic leader in the Third Ward, took an immediate dislike to D'Alesandro, starting a feud that would end years later with Palmisano's political demise.

"He always saw my father as an irritant," one of Tommy D'Alesandro's sons said. "Didn't like his style." Palmisano, a generation older than Tommy, offered to make him "president" of the Third Ward Democratic Club, a move to sideline him. Then he tried to block D'Alesandro from making a speech to the club seeking support. Joining the club required paying three dollars in dues, not a negligible amount for Tommy. He scraped it together with the help of friends, then argued that his membership gave him the right to speak. He delivered remarks he had been practicing in private.

On the night of the primary, D'Alesandro didn't have a radio to listen to the results, but Palmisano, who happened to live around the corner, did. D'Alesandro and some friends sat on the stoop outside his house, eavesdropping on the news and sometimes breaking into cheers "The first thing you know, the radio was thrown out in the middle of the street," D'Alesandro said. With his friends, he headed uptown, to the office of the *Baltimore Sun*; the newspaper posted vote totals on the side of its building on Election Night. He and Palmisano crossed paths, and the two engaged in some trash talk. "Everyone won but you," mocked Palmisano, who was running for the Democratic nomination for Congress. D'Alesandro asked, "Did you win?" Yes, he said. D'Alesandro replied, "If you won, I ran away with it because everybody was clobbering you."

It was 2 a.m. when the *Sun* reported the results from the First District for the Maryland House of Delegates: Thomas D'Alesandro Jr. came in fourth in a field of a dozen Democrats who were vying for six legislative seats from the district. In the overwhelmingly Democratic neighborhood, winning the party's nomination was tantamount to election.

In the general election in November, Tommy D'Alesandro would brag that he got more votes in his district than anyone else on the ballot, including Palmisano. It was the first of twenty-two consecutive elections that Tommy D'Alesandro Jr. would win, and for increasingly powerful posts.

On January 5, 1927, he took the train to Annapolis to report for his first legislative session. He dressed as a statesman, sporting an Oxford gray suit, polka-dot tie, and leather slippers, with a derby perched on his head. He was hailed as the youngest member of the state legislature. "I walked upstairs and I looked for Henry Clay, George Washington, and Abraham Lincoln," he recalled. "All I saw was a bunch of drunks."

He wouldn't stay in the state legislature for long. He had bigger plans.

———

Though Tommy D'Alesandro and Nancy Lombardi grew up on the same street, just a block apart, they didn't really know each other. He was six years older than she was, a big gap when children are small. When he was expelled from St. Leo's to make his way in the world, she was only seven.

But by the time she graduated from high school, from the Institute of Notre Dame, he was considered a catch.

As a newly elected member of the Maryland House of Delegates in 1927, he was invited to an annual reception for state legislators hosted by Governor Albert C. Ritchie. When the Baltimore *Evening Sun* noted that he didn't have a wife to take with him, D'Alesandro was besieged by letters from women across the state who were "perfectly willing to terminate his bachelor days." The newspaper story described him as a "dark-eyed young man" who was "regarded as attractive."

Nancy Lombardi had grown up by the time he noticed her, "a beautiful nineteen-year-old woman leaving St. Leo's church one Sunday morning," Nancy Pelosi said, retelling one of her family's favorite stories. "He followed her down the street and, when she stopped at a corner, went up to her and asked for a date." Unlike the women who had propositioned him by mail a year earlier, she did not swoon. "My mother's response was to tell the dapper legislator that she didn't know who he was and that she would not go out on a date unless her grandmother approved. Hence Daddy's courtship of Mommy's grandmother."

In short order, an engagement followed. "T.L.J. D'Alesandro to Wed Schoolmate," read the local newspaper headline. "Miss Annunciata Lombardi to Become Bride of Assemblyman September 30."

Their wedding—at St. Leo's, of course—was "a traffic-stopping event," Pelosi said. After all, Tommy was a gregarious pol on the rise who seemed to know everyone, in Baltimore and Annapolis. Every member of the Baltimore police and fire departments was invited. So were Governor Ritchie and the entire Maryland House of Delegates. On the morning of the big day, Tommy dispatched the St. Gabriel's Society Band, eighteen musicians strong, to serenade his bride as she got ready at home. (She demanded that he send them away.) After the ceremony, thousands of guests celebrated in the streets. By the time the groom cut the cake in the reception at Lehmann Hall, it was approaching midnight.

For their honeymoon, the newlyweds boarded a train to go to

Montreal, but D'Alesandro had such serious stomach pains that he debarked at Grand Central Station. A doctor in New York diagnosed appendicitis and recommended an immediate operation. "After a conference with his bride," the Baltimore *Evening Sun* reported, the couple instead returned home, where his own doctor diagnosed indigestion.

They moved into a newly built house at 245 Albemarle Street. They would live there for the rest of their lives.

He was twenty-five years old and on his way to winning a second term in the Maryland legislature. After his son and namesake arrived the next year, just about everybody would call the father Tommy the Elder. His wife was nineteen years old and formidable in her own right. After her daughter and namesake was born a dozen years later, just about everybody would call the mother Big Nancy, a nickname that fit her personality and, over time, her power. Her daughter would be known as Little Nancy.

Annunziata Lombardi had been born in Fornelli, Italy, in 1909, the second of five children. Her parents chose her name because she was born on March 30, five days after the Feast of the Annunciation. Her family immigrated to Baltimore when she was an infant, moved back to Italy for a few years, then returned to Baltimore for good. The family had more money and higher social status than the D'Alesandros. "Her grandmother had the first box at the Baltimore Civic Opera, and when she was a little girl, she gave Toscanini a bouquet when he came to Baltimore," Nancy Pelosi told me years later. The famed Italian conductor was a figure of veneration. "Then, when my father was mayor, Toscanini came back to Baltimore, like, twenty-some years later, and she gave Toscanini a bouquet of flowers—so as a little girl and as first lady."

Nancy Lombardi was a striking beauty, always perfectly groomed and elegantly dressed. In her wedding portrait, taken at Markiewicz Photos of Distinction on South Broadway in Baltimore, she displays the steady gaze and straight-backed posture demanded by the nuns who had educated her. Her dark curls are covered by a lace cap; a cluster of pearls on each side of her face holds back an enormous train of voile that cascades down her back and winds into a puddle in front of her feet. Her white dress has a modest V-shaped neckline, trimmed in lace, but the asymmetrical hem of the skirt is short enough in front to show a little leg. She is wearing white satin heels with bows tied at the ankles, and she holds an oversized bouquet of white roses and baby's breath, white ribbons trailing from their stems.

Unlike her husband, Big Nancy had a high school diploma, and not from St. Leo's but from the more exclusive Institute of Notre Dame across town, where she eventually would insist on sending her daughter. Again and again, she would challenge the conventions of the day when it came to her gender. At the time, women in this neighborhood generally were given the choice of being a homemaker or a nun, or perhaps a nurse or a teacher. Instead, she went to work as a clerk for a local auctioneering firm, A. J. Billig & Co. She proved to be so talented as an auctioneer that her employer suggested she go to New York to earn official certification.

She didn't go to New York to become a certified auctioneer, though, and she never realized her lifelong dream of becoming a lawyer. Two years after she graduated from high school, she married D'Alesandro, then ten months later gave birth to Thomas Ludwig John D'Alesandro III. He was born on July 24, 1929, three months before the stock market crashed and the Great Depression began. The next year, in 1930, Nicholas arrived. Then, in 1933, they were joined by Franklin Delano Roosevelt D'Alesandro, named in honor of the president who had been inaugurated for the first time just three days before the baby's birth. The president sent his namesake a handkerchief with "Franklin Roosevelt" stitched on it, a keepsake the D'Alesandros framed.

Over eleven years, the D'Alesandros would have seven children, the first six of them boys—Tommy the Younger and Nicholas and Roosie, then another Nicholas and Hector and Joseph—and finally, a girl.

Nancy Patricia D'Alesandro was born on March 26, 1940, a day after her mother's thirty-first birthday.

Big Nancy was organized and disciplined, the enforcer for her family and, at times, for her husband's political life. She was self-confident and comfortable with power, traits she would pass on to her daughter. She was a risk-taker. Indeed, she played the ponies, a regular presence at Pimlico Race Course, host of the Preakness Stakes, part of horse racing's Triple Crown. The gambling debts she later ran up with bookies who operated from Sabatino's and other restaurants in Little Italy would become the source of neighborhood gossip.

Tragedy struck the young family's life. When their second son, Nicholas, was three years old, in 1934, he fell ill with lobar pneumonia. Two days later, he died. Penicillin had been discovered a decade earlier, but the groundbreaking antibiotic wouldn't be readily available until the 1940s. Tommy D'Alesandro, who had briefly taken a patronage job with the Internal Revenue Service in New York, hurried back to Baltimore to see his son before he passed away.

Four days later, the priests at St. Leo's celebrated a Mass of Angels, conducted for children too young to have made confession and received Communion. Nicholas was laid to rest at New Cathedral Cemetery in Baltimore; later his mother and father and two of his brothers would be buried nearby. The child's body was placed alongside a previous generation of his father's family, John and Jaccintha Forppiano, his name etched below theirs on the simple granite gravestone.

His birth had been a happy occasion considered so newsworthy, given his father's office, that the newspapers covered it. "New Son in Family of Assemblyman," the *Evening Sun* reported. Less than four years later, so was his death. In the *Baltimore Sun*: "D'Alesandro's Child to Be Buried Monday."

More than a decade later, Big Nancy said the scars of her son's death still felt fresh. "That is the kind of sorrow that cuts into your bones and leaves you so numb you feel nothing," she said. "You think you will not live through it, but you do, and it leaves you with an immunity to lesser troubles." She had survived this heartbreak. Now she could ignore "criticism, or snubs, or disappointment," she said, as long as her children and husband were well and reasonably happy.

For the rest of her life, she said, not a single day went by when she didn't think of little Nicky. When Nicholas died, his mother was five months pregnant. When the baby was born that summer, they would christen him with the same name, Nicholas. But in the years that followed, Big Nancy would always say that she had six sons, and seven children, making the point that the Nicholas they had lost had not been forgotten.

Big Nancy would always be ambitious and creative, an entrepreneur by nature. She was constrained not by a lack of imagination but by the limits of opportunity for women in her day. "I often think she was born fifty years too soon," Nancy Pelosi said of her mother. "The truth is that my father and the times held her back." If not for that, she predicted that her mother's political career could have exceeded that of her father, or her own. "If she were starting out now," Pelosi declared, "I'm sure she would be president of the United States."

In 1936, Nancy D'Alesandro bought the copyright to a waltz called "I'm Dreaming," the reason unclear. She composed a prose poem to motherhood, one her daughter would later send to friends when their mothers had passed away. ("Motherhood cannot be understood," it said. "It has its overtones in all languages; like magic it weaves a pattern full of joys, tears, patience, love—each exalting like music of golden bells.")

She was an inventor, proposing some ideas that seemed ridiculous at the time but now sound prescient. "She used to say to me when I was a little girl, 'I know that this telephone can do more things,'" Nancy Pelosi told me. The daughter found that notion disconcerting, worrying about the repercussions of adding video—think FaceTime—to the telephones they had at home. "I was so afraid that she was going to be, like, 'You have to get dressed to answer the phone.'"

In 1942, when her husband was serving in Congress, Big Nancy founded the Velvex Beauty Company, devoted to products that promised smoother, fresher, younger-looking skin by using special oils and an electrical device that gave steam facials. Later she registered her company and patented her inventions.

The patent submissions show black-and-white drawings from various angles of the "Beautifier Vaporizer for Treatment of the Skin." The aluminum urn has a coil at its base, which heats water and oil when plugged in with an electrical cord. A small funnel at the top directs steam to the face of the user. (In 2018, the author's son bought a used Velvex "Beauty by Vapor" machine on eBay for $33.74, a metal tag at the bottom crediting "Nancy D'Alesandro Inc." It was still operational.)

She rented space on the ground floor of the building next to their home for a shop that offered her machines and creams and oils; she would describe them as "an old family beauty secret." The enterprise was featured in articles in the *Philadelphia Inquirer* and the *Baltimore Sun*. "Taxpayers whose faces are becoming lined with worry over politics may be comforted by the news that the Mayor's wife, Nancy D'Alesandro, has completed research on a process to refresh and beautify worn complexions," the *Sun* reported in 1949. She is "smooth-skinned and radiant," the reporter observed, and her device "enables her to face the public for about eight hours without even having to think about a powder puff."

What Big Nancy yearned to do was to practice law, a career in which women were then seen as an oddity at best. She had hoped to study law after she graduated from the Institute of Notre Dame. More than a decade later, just months after Little Nancy was born, she enrolled at the University of Baltimore School of Law.

"When my children grow up, I'll need another interest to keep me busy," she explained to Sara Wilson, who wrote a column called "The Woman's Angle" in Baltimore's *Evening Sun* that featured chatty discursions on fashion, food, and family. "Even now the house seems empty because three of the children are in school. Tommy is in the seventh grade; Roosie is in the second; Nickie started in the first grade this week. That leaves me only Hector and Jo-Jo and Nancy during the daytime."

The notion that having six children under the age of twelve, three of them not yet enrolled in school, would leave a mother with a lot of free time was surely a novel one, then and now. What's more, her husband was a member of Congress and rarely around to help. But she explained her plan for time management. She would attend three evening classes in the fall and up to five in the winter. "The children always go to bed at 7 o'clock," she said. She would be in class from 7:30 to 10:30 p.m. and study during the day.

"I spend most of my time in the front room here, anyway," she said. During the interview, she answered phone calls and chatted in Italian with a neighbor who dropped by for help in filling out a government form. In one of the photographs with the story, Joseph is sitting on top of her desk, drawing; another shows six-month-old Nancy in her lap, chewing on the cord of the phone, while Hector drapes an arm around his mother.

"Don't you see?" she said breezily. "The children take care of themselves. They play together, and the older ones look after the babies. Now that my eldest son is 11, there is little left for me to do. So I plan to go to school while I can."

Her restless energy was apparent. Despite her key role in her husband's political career, she wanted to do something beyond that, beyond being a wife and mother—something for herself. "I feel I should do something constructive to learn more," she said. "I was married a year after I finished school, and this has been my first chance to study."

But her carefully laid plans were soon upended. All at once, several of her sons developed whooping cough, demanding her time and attention. The disease was dangerous; the pertussis vaccine was just undergoing its first large-scale study in the 1930s. It was a terrifying time. Everyone remembered what had happened six years earlier, when Little Nicky had developed lobar pneumonia and died after just two days.

Her dreams of law school were over.

Her husband had never been enthusiastic about his wife's aspirations. "My father was no help," Nancy Pelosi told me. "I mean, he wanted her at home with the children. You get my point? I think he was more confining—not awful, but typical of the era. Why would he want her to have the independence of having a law degree?" When she wanted to invest in land in Ocean City, on Maryland's Eastern Shore, he said no. "I don't want to use the word chauvinistic, but I guess that is the word. It's just the way it was. He wanted her home."

She was home, but she was more than a homemaker. Tommy the Elder and Big Nancy were a fiercely loyal couple and a formidable political partnership. Their skills complemented each other. He was a charismatic campaigner; she was a meticulous organizer. She wrote the fight song for his first campaign for Congress, to the tune of Notre Dame's "Victory March," to be sung at rallies. ("Cheer, cheer for Tommy D'A / He is the winner of every fray / Cast your vote for Tommy D'A / The defender of the U.S.A.")

"She took an active part in my campaigns," her husband said, calling her "a beautiful, intelligent woman well-versed in the affairs of Baltimore." He also called her "an excellent cook."

As he rose in politics, she rose in influence. Over time, she became a trusted adviser in private and a recognized enforcer in public, someone to be reckoned with. Just an invitation to sit at her table at the annual post-election ravioli dinner held at St. Leo's could send a powerful message to insiders about who was welcome, about who was forgiven. She had clout even when her husband was no longer mayor.

During the 1984 campaign, just a month before Election Day, President Reagan made plans to visit Little Italy to dedicate a statue of Christopher Columbus, financed by local contributions and carved from white marble imported from Italy.

As Reagan's visit to the park approached, Vince Culotta put a poster in the window at Sabatino's Restaurant urging people to attend the celebration. "I don't think the poster was in the window for ten minutes and I get a phone call and it was Miss Nancy," he told me. She summoned him to her home a half block away.

"I'm very surprised at you," Big Nancy rebuked him. "All the things your father and Tommy did together when he was in office and all that. I can't believe you put that Republican poster in a window." He tried to defend himself, arguing that the event wasn't a partisan one, but he quickly gave up. He was muttering to himself as he walked back to his restaurant. "I said to myself, I was married, I had children, grown children, and I said to myself, 'I got to be crazy. I got that woman in there and she's in her eighties and she's telling me what to do.'"

Did he remove the poster?

"Oh, yeah," he told me. Of course.

An unsuspecting White House staffer had called the D'Alesandro house with an offer that most pols would consider appealing: a ride with the president to the event in his official limousine. Reagan could pick them up at their house. The woman's voice on the other end of the line replied, "Tell them not to come anywhere near our house after all he's done to poor people in our country." The woman's tone was so fierce that the staffer worried it might represent a threat to the president's safety.

The D'Alesandros' oldest son, himself a former mayor, was driving when the Secret Service called his car phone. Thomas D'Alesandro III pulled over to the side of the road to talk. The official relayed the disturbing conversation. Tommy the Younger assured him that his mother posed no actual physical threat.

When Reagan arrived in Little Italy that day, the D'Alesandros had decamped to her sister's place for the day. But the house at 245 Albemarle Street was plastered with "Mondale for President" signs in every window.

Decades later, the statue would be back in the news. On the Fourth of July in 2020, demonstrators protesting Columbus as a symbol of racism against indigenous peoples toppled it with ropes and threw it into Baltimore's Inner Harbor. Reporters in Washington asked Pelosi about the incident, suggesting that as an Italian American she might be dismayed.

But her response may have reflected her family's dyspeptic attitude toward the statue from its start. "People will do what they do," she said, shrugging.

———

Nancy D'Alesandro would push to give her daughter opportunities she never had, and she reveled in the lives of her granddaughters. In 1993, when Christine Pelosi graduated from the Hastings College of the Law at the University of California, then passed the California bar exam, she sent a formal invitation to her grandmother for the ceremony at which she would take the attorney's oath. She knew that Big Nancy, then eighty-four years old, wasn't likely to travel across the country for it, but she thought the embossed announcement might please her.

"I'm the second happiest person to receive this notice from the bar exam," Big Nancy wrote back in a letter that Christine framed. "How happy I am to see you accomplish what I could not 55 years ago."

Years later, Nancy Pelosi was onstage at the University of Baltimore School of Law commencement to receive a doctor of laws degree, albeit an honorary one. When she delivered the graduation address there in 2013, she recalled how much her mother had longed to attend the school, and to become a lawyer. "She had started law school, and she had seven children, and so four of them were sick at one time; she had to quit, and she never really could go back," she said. Then she quoted her mother's message to a rising generation. "You're living the dream that so many of us women had at that time," she said, "but it just really wasn't possible."

Before she died in 1995, Big Nancy cheered the rise of women in jobs she could never have dreamed to hold. "During the Clinton years…she would be so excited every time he appointed a woman—Madeleine Albright, Wendy Sherman," Nancy Pelosi told me. President Clinton appointed Madeleine Albright as the U.S. ambassador to the United Nations in 1993; she would later become the first woman to serve as secretary of state. Clinton named Sherman, a Baltimore native, as an assistant secretary of state in 1993; she later held senior posts at the State Department in the Clinton and Obama administrations.

By then, Big Nancy was a widow in her eighties, still living in the family home on Albemarle Street, her daughter a rising member of Congress from California.

"Every time a woman was appointed to something that she read in the paper, she would send me the clip," Nancy Pelosi told me. She would say, "Make sure you tell them good luck and I'm rooting for them!"

## CHAPTER TWO

# WELCOME TO AMERICA

*1932—Montenerodomo, Abruzzo, Italy*

Francesco Passalacqua was just a boy then. But a lifetime later, by then an old man in this Italian village, he could still remember when his cousin from the United States visited Montenerodomo, eager to see the place where his father had been born before emigrating across the Atlantic, never to return.

His cousin Thomas D'Alesandro Jr. was a charmer and a go-getter. Not yet thirty years old, he had been elected and reelected to the Maryland House of Delegates, representing Little Italy in Baltimore. Four years earlier, he had married his Italian-born wife at St. Leo's Roman Catholic Church there; they already had two young sons, Thomas and Nicholas. Eventually, they would have six boys in a row, and then, finally, a girl they named Nancy. Perhaps he saw this as the perfect moment to visit his roots, to report back to his father about his hometown.

Montenerodomo seems impossibly isolated. That helps explain why Tommy's father had left as a young man, and why he had never come back to visit. The town is perched on the spine of Italy, atop the Apennine Mountains. Getting there involves cutting off the main highway from Rome and traversing narrow, winding mountain roads. "Keep driving up, and then up, up, up," advised Francesco Passalacqua's granddaughter, named Francesca. The town was little more than a mountain spur of dark rock, she told us. Indeed, its ancient name was Montenero in Domini; *montenero* is Italian for "black mountain." But the trek to the village, going up to an elevation of more than three thousand feet, brought the reward of breathtaking views—on a clear day, of the Tremiti archipelago in the Adriatic Sea.

It was here that Tommaso Fedele D'Alessandro, the grandfather of Nancy D'Alesandro Pelosi, was born on September 11, 1868, to Giuseppe D'Alessandro and Lucia Rossi. (When he moved to the United States, the second "s" in his last name would be dropped; changes in the spelling of names weren't uncommon during the immigration process at the time.) His family cultivated the rocky land and kept a few donkeys. In his hometown, the views were spectacular but his horizons were limited. To this day, the village retains the air of a world apart, home to 680 souls divided into two rival neighborhoods. For years, they rotated the town's annual festival between the main squares on each side. Only recently had they built a central piazza on neutral ground, big enough to hold everyone for the feast day honoring St. Fidelis, the town's patron saint and the source of Tommaso's middle name.

Even now, Francesco—who was D'Alesandro's second cousin—spoke only a local dialect, difficult for outsiders to understand. In a conversation for this book, family members translated for him to standard Italian.

The young American caused a stir when he visited Montenerodomo during the window between two world wars, while Benito Mussolini and his Fascist government were in power. Even the car D'Alesandro drove was a novelty, drawing attention and admiration when he parked it in the square. He visited the Shrine of St. Gabriel, taking along Francesco's older brother. He asked to see the house where his father, Tommaso, was born.

Tommaso D'Alessandro had been twenty-two years old when he left Italy for the United States in 1890. He passed through Ellis Island, worked in New York, then ended up in Baltimore. In 1893, he married Marie Antoinette Foppiano, who had been born in Baltimore. She encouraged him to get more education, to raise his sights. (That fit a family pattern: Her ambition for her husband would be echoed a generation later by her formidable daughter-in-law, who would help propel Thomas Jr.'s political career.) In time, they would have a sprawling family of thirteen children. In their formal portrait, found in a cardboard box of unsorted memorabilia in their son's mayoral archives, an aging Tommaso and Marie are seated side by side. A youthful Thomas Jr. stands just behind—a triangle of solemnity and solidity in the New World.

In Baltimore, Tommaso found a backbreaking job as a laborer at the local quarry. He worked for the railroad, helping dig the tunnel under the city. He earned fifteen or sixteen dollars a month toiling at the enormous pumping station that opened in 1911 at the edge of the harbor, bringing modern sewage treatment to Baltimore.

After getting married, he opened a small grocery on President Street in East Baltimore, living above the store. That was the home in which Tommy D'Alesandro Jr. was born.

"My father didn't make out very well with the store," Tommy D'Alesandro said in an oral history he recorded when he was seventy-two years old. "Most of the people in the neighborhood were hard up and bought on credit—on the book, as they used to say—and when most of them didn't or couldn't pay, he went out of business." The family was always pressed for money. His father often worked two jobs. "He was a city laborer for many years and during World War I he worked at night at the Bartlett-Hayward munitions plant and worked for the city during the day. He had to, with thirteen children and a wife to support."

On the day his son was inaugurated at City Hall, in 1947, Tommaso was emotional. "This is a great country when you can be a city laborer and raise a son to be mayor," he exclaimed to a friend during the ceremonies. Five years later, at Tommaso's funeral, nearly twenty-five hundred mourners, congressmen and judges among them, gathered at St. Leo's for a man the *Evening Sun* described as "an old Italian-American with a merry heart."

After Tommy D'Alesandro visited his father's hometown, his Montenerodomo cousins began to follow his political rise from a distance. He was elected a member of the Baltimore City Council in 1935, a U.S. representative in 1938, and mayor of Baltimore in 1947. But years down the road, they were slow to realize they had a connection to another rising American politician. Francesco's sister, Anna, was the first to suspect their relationship to Nancy Pelosi. In 2007, Italian news outlets covered Pelosi's election as Speaker of the House—newsworthy because she was not only the first woman to hold the job but also the first Italian American. She was the daughter of a former mayor of Baltimore, one story said, and Anna put two and two together. "Just wait and see that she turns out to be our relative," she told the others after she saw a photograph of Pelosi. "This woman looks like us!"

Anna was right; she was Pelosi's second cousin. Francesca was Pelosi's second cousin, twice removed. In an interview for this book in 2019, at age thirty-two, the young woman bore such a strong resemblance that she could have been Pelosi's daughter. What's more, she and other family members had been active in local politics; perhaps it was in their DNA. "Who could have imagined it?" Francesca marveled.

When Nancy Pelosi made an official visit to Italy in 2009, the speaker of Italy's Chamber of Deputies, Gianfranco Fini, presented her with the birth certificates of her grandparents. "Oh, mamma mia, I wasn't expecting this," Pelosi exclaimed. The itinerary for that six-day trip took her to Rome and Florence and Naples, and to the Vatican, where she had a testy meeting with Pope Benedict XVI, but not to Montenerodomo.

The mayor of Montenerodomo, Antonio Tamburrino, had read about her Italian tour. He wrote Pelosi a year later with an invitation to visit, offering to present her with a key to the city and to make her an honorary citizen. He didn't get a response. He wrote again five years later, when she was scheduled to return to Italy to visit the international Expo 2015 in Milan. This time, someone from her staff called. But when he learned where the village was located, he demurred. The drive was too far and the town too remote, he told the mayor.

Indeed, none of the Montenerodomo kin had ever met Pelosi or seen her in person. They assumed they never would. Cosimo, Tommaso's brother, had come the closest. In 1956, he emigrated with their sister, Emilia, to Perth, Australia. As an old man, he visited the United States as a tourist and found a plaque outside Pelosi's congressional office on Capitol Hill. He took a picture of himself standing under the plaque, her name in bronze, and sent it back to the family in Italy.

It never occurred to him to step through the door and ask to meet his great-niece in person, or that she would have any interest in meeting him. "He told us, clearly one cannot just walk up to someone so famous," Francesca explained. "Even if we are relatives, we will never get close." Despite their family ties, she and her parents referred to her as "la Speaker" and "la Pelosi," not presuming the familiarity to use her given name.

Still, they felt a common bloodline and a shared attraction to politics. "We are just a tiny dot" compared to Pelosi's powerful role in politics, Francesca said, "but there is a bit of it in our blood." She expressed pride in their connection, however distant. "It is surely an honor," she told us in 2019. "She is pretty tough. With [President] Trump, she has to be at the top of her game, no?"

Nancy Pelosi credited her grit and stamina to her Italian heritage. "I've always thought I have more energy than anyone because I'm an Italian-American woman," she said. Her Italian-born mother was a crucial partner in her husband's political career. Her Italian grandmother had encouraged her husband to pursue bigger ambitions in a new land. Both women were willing to take risks. "I don't know that I would have the drive, and the energy, and the enthusiasm, and the spirit if I were not Italian-American," Pelosi said. "I really believe that."

Her grandparents were part of a massive wave of immigration around the turn of the twentieth century from southern Italy to the United States, a land of opportunity, albeit not one where everyone was ready to welcome them. Italians gained the unhappy distinction of succeeding the Irish as the target of anti-immigrant and anti-Catholic bias, as a prime example of the perils to American workers posed by an influx of cheap labor. They were the victims of mob violence and lynching, and Congress overhauled immigration laws to keep out Italians and Jews.

———

Tommaso D'Alessandro and Nicola Lombardi were born in villages just forty miles from each other, in the same mountainous part of Italy. But Nancy Pelosi's grandfathers wouldn't meet until their families settled across the street from one another in Baltimore's Little Italy.

Nicola Lombardi, Pelosi's maternal grandfather, was born on March 9, 1878, in Fornelli, Molise, to Giovanni Lombardi and Antonia Petrarca Lombardi. Fornelli was a "sister city" with Warwick, Rhode Island, and residents emigrating to America often would head there, at least at first, where a network of hometown connections could help them get started.

That was the pattern the Lombardi family followed. Antonia's brother had moved to Warwick and opened a shop near a cotton mill. The mill needed workers, and he urged his sister to send her children. Ernesto and Elvira, then twelve and sixteen years old, immigrated in 1897, taking jobs at the mill and finding housing for a time above Vaccaro's Bar. Their older brother, Nicola, arrived a year later. He was twenty.

Nicola would find his bride in America, another Italian emigrée, Concettina Millio, born on April 10, 1883, in Montagnareale, in Sicily. At age twenty, in 1903, she arrived in Boston from a ship that had departed from Naples. Two years later, she and Nicola were married. Soon afterward, they moved back to Fornelli, where Nicola's family had a pasta shop. Their return wasn't unusual. Unlike some immigrant groups, most Italians came to the United States not to flee religious or political persecution but to earn money. "Birds of passage," they were called, moving back when they had saved enough to buy a plot of land in their homeland.

In Fornelli, Concettina Millio Lombardi gave birth to four of their five children, including Annunziata, who would grow up to be Nancy Pelosi's mother. She was born on March 30, 1909, in the family's home at the top of Via Laurelli, near what had been her father's pasta shop. A century later, Villa Lombardi was still standing, now owned by a distant cousin.

When the shop fell on hard times, the family headed back to the United States, this time for good. Concettina's brother Emilio was living in Baltimore, so they moved there. Nicola opened a pasta shop on the edge of Little Italy, much like the one he had run in his Italian hometown. Annunciata was three years old.

Nancy Pelosi's mother would never return to Fornelli, but her maternal grandfather would visit several times. He returned at middle age, in 1922, when he was forty-four years old, and again as an old man, in 1949, in the aftermath of World War II. Then seventy-one, he attended a family wedding and stayed for six months, living in the home of some cousins. It was their daughter who was getting married.

The bride's nineteen-year-old brother was Romano Pilla. Decades later, at age eighty-nine and a man of few words, Romano remembered the visit. In an interview for this book, he recalled Nicola Lombardi as "a large man, very tall." As with Thomas D'Alesandro Jr.'s visit to Montenerodomo, Nicola's arrival in a car was the source of excitement. Many Italian families didn't own cars until the 1950s, and the transition to automobiles was even slower in such a small town.

After Nicola returned to the United States, he kept in touch with his relatives in Fornelli. In 1952, he sent a picture postcard that showed him and his wife with their grown daughter. By then, their daughter was married to Thomas D'Alesandro Jr. and the mother of seven, among them Little Nancy. "A memory of cousins: Nicola and Concettina Lombardi and daughter Nunziatina D'Alessandro," he inscribed on the back.

The postcard was part of a stack of yellowing family letters and photos that Nicola's cousin passed on to her son, Luciano Mascio, in 2017.

The postcard piqued Luciano Mascio's curiosity. A financial consultant at an Italian bank who lived in the nearby town of Monteroduni, he had never heard of his D'Alesandro relatives. The postcard's inscription prompted him to begin researching his genealogy with the help of a friend, Rita Ucci. He discovered his family ties to Thomas D'Alesandro Jr. and Nancy Pelosi.

For a time, Mascio and Ucci posted news of Pelosi's hometown ties on a Facebook page designed to connect the town with residents who had moved away. They called it "Fornelli nel Cuore" ("Fornelli in our Heart"). But they stopped posting items about her because of the heated responses they would draw, a reflection of the toxic politics in the United States. "Basically, every time we posted something about Nancy Pelosi, the people of Fornelli in America latched on to it," Ucci said. "The young people think she is too old-school. There are some people who say they are embarrassed because she is for abortion. Some who say she is bad, they say all kinds of things."

Still, they hoped Nancy Pelosi would one day visit Fornelli, where her mother had been born. If Nancy Pelosi would ever visit Fornelli, she would be "welcomed triumphantly," Ucci promised.

Mascio began: "I am convinced that even those in America who criticize her—"

Ucci completed the thought: "—would change their minds in the moment she draws near."

———

Thomas D'Alesandro Jr. and Nancy Pelosi would remember the experiences their family had in immigrating to the United States—both the hope of a new land and the sting of anti-immigrant sentiment. They would apply the lessons to those coming to America from other places and under different circumstances. D'Alesandro would become an active voice on behalf of Jews trying to flee Nazi Germany. A generation later, Pelosi would push for legal status for young people who had been brought into the country illegally as children, the so-called Dreamers.

During the back-and-forth on immigration policy with President Donald Trump, the signature issue of his 2016 campaign, Nancy Pelosi bristled at his demand that the immigration system be overhauled to rely more heavily on "merit." The president repeatedly proposed replacing family-based immigration rules with a system that would favor those who had higher levels of education and more financial resources.

"But I just want to just say something about the word that they use, *merit*," Pelosi told reporters one day on Capitol Hill, her disdain for the word apparent in her tone. "It is really a condescending word. Are they saying family is without merit? Are they saying most of the people who have ever come to the United States in the history of our country are without merit because they don't have an engineering degree?"

In other words, were they saying that her grandparents, who arrived without education or money, taking just about any job they could get, were without merit? That her father, who never graduated from high school but would become the groundbreaking mayor of a major American city, didn't deserve to be here?

## CHAPTER THREE

# LITTLE NANCY AND THE FAVOR FILE

*March 26, 1940—Baltimore, Maryland*

Nancy's birth made headlines.

"It's a Girl for the D'Alesandros," the *Baltimore News-Post* trumpeted over a four-column photo that showed the swaddled newborn. She had been born only hours earlier, on March 26, 1940, at St. Joseph Hospital. Her mother, propped up on pillows and wearing an embroidered nightgown, was holding the eight-and-a-half-pound baby; the beaming father and five brothers surrounded them. The *Baltimore Sun* had a more political take: "Tommy D'Alesandro Announces Another Sure Vote—It's a Girl." The *Baltimore Guide* offered a prediction that in retrospect seems prescient. "D'Alesandro Will Find New Boss in First Daughter," it said, adding, "We predict that this little lady will soon be a 'Queen' in her own right."

Her big brothers weren't enthusiastic about having a sister join their all-male ranks, her father told reporters, but the neighborhood was delighted. "The whole community was rooting for a girl," her oldest brother, Tommy, then eleven, would recall.

From the start, Nancy Patricia D'Alesandro would grow up in the public eye, her childhood suffused with politics, the high-minded and the nitty-gritty. When she emerged as an increasingly powerful member of Congress, her political lineage would go unrecognized by many because as an adult she had moved to the other coast and taken her husband's name. When she was first elected Speaker of the House in 2007, it was news to some that Nancy Pelosi's father had once been a powerful big-city mayor.

But in Baltimore during those days, just about everybody knew the D'Alesandro family. In their time, they were a local version of what the Kennedy dynasty would become on a national scale, their careers and controversies scrutinized, their home life breathlessly chronicled. Tommy D'Alesandro Jr. was an up-and-coming pol with a glamorous wife. At thirty-six, he had already served two terms in the state legislature and a stint on the Baltimore City Council, then been elected to Congress. He represented Maryland's Third District, centered in Baltimore. He had ousted a six-term incumbent, Vincent Palmisano, in the Democratic primary. Years earlier, Palmisano, a political leader who lived around the corner, had taken an instant dislike to the younger man when he wanted to run for Maryland House of Delegates. Later, it would be D'Alesandro who ended Palmisano's career by winning his House seat.

That would provide one of the political lessons that Nancy D'Alesandro Pelosi never forgot.

"Power's not anything that anybody gives away," she would declare. "You have to fight for it." It was a precept that her father had followed in challenging Palmisano. It was advice she dispensed to Democrats contemplating tough contests. It was the approach she would apply in her own career, winning a position in the House Democratic leadership that a rival had assumed he was in line to claim. That bitter contest put her on the path to become the most powerful woman in the history of American politics.

Tommy D'Alesandro Jr. had long been at odds with Vincent Palmisano. But the most painful grievance he nursed wasn't their clash of ambitions or their differences over fealty to FDR. It was Palmisano's failure to make even a gesture of sympathy to his family at its saddest moment, when three-year-old Nicholas died of pneumonia in 1934. "He didn't even have respect for me to come and visit my boy," D'Alesandro said decades later. He was an old man by then, but he hadn't forgotten. "I used to go see him when he was sick. I didn't think it was personal when you're in politics."

That was another lesson his daughter would never forget. She understood the power of paying respects, of sharing life's joys and hardships—a sincere gesture of humanity, to be sure, and one that built enduring relationships. Two former Senate majority leaders, Republican Bob Dole and Democrat Harry Reid, each told me with delight that she remembered their birthdays every year by sending her signature white orchids. "I don't agree with her philosophy, but I agree with her as a friend," Dole said. When we talked, he was a few weeks from celebrating his ninety-seventh birthday, and looking forward to the annual delivery.

At times of grief, she would make time for those who had lost a loved one, for allies and adversaries, for the prominent and the not so prominent.

When a Washington reporter who had covered her lost her mother, Pelosi sent a poem about motherhood that her own mother had written. On Election Day in 2018, when she faced endless demands for her time and attention, she sat for more than an hour at the apartment of a former classmate whose husband had just died, as though there was nowhere else she could possibly want to be.

And when congressional scholar Norman Ornstein was sitting shiva for his son, who had died in a tragic accident at age thirty-four, Pelosi came to his house and stayed with the grieving family for three hours even though it was a hectic time for her, during the opening days of the 114th Congress. "She didn't have to do that," Ornstein said. "She could have sent a note; she could have come, paid her respects, and left." That

was in 2015; when he told me the story five years later, he began to
weep at the memory.

She had the deep understanding of politics, bred in her bones, that is
particular to those for whom public office is the family business.

"What I learned from my father was everything," she said. "I didn't
learn like you learn lessons. I learned by osmosis. I breathed it in. You
can't articulate it. Politics is every minute of every day. It is part of you."
At a celebratory dinner at a restaurant in downtown Washington on
the day she was first sworn in to Congress, her brother rose to deliver
a toast. His sister was "a thoroughbred," Tommy D'Alesandro III pro-
claimed. She had been born for the political career she was then starting, he said, though it had taken some time for that to unfold.

A week before she was born, her father had announced his candidacy
for a second term in the House of Representatives.

"Even those who for political reasons oppose me will admit that I
have brought more to the Third District in the time I have been in Congress than was brought to it in the previous twelve years," he declared,
a swipe at Palmisano, his predecessor. The next Congress would face
grave responsibilities as the threat of war loomed, he went on. A year
later, on December 7, 1941, the Japanese attack on Pearl Harbor would
catapult the United States into World War II. D'Alesandro embraced a
strong defense, endorsed the leadership of President Franklin D. Roosevelt, and advocated free trade. He warned against "Communism,
Nazism, Fascism and excessive nationalism."

When his wife went into labor eight days later, D'Alesandro was
in Washington, on the floor of the House. He was lobbying for the
National Youth Administration bill, an FDR initiative to provide job
training for young people. He cast his vote for it before rushing to his
wife's side, arriving before the baby was born at 3:10 p.m.

"We were all christened into the Roman Catholic Church and the
Democratic Party," Nancy Pelosi said. During her first campaign, running for Congress in 1987, she objected to the caricature of herself as

a "wealthy dilettante," a socialite who only dabbled in politics. "Our whole lives were politics," she told Jerry Roberts of the *San Francisco Chronicle*. "If you entered the house, it was always campaign time, and if you went into the living room, it was always constituent time."

Even as a little girl, she learned to be wary of Republicans and their ways. When she accompanied her parents to a polling place one Election Day, a GOP poll worker handed her a small toy elephant as a souvenir. Sensing a trap, she recoiled and quickly handed it back. "He thinks I don't know what that is," she said years later, laughing.

She knew what it was, even then.

--------

In those days, no one in the family, including Nancy herself, thought she was destined for a career in politics. Her father's political ambitions for the next generation were invested in his firstborn son, who had an easygoing charm though he lacked his father's taste for partisan combat. In 1967, Tommy the Younger would be elected to a term as mayor of Baltimore himself. But when Nancy D'Alesandro was born, no woman had ever served in Congress from Maryland. Not until 2007 would Baltimore elect its first female mayor.

Decades later, from her suite on the second floor of the Capitol, Nancy Pelosi expressed exasperation with those who confidently asserted that she had yearned for office from childhood. "That's not who I am," she said. "I didn't even see myself in that kind of role." Countering that misperception was her chief motivation in writing her memoir, she told me. Interestingly enough, though, she titled the 2008 book *Know Your Power*.

Her energetic mother did have a career in mind for her only daughter, but it was in one of the few fields then open to women. She wanted her daughter to have "the freedom to fly away and experience life on my own terms," but she also wanted "to protect me from the world, with all its potential heartaches and disappointments," Nancy Pelosi said. "And in her mind, the answer to this dilemma was simple: I should become a nun."

When Democrats won control of the House in 2006, paving the way for her to become the first female Speaker, then-congressman Rahm Emanuel of Illinois gave her a kiss as she made her way to the podium to accept the endorsement of the Democratic Caucus for the post. "Your parents would be so proud," he whispered in her ear. She thought, "In that instant I was taken to Baltimore, to our home, and I thought, well, my parents would be so proud." Then she told her fellow Democrats about Emanuel's comment, and offered a clarification. "They didn't raise me to be Speaker of the House," she said. "They raised me to be holy, to be good, and that was their measure of what they would be happy about."

Big Nancy, who kept statues of the Blessed Mother in her home and religious books on her bedside table, made no secret of her plan for her daughter's future as a nun. That ambition was not uncommon for devout Catholic families at the time. "You know, her mother really wanted a girl—[after] five boys," Jeanne Lynch, a friend and classmate of Nancy D'Alesandro at Trinity College, told me. "I always had the impression that her mother promised God, 'Give me a girl and I'll put her in the convent for you.'" A fair share of Little Nancy's high school class would enter religious orders when they graduated in 1958, although not all of them would stay. "Her mother thought she would make a good nun," Mary Ann Campanella, a neighbor and childhood playmate of Nancy from Little Italy, told me.

Early on, though, Little Nancy decided the religious life wasn't for her, at least not the one her mother had in mind. "I didn't think I wanted to be a nun," she told the *National Catholic Reporter* years later. "But I thought I might want to be a priest. There seemed to be a little more power there, a little more discretion over what was going on in the parish."

Nancy D'Alesandro grew up serious about her faith and sheltered by her family.

She lived at 245 Albemarle, a narrow street in the middle of Little Italy. Her paternal grandparents lived at 235 Albemarle and her maternal grandparents at 204 Albemarle. Aunt Jessie lived at 314 Albemarle. Aunt Mary had settled around the corner, on Eastern Avenue. St. Leo the Great Roman Catholic Church, the center of neighborhood life, was two blocks away, on South Exeter.

To accommodate their growing family, her parents added a third floor to their row house, with an office for her father and bedrooms for her brothers. Nancy's bedroom was on the second floor, next to her mother's room. On the first floor, Big Nancy used the front room as an office to see a steady stream of her husband's constituents. She would convene meetings for her army of women volunteers in the club room in the basement.

She had a taste for finery. "My mother wanted three things," Nancy Pelosi told me. "She wanted oriental rugs, she wanted a piano, and she wanted a painting of the family." She had all three of them in her home, although after her death the family portrait would end up on display across the street, in a Little Italy restaurant.

A *Baltimore Sun* profile from 1948 described oyster gray curtains in the living room and red upholstered benches in the dining room. "In Mrs. D'Alesandro's room, decorated in shades of pink, deeper rose and blue, there is a canopied bed with a rose satin spread over white marquisette ruffles," wrote reporter Margaret Dempsey, who happened to be a groundbreaking female journalist. (The seven photos accompanying the story were taken by A. Aubrey Bodine, who would become a prominent photographer.) "There is a blue satin love seat, a built-in mirrored dressing room, Hollywood style, and a white telephone."

Mayor D'Alesandro's room on the third floor featured a mahogany bed with a gray spread, monogrammed in maroon. An easy chair sat in one corner, a phone beside it. In another corner stood a small statue of Mother Cabrini, an Italian immigrant who became a naturalized citizen. She had been canonized in 1946, making her the first U.S. citizen to be declared a saint. The mayor kept a vigil light burning before her statue.

Tommy the Elder was a traditionalist when it came to his only daughter, objecting even to the idea, when she was a young teenager, that she would cut her long hair. She was well behaved and usually respectful of the curfews her parents set. In short, she was the model of a teenage girl of the Silent Generation. (Later, she would become a more disruptive force in matters of politics and gender, albeit one who retained the manners and posture that the nuns had drilled into their charges.)

For now, Nancy D'Alesandro's defiance of her parents' rules amounted mostly to pedaling her bicycle on the street and taking surf mats to ride the waves off Ocean City, Maryland, during summers on the Eastern Shore. "It was the era of Elvis Presley, cling-on skirts, cinch belts, Peter Pan collars, circle pins, charm bracelets and an occasional— but they tell me not to say this—an occasional cashmere sweater set," she said, a posh pleasure. "It was my youth."

She never rebelled?

"It wasn't even an option," she said years later. "This is the '50s." But she acknowledged that she would sometimes sneak out at night during high school. "Don't tell," she added with a laugh.

A friend from those days, Ted Venetoulis, told me she reminded everyone of Audrey Hepburn. "She had a certain humorous innocence," said Venetoulis, who would have a political career of his own, elected as Baltimore County executive. He described her as bright and unpretentious and shy, as someone who would never try to make other people aware that her father was the mayor. Nancy was smarter and more studious than he was. "I remember she was doing a paper on Emily Dickinson," a poet unknown to him. "If she wasn't a linebacker for the Colts," he joked about Dickinson, "I wouldn't know who she was."

––––––––

Nancy's brothers attended elementary school in the neighborhood, at St. Leo's. But Big Nancy from the start insisted that her daughter enroll at the Institute of Notre Dame, her alma mater. It was on the other side of downtown Baltimore, on Aisquith Street. The School Sisters of Notre

Dame, founded in Bavaria in 1833, had traveled to the United States in 1847 to educate German immigrants, especially girls and women. The first school they opened in this new land was the Institute of Notre Dame in Baltimore.

By the time Nancy D'Alesandro enrolled in the school a century later, the students were no longer only German; they came from Catholic families across the city, from Irish and Italian and Polish neighborhoods. Barbara Mikulski, the daughter of a Polish American grocer, was four years ahead of Nancy. Mikulski would become a community organizer—challenging, among other things, the D'Alesandro political machine. In time, she would be the first woman elected to the U.S. Senate from Maryland and the longest-serving woman in the history of Congress.

Mikulski graduated in 1954, Pelosi in 1958, but they were aware of each other while schoolmates at Notre Dame. "We had a mayor's daughter, we had a classmate whose father was a judge, but we also had new immigrants who had come after World War II and all that," Mikulski told me. Each morning, Nancy D'Alesandro "arrived in a car; I arrived in a bus. But the great thing about these Catholic schools—we all wore uniforms; they treated us all the same."

"Nancy's father was the mayor and my dad was a letter carrier," classmate Linda Wanner told me. "That school was the great leveling field where girls could grow into womanhood not on the amount of money they had, but on their schoolwork and their charity."

At the time, there were few women in elective office. When Nancy graduated from high school, there were a total of sixteen women in Congress. That was presumably one reason why it never occurred to Barbara Mikulski or Nancy D'Alesandro or the other girls that a political career could be an option. Even so, the education at Notre Dame was rigorous and the expectations high. Years later, Pelosi could quote from memory the framed statement that hung in the school vestibule: "School is not a Prison, it is not a Playground, it is Time, it is Opportunity."

"We were educated where it had to be intellectual rigor and a life of service, those were the two things," Mikulski said. "You really had to be smart and you had to keep up. We had courses like speech, debating; you had to stand up, speak up, and not shut up.... We were taught to debate the Jesuit boys—meaning the boys from Loyola [High School]—and we were taught to stand up."

Nancy joined the school's debate team her freshman year; the designated topic would seem surprisingly current decades later: "Resolved: The Federal Government Should Initiate a Policy of Free Trade Among Nations Friendly to the United States." She wasn't a star debater, but she was known to be both tenacious and diplomatic. (Classmates from those days told me they could see flashes of the same style years later when they watched her on C-SPAN as she spoke on the floor of the House.)

When the students arrived at school each morning, Sister Mary Lenore Bowling, the principal, would be standing on the steps. She was there in part to make sure that no student's uniform, a simple light blue dress with a white princess collar, had been hemmed immodestly short. Between classes, the students would walk down the halls in single file and an imposed silence. At chapel each day at noon, "we would decide what sins we had committed in the morning and make resolutions to be a better person in the afternoon," classmate Ann Seeley told me. What possible sins might have been committed by the girls of Notre Dame? "Maybe we talked when we shouldn't have?" she suggested.

The nuns sought to instill a commitment to social justice, even among the girls who didn't plan to join a religious order. The engraved message over the threshold of the school's gabled double doors was PRO DEO ET PATRIA ("For God and Country").

When Nancy D'Alesandro was six years old, she visited Washington for the first time. The family was attending the swearing-in ceremony for her father's fifth congressional term. "My brothers were excited," she said. "As our car approached the Capitol, they kept saying, 'Nancy, look at the Capitol.' I said I didn't see any capitals. They insisted, and finally I asked, 'Is it a capital *A*, *B*, or *C*?'"

Joey pointed his sister in the right direction. "I didn't see the giant letters I expected," she said. "Instead, I saw a stunning building with a magnificent white dome."

A year later, her father was elected mayor, a job he would hold until after she had graduated from high school. But his prominence offered her no protection from the nuns' rules, or their ire. There was the time that her sophomore class dissolved into uncontrollable giggles during a performance before a school assembly in celebration of Shakespeare. One classmate and then nearly all of them were undone by language from *The Tempest* that struck them as embarrassingly suggestive: "Where the bee sucks, there suck I." At the Latin class that followed, Sister Mary Lenore singled out Nancy as though she was responsible, although she hadn't played any special role in her class's meltdown. "And you, a Latin scholar!" the nun scolded her in front of the rest of the class.

Nancy was among the top students, invariably prepared, a discipline she would continue for the rest of her life. She would devour *Time* magazine every week. The school chose her to compete in a news quiz that *Time* was sponsoring for high school students. A half century later, she still remembered with vexation the only question she missed: "What is a hatchback?"

"I didn't have the faintest, remotest idea," she told Karen Tumulty of *Time*. "I guess it's getting common usage, but at the time, it was the new car." She had never forgotten the question or, apparently, forgiven her misstep.

Little Nancy's unconvincing insistence to friends that she was winging it became the source of teasing. The description of her in her senior yearbook, *The Clarissian*, called her "pleasant and sincere...*tres* feminine," and then mockingly quoted her: "I haven't opened a book yet." For a time, the mayor's driver would bring her to school each morning—sometimes her father was also in the car, on his way to City Hall—but she didn't put on airs.

"She'd hop out and she was regular Nancy," said Karen Kadar, a friend and high school classmate. "For those four years, she was just Nancy."

If her father wasn't in the car, she would sometimes ask his driver to drop her off a block or two from school so she wouldn't be pulling up to the entrance in the mayor's limousine. By the time she was in high school, she was allowed to take the bus. "She didn't act like a diva," Mikulski said.

"My whole thing was just to be normal," Pelosi told me. "Just to be an unrecognizable, normal, 1950s teenager."

---

Outside the tall doors of the Institute of Notre Dame, though, she was not just Nancy. She was the adorable sidekick for her father's photo ops and the promising vehicle for her mother's unrealized ambitions. When Tommy D'Alesandro Jr. was sworn in as mayor for the first time, his seven-year-old daughter held the Bible and delivered her first political speech. "Dear Daddy, I hope this holy book will guide you to be a good man," she said solemnly, wearing white gloves and a frilly hat. A newspaper photo of the moment shows her father towering over her on the dais in front of City Hall, watching with a benevolent gaze. Another man is crouched next to her, holding a microphone from radio station WCBM to capture her words.

For years, an oversized oil portrait of the family was displayed in the living room of the D'Alesandro home, titled *Victory Night/May 6, 1947.* Nancy is front and center, as though perhaps the little girl was the one who had been elected mayor that day. Her mother sits to one side of her, Bible in hand; her father sits to the other side, clasping his daughter's hand and sporting his signature bow tie. Standing behind them are her five brothers, dressed in suits and ties. Everyone is wearing subdued black and tan except Little Nancy, whose bright white dress is iridescent, with a matching headband and shoes and socks. Hanging over the fireplace mantel behind the family is a portrait of George Washington.

(The painting of the family eventually ended up on the wall at Germano's Piattini, one of Little Italy's iconic restaurants. After Big Nancy died in 1995, it was eventually taken across the street to hang on display, with updated commentary. "Be careful with Nancy's painting," a small sign next to it warned visitors in 2019. "She will impeach you." The message had a weird resonance for one accidental diner during President Trump's impeachment. Adam Schiff, the California congressman who was the lead impeachment manager, happened to go to Baltimore with his wife on a Saturday during the Senate trial; they searched online for a restaurant with vegan options. They ended up at Germano's. Schiff called Pelosi on his cell phone to report that he was looking at her portrait as a child. "It's spooky, right?" she told me.)

From the day she was born, Little Nancy was a familiar figure to anyone who read the city's newspapers. At age seven, she was at City Hall to present a key to the city to an esteemed visitor from the Vatican, the Right Reverend Monsignor Lucinio Reflee, conductor of the Roman Singers of Sacred Music. When she was eight, the city named its new forty-six-foot harbor patrol boat the *Nancy D'Alesandro*. At nine, she christened the city's new fireboat, *Cascade*, a refurbished submarine chaser from World War I. At thirteen, she was christening *The Mainliner Baltimore*, a twin-engine Convair that United Airlines was using to begin regularly scheduled flights at what was then named Friendship Airport.

"Little Nancy, with her long, beautiful hair and gamine face, is the princess in the ivory tower, the fairy child, whose school average is 97, the daughter who came after six sons," the *Baltimore Sun* gushed in a profile of her mother.

She was twelve years old when her parents took her with them to her first Democratic National Convention, in 1952 in Chicago. She brought along a toy donkey she named Adlai after that year's presidential nominee, Illinois governor Adlai Stevenson.

Four years later, she filled in for her mother at a dinner being held for a rising young senator from Massachusetts. Knowing how enamored her daughter was with John F. Kennedy, Big Nancy feigned illness and sent Little Nancy in her stead, to be seated at the head table, next to JFK. He was the guest speaker at a dinner sponsored by the United Nations Association of Maryland; his book *Profiles in Courage* had recently been published. A group of high school students invited Nancy to sit at their table, with her peers. "What do I do?" she would later recall to an audience at the JFK Library that included Senator Ted Kennedy. "I'm usually so courteous and accept that lovely invitation but, Teddy, it just wasn't going to happen," she said to laughter. "So I said to them, 'I'd be so honored but I'm taking my mother's place tonight and I couldn't possibly leave this empty seat.'"

A photographer snapped a photo of her standing next to Kennedy. "Save this picture," a woman at the dinner told the sixteen-year-old. "One day he may be president." She took the woman's advice. The photo shows JFK in a tux, looking at Nancy, who is smiling shyly at the camera. She is wearing over-the-elbow white gloves and a formal gown, a cinched belt over a wide gathered skirt.

———

Her father was a master of the outside game of politics. "A phenomenal natural politician," his daughter would say at a time she was in a position to judge. He was the sort of indefatigable campaigner who drew energy from crowds, a skillful storyteller with an oversized personality. More than once after his annual reception for constituents on New Year's Eve, he would shake so many hands and with such enthusiasm that his battered right hand would have to be bandaged. His daughter sometimes stood beside him in the reception line, shaking hands herself, wearing white gloves.

She also learned politics from her mother, a master of the inside game.

Big Nancy knew how to rally women's groups and deploy them, how to grant favors and then cash them in, how to keep score. "She was always there when I needed her," Tommy the Elder said of his wife shortly before he died in 1987. "Every election I ran, Nancy was pregnant. But she'd organize the ladies to address envelopes, write letters and make fliers. Every night she had the ravioli and lasagna parties with the neighborhood ladies. She did the work."

"She was the powerhouse of Albemarle Street," California congresswoman Anna Eshoo, one of Pelosi's closest friends, told me. "She knew where every vote was. She was really like a director of social services."

She trained her daughter how to keep the "Favor File," a distinctively D'Alesandro system during those days before computers. It became the stuff of local legend, taking the classic rewards of political machines to a new level. Constituents would line up on the sidewalk outside the house on Albemarle Street, seeking, well, favors. They would file in past presidential portraits of FDR and Harry Truman and take a chair on one side of a big desk. Big Nancy would be seated on the other side, ready to chat in Italian if an immigrant didn't speak English. Little Nancy was often seated by her side, taking notes in her careful hand.

The system started when Tommy D'Alesandro was a congressman and expanded when he was mayor. "When someone came in with a request, Mommy wrote it down on a piece of yellow paper and put it in a folder," Nancy Pelosi recalled. Later, the notations would be typed on index cards and filed. "Then, when that person got on his or her feet and someone else came in looking for similar help, my mother would take out the slip of paper and call on the first person to help the second." Those who got help could also be deployed at election time to stuff envelopes, pass out flyers, attend rallies. And, of course, to vote.

Even when she was too young to open the door to strangers, Little Nancy was taking notes and making phone calls. "When I was a little girl, I knew how to tell somebody who to call to get on welfare, into a project, a bed in a city hospital, you name it," Pelosi said. "That's what our home was about." A childhood playmate, Mary Ann Campanella, told me that her friend at age eight or nine already had a political sophistication the rest of them lacked. "She knew the word 'constituent,' which we didn't," she said dryly.

The D'Alesandro home had a phone number just about everybody in the city seemed to know—Calvert 4890—and so many callers that eventually nine phone lines were installed. "I say this braggadociously: I don't know anyone in Baltimore who knew more people and did more favors than my mother and father in their heyday," said her brother Tommy D'Alesandro III, himself a former mayor. "That was the atmosphere into which Nancy was born."

For a time, wanting for space in the small row house overflowing with six children, her father would store copies of the *Congressional Record* under Nancy's bed.

Nancy D'Alesandro's childhood was a master class in politics—not the philosophical but the pragmatic. It was about how to help constituents land a job or find an apartment, how to get an ailing grandmother admitted to a hospital or an errant son sprung from jail. It was about forging alliances and building coalitions across ethnic lines, favor by favor, for the long haul.

She learned from a charismatic father who had never lost an election and an ambitious mother who organized the grass roots. The challenges of having five older brothers forced her to figure out how to assert herself. The teachers in her all-female school expected girls to take positions of leadership—"to stand up, speak up, and not shut up," as Barbara Mikulski put it. Early on, Little Nancy gained the poise to appear before cameras at a photo op and the bones to negotiate a government bureaucracy.

The combination of it all would make her formidable and fearless, although decades would pass before she recognized the possibilities for herself as a candidate, as an officeholder, as a leader.

Working on the Favor File, Little Nancy learned to listen, to understand not only what someone said but what they meant. Those were skills that would later help make her an effective legislative captain, when her constituents weren't voters lined up on the sidewalk but fellow politicians in the corridors of the Capitol. At meetings of the House Democratic Caucus, Pelosi could be endlessly patient in hearing out other members of Congress—a loquacious group—while her colleagues became restless. Allies say her command of Democratic ranks was grounded in her ability to figure out what was motivating others, sometimes with more clarity and insight than they had themselves.

———

Tommy D'Alesandro Jr. was born to be mayor of Baltimore, and during a time when big cities were booming. It was a role he relished more than being a member of Congress. He was no longer one vote out of 435 House members, working his way up the seniority ladder in committees. As mayor of his hometown, he had the power to get things done. Big things.

"He had a love affair with the city of Baltimore," Nancy Pelosi said. "He loved the city, and he loved being the mayor."

He brought back major-league baseball to the city—no easy task, getting the St. Louis Browns to become the Baltimore Orioles—and he thought big. During his twelve years as mayor, the city paved hundreds of miles of streets and opened eighty-seven new schools, including some that replaced second-rate facilities that had been assigned to Black students in those segregated days. He opened the Baltimore Harbor Tunnel and dedicated Friendship International Airport. He was so proud of the new airport that he overcame his phobia of flying so he could accompany President Truman aboard Air Force One for its inaugural arrival.

"I said 300 Hail Marys, 50 Our Fathers and the best doggone Act of Contrition of my life," he said afterward.

D'Alesandro's political strength was grounded in working-class neighborhoods, albeit more in White precincts than Black ones. When he was first elected mayor, in 1947, he carried two-thirds of the vote in White working-class wards, 44 percent of the Black wards.

In 1948, he accepted on behalf of the city a bronze statue in Wyman Park honoring Confederate generals Robert E. Lee and Stonewall Jackson, side by side on horseback. A Baltimore banker, J. Henry Ferguson, had bequeathed $75,000 for the monument honoring his childhood heroes. "Today, with our nation beset by subversive groups and propaganda which seeks to destroy our national unity, we can look for inspiration to the lives of Lee and Jackson to remind us to be resolute and determined in preserving our sacred institutions," D'Alesandro told a crowd of three thousand, among them Governor William Preston Lane Jr. The statue wasn't controversial then, but it was later. In 2017, after violent protests in Charlottesville, Virginia, over Confederate statutes there, the Baltimore City Council ordered it removed.

That said, D'Alesandro had an admirable record on one of the most racially charged issues of the day, the desegregation of public schools. Almost six months before the Supreme Court handed down its landmark decision in *Brown v. Board of Education* in 1954, a reporter asked him how the city would respond if the court ordered desegregation. "It will be my duty and the responsibility of the Board of School Commissioners to carry out the mandate of the Supreme Court," he replied.

When the high court ruled that racial segregation in public schools was unconstitutional, D'Alesandro said he agreed with it. "I asked the nuns," he said. "They said it was right, so I went with the nuns." Baltimore became one of the first major cities in the country to desegregate its schools citywide.

The court decision accelerated White flight to the suburbs across the country, increasing the percentage and the power of African Americans in urban centers. In Baltimore, the population was about one-fifth Black when D'Alesandro was first elected mayor, in 1947. By the time he left City Hall, in 1959, it was more than one-third Black. By 1980, African Americans comprised a majority of the city.

Tommy D'Alesandro ruled in an era when big-city mayors had a certain swagger, from Fiorello La Guardia in New York to Richard J. Daley in Chicago. It was a time of bosses and patronage, of walking-around money on Election Day and no-show jobs afterward. Jack Pollack, a local businessman and political ally, once asked D'Alesandro to give a friend a city job, prompting an exchange that became the stuff of local legend. "What can he do?" the mayor asked.

"Well, he really can't do anything," Pollack acknowledged in a conversation witnessed by an associate, one who would later become a judge.

D'Alesandro was unfazed. "Good," he replied. "Then we don't need to break him in."

But the norms of politics were changing, and the scrutiny was increasing. Scandals both personal and political were about to catch up with Tommy the Elder and the D'Alesandro family.

# CHAPTER FOUR

———

# SCANDAL

*August 5, 1953—Vienna, Austria*

A triumphant Thomas D'Alesandro Jr. was returning to the continent that his father had left six decades earlier, when he had emigrated from Italy with little in his pockets except hope.

His father, Tommaso D'Alesandro, had found work in Baltimore as a laborer, digging railroad tunnels and swinging a pickaxe. Now the son, elected and reelected as the city's mayor, was part of a distinguished delegation from the U.S. Conference of Mayors, chosen to attend the International Union of Local Authorities conference. Representatives from thirty-one countries were gathering in Vienna, a city still under occupation in the wake of World War II. Meeting at the sumptuous Bristol Hotel, they were studying ways to preserve world peace and foster democratic local government. Those high-minded topics had been made more pressing by the battle against fascism that had been won just eight years earlier.

The ten-week tour of Europe would be a glorious journey, the capstone of his career—until, that is, it ended amid crisis.

D'Alesandro made the most of the trip. It stretched from one season into the next, from late May to early August 1953. He and his wife used the occasion for an early celebration of their twenty-fifth wedding anniversary, which fell in September. He sailed on the *Queen Mary* for the first leg of the journey, to London, with their eighteen-year-old son Nicholas. The teenager then returned to Baltimore while Big Nancy and their three youngest children—Hector, Joseph, and Little Nancy—met up with her husband in Europe once their school terms were over. The two oldest boys didn't accompany them.

Tommy D'Alesandro III, of draft age at twenty-three years old, was otherwise occupied fulfilling his military obligation in the U.S. Army. There had been a dustup about that a few days after the elder D'Alesandro left for Europe.

Drew Pearson, the most widely syndicated political columnist in the country, accused Mayor D'Alesandro of pulling strings to try to make sure that his firstborn son wouldn't be deployed to Korea, where thirty thousand U.S. soldiers had been killed in a war that still raged. According to the column, D'Alesandro had enlisted the help of Maryland senator John Marshall Butler, who talked to the Army's lobbyist on Capitol Hill, who arranged to have the younger D'Alesandro pulled out of basic training at Fort Indiantown Gap, Pennsylvania. At the time, "The Gap," home to the 5th Infantry Division, was training thousands of soldiers as replacement troops for Korea. The mayor's son, who had just graduated from the University of Maryland Law School, was transferred to the Judge Advocate General's office and sent instead to Camp Breckenridge, Kentucky. Those assigned to the Army's legal office usually didn't see combat.

Maryland's other senator, J. Glenn Beall, a Republican, had declined D'Alesandro's request to intervene, Pearson said, but Senator Butler agreed. Butler was not only a Republican but also an acolyte of the red-baiting senator Joseph McCarthy of Wisconsin. Still, he told the columnist, he agreed to help because Tommy the Elder was a friend. For his part, D'Alesandro denied seeking a political favor. He said he had just called the senator asking for information.

D'Alesandro's second-born son had stayed in the States, too. Franklin Delano Roosevelt D'Alesandro, then twenty years old and known to everyone as Roosie, had no interest in going to Europe. He preferred to take it easy for the summer after his sophomore year at Baltimore's Loyola College, where he was majoring in business administration. He worked at his father's insurance company for a few hours each day, then went bowling or to the movies with his girlfriend, Mary Ann Jankowski.

The timing of the Vienna conference was fortuitous, just after the coronation of Queen Elizabeth II; the twenty-seven-year-old princess would go on to hold the longest reign in British history. Mayor D'Alesandro was invited to be one of those representing the United States at the royal ceremony in London.

The following day, the visiting mayors met with members of the London County Council. D'Alesandro wanted to go to Ireland to visit the tiny town there named Baltimore. Later, in France, he went to see the grave of his youngest brother, John B. D'Alesandro, at the Lorraine American Cemetery and Memorial. The Army private, thirty-three years old and the father of three young children, had been killed just before the Battle of the Bulge began, near the end of World War II. Mayor D'Alesandro scheduled a stop in Germany as well, in Stuttgart.

After the conference in Vienna, D'Alesandro joined his wife and three youngest children in Paris.

"I didn't even want to go because I was leaving my friends," Pelosi told me. "It was summer; I was like, 'I don't want to go! I don't want to go! I don't want to go!'" Her parents made her go, of course. It was her first trip abroad; she called it a "transformational" experience, full of adventures. The D'Alesandros were made honorary citizens of Rome. When they went to Bologna in northern Italy for her father to deliver a speech, "we were scared because they said the Communist Party ruled the city," she recalled with a laugh, "and we're like, 'The Communist Party? Why are we going there?'" (The city government of Bologna was then a showcase for the Italian Communist Party, the PCI.)

They toured Florence, Venice, and Milan. Mayor D'Alesandro had an audience with Pope Pius XII at the Vatican. After a brief stop in

Switzerland, the family sailed home in grand style, aboard the SS *United States*, the first superliner constructed in America. On its maiden voyage a year earlier, it had broken the speed record for crossing the Atlantic.

When the ship docked in New York City on August 4, however, D'Alesandro was confronted by allegations of scandal. City Hall aides and son Roosie were there to warn him of trouble brewing in Baltimore, a jolt after seventy days of ceremony, celebration, and sightseeing. The repercussions would undermine D'Alesandro's health, landing him in the hospital for months after a nervous collapse, and undercut his aspirations for statewide office.

First, the political: A grand jury was investigating alleged irregularities by Baltimore's off-street parking commission, aides told the mayor. At issue were contracts using municipal funds that the agency had awarded to businessman Dominic Piracci for construction of downtown garages. Piracci was one of the mayor's cronies, not to mention a member of the family by marriage; Piracci's daughter had married D'Alesandro's eldest son a year earlier. (The marriage of Tommy the Younger to Margie Piracci was too big for St. Leo's, the neighborhood church in Little Italy. Instead, it was held at the Baltimore Basilica before a throng of more than five thousand guests. "Baltimore's equivalent of a royal wedding," the *Baltimore Sun* later wrote.)

D'Alesandro faced a flurry of questions from reporters who gathered at his suite in the posh Essex House hotel, where he and his family were spending the night before returning to Baltimore. He projected confidence. "If anything is wrong, we will right it," he assured a *New York Times* reporter. The headline on the story was remarkably understated: "Baltimore Mayor Here," it read. "Back from Europe, He Learns of Unpleasantness at Home."

Second, and worse, the personal: Roosie was likely to be arrested the next day on charges of rape. He was one of fourteen young men who had been implicated in the sexual assault of two girls, thirteen and eleven years old. Two weeks earlier, the girls, cousins who had run away from their home in East Baltimore, allegedly had gone on an all-night joy ride with four of them, including Roosie. Then the young men paid ten dollars to rent a furnished two-room apartment, where the girls stayed for a week. They were the victims of rape and other "perverted practices," according to the grand jury indictments. One of the indictments was for an unidentified "John Doe" that one of the girls had heard being called by the name "Rudy" or "Rootie."

Roosie returned to Baltimore Tuesday night. At midday Wednesday, he and his girlfriend were among the contingent on hand at the Mount Royal train station to welcome home his parents and Hector, Joseph, and Little Nancy. The Baltimore & Ohio train pulled in right on time, at 12:38 p.m.

From that moment on, Mayor D'Alesandro would be immersed in frantic efforts to defend his son and protect his family.

When they arrived at home in Little Italy, he called his son into the master bedroom. "He said to me: 'Tell me the truth. Did you have anything to do with any girls?'" Roosie later testified. "And I told him the truth and said 'no.'" That was enough for his father and his family.

Reporters camped out on the street recorded, minute by minute, the comings and goings of the city's powerful. At 3:15 p.m., Joseph Sherbow, a prominent former judge, arrived; he had been hired as Roosie's defense lawyer. At 5:10 p.m., Roosie walked out of the house in a blue suit and climbed into the car for the short drive downtown, to stand in a lineup at Baltimore police headquarters.

At the station, the police commander told Roosie to take off his suit jacket and tie; during the alleged crimes, none of the young men had been so formally dressed. His shirtsleeves were rolled up and his collar open when he stood with five other young men in a row against the wall in the third-floor room. The lineup began at 5:30 p.m., the girls behind a screen that shielded them, each in turn. The younger girl identified Roosie as the man she saw through a door in the apartment that was ajar. But she remarked that the man whose nickname she had heard as "Rudy" had seemed taller in the apartment than he did in the lineup.

Fifteen minutes later, a police officer filled out the Central Police

Station docket with Franklin Delano Roosevelt D'Alesandro's name and the charges against him. He was booked and fingerprinted; his mug shot was taken. He waited in the police commander's office while Sherbow hurried to the courthouse to request bail. By 7:15 p.m., Roosie was headed back to Little Italy.

The mayor's friends and supporters had scheduled a "Welcome Home" banquet that evening at the Emerson Hotel, which had long served as headquarters for the Maryland Democratic Party on election nights. Tommy the Elder showed up, delivering a defiant one-sentence statement to reporters before he walked in. "I hope that the oldest and most respected law in our country, that a man is innocent until proved guilty, holds good for a mayor's son as well as anyone else," he said.

At the dinner, D'Alesandro was presented with a miniature pair of boxing gloves "for the political battles to come." The *Evening Sun* published a jovial account of the evening, "Welcome Banquet Honors Mayor on Return." Next to it was a more sobering headline: "Son of Mayor out on Bail in Morals Case."

Police also arrested the three other young men who allegedly had picked up the girls. The stories in the morning newspapers focused squarely on the mayor's son, of course. "D'Alesandro's Son, 20, Accused in Rape Case Involving Child of 13," the *Baltimore Sun* headline read, next to a photo of Roosie taken during happier times. It was the first of months of front-page headlines about the charges against the mayor's son.

"It was an awful scandal," Mary Ann Campanella told me, one that transfixed the neighborhood and the city. In 2019, at age seventy-seven, she still lived in the same house in Little Italy where she had lived then, when she was a childhood friend of Little Nancy, the girl down the street. "It was a disgrace on the family."

———

Three months later, Roosie was acquitted.

After just twenty-five minutes of deliberation, the jury of twelve men voted unanimously to find him innocent. The young D'Alesandro would be the only one of those charged in the case to win acquittal; the other thirteen were all convicted. Several were given sentences that ranged from eighteen months to two years, although Judge W. Conwell Smith ordered some of them released on probation after they had served sixty days at the State Reformatory for Males.

During his three-day trial, the first of the group, Roosie denied ever meeting the two young girls. Denied riding in a car with them. Denied taking them to a furnished room to stay for a week. Denied raping the thirteen-year-old.

His girlfriend and her parents bolstered his alibi, saying he had eaten dinner and sometimes slept overnight on a couch in their living room during some of the days in question. It was during a crucial week while most of his family were traveling abroad. That's why his mother had arranged for him to spend time at the Jankowski household, Roosie said.

Young D'Alesandro was a victim of mistaken identity, his lawyer told the jury—referring to him in court as "Frank" rather than "Roosie," which was so similar to the nickname the girl remembered. Sherbow noted that the eleven-year-old girl who picked him out of a lineup had remarked then that he had seemed taller in the apartment. Perhaps to reinforce the case for confusion, Roosie's three younger brothers showed up each day in court and sat on the front bench with him, all wearing identical blue suits.

"I have no hesitancy in saying to you that if the case was submitted to me without the aid of jury, I would have no hesitancy in saying not guilty," the judge told the jury before it began its deliberations. The prominent position of the defendant's father shouldn't be a factor, one way or the other, he went on: "It would be infamous and outrageous if this boy were dismissed out of favor. It would be equally infamous and outrageous if he were convicted merely out of prejudice."

When the verdict of "not guilty" was read, Mayor D'Alesandro, who had sat in the courtroom throughout the trial, stood up, wept, and embraced his wife.

Through it all, family and friends tried to shield thirteen-year-old Nancy from the firestorm. "We kept quiet about it," Karen Kadar, a classmate at the Institute of Notre Dame, told me, then referred to herself in the third person. "What would you say? I remember my father and somebody he knew talking about it, but it went right over Karen's head. It was more puzzlement than anything." Nancy was their friend, and that was all that mattered to them, classmate Linda Wanner added. Nothing changed that.

"It was just something that we never talked about—never talked about it," said Ted Venetoulis, the high school friend who was later elected Baltimore County executive. "I'm sure she was hurt by it all." The episode was tough on the whole family, he said. "They grappled with it, and survived, and did extraordinarily well" afterward. "And Nancy, she went through it," Venetoulis told me. "It probably strengthened her, I think."

Pelosi told me that those months of legal problems—her brother's prosecution and her mother's testimony in a corruption trial that followed—had no effect on her. She never doubted her brother's innocence.

"We loved him and trusted him, and it was never any question," she told me, calling him "a beautiful, lovely person." She said it was either a politically motivated prosecution aimed at hurting her father or a case of another defendant trying to shift the blame to someone else. "I thought it was so unfair, because I thought somebody was trying to accuse him of something because they were trying to besmirch my father," she told me.

Her father was the first Italian American and the first Catholic to be elected mayor, she noted, operating in a "competitive world" of Baltimore politics. "It was like that because of Daddy," she said. "They're always trying to take him down."

At a formative age, Nancy D'Alesandro had gotten a brutal lesson about public life, about the scrutiny and the headlines it could bring. She saw her family close ranks, her parents persevere, her father run for and win reelection after it was all over. It was a case study in taking a punch, then keeping your head up. Consider how she would describe her job in politics years later: She said she would begin each day by donning "a suit of armor."

Roosie D'Alesandro's legal troubles weren't over with his acquittal. Trials for three other defendants followed in the next two weeks, also presided over by Judge Smith. All of them were convicted of statutory rape or perverted practices, and all of them implicated D'Alesandro. They hadn't been witnesses at Roosie's trial because he had gone first. Since their own trials were pending, their Fifth Amendment right against self-incrimination had meant they couldn't be compelled to testify.

The judge ordered the state's attorney to open a perjury investigation. In December, a grand jury indicted Roosie for lying, calling his testimony at his trial "willfully and corruptly false."

Roosie D'Alesandro's second trial lasted longer than the first. At this point, prosecutors noted, eight other witnesses had given testimony that conflicted with his denials. Those witnesses included two police officers, members of the protective detail at the mayor's home, who said they had seen Roosie with the other boys on that first, crucial night in question.

The jury deliberations lasted longer, too. After more than six hours, they voted to acquit. When the verdict was read, Big Nancy reached out for her son and wept. Mary Ann Jankowski, the girlfriend who was now Roosie's fiancée, grabbed his hand and kissed it. When court was adjourned, the young man planted a kiss on the face of his lawyer. "Mayor's Son Acquitted in Perjury Case," the *Baltimore Sun* blared in a banner headline across the front page the next morning.

———

Big Nancy and Tommy the Elder were having legal troubles of their own.

On the day his son was acquitted of the morals charge, the mayor had been summoned to testify before a grand jury investigating city corruption. D'Alesandro asked for his appearance to be delayed for a day so he could be in Youth Court for the end of Roosie's trial. In the *Baltimore Sun* on the morning of November 6, 1953, the headline at the top of the page on the right had good news for D'Alesandro and his family: "Mayor's Son Acquitted in Morals Case." The headline at the top of the page on the left had a disquieting note: "Mayor Testifies Before City Jury."

The grand jury had been meeting for three months, ever since D'Alesandro returned from Europe. It was looking into allegations of fraud involving $10 million in city contracts to build off-street parking garages. The mayor was the final witness. While grand jury proceedings are secret, he testified in such a booming voice that reporters loitering in the courthouse hallway could hear some of what he was saying, not to mention the sound of him pounding the table for emphasis.

His wife already had been ordered to appear before the grand jury. She would be called to testify in public at the trial of Dominic Piracci that followed five months later. Piracci had written six checks to Nancy D'Alesandro for amounts that totaled $11,130.78. As rumors of an investigation began to circulate, Piracci had erased her name and the names of some city officials from the Piracci Construction Company ledger. He testified that he erased the names not because the payments were illegal but simply to avoid embarrassing important people.

When she testified in court, on April 8, 1954, the courtroom was jammed with city and state officials and spectators. Her son Roosie was with her. The *Evening Sun* splashed the story across the top of the front page with the sort of double-decker banner headline reserved for war. The reporter noted that she wore a blue suit and a small yellow straw hat.

Nancy D'Alesandro testified that none of her financial dealings had anything to do with the disputed contracts to build off-street garages. She said $1,500 of the money was a gift from Piracci for his daughter and her son, who had gotten married the year before; for logistical reasons, he had given the money to her and she had passed it on to them. She had borrowed the rest of the money to pay off a series of bank loans for her various business enterprises, she testified. She produced paperwork that showed she had paid the loans back, and said she had protested to Piracci when he told her he had erased her name from the ledger, as though she had done something wrong.

Her friends and neighbors speculated that she needed the money for another reason—to pay off her gambling debts, an open secret in the neighborhood, although not one that was mentioned in the newspapers of the day. "She was always out at the track," Frank DeFilippo told me over lunch at Sabatino's, one of the Little Italy restaurants where bookies regularly conducted business in those days. DeFilippo covered politics for Baltimore's *News American*, then became a top aide to Maryland governor Marvin Mandel, a Democrat. Of the D'Alesandros, he said, "She loved the horses and he was always fending off the bookies."

Piracci was convicted of two counts of conspiring to obstruct justice in the grand jury investigation and fined $4,000, although Governor Theodore McKeldin, a Republican, would later grant him a pardon.

By the time his friend was convicted, Mayor D'Alesandro had already spent more than a month in the hospital for an ailment never fully explained to the public. He had checked into Bon Secours Hospital on the night of March 10, 1954, "for a checkup and a rest," the Associated Press reported.

He had been hospitalized two years earlier as well, spending about a month at Mercy Hospital for what was described as "grippe"—that is, the flu—and high blood pressure. His doctor blamed "overwork" and prescribed a Caribbean cruise to recover, which the mayor took. A photo in the *Evening Sun* showed him leaving the hospital, hand in hand with his elegantly dressed wife, who was wearing a fur stole. Dressed in a suit and tie, his dark shoes polished to a sheen, he was tipping his fedora.

Two years later, when D'Alesandro was hospitalized for a longer stretch, it fell to Big Nancy to represent the family in the public eye.

When Roosie was acquitted of perjury, she was in the courtroom. The family rushed to a pay phone to let his hospitalized father know. When Roosie got married at St. Katharine of Sienna Catholic Church, his mother was the one photographed leaving the church, beaming in a broad-brimmed hat; she greeted the eight hundred guests at the reception. The bride and groom had gone to the hospital before the wedding to receive his father's blessing.

Perhaps most surprising of all, when professional baseball returned to Baltimore after the absence of more than a half century, the mayor wasn't in the parade—an extravaganza featuring thirty-two floats and twenty marching bands—or at the Orioles' opener in Memorial Stadium. Vice President Richard Nixon threw out the first ball. "Missing, and missed, was the personality who had perhaps done more to bring big-league baseball back to the city than any other—Mayor D'Alesandro, who lay ill in Bon Secours Hospital," the Baltimore *Evening Sun* reported on its front page. Fifty years after Baltimore lost its team, he had brought the St. Louis Browns franchise to town, persisting even after the American League twice turned him down.

Not until July did D'Alesandro emerge back into public view, and only after the *Baltimore Sun* began to question the long absence of the mayor, by then missing from City Hall for four months. When he showed up at the office, he had lost forty or fifty pounds. "A roly-poly wisecracker, D'Alesandro went into the hospital with personal and official trouble over his head," the Associated Press story noted.

"During much of that five month period," the *Sun* later said, "friends and political enemies alike doubted that he would ever run for office again."

———

The calamities swirling around him didn't extinguish D'Alesandro's political ambitions. Indeed, it may have stoked them. He hadn't gotten as far as he had by showing hesitation or acknowledging weakness. In a lesson his daughter would follow, no one had given him power; he had taken it. As he liked to point out, he had never lost an election. By that point, he had won twenty-one of them in a row.

Now he wanted to be governor.

When he campaigned for other Democrats on the ballot in 1952, he would grin when he was introduced as "the next governor"—that is, the suggestion that he would be headed to the statehouse when the office was up for election in 1954. On August 22, 1953, even though a grand jury was investigating City Hall, D'Alesandro declared his gubernatorial campaign with a lengthy written statement extolling his achievements in the past and outlining his vision for the future.

The primary was still ten months away. The early announcement was intended to be peremptory, a message to potential rivals. (That was another example his daughter would follow decades later, announcing her campaign for House whip before the opening existed.)

His statement alluded to what the *New York Times* two weeks earlier had delicately referred to as the "unpleasantness" of current events. "As a candidate for Governor, I expect a continuation of the political smears and groundless insinuations which were begun two or three months ago in an effort to keep me from becoming a candidate," he said. "These attacks do not frighten me and I am confident that they will not impress the people of Maryland, in whose intelligence and fairness I have complete confidence."

But five months later, before the campaign had gotten into full gear, he withdrew from the race. He never formally filed the paperwork to run. This time, there was no lengthy declaration or lofty language, just a 152-word statement announcing that he wouldn't be running.

Tommy D'Alesandro wasn't ready to leave politics, though. A year later, in 1955, he decided to seek a third term as mayor. He won, but only after a bruising Democratic primary in which the integrity of his administration came under fire. The residents of Baltimore "are tired of the scandals, the trials, the mockery of our civil rights," one of his challengers, Barton Harrington, declared. The first plank of the platform released by rival Arthur Price promised, "Drive corruption, favoritism and mismanagement from the City Hall." D'Alesandro decried his challengers—"the bums!" he called them—and defeated them.

He had a powerful selling point, the centerpiece of his reelection campaign. He boasted that he was the mayor who brought major-league baseball back to Baltimore.

He managed to hold the Democratic nomination and then win another four years in office, and by double digits, though his margin of victory was smaller. Four years earlier, he had won a second term by a yawning 29 percentage points. This time, despite the Democratic tilt of the city, he won a third term over his Republican challenger by 11 points.

In another sign of changing times, the Maryland Democratic Convention in 1956 ousted D'Alesandro as the state's national committeeman in favor of Michael J. Birmingham, a victory by an insurgent faction over the old guard. Anti-D'Alesandro candidates won other posts in Baltimore's delegation to the Democratic National Convention in Chicago that would nominate former Illinois governor Adlai Stevenson for president.

Tommy D'Alesandro still aspired to statewide office. In 1958, he narrowly won the Democratic nomination for the U.S. Senate, defeating George P. Mahoney by two percentage points. (Mahoney led the faction that had ousted D'Alesandro as national committeeman two years earlier.) But the Baltimore mayor lost the general election in another close contest to the Republican incumbent, J. Glenn Beall.

D'Alesandro's lifelong record of electoral victories had been broken.

A year later, in 1959, D'Alesandro ran for an unprecedented fourth term as mayor of Baltimore. It would be his final race. After two decades of being the powerhouse of Baltimore politics, D'Alesandro was trounced in the Democratic primary. The candidate who won the nomination and later the general election was J. Harold Grady, a former FBI agent and state's attorney who ran as a "good government" candidate.

The primary drew record turnout, and the results were reported in a banner across the top of the front page of the morning papers.

"Grady Beats D'Alesandro by 33,000," the top deck of the *Baltimore Sun* screamed. "D'Alesandro fatigue" cost him reelection, Matthew Crenson, a political scientist who wrote the definitive history of Baltimore, told me. "People were tired of him by then. There had been this accumulation of accusations of special dealing and vote manipulation and all sorts of other stuff."

Down the road, President Kennedy would appoint D'Alesandro to the Federal Renegotiation Board, a panel that reviewed federal contracts and a political reward for a supporter. Years after that, Maryland governor Marvin Mandel would appoint him to the state parole board. But the remarkable elective career of the ebullient candidate known to everyone as Tommy the Elder—the youngest member of the state legislature, the challenger who had ousted an incumbent of his own party from Congress, the big-city mayor who hobnobbed with presidents—was over.

On Election Night, he made no excuses. "I have no alibis, boys," he told reporters. Would he back Grady in the general election? "Hell, yes!" he replied. "I'm a Democrat, and I'll live a Democrat and die a Democrat!"

## CHAPTER FIVE

# A VIEW OF THE CAPITOL

*1958—Trinity College, Washington, D.C.*

Gene Raynor was a teenager in Little Italy when he began to work as an errand boy for Tommy D'Alesandro Jr. Raynor had been a kid at loose ends after his parents divorced; he found his footing as an all-purpose gofer for the mayor, the start of his own long career in politics. Which is why he was in the D'Alesandro kitchen when Tommy the Elder and Big Nancy were arguing about where their daughter, who was about to graduate from high school, would attend college.

"Nancy wanted to go out of town," said Antero Pietila, a *Baltimore Sun* reporter for thirty-five years who counted Raynor as a source, on this story and others. "Mrs. D'Alesandro says that the matter has been resolved and that we have agreed with Nancy where she's going to school," to Trinity College in Washington. "The mayor says, 'Over my dead body.' And she shoots back, 'It can be arranged.'"

"Daddy had hoped I would go to college in Baltimore and live at home," Nancy Pelosi said in a less provocative recollection of the family debate. "Poor Daddy! With Mommy as my ally, he didn't stand a chance."

Baltimore was their anchor. Tommy D'Alesandro Jr. had been born there; Nancy Lombardi had moved there from Italy as a toddler. They had lived in the same row house, at 245 Albemarle Street, since the day they were married; they would stay there until the day they died. Their seven children were all born in Baltimore, and all their sons spent their lives in the city. Indeed, two of them continued to live in the family home for years after their parents had passed away. The boys were protective of their only sister, the baby of the family.

That was one reason she was eager to leave, even if she ventured no farther than Washington, thirty-seven miles from her front door to Trinity's leafy campus. "I wanted to be independent," she said. "And they were always, you know, 'Oh, you can't do this, you can't do that.' Telling me all the things I couldn't do." She settled on Trinity with the calculation that her parents were more likely to agree to let her leave Baltimore if she proposed a Catholic school that enrolled only women, and one that was close to their hometown.

It was a tumultuous time for the D'Alesandro family. Her father's remarkable political career was on the decline. Despite scandal and a long hospital stay, he won a third term as mayor in 1955. But the next year, in a rebuke to the political machine that had ruled for so long, he was ousted as the Democratic national committeeman for Maryland. In 1957, he dropped out of the race for the Democratic nomination for governor. When Nancy graduated from high school in 1958, from the Institute of Notre Dame, her father was in the middle of a heated campaign for the U.S. Senate.

When the big day arrived to enroll at Trinity, Nicky was supposed to drive his sister and mother to Washington, only to have his car conk out. They ended up piling in the Mercury of a friend of Nicky named Peter Angelos, who drove them to the campus instead. (Then a law school student, Angelos went on to gain wealth and fame, serving a term on the Baltimore City Council and buying the Baltimore Orioles.) During the drive, Nancy, eighteen years old, was excited but acted as though "she had everything under control," Angelos recalled. She gave no hint of how homesick she would feel once they drove away; she would secretly cry at night for the next two weeks. It was the first time she had spent any extended period away from her family.

Her departure for college was a declaration of independence for her and the culmination of a dream for her mother. Big Nancy had a sharp mind and an entrepreneurial spirit, but her own education had ended at high school. With six children at home, she had enrolled in law school classes at night but had to drop out when her sons caught whooping cough and needed her. The demands of her family and the expectations of her era meant she never had the chance to spread her wings. She was determined that her daughter would.

"It was an old-fashioned Italian family, and the boys are everything, the men are everything," Rosalind Wyman, a close friend and Democratic doyenne, told me years later. "But her mother was a very important influence on her, and she says, 'Nancy, you can do things. It just doesn't have to be your brothers.'"

"My father was a committed parochial guy," Nancy's oldest brother said. "My mother was for opening the windows."

The drive to Trinity only took about an hour, but it changed everything. Turning onto the campus driveway for the first time was like "entering Shangri-La," Nancy Pelosi recalled. For once, she wouldn't be known first and foremost as the mayor's daughter. She didn't have to be called "Little Nancy" to distinguish her from her formidable mother; she could just be "Nancy" now. She escaped the oversight of five older brothers. Even though she was heading to school in the nation's capital—and at a time of excitement around the presidential prospects of a handsome young Catholic senator named Jack Kennedy—the setting was a respite from the political world she had been immersed in since the day she was born.

"For me, it was a break from politics," Nancy Pelosi said, "a nice break."

Her opportunity for anonymity was threatened at the start. At the school's welcoming reception that first day, she didn't know a soul. Another new student came up to chat and spied her name tag. "Nancy D'Alesandro," she read aloud, then asked, "Is your father running for Senate?"

"How did you know?" Nancy replied in a whisper.

The young woman turned out to be Martha Dodd. Her father, Thomas Dodd, was also running for a seat in the U.S. Senate, from Connecticut. He would win, and her brother Chris Dodd would later serve in the Senate as well. She had seen campaign billboards for Tommy D'Alesandro as her parents drove her through Maryland on their way to Trinity. "We agreed that we wouldn't talk about it to our classmates," Pelosi said. "Thus began my new, normal existence."

Whether she realized it, though, the other students immediately figured it out. "The first thing I heard in that fall was, 'Be careful with your radio; don't have it up too loud because the commercials for the Republicans in Baltimore'" were attacking Nancy's father, classmate Jeanne Lynch told me. "It would be embarrassing to have her walk down the hall and hear it, so we were kind of careful to keep the radio down. I didn't know her, but I didn't want to start out by hurting her feelings."

"Everybody knew," said Carol Curran, another classmate. "But we were like, 'If they said something bad, turn off the radio.'"

That conspiracy of silence protected Nancy's privacy. Her father would lose his campaign for the Senate that November. The next year, he would be defeated again, this time in his bid for the Democratic nomination for an unprecedented fourth term as mayor, the last campaign he would run. Nancy didn't raise the topic, and no one else asked. "All four years, I never heard anybody having a conversation like that," Curran told me.

After she received her bachelor's degree in history from Trinity in 1962, Nancy D'Alesandro landed a job as a receptionist for a newly elected Maryland senator as she prepared for her wedding. Once married, she moved with her new husband to New York City, then across the country to his hometown of San Francisco.

"Although my roots were in Baltimore, and that is where my journey began... it was my brothers who stayed close to home," Nancy Pelosi said. "I was the one, it seemed, who was destined to fly away."

———

The stately brick buildings of Trinity College stood on a rise of land in Northeast D.C., in Edgewood. With adjacent Brookland and Michigan Park, the neighborhood was dubbed "Little Rome" because of the cluster of Catholic institutions in the vicinity. On a clear day, the fourth floor of Trinity's Main Hall offered a spectacular view of the Capitol, three miles straight south on a small hill of its own. The gleaming dome was a striking sight at sunrise and sunset.

But the vistas for the young women on campus were decidedly limited.

The first Catholic liberal arts college for women in the country, Trinity had been founded by the Sisters of Notre Dame in 1897 because Catholic University of America, located down the road and across the street, admitted only men at the time. The nuns wanted young women to have the same opportunity for higher education. Even so, students who enrolled in the fall of 1958 understood that they could pick from three crucial choices that would define their futures: Join a religious order. Embrace what the nuns called "single blessedness" (the students called it being an old maid). Or marry. Nearly everyone settled on marriage.

Within a decade or so, with the explosion of the women's movement, those options would seem impossibly constrained. Women on campuses and elsewhere would feel increasingly empowered to challenge stereotypes, pursue careers, demand equality. That social revolution would undermine the appeal of many women's colleges, prompting some to open their doors to men and others to close their doors entirely. Over time, Trinity would recast itself as a school that served young women and some men in the community, many of them African American or from immigrant families, striving for the middle class.

At the moment, the Trinity class of 1962 generally accepted the norms of the day and the dictates of the nuns. The dress code required students to wear skirts. As freshmen, their curfew was initially set at 10:30 p.m., then extended to 11 p.m. When they left campus, they would flip over a card with their name on it, noting the time they expected to be back. When they returned, if they missed curfew even by just two or three minutes, they were required to note it. Being late for a total of twenty minutes in a week meant being "campused," not allowed to leave on the next Saturday. Male visitors were restricted to the "smoker," a community room in Cuvilly Hall, the newly constructed dorm, where burgers were for sale and a bridge game was often under way.

The nuns were cloistered, so none of them lived in the dorms to police the students' behavior. That wasn't necessary. "It was an honor system, and, in general, it worked," Jeanne Lynch said. Carol Curran agreed. "I'd say 99 percent of us did exactly that."

Nancy D'Alesandro admitted to few rebellions, except for the time she and a friend snuck down to the dining hall at night and swiped ice cream bars. The freezer was locked but the lid could be lifted to create just enough of a gap for a hand to slip inside. "We would have bought the ice cream if they would have been there to sell it," she said. "But it was there, and it was challenging. What we did learn was that in the dark of night, it was hard to tell the flavors apart."

That obedient mien—the biggest rule flouted during her college years was swiping an ice cream bar after hours?—is hard to square with the tough-minded political leader who would later challenge the male Democratic establishment and confront presidents, but there it is.

There were some early signs of the changes ahead for women. When Nancy D'Alesandro was a freshman at Trinity, Sister Margaret Claydon, a Trinity graduate and English teacher, was named the school's new president. At age thirty-six, she became one of the nation's youngest college presidents. Nancy would remember her as young, sophisticated, and successful, "a symbol of strength and empowerment." During her sixteen years in the job, Sister Margaret would drop the curfew rules and the maid service in the dining halls. She would extend enrollment to women whose education had been interrupted by marriages, children, or jobs.

"Educated women must have definite views and standards," she declared at a press conference sufficiently forward-leaning that it drew the attention of *Time* magazine. "They must know the good from the bad, and be able to say why. A woman must not only know facts—she must have ideas about them."

At Trinity, she said, "We're not in the business of training committee women or bridge players."

With a campus in Washington, Trinity enrolled the daughters of ambassadors and politicians. Barbara Bailey, a member of the class of 1958, was the daughter of John Bailey, a power broker from Connecticut and onetime Democratic national chairman; later, as Barbara Kennelly, she would become a groundbreaking member of Congress. Kathleen Gilligan, class of 1970, was the daughter of Ohio governor John Gilligan; as Kathleen Sebelius, she would be elected governor of Kansas, the first daughter of a governor to be elected governor herself. Later, Kellyanne Fitzpatrick was a member of the class of 1989; as Kellyanne Conway, she would become the first woman to run a winning presidential campaign. She later served as a senior White House counselor for President Donald Trump.

And Nancy D'Alesandro, class of 1962, the daughter of the mayor of Baltimore, as Nancy Pelosi would become Speaker of the House. The inscription next to her graduation portrait in her senior yearbook: "Solemn she is rarely seen yet thoughts and deep are there."

With the benefit of hindsight, Jeanne Lynch recognized clues in the political science classes they shared for the path her friend would one day take. "Nancy was always fascinated with the process," she told me. "The rest of us were into policy, economics, socialism—you know, all that kind of stuff. But Nancy was into how you get the votes out, how you get control, how you get the power. I thought that was the boring end of it, and I thought, 'Well, I don't know why she's so interested in that.'"

Years later, she understood why. "Once it came out that she was taking over the Democratic Party in California, you knew she was on her way, and it suddenly all fit," Lynch said. "It was like the pieces of a puzzle falling into place."

————

Nancy's father had been an FDR man and then embraced JFK. His support mattered; big-city bosses in those days were Democratic power brokers. In January 1960, Tommy D'Alesandro had stepped down as Baltimore's mayor, courtesy of the voters. But after more than eight years in Congress and twelve years in City Hall, he still had political juice. At the Maryland Democratic convention in May, the *Baltimore Sun* reported that he "proved the hit of the lot" when he rallied Kennedy supporters. "He'll get the nomination—and he'll get it early," Tommy the Elder predicted to cheers. He was elected as a delegate to the Democratic National Convention being held that summer in Los Angeles. Because of his fear of flying, he and his wife and daughter crossed the country by train. They stopped in San Francisco on the way, the first time Nancy saw the city she would adopt as home a few years later.

A convention delegate and a Democratic VIP, Tommy D'Alesandro Jr. got front-row seats and special passes at the convention.

"It was the most exciting thing," Pelosi remembered decades later in a speech at the JFK Presidential Library and Museum. Massachusetts senator Edward M. Kennedy was in the audience as she talked about his brother. She called the experience "thrilling in every respect." In part, that was because Jack Kennedy was the first Catholic nominated for president by a major party since 1928, when New York governor Al Smith had been crushed in a landslide by Herbert Hoover. When she spoke at the presidential library in 2008, she wore a campaign pin that said "Youth for Kennedy" over the outline of a donkey. She had bought it at the 1960 convention and saved it ever since.

In his acceptance speech at the Memorial Coliseum, John Kennedy tackled concerns about his Catholicism head-on. "I am fully aware of the fact that the Democratic Party, by nominating someone of my faith, has taken on what many regard as a new and hazardous risk—new, at least, since 1928," he began. His nomination reflected the delegates' trust in the fairness of voters, he went on. "I hope that no American, considering the really critical issues facing this country, will waste his franchise by voting either for me or against me solely on account of my religious affiliation. It is not relevant."

What his address is most remembered for was his signature call for what he called a New Frontier. "But the New Frontier of which I speak is not a set of promises—it is a set of challenges," he said. "It sums up not what I intend to offer the American people, but what I intend to ask of them."

The next night, as a special treat, her parents let Nancy choose a restaurant for dinner. She picked Romanoff's in Beverly Hills, a favorite of Hollywood's old guard. When the waiter brought the menus, her father blanched. "Wow, look at these prices," he protested. "How did you ever find this place? Why are we here?" His daughter replied, defensively, "Well, this is Hollywood and it costs a lot of money here."

Then, suddenly, all was forgiven. "The door opens and in walks John F. Kennedy and his entourage, and all of a sudden this place is perfect," Pelosi recalled. "He came right over to the table. 'Mr. Mayor, how are you? Thanks for all you're doing to help and all the rest.'" She was glad she was wearing her "Youth for Kennedy" pin. And the pricey menu? After JFK's greeting, her father no longer minded. "The prices just seemed to melt," she said.

In Washington the next January, she attended Kennedy's inauguration in the freezing cold, eight inches of snow covering the ground.

———

Nancy D'Alesandro wanted to attend law school, a step that her mother had longed to do herself. Even though Big Nancy had gotten married at age nineteen, and happily, she encouraged other young women to take their time before settling down. "I think it's fair to say she didn't recommend marrying young," her daughter said. "Whenever she heard that a young woman was getting married, she'd say, 'I don't know why she's rushing into this. She has all this talent, all this spirit and intelligence—why does anyone have to get married so young?'"

That wistful view reflected her own thwarted ambitions. It was advice her daughter was inclined to follow. She took the LSAT, the Law School Admission Test, a sign of how seriously she was considering law school. Then she met Paul Frank Pelosi.

He was a student at Georgetown University, the Jesuit school on the other side of town. In 1961, between their junior and senior years, she enrolled in a summer school class at Georgetown on the history of sub-Saharan Africa. But he didn't make an impression on her—nor she on him—the first time or two they casually met. One day they were gathered with mutual friends at Teehan's, a hangout near campus, when one of her friends asked him where his classes were being held. When he answered, she remarked, "Oh, you're right next door to Nancy."

"Nancy who?" he asked.

Soon after that, Nancy was in the living room of Denny Meyer, a Georgetown law student who was engaged to her roommate and best friend, Rita Murray. Suddenly Paul Pelosi was standing at the open window. "What are you guys talking about?" he asked. They were discussing the Korean War; the armistice had been reached a few years earlier, in 1953. Paul joined the conversation as Nancy said she had to run out to pick up some clothes before the cleaners closed. He pulled out a laundry ticket and said, "While you're there, will you pick up my shirts?"

Her response to his presumption was telling and set the landscape for the relationship that would follow—traditional in many ways, but not one in which she was a timid helpmate. She took the ticket, put it in her pocket, picked up her clothes, and came back. "I thought I had more shirts than that," Paul said. "I forgot all about your shirts," she replied. Like her mother, she didn't swoon the first time she met her future husband.

He began to sit in on her class, taught by renowned history professor

Carroll Quigley. (When Georgetown graduate Bill Clinton was accepting the Democratic nomination for president in 1992, he would cite JFK's call to service and Quigley's course on civilizations as defining influences on his life.) That summer, Sargent Shriver, a Kennedy brother-in-law who a few months earlier had been appointed the first director of the Peace Corps, spoke to the class. Paul asked Nancy if she'd like to go out for a beer afterward.

"A beer?" she replied. "I don't think so." She rarely drank alcohol, then or later.

"How about dessert?" he persisted.

That was a more appealing offer; she was a fervent fan of chocolate, then and later.

"When we started dating, she was smart as hell and very knowledgeable," Paul Pelosi told me. He described her as beautiful, shy, and serious. Her dark brown hair was cut short and curled behind her ears. She would describe him as a "lovely, calm person" and a "good sport." He was tall and handsome, with a mop of hair. They had each turned twenty-one years old that spring—indeed, within three weeks of one another.

Both had endured difficult experiences in life that had given them more gravity than many of their peers. By the time she left for college at age eighteen, Nancy D'Alesandro had seen her family play, and survive, political hardball. When Paul Pelosi was sixteen years old, he was behind the wheel in a tragic automobile crash that killed his older brother.

At the time, Paul was a student at St. Ignatius Academy in San Francisco, one of four sons of a successful wholesale druggist in the city. Just before 1 a.m. on a February night in 1957, he picked up his brother David John Pelosi at the home of a girlfriend. David, three years older and a student at the College of San Mateo, suggested a ride down the peninsula.

At 2:40 a.m., they were traveling about 55 miles an hour down

Skyline Boulevard when David cautioned his brother to slow down because they were entering a "bad stretch" of road. Paul told California Highway Patrol investigators later that he tried to "gear down" the sports car. But it careened across the highway and bounced off an embankment, landing upside down on the shoulder of the road.

Both brothers were trapped underneath. His collarbone broken, Paul managed to struggle free and summon help. When the highway patrolmen arrived, they jacked up the car to try to extricate David. But he was already dead, apparently strangled by a neck brace he was wearing; he had injured his neck making a shallow dive at Lake Tahoe the previous summer.

Three months later, at the inquest in Redwood City, a coroner's jury cleared Paul of blame and recommended that signs warning of sharp curves be erected along that stretch of road. Nancy Pelosi said later that the family's Catholic faith sustained them when they lost "dear David," as his mother would always call him.

When their senior year in college began, Paul Pelosi and Nancy D'Alesandro began to date, a romance developing, slowly. One day after Mass in the university's Dahlgren Chapel, walking along the edge of the small Jesuit cemetery, she asked him, jokingly, "What are you going to do when you grow up?"

"I'm going to come looking for you," he said.

A year later, in the chapel, he proposed and she accepted. Afterward, they drove to Baltimore and Paul asked her father for her hand in marriage. He agreed, but with a condition: "More than anything else, Daddy did not want to be the one to tell his wife," his daughter recalled. "He told us we had to do it."

When they did, Big Nancy looked almost sad. "Oh, my," she said to her daughter with tears in her eyes. "I thought you'd always be with us." Little Nancy didn't say aloud the response that ran through her mind: *"You also thought I was going to be a nun."* Instead, she said, "Mommy, I love Paul. I want to marry him."

———

They graduated in the spring of 1962, but their wedding wouldn't take place until September 1963. Paul Pelosi was studying economics at New York University's business school. Nancy D'Alesandro applied for her first job on Capitol Hill, as a receptionist for Daniel Brewster, a newly elected Democratic senator from Maryland.

When Nancy D'Alesandro applied for a job, "I grabbed her with both my hands," Brewster, who died in 2007, told Marc Sandalow for his biography of Pelosi, published in 2008. The D'Alesandro name mattered in Maryland, and Nancy's father had been a key supporter of Brewster in his campaign. "It was probably the most exciting and quickest hire that my father ever had," Brewster's son, Gerry, told me. "He hired her on the spot." Senator Brewster ordered nameplates for all his staffers, but he made hers larger than the others.

"My father knew right away that he wanted Nancy D'Alesandro to be the face of his Senate office, to be the one that greeted people when they came in," Gerry Brewster said. "So hers was literally the very first desk in the only doorway going into the Senate suite for the public to access." She welcomed visitors, answered the phones, opened the mail, arranged tours of the White House and the Capitol, and helped draft responses to queries from constituents.

Matthew Crenson, then an undergraduate at Johns Hopkins University, was working occasionally as a gofer and driver for Vincent Lanasa, a political hack from northeast Baltimore known to all as Murph. Crenson would become a political science professor at Johns Hopkins, the author of *Baltimore: A Political History*. He met Nancy D'Alesandro when he drove Murph to Washington one day to meet with Maryland's new senator.

"Murph looked like he was sent from central casting to be a machine politician," Crenson told me. "He was fat; he smoked cigars and, you know, wore a fedora all the time. He had dropped out of school in the fourth grade." But when Murph arrived at Brewster's office, Nancy

D'Alesandro "treated him like visiting royalty. He was the center of her attention." He was, of course, completely charmed. No one had to tell the daughter of Tommy the Elder and Big Nancy who Murph was, or why he mattered.

In one of those remarkable coincidences, Brewster also hired a clerk named Steny Hoyer, a University of Maryland senior who had already been spotted as a political up-and-comer. He was vice president of the Student Government Association and a member of the Young Democrats.

Some accounts describe Nancy D'Alesandro and Steny Hoyer as interns in the Senate office; in fact, congressional records from the time show both as congressional staffers. She was listed as a secretary and he as a clerk. She was hired at twice his salary. (Pelosi found that impossible to believe, when I told her congressional records showed that; she insisted he must have been working fewer hours than she was.) She was paid $1,360.45 for the first quarter of 1963, about $106 a week. He was paid $629.67 that quarter, about $49 a week. During the second quarter, she was paid $1,391.37 and he was paid $725.18.

The staff directory for the 88th Congress shows Senator Brewster with fifteen staff members. "D'Alesandro, Nancy—secty" is listed just above "Hoyer, S. Hamilton—asst."

"A great sort of irony of history," Hoyer told me with a laugh. "Nancy's sitting ten feet from me being a receptionist and I'm processing [military] academy appointments for Senator Brewster, you know, and these two kids end up for two decades being the leaders of the Democrats in the House of Representatives."

Leaders, and rivals. The enmity between them was all but open after they competed for Democratic whip in 2001. Their relationship got worse five years later after she backed the challenge by her old friend John Murtha of Pennsylvania to Hoyer as majority leader. The source of the friction would become the topic of endless gossip on Capitol Hill. Idle speculation that they might have dated while both were working in Brewster's office, besides being a bit of a sexist trope, doesn't meet the commonsense standard. At the time, he had recently gotten married and she was engaged. "We weren't friends; we were coworkers," Hoyer told me. "She was delightful, and we had a good relationship."

Friends who were close to Pelosi at the time told me Hoyer had treated Nancy D'Alesandro in the dismissive, superior way that men of that era (and not only that era) often treated women. He was graduating from the University of Maryland; she had just graduated from Trinity College. But he landed a job that would put him on track to deal with legislation; she was hired as the receptionist who greeted visitors.

However, both Pelosi and Hoyer told me their relationship in Brewster's office was cordial and mutually respectful. Her friends who said otherwise may have confused Hoyer with another staffer in the Senate office who was "a little bit chauvinistic" toward her, Pelosi said. Hoyer denied there was any basis for the criticism. "I can't believe I really treated her any differently than I would have treated any other colleague," he told me.

The most likely explanation for the tension in their relationship is the most obvious one, in politics and the workplace. They competed for the same job. One of them got it.

At the time, neither of them could have imagined how their political ambitions would one day intersect and collide. Hoyer's career was on the rise. After four years as a staffer in Brewster's office, he won a seat in the Maryland State Senate. Nine years later, he was elected its president, the youngest person to hold the post in the state's history. In 1981, he was elected to the U.S. Congress, eventually ranking as the dean of the Maryland delegation.

Pelosi would have a more circuitous path and a slower start in politics. Hoyer had been elected to his fifth term in the U.S. House by the time she won a congressional seat herself, an unexpected candidate in a special election. In time, though, she was the one who would move into the Speaker's office.

For now, she left Capitol Hill when she got married. The Reverend Felix Cardenas, a D'Alesandro cousin, performed the ceremony at

Baltimore's Cathedral of Mary Our Queen. She wore an embroidered lace mantilla and carried a bouquet of white glamelias, a composite bouquet arrangement fashioned from gladiolus petals. There was a maid of honor and five bridesmaids and three flower girls; all her brothers served as ushers. "Mrs. Paul Pelosi was Miss Nancy D'Alesandro before her marriage," the caption on her photo in the *Baltimore Sun* read.

They spent their honeymoon in Puerto Rico, then moved to New York City—to a new home, and a new job for Paul, at First National City Bank, and, soon, a slew of children. Nancy Corinne, named after her grandmothers, arrived less than a year later. When Nancy and Paul Pelosi left New York City in 1969, they would have four young children in tow.

# CHAPTER SIX

## "PROPER PREPARATION PREVENTS POOR PERFORMANCE"

*January 23, 1969—New York, New York*

Nancy and Paul Pelosi had five children in the span of six years and one week, practically a biological marvel. "The week Nancy turned six, we had our fifth baby, Alexandra," she said. She was then thirty years old. "The Catholic way," she wryly called it years later when she delivered the commencement address at Trinity Washington University, her alma mater. Looking back, there were those who saw the arrival of her children as a delay in starting down the political path that would follow, a prorogation that no man would have had to face. Her children were born between 1964 and 1970, in the wake of publication of the landmark *Feminine Mystique*. The women's movement was taking hold, opening doors of opportunity and a window into the resentment many women felt about traditional roles.

But Nancy Pelosi expressed no frustration, then or later, about her days of raising four daughters and a son. They equipped her to succeed in the unexpected career that followed, she said. After she became the most powerful woman in the history of the country, she said her children had been more influential in shaping the leader she became than even her formidable parents.

"I really was forged by my children," she said. "Having five children in six years and understanding the difference in personalities, from one to the next, is a real lesson, but also you become so disciplined in terms of schedule and use of time and respect for everyone's needs that I think I'm a much different person coming out of raising my kids than I was going in."

Being the parents of five young children was "master-class training" for what would be ahead for his wife, Paul Pelosi told me. "You've got to be on top of it and organized," he said. "Being an arbitrator, booster, and enforcer, you've got to handle a lot of balls in the air all the time." Later, in politics, "One of the secrets of her success is that she can handle a lot of balls in the air at the same time and keeps things in their proper slot with a calm, confident attitude."

She would use that experience as a recruiting tool, a fund-raising appeal, a source of humor. She would use it to bait a president when she accused Donald Trump of throwing a temper tantrum. "I'm a mother of five, grandmother of nine," she told reporters after he angrily walked out of a White House meeting with her. "I know a temper tantrum when I see one."

She insisted that she wasn't restless when her life revolved around changing diapers, fixing dinner, and taking toddlers to the park. "I was personally content because for me, there was nothing more exciting than having and caring for new babies," she said. As her children were growing up, she and her husband would joke that they wanted to send them outside in the rain to shrink them and start over. Decades later, a photo from a Capitol Hill news conference showed three other female members of Congress intent on the TV cameras, discussing some important policy issue. The Speaker of the House is standing to one side, eyes closed and a look of bliss on her face as she cuddles a baby someone had brought to the event.

One of her daughters sent the photo with a teasing note to the family's private group chat. "Okay," it read. "Who's going to give her a new baby?"

But Nancy Pelosi, like her mother, harbored ambitions to go to law school when the children were older. She believed there would be a time for that and more. "I always knew that I did not want to deal only with the meals, the laundry, and the house forever," she said. Even during the most demanding days of motherhood, when she was "in my own little world," Nancy Pelosi remained an active Democrat. "I even volunteered during the 1966 midterm elections, though I certainly don't claim to have done very much—just some leafleting for Democratic candidates (while pushing my babies in a stroller)," she said. Her children gave her cover to roll past New York City doormen and ignore "no solicitation" signs in a way other get-out-the-vote volunteers couldn't. "I was a mom with three babies in a stroller," she said. "Who was going to stop me?"

That activism was a surprise to her close friends from college, a time that had been something of a respite from politics for Nancy D'Alesandro. Carol Curran was a classmate from Trinity who also moved to New York after graduation and marriage. She called the Pelosis' Manhattan apartment one day and asked for Nancy. "No, no, she's not here; I'm watching the kids," Paul Pelosi told her. "She's a delegate."

"I said, 'Oh, okay, great,' and I hung up," Curran told me. "And I said to [my husband] Frank, 'What's a delegate?'"

In Baltimore, Nancy's oldest brother, Thomas D'Alesandro III, was elected mayor in 1967, following in their father's footsteps. But father and son divided their allegiances in the 1968 Democratic presidential race. Tommy the Elder backed the establishment candidate, Vice President Hubert Humphrey; Tommy the Younger supported the insurgent, New York senator Robert Kennedy. At the Maryland state convention, the D'Alesandros squared off in the battle for convention delegates. "It was a serious, generational fight," Nancy Pelosi said.

Tragedy ended it when Bobby Kennedy was assassinated as he celebrated winning the California primary. Two months later, Nancy and Paul Pelosi went with her father and brother to the tumultuous

Democratic National Convention in Chicago, which was scarred by street protests and a police crackdown. "Paul and I had a foot in both worlds," she said. "We were able to go onto the convention floor, and also get into the park across from our hotel to see the confrontations between the antiwar protestors and the baton-wielding police."

She opposed the Vietnam War but supported Humphrey when he was nominated, despite criticism by antiwar activists that he should have broken sooner and more decisively with President Lyndon Johnson. Always a pragmatist, she was focused on the imperative to elect a Democrat to the White House. "I stuffed many 'Humphrey for President' leaflets under apartment doors that fall," she recalled, "visibly pregnant with my fourth child, and with my little girls in a stroller."

Party loyalty was a lesson she had learned from her parents. Four years later, "they weren't all that crazy about [George] McGovern," Pelosi told me. The liberal South Dakota senator would carry only Massachusetts and the District of Columbia against Richard Nixon in 1972. But the D'Alesandros backed him anyway. "It became a sort of, 'You're either with us or you're not' kind of thing," she said. "It was, 'This is what we believe in.'"

———

January 23, 1969, would be a momentous day for the Pelosi family.

Nancy Pelosi gave birth in a New York City hospital for the fourth time in four years. They named the new baby Paul Jr., his father's namesake, a brother joining three older sisters. That same day, Paul Sr. was offered a job with a financial services company in San Francisco. It was the city where he had grown up, where his mother lived, where his brother had been elected to his first term on the city council. The job was with a new company that leased computers to businesses in what would become known as Silicon Valley.

"If we're ever going to go to California, now is the time," Paul Pelosi told his wife. Four weeks later, they were heading west.

Just managing the plane ride was a test of their organizational and

parenting skills. Paul Jr. was a babe in arms. Jacqueline was a toddler, eighteen months old. Christine was two and a half. Even Nancy
Corinne, the oldest, was only four. On the flight, they sang round after
round of "California, Here We Come." (The reaction of their fellow
passengers on the cross-country trip has been lost to history.)

Nancy Pelosi, then twenty-eight, didn't flinch at the idea of cart-
ing her growing brood across the country, though she loved living in
New York. She was already the only member of her close-knit family to
leave Baltimore, attending college in Washington, D.C., then moving
to New York. But she did make two demands before agreeing to resettle
three thousand miles away.

First, to have the *New York Times* delivered at home. "That was
harder in those days," she said later. Sometimes the paper would arrive
a day or two late. "But I had to keep in touch. Do that daily crossword
puzzle. It kept my brain going." Second, not to stay in somebody else's
house. "I am a person who needs my own space," she told her husband.

It was only after the plane had taken off from New York that Paul Sr.
turned to her gingerly. "My mother would be *so sad* if, on our very first
night in San Francisco, we didn't stay in her home," he said. His father, a
successful businessman who owned Kearny Wholesale Drugs, had died
two years earlier, collapsing in front of their house at age sixty-six. Now
his mother was eager to see her grandchildren. "Come on, Nancy," he
coaxed her. "We'll just go there for one night, and then we'll move on."

They would end up staying with his mother for four months.

In some ways, the household in the Marina District of San Francisco
was familiar for Nancy D'Alesandro Pelosi, not unlike the one she had
left back in Little Italy. Paul's parents had immigrated from Italy and
reared four sons in San Francisco. But keeping the preschoolers under
some semblance of control in borrowed quarters and under the gaze of
her blunt-spoken mother-in-law was no easy task. One Sunday morning in the breakfast room, the baby boy in her lap and the three girls
playing at their feet, Nancy and Paul looked at each other and had to

laugh over the mayhem. "At least we're happy," Nancy said to him. "Just think of what you'd be without us."

Eavesdropping from the next room, her mother-in-law spoke up. "An attorney!" Corinne Pelosi shouted. That had been her aspiration for her son, a dream that in her view had been thwarted by his marriage and the quick arrival of a clutch of children. (Actually, Paul had long before lost interest in law school.)

In San Francisco, they discovered to their dismay that many landlords were less than eager to rent to a family with four young children. A household with four dogs would have been more welcome, Nancy Pelosi concluded with exasperation. Finally, she found a big house that had already been childproofed. The backyard had a swing set and a sandbox. The owners were willing. She was ecstatic.

As they were negotiating the final details, she asked, casually, why the house was available. Her husband had been appointed to a top job in the Department of Health, Education, and Welfare, the woman said proudly. "So we'll be going back East to join the Nixon administration."

As a little girl, Nancy D'Alesandro had once refused to accept the gift of a toy elephant from a poll worker because of the partisan symbolism she understood even then. Now, as desperate as she was to move out of her mother-in-law's domain, she knew that this was an arrangement she could not abide. She had volunteered for Humphrey's presidential campaign the previous fall, a time when she was the mother of three young children and pregnant with a fourth. When Nixon won, she had cried for three days.

She told her astonished real estate agent, "I could never live anyplace that was made available because of the election of Richard Nixon." The deal was off. Nancy and Paul Pelosi finally gave up looking for a place to rent and instead bought a big house in affluent Presidio Terrace, one that needed some work.

That prospective landlord who had gone to work for Nixon was Lewis Butler. "All I knew was that a tenant had backed out," he told me more than a half century later. His wife was handling the rental of their house while he moved to Washington for his appointment in the Nixon administration as assistant HEW secretary for planning and evaluation. The real estate agent didn't tell them why the family with four children decided at the last minute not to sign a lease. They soon found another tenant.

As it happened, Butler's tenure in Washington didn't last long, ending in a way Nancy Pelosi would have approved. In 1971, he became one of the first Nixon administration officials to resign to protest the Vietnam War and the U.S. bombing of Cambodia.

Butler returned to San Francisco and eventually became a founder of the Ploughshares Fund, a nonprofit organization with a mission of reducing and eliminating nuclear weapons. After Pelosi was elected to Congress, they worked together on converting the Presidio from a U.S. Army base into a national park at the northern tip of the San Francisco Peninsula, an arduous process that she pursued for years. During a meeting on that project, Pelosi told him about the time their lives had intersected before. Later, when Butler was invited to a reception at Pelosi's house, she regaled the group with the story of her principled refusal to rent his house.

"It tells you a lot about Nancy, how she's political right down to her core," Butler told me admiringly. In 2019, he was still living in the same big house. "No event in her life wasn't political, including renting a home. She was born that way and raised that way in Baltimore."

———

Nancy Pelosi devised an unofficial family motto and drilled it into her children: "Proper preparation prevents poor performance." Inelegant, perhaps; she would never be known for eloquence. But it was memorably alliterative and applicable to almost any situation. She repeated it so often that the family would shorthand it as "The Five P's."

Which is not to say things were always under control in the Pelosi household.

"Some days I didn't even have time to wash my face," she said of the era dominated by the demands of babies and toddlers. When she was carpooling her children to school in the morning, she would occasionally just throw a coat over her nightgown for the drive. There was the time that California's young governor Jerry Brown came down from using an upstairs bathroom and asked, "What's the name of your cat?" Until that moment, Nancy Pelosi had been unaware that her children were keeping a cat in the attic, albeit not for much longer.

Years after the fact, she and her husband discovered, to their alarm, that daughter Alexandra as a teenager had been sneaking out of the house late at night to play grunge during the graveyard shift at the University of San Francisco radio station.

"Makes going to work look easy, doesn't it?" she would say later, when she was Speaker.

Snafus aside, Pelosi implemented a system that was virtually military. "Methodically planning each troop movement with precision and diplomacy was vital to the stability, ethos, and growth of the family," one of her daughters would write, without apparent irony, in a 2019 book titled *The Nancy Pelosi Way*. Nancy Corinne, named after her two grandmothers, was the oldest, the big sister in charge. She was followed in short order by Christine, the bookworm-turned-activist, then Jacqueline and Paul Jr. Finally, Alexandra, the free spirit. ("She was a character," Rosalind Wyman, the Democratic doyenne from Los Angeles, told me, describing Alexandra's youthful purple hair and thrift-shop clothes. She once showed up at Wyman's estate driving a dilapidated truck she had named Bumpy.)

Each morning, the children were required to make their beds and were encouraged to straighten their rooms before coming down to breakfast. School lunches were prepared assembly-line style, no special requests accommodated: wheat bread, lunch meats, apples, pretzels. The girls would line up to have their hair braided or pulled into pigtails. "One day, in our haste, Jacqueline went to school with one of each," Nancy Pelosi said with chagrin. Their mother was known for weaving braids so tight they could pinch, their father for ones so loose they might unwind by the time the girls got off the bus at the Convent of the Sacred Heart Elementary School.

After school, the children would have a snack, do their homework, and be sent outside to play, often at the nearby playground at the Presidio, an active military installation that also had a park open to civilians. When it was time for dinner, their mother would ring an oversized brass cowbell on the porch to call them home, a scene that sounds more Kansas than California. As soon as the dinner dishes were cleared, the table was set with cereal bowls, ready for breakfast. "It was always planning ahead," daughter Christine told me. "It was very organized and very focused on—we're eating one meal; now we're planning the next one." Before bedtime, Nancy Pelosi would press the girls' plaid Catholic school uniforms for the next morning. The children were responsible for polishing their white school shoes.

She valued efficiency and teamwork, then and later. "Let's have some cooperation," she would say, another favorite axiom. She would run a load of laundry, pull the clothes out of the dryer into a pile, and have the children retrieve and fold what they wanted for themselves. Even when they weren't wearing their school uniforms, she would often dress them in the same colors to make it easier to keep track of them. "She might say, 'Okay, everyone, white pants and yellow turtleneck,'" daughter Christine said. "Then there would be a race to the laundry room because with everyone being relatively close in age and size, the first one would get the best clothes and the last might have a grass stain or frayed hole to contend with."

The lessons learned from being reared in a political family in Baltimore were helpful when she ran for office, Nancy Pelosi said, but she found the organizational skills required of managing motherhood in California just as relevant. "As one of my friends once said about me, 'I knew she was going places when I would go to her house and see those little children folding their own laundry and organizing it into stacks!'" One daughter described it as "synchronized chaos."

Christine called her a "hands-on mom," one who served as class mother at their schools and fashioned their costumes at Halloween. She refereed the inevitable sibling rivalries. She tried to treat all her children fairly but not the same, depending on what they wanted and what they needed. She would figure out what mattered to each of them, sometimes more than they understood themselves. They knew that they could confide in her, that she could be trusted to keep their secrets. "Everybody was always fighting somebody," her daughter recalled. "There was always one of those San Francisco coalitions forming. You could have three on two, and four on one, and five against her, and one-one-one-one-one at any hour of the day."

In other words, Nancy Pelosi perfected the art of forging bonds amid shifting dynamics, experience that would prove crucial later.

She empathized with Paul Jr., the only boy in a family with four sisters, just as she had grown up as the only girl in a family with five brothers. He "was determined to carve out his own path early on, and I could certainly relate to his situation," she said. There was the question of schools. In Baltimore, her brothers had gone to the local parochial school, St. Leo's, but her mother had sent Nancy to the girls' academy across town, the Institute of Notre Dame. "When he was old enough to begin kindergarten, Paul balked at the idea of going to the same school as his sisters, the Convent of the Sacred Heart," his mother recalled. "He made his views known during his defiant interview at the school when he was five."

Paul ended up at the school of his choice, Town School for Boys, where girls in general and sisters in particular weren't allowed. On the first day, he came home with his name tag tied with yarn around his wrist. His sister Jacqueline told him he was supposed to wear it around his neck. "At my school, my teacher said I can wear it anywhere I want," Paul retorted. "You don't go to my school, you weren't there, so you couldn't possibly know."

It was a historic day, his mother said. "It was Paul Jr.'s declaration of independence from the tyranny of a household of girls."

She was strict but she also had a whimsical side, a quality outsiders often didn't see. Christine's favorite childhood memory was of the times her mother would let loose. "She would just dance wildly around the kitchen," Christine said, to the music of disco and Cher. "She would just always, always, always dance. She's not a good singer, but she doesn't let that stop her. She's a great dancer, and she always dances."

Once she had grandchildren, her relationship with them had some whimsy, too. She would keep in touch by text, often communicating via emoji: A plane if she was traveling. An American flag if she was in her office. Streams of hearts and smiles that could make them roll their eyes. In 2016, at age seventy-six, she took two of her grandsons to see the band Metallica in Central Park.

"Aside from all Nancy's accomplishments...she is *fun*," Rita Meyer, her best friend from college, told me. A regular visitor to Pelosi's Georgetown penthouse reported that her refrigerator was often bare but her freezer was always stocked with chocolate ice cream. In April 2020, after displaying a trove of Dove bars and Talenti gelato in her San Francisco kitchen on CBS's *The Late Late Show with James Corden*, she tweeted, "We all have found our ways to keep our spirits up during these trying times. Mine just happens to fill up my freezer."

When her children were growing up, some of the advice Nancy Pelosi gave them then was the same guidance she would later give to political hopefuls, or take herself, including when dealing with the famously provocative Trump. "Don't take the bait," she would tell her children when they were being teased. After they got into scuffles, she would dismiss their plaintive cries unless they were really hurt. "Throw a punch, take a punch," she would tell them, quoting her father. Her attitude was matter-of-fact. "She was like, unless someone's bleeding or like there's a broken bone—you play rough, you get hurt," one daughter said.

And this counsel, offered during family competitions in cards and backgammon. "First you need to learn how to play the game," she would tell them. "Then you need to learn how to win the game."

———

By the time her children were all enrolled in school, "I was so super-charged that I was ready to do more," Nancy Pelosi told an interviewer in 1984, when she was head of the host committee for the Democratic National Convention. "I used to think as I was sitting in the park for eight hours a day watching them play, that when they're in school, and I have enough time, I could do something—like feed all the hungry people in the world."

Now she had the space to expand her work as an organizer and a fund-raiser.

Politics were always a family affair. "I was indoctrinated into a Democratic Party cult from a very early age," daughter Alexandra joked. "She modeled our house in San Francisco after the house where she grew up in Baltimore. Our house was like a VFW hall. She'd be working the issues from there, stuffing mailers, having parties." At political events, the children were enlisted to take coats and pass hors d'oeuvres. When they were put to work sorting political mailings by zip code—the postal rate was lower that way—they would form an assembly line. While stuffing and sealing envelopes, they would sing their own lyrics to a popular spiritual: "He's got the stuffers and the mailers in his hand." When a reporter showed up at her house for an interview before the 1984 convention, she spied the five teenagers at work, putting together press kits.

Nancy Pelosi would pile the children in her Jeep Wagoneer and drive thousands of miles for community events and political meetings from Napa to the Central Valley. They once survived a harrowing car accident on their way to the Garamendi family's annual Basque barbecue in Stockton, when the Jeep flipped over several times. Paul Pelosi Sr. helped get all of them out of the car safely.

Paul Pelosi helped raise money and joined strategy sessions during his wife's first congressional campaign, in 1987, but after that he made a deliberate decision to step back from the political maelstrom. "What I've tried to do is stay out," he told me in a rare interview, to make it clear that she was the official, not him. "From the get-go, when she first ran... in 1987, that was pretty much an old boys' club." People would "come to me and say, 'Hey, you've got to talk to your wife about whatever.'" He would tell them, "'You have an issue, talk to her.' So people would eventually get that and did that, and then as they did it more and more, they realized how good she was, and she was the one to speak with."

She respected his wishes to keep some distance from politics. "I think one of the reasons why we have a good working relationship is that I try not to make too many demands on Paul's time as far as the political stuff is concerned," she said. As a member of Congress, she flew home to San Francisco almost every weekend. He would often spend one week a month in Washington, where he was active at Georgetown University, his alma mater.

He was by her side for the big events, but he wasn't consumed with politics in the way that she was. He was calm; she was combustible. "Sometimes I may stun him with the ferocity of my sentiments about certain issues," Nancy Pelosi said with a laugh, "because he's a gentleman, a lovely, calm person." "My father doesn't like talking about politics," one daughter told me, "so we don't talk about it at the dinner table."

Nancy Pelosi didn't mind that her husband wasn't particularly political. Indeed, she may have appreciated that about him. "He's a businessman," she said. "He likes sports. He plays golf and tennis. He's normal."

That said, it was not the life Paul Pelosi or Nancy D'Alesandro had imagined when they married. "He does from time to time say, 'This isn't what I bargained for.' Or 'How did this happen?'" Nancy Pelosi said. "Here we were just getting married, happily having our children and the rest, and then boom, all of a sudden, one thing and another."

Paul Pelosi's business success and the couple's growing wealth helped give Nancy Pelosi financial freedom and membership in elite social circles, an asset in fund-raising and politics. He described himself as his wife's "enabler," providing the financial stability that "let her go there completely on her own terms, not owing anything to anybody." His San Francisco investment firm, Financial Leasing Services, later FLS Inc., had extensive holdings in real estate and venture capital investments. By 2018, the nonpartisan Center for Responsive Politics estimated Nancy Pelosi's net worth at $115 million, making her the seventh wealthiest member of Congress at the time.

Paul Pelosi provided another service for his wife: personal shopper. She had never been much for clothes shopping; her husband had done much of that for their children when they were young. As she rose in politics, he would often find outfits for her to wear. When she became the first female Speaker, a spate of profiles of her clothes appeared, a scrutiny that Denny Hastert and Newt Gingrich didn't face. A *Baltimore Sun* story on the way she dressed declared that she was "Suited for Politics." The *Desert Sun* in Palm Springs, California, offered advice on local stores for readers who wanted "to look like a polished politician yourself." The story was headlined, "How to Get the Nancy Pelosi Look Here."

That said, Pelosi rarely encouraged attention to what she was wearing. She favored classic lines in the solid, bright colors that look best on TV. Her tailored clothes complemented but didn't overshadow the authority she aimed to project. "Consciously, comfortably and authoritatively female," wrote Robin Givhan, the Pulitzer Prize–winning fashion correspondent for the *Washington Post*. She described the Giorgio Armani designs Pelosi often wore as "a kind of professional armor" for powerful women.

She did have an unintended impact on the fashion world. The distinctive red coat she wore coming out of the West Wing after a contentious meeting with President Trump became a meme. For the next fall season, the *Wall Street Journal* identified a trend in its fashion report. "The Pelosi Effect," they labeled it, showing bright red coats from the runways of five top fashion designers.

———

One of the Pelosi children would follow their mother into politics, and one would follow their father into business; another became a journalist. Having such a famous last name can open doors but also create complications. Christine, seen as a potential contender to succeed her mother in Congress, would divide the political world into first-name friends and last-name friends. "First-name friends are people who are interested in you from the minute they meet you," her sister Alexandra explained. "Last-name friends are the people who want to be your friend once they hear your last name."

Christine worked on Capitol Hill for four years as chief of staff to Massachusetts representative John Tierney. Settling in San Francisco and marrying filmmaker Peter Kaufman, she ran "boot camps" for aspiring leaders in politics and nonprofits and was a member of the Democratic National Committee. She also became one of her mother's most fervent defenders, on social media and in person. At a Democratic National Committee meeting in 2003, she upbraided former Vermont governor Howard Dean, then an aspiring presidential contender, after a speech in which he blasted "the Democratic leadership" for supporting unilateralism in Iraq. Her mother hadn't, she told him. Dean backed off as friends around Pelosi chanted, "Don't dis the mama."

Nancy Corinne was working in the hotel hospitality industry when she married Jeff Prowda, at the time an administrator of the special education programs for the San Francisco Unified School District. They later moved to Scottsdale, Arizona. Paul Jr., a lawyer with an MBA, worked in finance in San Francisco; on New Year's Eve in 2018, his Instagram account showed him socializing with Ivanka Trump at Mar-a-Lago, Trump's resort in Palm Beach, Florida. (At one point, President Trump promoted a debunked conspiracy theory accusing Paul Jr. of wrongdoing in Ukraine, an accusation declared false by independent fact-checkers.) Alexandra became a documentary filmmaker based in New York; she married Michiel Vos, a Dutch journalist and filmmaker.

Jacqueline settled in Houston, where she taught art to children with special needs and others. She was the first to marry, to Michael Kenneally. He had roots in Ireland and, by the way, turned out to be a Republican.

She didn't try to change her son-in-law's political beliefs, Nancy Pelosi said. She was focused on the next generation: "We're just fighting for the hearts and minds of the children."

––––––––

Nancy Pelosi saw parallels between being the mother in the house and the Speaker of the House. "Nothing prepared me for being Speaker of the House more than the values, discipline, diplomacy, interpersonal skills, the logistics, the quartermastering—all that you have to do to raise a family while never taking your eye off the children," she said.

It was a point she would make in recruiting women to run for Congress, especially to those who demurred that they were "only a homemaker" and therefore unqualified to run for office. She would tell them that the skills that made her an accomplished legislator, in being able to manage chaos and motivate people, were those she had honed as a mother. In that role, she had learned to command, to delegate, to understand what appeals would resonate best with each individual. To lead.

Her children saw the parallels, too. "I knew the face," Nancy Corinne said when she watched the early showdowns between her mother and President Trump once Democrats regained control of the House. It was the face Nancy Corinne and her siblings might see if they skipped out on chores or snuck out to a movie. It was a face that said, *You children wouldn't have done that.* "It made you feel worse because of course we had done it," she said. "It'd be better if she'd just get mad at you."

Nancy Pelosi displayed *the face* at the first Oval Office meeting after the 2018 midterm elections—the session where Trump suggested she was in a politically weakened position. "Mr. President," she replied icily, "please don't characterize the strength that I bring to this meeting." In an interview on CNN afterward, anchor John Berman asked

Alexandra how her mother would approach meetings with the president. "She'll cut your head off and you won't even know you're bleeding," she replied. "That's all you need to know about her. No one ever won betting against Nancy Pelosi."

A few weeks later, at his State of the Union address, President Trump called for an end to the "politics of revenge, resistance, and retribution." That drew exaggerated, arms-extended applause from Speaker Pelosi— a gesture instantly seen on social media as sarcastic, although she said she didn't mean it that way.

That scene took Christine back to her teenage years. She offered to translate her mother's message for the uninitiated: "She knows. And she knows that you know. And frankly she's disappointed that you thought this would work. But here's a clap."

## CHAPTER SEVEN

# RUNWAY

*June 23, 1975—San Francisco, California*

Politics didn't play a role in the Pelosis' decision to move west. The notion of running for office hadn't entered her mind or occurred to her husband.

"I knew that she wanted to go on to law school, have a professional career; that was the goal," Paul Pelosi told me. "She was interested in the issues and public service, but I never, ever thought that she would be an elected official." She had "absolutely no interest" in doing that, he said. "I would have bet anything that she never would have actually run for office herself. Actually, I was the one who thought I was going to run for office."

He had been elected student-body president of Georgetown's School of Foreign Service, although his interest in elective office waned when he was immersed in the world of business and finance after graduation.

Still, the serendipitous reality was that San Francisco's political landscape echoed the Baltimore of Nancy D'Alesandro's heritage. It was a port town that was populated by tribes, reminiscent of the ethnic neighborhoods that had surrounded Little Italy. There were the Italians, the Chinese, the gays, the Jews, the hippies, the environmentalists, the shipyard unionists, and the Masters of the Universe in the burgeoning

Financial District, where construction of the Transamerica Pyramid had just begun. Here, as in Baltimore, successful politicians had to build coalitions. Democrats dominated and bosses ruled.

Nancy Pelosi would call Baltimore "a proper introduction to politics in San Francisco."

With a population of fewer than a million people, the city boasted twenty-seven officially chartered Democratic Party chapters in 2015, from the Raoul Wallenberg Jewish Democratic Club to the Filipino American Democratic Club to the Black Young Democrats of San Francisco to the Harvey Milk LGBT Democratic Club. "Roughly one party franchise every few blocks," veteran California political reporter Mark Barabak reckoned. "San Francisco is the closest thing to an East Coast enclave set over the Pacific, a place, like New York or Boston, where politics is a passion, a sport, something everyday people fuss and fight and scheme over."

Nancy and Paul Pelosi bought a big house on a leafy cul-de-sac next to the Presidio, the sprawling military post that had been established in 1776 by the Spaniards. She described herself as a full-time mom who volunteered. She volunteered at the San Francisco Library and joined the board of the Leakey Foundation, sparking her interest in the origins of humans and the behavior of primates. When they were older, her children would go on a dig in Kenya with famed paleoanthropologist Richard Leakey.

The Pelosi house itself became a political asset. With a prime location and big rooms and not much furniture, it was ideal for fund-raisers. "You have a big house," a woman who also volunteered in politics said approvingly. "We'll be using it for Democratic Party events." Pelosi had a built-in staff, too. She would enlist her children to collect the coats and pass the hors d'oeuvres.

"There never was any *decision* to go into politics," Nancy Pelosi said later. She had been working on campaigns since she was a little girl; she had never really stopped. Before long, she was president of the neighborhood's Presidio Terrace Association and the host for a stream of political hopefuls. They were raising money and making connections to run for the local Board of Supervisors and the state legislature and the U.S. Congress and, eventually, for president. "You just discover it's in your DNA, in your blood," she said.

Her abilities as a fund-raiser would eventually help propel her to the Speaker's chair and keep her there. In California, she became friends with the tech entrepreneurs and the Hollywood royalty willing and able to donate huge amounts to campaigns. With her history in politics, and her conviction that she was working on the side of the angels, she had no qualms about pressing for contributions.

San Francisco mayor Joseph Alioto lived three doors down the block. Alioto was the son of a Sicilian immigrant and a graduate of the law school at Catholic University of America, across the street from the Trinity College campus that Nancy had later attended. He knew the D'Alesandros; he was especially close to Nancy's brother Tommy D'Alesandro III, who had been elected mayor of Baltimore on the same day that Alioto had first been elected mayor of San Francisco. He knew the Pelosi family, too. When Paul was growing up, he had been a youth coach for Alioto's children.

"So what are you doing, Nancy?" Alioto asked when he phoned one afternoon, on the cusp of summer in 1975. It was 5 p.m., and he assumed that he knew what women were doing at that time of day. "Making a great big pot of *pasta e fagioli*?" he suggested, the hearty Italian soup of pasta and beans. But perhaps he didn't know her that well. "No, I am not making *pasta e fagioli*," she replied. "I'm reading the newspaper."

Alioto got down to business: He wanted to appoint her to the San Francisco Library Commission. It would give her official recognition for the volunteer work she already was doing, he told her. She instantly understood that it would also give the mayor another friendly vote on the commission to support Kevin Starr, the new city librarian who had been shaking things up. (Starr would go on to become California state librarian and the author of the signature multivolume history of the state, called *Americans and the California Dream*.)

"Now, Kevin needs you, and I need you," Alioto told her. "And besides, what's all this about volunteering and getting no official recognition? One day you might want to run for office; it will help that you were recognized in the city as a commissioner."

"Mr. Mayor, I have absolutely no intention of running for office," she replied.

"Nancy, you love the library; this is perfect for you," he persisted. "Why don't you think about it?" She did, and she accepted. The appointment prompted the first mention of her name in the San Francisco newspapers since her wedding announcement. In the *Examiner*, the three-paragraph story was headlined "Mayor Alioto Appoints Neighbor." Besides her status as a neighbor, the story also identified her as the sister-in-law of supervisor Ronald Pelosi.

There was another brief mention in the *Examiner* three weeks later. "While Nancy Pelosi was sworn in as a library commissioner yesterday, her five children, 4 to 11, played tic-tac-toe on Mayor Alioto's desk," Jack Rosenbaum wrote in his chatty "My Town" column, immortalizing her first oath of office. "Once, while the mayor was in full oratorical stride, he leaned over and with his pen finished one of their games without losing a comma."

At age thirty-five, she discovered that she liked having an official position, being able to convene hearings, to cast votes. She began to think about her possible political role in a different way.

"We're at one of these meetings, and somebody said, 'We really need to get this bond initiative; does anybody know Leo McCarthy?'" Pelosi told me. McCarthy, a Democrat, was then the Speaker of the California State Assembly. "I thought, 'Well, I know him from church,' and then I realized I wasn't going to be able to do what I wanted to do for the library by being a library commissioner only. We needed the state legislature to support libraries. You can't get things done that are important to people's lives" without a bigger platform. "That sort of drew me back into politics."

Mayor Alioto was the first of a series of benefactors who recognized

Nancy Pelosi's political potential before she saw it herself. (That was a common experience for female candidates of her generation, and the next.) After encountering her as an organizer and a fund-raiser, some of the most prominent Democrats in the country—California governor Jerry Brown, New York governor Mario Cuomo, Senate majority leader George Mitchell of Maine—would privately urge her to run for office, though she didn't take the advice until it came from another woman, Sala Burton.

———

Nancy Pelosi would soon prove her political credentials on a bigger stage than the San Francisco Library Commission.

In 1976, Jerry Brown, California's new governor, decided to jump into the Democratic presidential race even though the early primaries were already over. Nancy Pelosi didn't know Brown well, but her in-laws did. Jerry Brown and Paul Pelosi's brother David had been classmates at St. Ignatius High School. She had cohosted a fund-raising dinner for Brown early that year, and she liked his focus on environmental issues and his "small is beautiful" mantra. "After the dinner, I said to myself, 'He's the one person who really seems to be able to strike a chord with all in the party,'" she said.

Even so, she had doubts about his strategy to derail Democratic front-runner Jimmy Carter. The former Georgia governor, who had been campaigning for the nomination in earnest for more than a year, had unexpectedly won the Iowa caucuses and the New Hampshire primary. Brown was calculating that a big victory in the California primary could give him momentum into a brokered national convention. But his home state didn't vote until June 8, the last day of the primary season. Carter might already have the nomination in hand. "If Jerry Brown wants to run for President, we shouldn't wait for California," she told Leo McCarthy, the state legislative leader who was also chairman of Brown's presidential campaign. "By then it's going to be too late—there will already be a nominee."

She had a different idea: Challenge Carter in Maryland. Its primary was earlier, on May 18. The Maryland secretary of state had declared that a recognized candidate in any state would automatically be on the ballot unless he or she ordered it removed. It was a state she knew well, and where she had connections. Pelosi wrote a memo making the case for a Maryland campaign and listing some local officials who might help. They included her brother Tommy D'Alesandro III, who was a former Baltimore mayor, and her high school friend Ted Venetoulis, then the Baltimore County executive. Encircling the city of Baltimore, it was the largest county in the state.

At the time, Jerry Brown hadn't even realized that Nancy Pelosi of Presidio Terrace had political roots in Maryland. "I'd never been to Baltimore," he told me in an interview years later, after he had finished a second stint as California governor. "In fact, I didn't even know her name was D'Alesandro until I went to Baltimore." He agreed to think about her idea.

Nancy Pelosi called Venetoulis. "My governor wants to run for president, and we think he ought to come to Maryland," she told him. He replied, "Well, Nancy, you know, we don't have a lot of time." He wasn't even sure if they could make the deadline to file a slate of convention delegates. Venetoulis told her, "Why don't you have him call me, and let me talk to him?"

Venetoulis, who as Baltimore County executive had a robust grassroots organization, told me about his unusual introduction to Jerry Brown. On a Friday afternoon, he had gone to a favorite Baltimore hangout, the Last Chance Bar and Grill, to meet with some precinct workers. The tavern owner came over to say Venetoulis had gotten a call on the bar's pay phone.

"This is Jerry Brown," the caller said. "Nancy told me to call you."

After exchanging pleasantries, Brown said he was considering campaigning in the Maryland primary, although he had no organization and no known support in the state. "Governor, you know, it's awfully late," Venetoulis cautioned him. He had already been approached by other presidential hopefuls seeking his help, among them Congressman Morris Udall of Arizona and Senator Henry "Scoop" Jackson of Washington State, but he hadn't endorsed anyone yet. Over the pay phone in the bar with an apt name, Venetoulis and Brown talked for an hour.

"Okay, here's the deal, Governor," Venetoulis finally said. If they moved ahead, the Californians would raise the money; the Marylanders would call the shots. He would have to commit to the sort of grassroots campaigning that wasn't required in California, where campaigns were often waged via TV ads. "You're going to have to campaign in the streets, because we believe in a ground game," Venetoulis told him. He also needed to make sure Tommy D'Alesandro III would be on board. And Nancy Pelosi would have to join them for the duration of the campaign. Their efforts would be as much for her as they were for him, he made clear.

"She's got to be here with us because if we're going to do this thing, we're doing it because of her," Venetoulis told Brown. Then he added, almost as an afterthought, "Although we like you, and you're terrific, and all that."

The phone conversation was on the afternoon on April 2, 1976. The deadline for a presidential candidate to remove his name from the ballot was an hour or so later, at 5 p.m. Brown left his name on the ballot but waited another three weeks before deciding to actively campaign in the state. Then he called Venetoulis again—this time at home, and at 11 p.m. in Sacramento. Which made it 2 a.m. in Baltimore.

He was running.

What followed was an unlikely alliance between the New Age governor of California and the Old World ward bosses of Baltimore, an alliance forged by Nancy D'Alesandro Pelosi.

The coalition behind Brown became even more peculiar when he was endorsed by Maryland governor Marvin Mandel. Venetoulis was a reformer, but Mandel was a machine pol of the old school, from East Baltimore. He was in a spot of trouble at that moment, scheduled to go on trial in a few weeks on federal charges of mail fraud and racketeering.

Legal troubles or not, Mandel still had political juice, and he didn't have a candidate in the race. He had been inclined to support Scoop Jackson or former vice president Hubert Humphrey, but Jackson faltered in the early contests and Humphrey decided not to run. Admittedly, the Mandel machine seemed an odd match with Jerry Brown. "The whole point was to bring the Old Guard and the Young Turks together," Frank DeFilippo, a Mandel aide, told me years later. It sent a message when another veteran of the Old Guard, Tommy D'Alesandro Jr., Nancy's father, showed up for the meeting where Mandel made the pitch to his lieutenants to back Brown. They gathered at the old Hilton Hotel downtown, on Fayette Street.

"Marvin gave the party call," DeFilippo said. The governor started by acknowledging his current legal difficulties. "He says, 'Do me a favor. I don't have any walking-around money right now, but I'll take care of you later. I'd like to see Jerry Brown win.' It was a do-this-one-for-the-Gipper kind of speech." In truth, Mandel was motivated less by his belief in Jerry Brown and more by his antipathy for Jimmy Carter. Ambitious and a loner, Carter had made no friends at National Governors Association meetings. "Everybody hated Jimmy Carter," DeFilippo said matter-of-factly.

Venetoulis and the younger Tommy D'Alesandro escorted Brown on a tour of the state, rolling campaign stops arranged on the fly. The governor's girlfriend, singer Linda Ronstadt, came along for the ride; sometimes the Eagles, a hit rock band she had helped forge, would show up to perform. Brown spent some nights at D'Alesandro's house, some nights at Venetoulis's. At 3 a.m. one night, Venetoulis was awakened by yet another phone call—this time from actor Warren Beatty, who insisted he awaken Brown so they could talk.

In the end, Brown didn't succeed in denying the Democratic nomination to Carter, who had accumulated the delegates he needed by the time the Democratic National Convention opened in New York City that July. But the Maryland campaign was in some ways the high point of the California governor's campaign. To the surprise of Jerry Brown and the chagrin of Jimmy Carter, Brown managed to win a state he had never visited before arriving to campaign. Where he had started late and without any political organization of his own. At the urging of a political volunteer from San Francisco.

"There are fifty states," Brown said. "The first state I ran in was Maryland—why Maryland? Well, because of Pelosi."

Brown won big, defeating Carter by double digits, 49 percent to 37 percent. It gave him a boost for wins that followed in the Nevada and California primaries. "That was a huge victory, just out of nowhere," Brown mused to me decades later. "I mean, it seemed pretty implausible to me at the time." The front-page headline on the next morning's *Los Angeles Times*: "Californian Slows Carter Bandwagon."

A few days later, when he arrived back in Sacramento, he gave credit where it was due. "Nancy Pelosi was the architect of my Maryland campaign," he told the welcoming crowd.

That August, she attended the Democratic National Convention in Madison Square Garden as a delegate from California and a new member of the Democratic National Committee. She would later cite her role in Jerry Brown's 1976 presidential campaign as the pivotal event in starting her on the path from homemaker to House Speaker.

"My political hobby had suddenly taken a serious turn," she said. "I think Mayor Alioto would have agreed that I now had at least one foot outside the kitchen."

————

Jerry Brown offered Pelosi a reward: the post of California Democratic chair. She demurred, something few ambitious men would have done. That seemed like an overreach, she protested; she had never even attended one of the party's State Central Committee meetings. "Please find someone else," she told him. Then Leo McCarthy suggested she take instead the job of Northern California chair, overseeing the political operation in half the state. She agreed, but she continued to downplay her standing and her aspirations. The slogan on her campaign flyer read, "Nancy Pelosi—Volunteer."

After two terms in that job, she became state chairman, this time on her own credentials.

She took over a California Democratic Party that had been shaken by Ronald Reagan's victory in 1980, a landslide nationwide and in his home state. In California, Reagan had crushed Jimmy Carter by nearly 17 percentage points; the GOP also had picked up three congressional seats. Pelosi moved to tighten the Democratic organization, build a more dependable fund-raising operation, and invest in a new computer-aided voter-registration program. Two years later, for the 1982 midterm elections, she shaped a new Democratic attack. TV and radio ads declared, "Reaganomics don't work." The message resonated as the country felt the effects of an election-year recession.

"The party under Pelosi is doing more than it has in the last 15 years," state assemblyman Art Agnos, later elected mayor of San Francisco, told the *San Francisco Examiner*. "She's had a galvanizing effect on the party." In the midterms that November, California Democrats picked up five House seats, reversing the GOP's 1980 gains in the state and more.

Pelosi gained useful experience in holding together disparate Democrats. "People frequently talk about the differences between northern and southern California, but what I learned is that the real difference in California is between east and west," she said. "Inland California voters tend to be moderate. On the coast, they tend to be progressive." She tried to "calibrate our issues" to unite them, an approach she said would later serve her well in national politics.

Then she did one more thing: pushed to bring the Democratic National Convention to San Francisco in 1984.

"She was a booster there," Walter Mondale told me, recalling the convention that nominated him for president. "One of the reasons we put our convention there is we had friends like Nancy who'd back us up, and Dianne Feinstein, too." Pelosi chaired the host committee.

Feinstein, later a U.S. senator, was then the mayor of San Francisco. The two women were allies on this and had a cordial relationship afterward, although they reflected different strands of the city's Democratic politics.

Mondale, the former Minnesota senator who had served as Carter's vice president, would make history in two ways that year, one happier than the other. He would lose a record forty-nine states to Reagan in November. Before that, he would choose as his running mate New York representative Geraldine Ferraro, the first woman nominated by a major party for national office.

Pelosi would savor the memory of the thunderous response Ferraro received when she was introduced onstage in San Francisco. "Nothing could describe what happened on the floor of that house when she was nominated and accepted the nomination for that convention," she said. "Really, in my life, there are very few things that would match when Geraldine Ferraro was nominated, and when she accepted the nomination."

Unfortunately for the Democrats, the convention was the high point of what turned out to be a difficult campaign for Ferraro, who was hit by questions about her finances and her husband's business interests in New York. It was a disastrous campaign for Mondale.

That convention also marked a turning point for Pelosi's view of herself. She was chair of the host committee and also chair of the Compliance Review Commission, which oversaw state delegate-selection plans. In a conversation with Louisiana representative Lindy Boggs—an "elegant and politically astute" mentor, Pelosi called her—she said she was thinking about giving up one of the positions; perhaps it was too much. "Darlin', no man would ever, ever have that thought," Boggs told her in her Southern drawl. "Nancy, know thy power."

Nancy Pelosi kept both jobs, and she took the lesson to heart. A quarter century later, after she was elected Speaker, she passed on the advice. She titled her 2008 memoir *Know Your Power: A Message to America's Daughters.*

In the wake of Mondale's Election Day thumping, Pelosi herself would suffer the only defeat in any election bid of her career.

"People came to me and said, 'Everything you've done is [preparation] to be chair of the DNC,'" Pelosi told me. "'You've been a state party chair; you've been chair of the Platform Committee; you've raised money for the whole kit and kaboodle. You have been the chair of the Delegate Selection.' It was called the Compliance Review Commission, how you comply with the delegate selection. 'You've done every piece—the organizational piece, the money piece, the platform piece, the management piece, and the rest.'"

She decided to run for national party chair, a crucial job at a time when Reagan's romp to reelection was raising questions about the Democrats' direction. That said, she thought it was unseemly to begin campaigning for it before the presidential election was over. If Mondale managed to unexpectedly win, he would be the one to choose the new party chair. "I said, 'I won't even think of running for something that is predicated on our losing,'" though she acknowledged that a Democratic victory looked like an increasingly distant prospect. "I'd hoped we could win, but it wasn't looking that great."

Her rivals felt less constraint. "Everybody else was running and I'm waiting for us to lose in order to run," she recalled. "I was late in the game." On November 15, eleven days after the election, she formally announced her candidacy.

Even so, she thought she had a strong chance. She had been credited with revitalizing the Democratic organization in California, the most populous state in the nation. She was endorsed by top Democrats in California and her native state of Maryland. New York governor Mario Cuomo supported her, calling her "a youngish person with a clear commitment to the future," a commitment he said was demonstrated by the fact that she had five children. "She has a nice pragmatism to her," Cuomo said.

She planned a campaign budget of $100,000 to win over an

electorate of the 378 members of the Democratic National Committee and rented offices in Washington to serve as her headquarters. She flew to the Virgin Islands to lobby a meeting of the state Democratic chairs. The headline on a column in the Baltimore *Evening Sun* asked, "Can a D'Alesandro Save the Nation's Democrats?"

There were a half dozen other candidates, including former Nebraska congressman John Cavanaugh, former Mondale aide Duane Garrett, Washington political consultant Robert Keefe, and Democratic activist Sharon Pratt Dixon. Former North Carolina governor Terry Sanford eventually jumped into the race. But her chief rival from the start was Paul Kirk Jr., the DNC treasurer, a longtime adviser to Massachusetts senator Edward M. Kennedy, and the candidate backed by Big Labor.

Democratic power brokers had a vision of the DNC chairman they believed could rebuild the party, and it wasn't a description that fit her, although it wasn't a perfect fit with Kirk either. "The short form is more crudely put: white, southern male," political reporter Dan Balz wrote in the *Washington Post* assessing the race. His story didn't portray Pelosi as a serious contender. The penultimate paragraph mentioned her name in passing, on a list of "others who have announced."

She faced a whispering campaign about the political risks of electing a woman, an Italian American, a Catholic. She was accused, inaccurately, of having accepted contributions from the gun industry for the 1984 convention. "They made up stuff," she told me, her ire fresh decades later. Geraldine Ferraro's disappointing performance on the ticket was cited by some as a reason not to entrust another woman with such a prominent role. In his syndicated column, Washington graybeard Joseph Kraft dismissed Pelosi as "an overbearing player of feminist politics."

For the only time during her political career, Pelosi would complain publicly about being the victim of sexism.

"Everywhere I go, they tell me, 'If you were a man, this would have been over a long time ago—slam dunk,'" Pelosi complained to a breakfast of Washington reporters, a standing group organized by the *Christian Science Monitor*, a few days before the vote. "I have all the credentials.

Paul Kirk's credentials are that he's been associated with Teddy Kennedy for 15 years" and had the backing of labor leaders.

She singled out for criticism John Perkins, the AFL-CIO's top political operative, for pushing an "anti-woman line." While the labor federation hadn't officially endorsed a candidate, she accused him of questioning her intelligence, of describing her as an "airhead." Cuomo confirmed that Perkins had said "something like that" about Pelosi in a conversation with one of his aides. Contacted for comment, Murray Seeger, a spokesman for the AFL-CIO, issued a mocking denial that seemed designed to make sure no one had missed the point. "He has certainly not called her an airhead, a female airhead or a Baltimore airhead," Seeger said.

Paul Kirk Jr. told me he heard about the sexist jabs, "and I remember saying to my staff, 'Look, if that's coming from here, you better knock it off.'" The fiercely contested race left some wounds, he said, although he and Pelosi later became allies; she attended his swearing-in in 2009 when he was appointed to complete the Senate term of Ted Kennedy. "It took a while for the dust to settle," he said.

At the time, Jack Germond and Jules Witcover, leading political columnists of the day, described the furor as a "catfight," a word with sexist overtones. "Pelosi's complaints sound like the lament of somebody on the short end of the arithmetic," they wrote.

She was on the short end of the arithmetic, and one of the things she knew how to do was count votes. On the day of the DNC election, she withdrew her candidacy, throwing her support to Sanford. If he won, Sanford had agreed to appoint her as the DNC's finance chairman. But Kirk prevailed.

Pelosi sounded disillusioned in her speech withdrawing from the contest. Six months earlier, Democrats had rejoiced over the groundbreaking nomination of Geraldine Ferraro for vice president, she told the DNC members, meeting at Washington's Shoreham Hotel. Now they seemed afraid that choosing a woman to lead the party would alienate male voters. "It is clear to me that many of you felt that the wrong message would go out if a woman was elected chairman."

Kirk's election signaled the politics of "yesterday," she said, not bothering to hide her scorn. "It's not the politics of tomorrow."

————

Pelosi told me that she learned more from that loss than she did from any victory.

She developed a tougher skin against political attacks, including those lobbed by people she thought were her friends. She knew not to assume the old boys' network would make room for her, regardless of how she had delivered for them. More than a decade later, when the job she wanted was in the House Democratic leadership, she started so early— remembering the cost of waiting until Mondale's defeat—that her chief rival complained she was jumping the gun. She went ahead anyway.

And she would almost never again complain publicly about being the victim of sexism. "Don't agonize; organize," she said then, a personal mantra. And later: "No whining; just winning."

"I tell you, I would never be in Congress if I had not run for that," she said of the DNC race. We were talking in the Speaker's suite in the Capitol, a considerably grander office than the one she once lost at Democratic headquarters. "These are people that I knew, that I worked with all the time, that I'd helped so much in different things with their initiatives, their whatever, and all of a sudden they had turned on me," she said.

"Her race for national chair was a heartbreaker," California representative Anna Eshoo, one of Pelosi's closest friends in Congress, told me. "But I remember saying to her after that, I said, 'Nancy, God has something else in store for you.' I remember she said to me, 'You have a direct line?' And I said, 'Well, I don't know about a direct line, but I truly believe that. I truly believe that.' And I did; I did."

When a door for elective office suddenly opened in 1987, her DNC defeat had prepared her to walk through it. It had "strengthened" her. "I knew exactly what to expect," she said. "Two years later, when Sala [Burton] asked me to run for her congressional seat, I was battle-ready."

# CHAPTER EIGHT

---

# SALA

*April 7, 1987—San Francisco, California*

Sala Burton was dying.

"She looked like Mother Earth," Nancy Pelosi wrote in the opening passage of her 2008 book *Know Your Power*, which was part memoir, part advice column. "She spoke with a Polish accent; she didn't drive a car. She gave off an intense warmth—if she liked you. She was passionate about what she believed in, but very dispassionate about her politics."

Sala had been the soft-spoken partner of her outspoken husband, Phillip Burton, the leader of a Northern California political machine and a liberal lion in the U.S. House of Representatives. A ten-term representative from San Francisco's main congressional district, he had come within a single vote of being elected majority leader in 1976. (He would be immortalized in a majestic political biography, *A Rage for Justice*, by journalist John Jacobs.) Burton was just fifty-six years old in 1983 when, late one night in San Francisco, he turned to his wife and said, "Jesus, Sala, I don't feel good." An aortic aneurysm had ruptured in his abdomen; he collapsed and died before the ambulance could get him to the hospital. Sala won the special election to complete his term and was reelected the next year.

Now she was facing her own health crisis. In early 1986, she underwent drastic surgery for colon cancer. Nearly her entire colon was removed; her doctor told her she would be lucky to live another year. She confided in almost no one about what was happening, even after she had to check back in to the hospital in August. Then the *San Francisco Examiner* got wind of it. "Sala Burton's secret surgery. Colon cancer," the front-page headline blared two months before Election Day. "I'm recuperating and I'll be raring to go," she assured reporter David Johnston, who said she sounded "tired but upbeat."

Unable to campaign, she won 75 percent of the vote and a third term in the solidly Democratic district anyway.

On Election Day, she showed up for lunch at the Washington Square Bar and Grill, a San Francisco institution favored by pols and reporters. "How ya doing?" one diner shouted. "I'm in better shape than you," she replied; then she spied Herb Caen, the legendary (and balding) *San Francisco Chronicle* columnist. He had reported rumors that she was undergoing chemotherapy. "And you will notice that I have more hair than you!" she teased. His good-natured response: "Like who don't?"

Bravura aside, the seriousness of her illness was impossible to miss. She had always been a big woman, and a vigorous one. Now she was thin, almost gaunt; she could no longer manage to walk up a flight of stairs unassisted. Maneuvering began behind the scenes—"gingerly," as the *Los Angeles Times* reported—by those interested in running for her seat, potentially a lifetime sinecure for a Democrat. A new election would be a test of the rising power of the gay and lesbian community in San Francisco, and of the ebbing power of the Burton machine her husband had forged. Harry Britt, an openly gay member of the Board of Supervisors, was ready to run for the seat. He would make history if he won. At the time, no openly gay candidate had ever won his or her initial election to Congress.

When Sala Burton didn't attend her swearing-in ceremony at the Capitol in January 1987, speculation surged. "S.F. Politicos Express Concern—and Start Jockeying," Jacobs reported in the *San Francisco Examiner*. His story mentioned five prospective candidates. Nancy Pelosi wasn't one of them.

She wasn't seen as an obvious contender, much less the favorite. She would later tell people that when she first heard Sala Burton was interested in having "Pelosi" run to succeed her, she assumed she meant her husband, Paul Pelosi. He had political connections of his own; his brother Ronald had been president of the San Francisco Board of Supervisors. When John Burton first heard that Sala, his sister-in-law, was interested in having "Nancy" run for her seat, he assumed she meant Nancy Walker, then a member of the Board of Supervisors.

"I said, 'Oh, she's for Nancy—Nancy Walker?' " John Burton told me, remembering the conversation he had that day at a downtown coffee shop with Agar Jaicks, a leader of the San Francisco Democratic County Central Committee. "I said, 'That's great!' " Jaicks corrected him. "Not Nancy *Walker*," he said. "Nancy *Pelosi*."

A *Los Angeles Times* article a few weeks later mentioned Nancy Pelosi, but it quoted Paul Pelosi before it quoted her, and it identified her as "a San Francisco socialite" before citing any of her political credentials. She had run the state Democratic Party and was known as a successful fund-raiser, but she had never sought public office. Some dismissed her as one of those wealthy dilettantes who liked to dabble in politics.

It was the same rap that had enraged her when she ran for Democratic national chairman two years earlier. Like many women of that era, when the power brokers were almost entirely men, she was routinely underestimated. That is, by those who hadn't worked closely with her. Behind the scenes, those who knew her best had been encouraging her for years to consider running for mayor, for Congress, for governor, for whatever.

When John Burton announced in 1982 that he wouldn't seek a sixth term in the U.S. House—he was fighting an addiction to cocaine—Phillip Burton sounded out Pelosi about whether she might be interested in seeking the seat. (Phil Burton had gerrymandered the district, in Marin County and northwestern San Francisco, to make it more Democratic and thus friendlier for his brother.)

After the 1984 Democratic convention in San Francisco, New York governor Mario Cuomo urged her to run for office, too. She and Cuomo were close. They had met in 1980 when President Jimmy Carter named both to an official delegation bringing aid to Italy after the devastating Irpinia earthquake. (When she finally ran for the House in 1987 and won, Cuomo called and congratulated her in Italian, and she was poised to play a major role if he had decided to run for president.)

And Maine senator George Mitchell had encouraged her to run for governor of California. When Mitchell chaired the Democratic Senatorial Campaign Committee in 1986, he enlisted Pelosi to lead the organization's fund-raising. Those were the midterm elections in which Democrats regained control of the Senate.

"I told her, 'I really think you've got the ability and the commitment and the energy to serve in public office,'" Mitchell told me. He was urging her to consider it just months before Sala Burton's illness became common knowledge. He told Pelosi, "I think you'd be a terrific governor of California, and I think you ought to think about running for it at some point."

She had always demurred. "I don't want to run for anything," she said flatly in 1984.

Thanks to Sala, though, her attitude was changing.

"Sala simply said she had to convince Nancy to run, that Nancy was the logical person to continue the legacy," William Sweeney, a top Democratic operative who was close to Sala Burton, told me. "One of the last times I saw Sala she said, 'This is what I'm going to do.'"

Nancy Pelosi knew better than most about Sala Burton's dire diagnosis. They were friends. When Pelosi visited Washington, she often stayed overnight at Burton's town house. Pelosi's oldest daughter, Nancy Corinne, had been an intern in Burton's congressional office. When Nancy Corinne was a student at Mount Vernon College in Washington, she convinced her parents to let her take the family's old Jeep Wrangler to school with the argument that she needed it to chauffeur Sala around town. "It was quite a sight to see Nancy Corinne driving the dignified Sala Burton around Washington in a car with removable windows," Nancy Pelosi said.

Now Sala Burton told Nancy Pelosi she wanted to endorse her as her successor. Pelosi wasn't the only possibility she considered, but she was the one she settled on. Her embrace would provide a major boost, albeit not a guarantee of victory. It could convince some potential rivals to stay out of the race. It would make her an instant contender.

First, Nancy Pelosi conferred with her husband. "Yes, you should run, and you'll win it," Paul Pelosi told her, "but only if you want to do it, not because other people think it's a good idea." Then she talked with her children; they were on board. Alexandra, heading into her senior year of high school that fall, was the youngest and the only child still at home. She had always been a handful—their most rebellious child, and the one who took the longest to find her way. "In some ways, our most challenging child," as her mother diplomatically put it. A campaign for Congress, not to mention winning the seat and working in Washington, would affect Alexandra's life more than those of her siblings.

"So I went to her and I said, 'Alexandra, Mommy has an opportunity to run for Congress,'" Nancy Pelosi said. "'I love my life. I love being home with you. But if it's all right with you, for a few days a week, I'll be in Washington, if I run for Congress and if I win.' And she said something to me that I had never heard before. She looked up— now, she's sixteen, young for her class—she looks up to me and she said, 'Mother, get a life.'"

With that eye-rolling reply, a teenager's commentary on the cluelessness of parents, Nancy Pelosi felt free to walk through the door that Sala Burton had opened.

With the benefit of hindsight, her decision seems obvious, even inevitable. Pelosi had been raised in a political family as a child and immersed in the political world as an adult. Her offspring were unsurprised. "It's about time you're doing that," they told her. Down the road, some reporters and opponents assumed that she had always known that she would run for office eventually, or at least that it was a possibility. They saw her protestations as a convenient myth.

But in fact this was a breakout moment, an instant of transformation for a woman who had grown to adulthood before the women's movement took hold. Until the 1987 special election, Nancy Pelosi had been following in her mother's footsteps, as the organizer behind the scenes, the person who made it possible for others to get elected. From then on, she would be following in her father's footsteps, the candidate running for office and holding it.

She went from being the power behind the throne to being the person sitting atop it.

In Washington, Sala's health continued to decline. On the day the newly elected Congress was being sworn in, on January 6, 1987, she showed up at the Capitol but had to return home before the ceremony, too weak to stay. California congressman Don Edwards stopped by to administer the oath of office in her living room. Within a week or two, she was admitted, once again, to George Washington University Hospital. She would never leave.

Sala asked her inner circle of friends and allies to the hospital to meet with her one last time. John Burton, Nancy Pelosi, and Agar Jaicks flew on the same commercial flight from California to Washington. The capital had been all but shut down that weekend by a foot of snow. Close colleagues from Congress, Mary Rose Oakar of Ohio and Don Edwards, were there. So was Sala's daughter, Joy.

There was no time for tears. Sala Burton was all business. Everyone understood what was ahead. Even so, John Burton was shocked by how gaunt his sister-in-law looked; he could see that she was gritting her teeth in pain. Nancy Pelosi already knew what Sala Burton was going to ask her.

"You know, Nancy, I would like to see you run, but you should not run unless you want to run," Sala Burton told her. "You have to want that office." She acknowledged that Pelosi had to weigh the impact not only on her but also on her family. "You have five children. You have a husband. You're going to have to take that into consideration." But if Pelosi wanted to run, she told her, she would endorse her. That was no small gift.

"Sala, please don't talk this way," Nancy Pelosi finally replied. "You're breaking my heart."

She offered comforting assurances that none of them believed. "I expect you to get well. I want you to get well. And I want you to be able to finish out your term," Nancy Pelosi said carefully. "But if you decide at some point that you are not going to run for it, I'd be honored to be able to run for the Congress of the United States."

In an interview years later, John Burton described the moment to me. By then he was eighty-six years old, a recovering cocaine addict who had survived a series of health crises. But he retained the bent for political declarations and profanity-laced tirades that had made him a legend in California politics. He had been a skeptic about Sala's choice, he said. He was not at all sure he wanted to go along.

"She called us back to Washington and basically lays hands on Nancy, whom I did not know," he told me, sitting at his favorite coffee shop near his office in downtown San Francisco. He noted that Pelosi had been aligned more with the Democratic machine led by Leo McCarthy than the rival Burton organization. That said, Nancy Pelosi already had reached out to him and given him an opportunity to raise objections, a courtesy that he appreciated. "She said, 'If my running would damage the Burton name, the Burton reputation, I don't have to run,'" he recalled.

When they met with Sala, "I thought we were going to get the bullshit that 'she's a friend of mine, she's a friend of Phillip's,'" John Burton said. But that wasn't what Sala Burton, dispassionate about politics, said about Nancy Pelosi. "She starts talking about, 'She's smart, she's tough, she's operational,'" Burton said. He remained unconvinced. "Is she bullshitting us or what?" he said to Jaicks afterward. Despite his doubts about her decision, John Burton decided to accede to her wishes. Only later would he see the skills that his sister-in-law had recognized. "She saw the greatness of Nancy Pelosi before any of us," he told me.

The others left the hospital room, leaving Sala Burton and Nancy Pelosi alone.

"You've got to be ready," Sala told her with all the force she could muster, a diminished figure propped up in a hospital bed, surrounded by IVs and medical monitors. "Are you ready?"

Yes, Nancy Pelosi replied. She was ready.

She went downstairs to the lobby of the hospital and headed to a pay phone, a necessity in that era before cell phones were ubiquitous. She called George Mitchell to confer; they had worked together the year before on the Democratic Senatorial Campaign Committee. Then she called Peter Kelly, a top Democratic operative she had worked with closely for years, at the 1984 convention and at the Senate campaign committee. She told him about her conversation with Sala Burton. "What do I do?" she asked him. "Is that something that I should think about?"

Kelly, an ebullient man, responded by singing the refrain from "Olive Tree," a song from the Broadway musical *Kismet* about the rewards of ambition.

> *Why be contented with one olive tree when you could have the whole olive grove?*
> *Why be content with a grove when you could have the world?*

"I sang the song to her," Kelly told me. "And she said, 'Got it.'"

Sala Burton wasn't ready to let journalists or her constituents know what was happening, at least not all at once. After the meeting that Saturday, John Burton told a handful of California reporters who had gathered downstairs at the hospital that his sister-in-law had no intention of resigning and planned to finish out her term. But she had decided not to seek reelection in 1988, he said. Three days later, in her San Francisco office, John Burton read another statement to the news media, still not disclosing her catastrophic prognosis but announcing that she was supporting Nancy Pelosi as her successor.

He wanted to make sure he revealed the endorsement before she died, so there could be no question about whether it came from her.

"I strongly believe that no individual can give a Congressional district to another, nor, in our democracy, can, nor should anyone be anointed to public office," the statement said. "However, as a person who has been active in the political affairs of this city for most of my adult life, I feel an obligation to make my thoughts known to my friends and supporters. It is in that spirit that I support and will recommend to my constituents the candidacy of Nancy Pelosi, a respected leader and former Democratic State Chair."

Five days later, Sala Burton died. Nancy Pelosi's elective career was launched.

Pelosi said she had never seriously thought about or wanted to run for office until Sala Burton pushed her to do it. A few years earlier, it had been another woman, Louisiana representative Lindy Boggs, who had urged her to embrace powerful posts in the Democratic Party, putting her on track to be a contender for this campaign. "Sometimes it takes the encouragement of someone who knows us well to propel us forward in ways we never would have dreamed," Pelosi said. That was particularly true for female candidates, then and later, who often assumed that some other person, generally a man, would be better qualified or more electable than they would be. Indeed, both Sala Burton and Lindy Boggs had been first elected to succeed their husbands when they died in office, one of the most common early routes to Congress for women.

Decades later, sitting in the Speaker's office, Pelosi dismissed the assumption by some that this course was somehow preordained, the result of a master plan, the realization of an ambition that had been forged on her father's knee. "People were saying, 'She knew since she was five years old, she wanted to be Speaker of the House,'" Pelosi told me, her tone mocking. She waved her right arm in the air as though to physically dissipate the thought. "I had absolutely no interest, ever, in running for political office until I did," she said.

Once she was running, though, she was running hard.

———

Nancy Pelosi was forty-six years old when she started her first campaign as a candidate. It had been more than two decades since she held her first full-time paying job—which had been, coincidentally, on the congressional payroll. She had been hired as the receptionist for Maryland senator Daniel Brewster in the interval between her college graduation and her wedding. In contrast, by the time her father was forty-six, he had already won five elections to Congress and was serving as mayor of Baltimore.

Unfortunately, she had not inherited his gifts as a campaigner.

Behind the scenes, she was a master strategist and tactician, but at center stage she often came across as uncomfortable and scattered. "She was kind of all over the place verbally," recalled Douglas Foster, who produced the only debate of the campaign. Sometimes she would struggle to speak in full sentences and stay on point; at other times she could seem programmed and stilted. She had her mother's political smarts but not her father's storytelling skills, nor his gregarious personality. She was ambitious but she was also shy. Her proper mien was not necessarily a political asset, particularly in the rough-and-tumble of a competitive contest like this one. Jerry Roberts, then the political editor of the *San Francisco Chronicle*, called her "extremely disciplined and annoyingly on message all the time," an assessment that reporters in Washington would echo in future years.

Scott Shafer, then a young Democratic operative, was credited with an observation that would describe Pelosi through much of her career. "She's really, really good with the things you can't see, and really, really bad at the things you can," he told me. "The things that everyone sees her do are the things she does least well—press conferences, speeches, impromptu remarks, television appearances. And the things that she's so good at are...all the things she does behind the scenes that nobody really sees unless you're in the room with her."

Though she would work over the years to improve her communication skills, including consulting with a speech coach, that would be a challenge for her even decades later.

KQED, the public broadcasting station in San Francisco, was hosting the only televised debate of the campaign. As a special election, the primary was open to contenders from all parties. If no candidate managed to carry 50 percent of the vote, the two top finishers from different parties would compete in a runoff election. Fourteen candidates had signed up, and the station decided that all of them would be invited to participate in the debate.

The candidates, seated on three levels of risers onstage, represented not only the Democratic and Republican parties but also the Libertarian Party, the Humanist Party, the Socialist Workers Party, and the Peace and Freedom Party. One candidate was a follower of Lyndon LaRouche, a cultish figure on the fringe of American politics. It was the sort of freewheeling encounter that would reward verbal agility and chutzpah.

Pelosi almost didn't show up for it.

Her campaign manager, Clinton Reilly, was getting increasingly nervous about how his candidate would fare. "She can get ahead of her skis when she's talking," Foster, the debate's producer, told me. "He could see that she wasn't necessarily going to be good on television." Three days before the debate, Reilly called Foster to say Pelosi wouldn't be there because of a scheduling conflict with an event featuring Maryland senator Barbara Mikulski.

"If you're telling me that a well-run campaign like yours didn't notice a scheduling conflict between an hourlong debate on the PBS television station in San Francisco and a visit by Senator Mikulski, I just can't believe that," Foster told him. He accused Reilly of already trying to undermine the debate by fomenting fears among the secondary candidates about whether it would be fair to them. "Either you're incompetent or you're lying, and I choose to think that you're lying."

The argument between the two men was heated. A few hours later, Foster called Reilly back with a warning. "Clint, I've really been thinking about the decision that you've made. I think your candidate is going to regret it." He would be "obligated" to put an empty chair onstage with her name on it, he warned. Later, he called Pelosi's home and told Paul Pelosi the same thing, just to make sure Nancy Pelosi knew.

For a novice candidate, one who had already been depicted by her rivals as a dilettante, her absence could have been damaging, perhaps even fatal, particularly in a race that would end up being decided by a razor-thin margin. But there were also risks in participating in a debate guaranteed to be raucous. "At the time, just so you know, the theory was that if there are thirteen clowns in a ring, and a sane person jumps in, she looks like the fourteenth clown," Pelosi told me. She said she didn't remember the dispute, but she acknowledged, "Clint could have done that."

The Pelosi campaign never called Foster back with word of whether she was going to show up. Five minutes before airtime, she did.

———

Tom Spinosa, one of four Republicans onstage, opened the forum by calling for the bombing of the headquarters of Nicaragua's Sandinista government—oh, and of Ayatollah Khomeini of Iran, too. Those might not be decisions typically made by a freshman member of the House, not to mention one from the minority party, but his impassioned declaration did reflect the GOP's determination to oust the leftist regime of Nicaraguan president Daniel Ortega. (That determination had ensnared President Ronald Reagan in the Iran-Contra scandal, then the subject of a congressional investigation.)

"Wouldn't that cause a war?" moderator Spencer Michels asked.

"How could they fight after they'd been bombed out of existence?" countered Spinosa, who was sporting his signature black fedora.

Michels started to pose a question to Nancy Pelosi, one she had been expecting. "Harry Britt has charged in several forums that you don't represent the struggling people in San Francisco," the KQED anchor began. Before she could respond—indeed, before Michels had finished asking the question—the Peace and Freedom candidate, Ted Zuur, jumped from his seat and stood squarely in front of the camera.

"This show is a fraud!" he bellowed. "The most important issue is that Reagan—"

"Okay, could you sit down?" Michels asked, trying to regain control.

Zuur was undeterred. "—and Bush and the Contras and—"

"Ted, Ted," Michels said pleadingly.

"Nobody is addressing the issues!" Zuur continued, his voice getting louder. "I think the president must resign!"

"Could you sit down," Michels said more firmly—this time a demand, not a question.

"I think everyone here should take a stand on it," Zuur insisted.

Michels finally summoned a reluctant security guard. Zuur, a burly and determined man, easily shook him off. After a moment, the guard put his arm on the candidate's shoulder and managed to escort him offstage.

"Excuse me," Zuur shouted as he exited. "I'm not finished here."

The other candidates looked a little stunned at the eruption. Then Pelosi spoke up. "If I could address those two things," she began, turning back to the question that she had been waiting to answer.

Not quite yet, as it turned out. Carol Ruth Silver, a fellow Democrat and a member of the Board of Supervisors, interrupted to complain that Pelosi had loaned $250,000 of her own money to her campaign. "How can she relate to people like me, a single parent, working mother?" Silver demanded. "She's never had to meet a payroll. She's never had to worry about child care. She's never had a kid in the public schools. She's never worried about the things that most of the people of San Francisco have."

Only then did Nancy Pelosi manage to get the floor.

Her wealth gave her an independence that the others didn't have, she argued. "Especially the four supervisors who were reported this week to have received $1,000 each from the Embarcadero Center, and then voted to give them a street," she said pointedly, a charge aimed at Silver and three other Democratic contenders, including Harry Britt. "So if you want to talk about independence, let's talk about independence.

"Second of all, I don't think you have to be sick to be a doctor or poor to understand the problems of the poor," she went on. For her, this would be the most crucial exchange of the evening—the essential exchange of the campaign, and perhaps of her political career. She defined herself not as a wealthy socialite but as a loyal Democrat. "I have spent my life committed to the ideals of the Democratic Party, and I believe that I have recognition in Congress for my commitment to the principles of the Democratic Party, for my determination to get the job done, and in my skill in getting the job done."

She spotlighted her powerful connections, connections that could help her deliver for the district. "I don't think it hurts—Democrats in the United States Congress recognize me as the person most responsible for winning the Senate for Democrats," she declared, referring to her work the year before as finance chair of the party's Senate campaign operation. Democrats had scored a net gain of eight seats, wresting control from the GOP.

It was clear that she had prepared the response and practiced it beforehand; she finally was able to deliver it over the din of the debate. She had been the main focus for attack throughout the one-hour forum. She didn't dominate the evening, but she survived it.

Clint Reilly, who had been watching the debate on a monitor in the overflow room, wasn't so sure. When Foster came out of the control room after it was over, he saw Reilly approach. "Clint came up with his fists raised like he was going to clock me, and he shouted, 'You set up my client for a gang fuck.' And if I remember right, it was the political writer from the *Chronicle* who pushed his way in and held Clint back."

In the heat of the moment, Reilly thought the debate had turned out to be a bad idea, but that wasn't the consensus of the news coverage that followed. Harry Britt, her top competitor and a more experienced candidate, was more fluent and projected more confidence. But Nancy Pelosi had held her own in what amounted to a political brawl.

"I think it was her breakout moment that showed people she had the capacity to rise to a position of being a power in her own right," Foster said. "Until then, she had been the person who made it possible for other people to have careers, without much of a sign that she herself could become a political power."

Before she left the studio, Nancy Pelosi walked over and gave Foster a knowing look and a half-embrace. "Thanks," she told him, in what he interpreted as a reference to his surreptitious call to her husband. "I think that was good."

———

She was fortunate that the campaign was just sixty days long and that the primary in a special election was open to all parties. That softened the advantage that the most liberal candidate would have had in a regular Democrats-only primary. (Decades later, California voters would pass a referendum making all primaries open, a boost to more moderate contenders.) Most of all, she was lucky that few voters usually bothered to turn out in special elections, making a grassroots organization matter more.

Nancy Pelosi was not the most charismatic candidate or persuasive debater in the field, but none of her rivals knew as much as she did about how to build an organization.

On the five-hour flight back to San Francisco after the hospital meeting with Sala Burton, she and Jaicks started strategizing. They were seated across the aisle from each other in the coach section of the plane. One row ahead of her, he spent much of the flight twisted around and leaning over to talk. John Burton, seated in first class, came back occasionally to weigh in.

They knew the timetable was going to be short. Sala was failing; she would die the next week. California governor George Deukmejian would then set the date of a special election to take place within sixty days. It would end up being on April 7, 1987.

On February 12, Nancy Pelosi formally announced her candidacy at the old Jack Tar Hotel on Cathedral Hill.

The supporting cast around her was calculated to signal her political muscle. Former mayor Joseph Alioto, who years earlier had urged her to accept his appointment to the San Francisco Library Commission because it would give her a credential if she ever decided to run for something, was there. So was John Burton, who had agreed to be her campaign chairman, testimony to her backing by the Burton machine. And Del Martin and Phyllis Lyon, activists who in 1955 had cofounded the first social and political organization for lesbians in the United States. They were key in her efforts to make at least some inroads among gay and lesbian voters drawn to Harry Britt.

Pelosi declared herself the front-runner, but her campaign's internal polling showed that Harry Britt started with a lead. She had the endorsement of Sala Burton, but he could claim the imprimatur of Harvey Milk, the revered gay Board of Supervisors member who had been assassinated in 1978. Days before he was killed, Milk had recorded a sort of political will endorsing four gay leaders. Britt had been one of them. Dianne Feinstein, then the mayor of San Francisco, had appointed Britt to replace Milk on the board.

That said, Britt could be abrasive. His commitment to addressing the burgeoning AIDS crisis wasn't in doubt, but critics questioned if he would be able to build the sort of Washington coalition needed to win more federal resources to care for those who had the disease and to prevent more people from getting it.

That was the card Pelosi played. At her announcement, she endorsed the same liberal policies that her Democratic competitors had, to ban offshore oil drilling and end foreign military interventions and, especially, to battle the AIDS epidemic as "a very top priority." Then she spotlighted what she said was distinctive about her. "I believe the No. 1 issue in the upcoming campaign will be who can accomplish the most for San Francisco," she said.

Her campaign slogan was that she had "a voice that will be heard." In other words, all the candidates could talk; she was the one who could deliver. That may have seemed presumptuous for someone who had never held elective office. But while she hadn't been in a position to wield power herself, she knew many of those who were. She had raised money for them, and she knew something about forging coalitions and striking deals.

The slogan was repeated at rallies, plastered on flyers, and used in her TV ad, the only one aired by any campaign in the expensive broadcast market during those days before the profusion of cable channels. It was a talking point repeated by allies. It was so ubiquitous that it became the source of humor.

At a crowded candidates' forum at the Jewish Community Center one night, Nancy Pelosi was responding to a question about her stance on Catholic doctrine on artificial insemination when a voice from the back of the library shouted, "Louder!"

"It's okay," Pelosi yelled back to laughter that rippled through the room. "I'm the voice that will be heard!"

She demonstrated her powerful connections in another way: by swamping her rivals in fund-raising. A $1,000-a-plate luncheon in Washington raised $60,000 and drew eight Democratic senators, including George Mitchell. She raised more than $650,000 in a campaign that lasted just sixty days. That was three times as much money as Harry Britt raised. It was twice as much as the money raised by all the other Democratic contenders combined.

She was also working the inside game.

At the time, Stephen Morin was the highest-ranking openly gay appointee in California government, a psychologist and mental health expert who was working on the AIDS issue. Like Nancy Pelosi, he had grown up in politics; his father had been a member of the county Democratic committee in western Massachusetts who had worked on John F. Kennedy's Senate and presidential races. "Out of the blue Sala died, and everybody was jumping in this race, and some people approached me and said, 'Get into this race,'" Morin told me. Some allies worried that Harry Britt's brusque manner made him a flawed candidate. "So I got a group together around my dining room table, and we hashed out what that would look like." At the end of the evening, he wasn't sure what he was going to do.

"The next morning, the phone rings, and it's Nancy Pelosi," he said. "She wants to have breakfast, so off I go and we have a two-hour breakfast." She had somehow heard about his meeting the night before, and she wanted to make the case that he should support her, not run himself. "It was pure Nancy Pelosi," he recalled. "She said, 'You have amazing credentials. I mean, this is perfect for you—but I'm going to win.'" She laid out fund-raising and strategic details that dwarfed anything her rivals had in the works, and anything Morin could do.

He was interested in running to influence federal policy on AIDS; she persuaded him that she had the same priority. Indeed, after she was elected, she would hire him as the first staffer in Congress devoted specifically to AIDS policy. During the campaign, Morin's support helped her counter criticism that she wasn't involved with the gay community.

Her campaign targeted gay voters to reduce Harry Britt's advantage with that significant voting bloc. That was no easy task in those days before technological innovations made microtargeting routine. Instead, her campaign worked with the information they had. If two men were listed at the same address and were within twenty years of each other in age, they were sent a campaign brochure focused on AIDS and other issues of particular importance to gay voters.

A brochure that targeted female voters showed eight locally prominent women who had endorsed her. Another brochure had the same template but included photographs of eight African American supporters. A mailing designed for Italian American voters on the west side showed Nancy Pelosi at the center of her large family, with smaller photos labeled "The D'Alesandro Family" with her as a little girl and a third picture of Paul Pelosi's parents. The candidate was "steeped in the traditions of her Italian Catholic childhood," the caption said.

In 1987, having children wasn't generally viewed as a political asset for a female candidate. There were few women running for office, and those who were generally tried to make the case that they were as tough as their male counterparts, not different from them. A memo sent out the next year by Emily's List, a political action committee formed to help elect Democratic pro-choice women, warned that they must "fight throughout their campaigns to establish their qualifications, power, toughness and capacity to win."

Power and toughness, not the softer attributes of compassion and motherhood. At the time, having children could even be seen as a political liability.

"Many people assumed that I still had little ones at home," Pelosi recalled. "I was asked over and over again, 'Who is taking care of your children?' My answer was, 'My children are grown and are taking care of me.' In 1987, even among the progressives who wanted to see more women in public office, some were uneasy with the idea of a mother running for Congress who still had young children at home."

Her opponents were campaigning, too, of course. "Nancy Pelosi says her 'voice will be heard.' But to whom would she listen, and for whom would she speak?" a flyer from Harry Britt's campaign asked. "You *know* he's on *your* side." Britt's campaign sent a mailer to fifty thousand voters and aired a thirty-second radio ad that said Pelosi had been "missing in action" while he had fought to get funds to fight AIDS, a disease that was devastating the city. He had sponsored anti-pollution and rent-control legislation. The ad featured a mythical "Inspector Reilly, Missing Persons Squad" on a doomed quest to find her.

Another Democratic contender, Bill Maher, financed by tens of thousands of dollars that reportedly had been steered to his campaign by Harry Britt, attacked Pelosi as an elitist. "Going to Congress is not a reward for meritorious service to the party," he told reporters. "We had a system that used to work the way she wants. It was called vassals and lords." In a campaign mailing, he mocked efforts by the Burton machine to "anoint" Pelosi as Sala Burton's successor. It featured a photograph of the coronation of Queen Elizabeth II by the archbishop of Canterbury in 1953. The caption sarcastically asked, "Why not a Pelosi?"

Maher dubbed her "a party girl from the party." Campaign signs asked if voters wanted "the legislator...or the dilettante?"

A week before the election, a *San Francisco Examiner*/KRON-TV poll showed Pelosi's earlier lead of 18 points cut to 11 points. Half of those surveyed were still undecided.

Nancy Pelosi's father was too sick to travel; he would die of a heart attack that summer. But he wasn't too sick to offer political advice to the daughter he never imagined would run for office. He dispatched her oldest brother, himself a former mayor of Baltimore, to take a look.

Tommy D'Alesandro III visited his sister's headquarters at 666 Mission Street. Oversized balloon-shaped posters were plastered on the ground-floor storefront and a giant banner was strung across the second-floor windows. (Her forty-seventh birthday fell in the middle of the campaign to represent the Fifth Congressional District; staffers presented her with a sheet cake decorated with the message "Take the Fifth!") Tommy the Younger reviewed the precinct maps, the lists of volunteers, the voter-registration files, the get-out-the-vote operation.

"When he called our father, Daddy said, 'So how is it? What's her campaign like? Does she have a good organization?'" Nancy Pelosi said. Her brother registered his approval. "She's true to her roots," he told Tommy the Elder. "She's going to give them a run. It's just a question of what the other side has."

That was the crucial question. Harry Britt had the enthusiasm of gay and lesbian supporters eager for a breakthrough; they were all but certain to show up at the polls. What about her voters? She was counting on support from younger women, from older, ethnic Democrats, and from Republicans. She was leading in the public polls, which might make her supporters feel complacent. Heading into the final week of the campaign, Nancy Pelosi applied what she called "the most important D'Alesandro rule of all," something so crucial she would refer to it in capital letters: "Count Your Votes."

The campaign calculated the likely results based on various turnout models. The conclusion wasn't reassuring. "If things broke poorly for me," she said, "and the best-case scenario happened for my opponents, I would lose by five hundred to a thousand votes." They decided to fortify the get-out-the-vote effort with the goal of delivering five thousand additional Pelosi supporters to the polls, "a number chosen because it would, we hoped, give us a wide, safe margin." As it turned out, she would need almost all of them.

When the votes were being counted, Pelosi and Britt were locked in a dead heat.

"Election Night was very tense," Morin told me. "I was sure we were going to win, but the early returns did not come in that way, and we're all going, 'Uh-oh.'" At the watch party, word circulated that John Burton and Leo McCarthy, then the California lieutenant governor and a mentor, were enlisted for the ticklish task of warning the candidate, "to just prepare her that it was going to be closer than expected."

In the ballots cast at polling places that day, it was all but a tie. Pelosi led Britt by only 450 votes. But she began to build a lead when the absentee ballots were counted. Among absentee voters, Pelosi led Britt by 3,540 votes, providing the lion's share of her narrow margin of victory. That was no accident. Her campaign had used a network of local house parties to convince irregular voters, those who couldn't be counted on to show up at the polls, to sign up for absentee ballots. The 27,000 absentee ballots made up about a quarter of the total vote.

Pelosi had also made a quiet and crucial appeal for GOP support.

Her campaign had drafted a letter labeled "Republican voter alert" and decorated it with the party's familiar elephant logo to mail to Republicans in the district. The message was a risky one that could inflame Democrats, if they heard about it. Local reporters covering the race heard that Nancy Pelosi was leery about sending it, that Paul Pelosi gave the final go-ahead.

The signatures on the letter included George Christopher, the last Republican who had been elected mayor of San Francisco, nearly a quarter century earlier. "It is clear that the next member of Congress from San Francisco will be a Democrat," the letter read. "In a close election, we as Republicans have the ability to decide who our member of Congress will be."

The message: If a Democrat was inevitably going to win, why not back the Democrat they liked most—or, put another way, disliked least? The letter touted Pelosi as someone who "will provide our city with the type of balanced representation that is long overdue." Another campaign mailer sent by the Pelosi campaign to the more conservative neighborhoods in the district sounded almost Reaganesque. "The individual tax burden is too high," it declared. "We need a representative who will fight all efforts to raise the personal income tax."

When the ballots were counted, Britt led Pelosi by wide margins in the most heavily Democratic precincts—in Noe Valley by 1,335 votes, in Mission by 1,273 votes, in Upper Market by an overwhelming 4,027 votes. Turnout had spiked in Upper Market, a largely gay neighborhood. But Pelosi had swamped Britt in outlying neighborhoods—in Sunset by 3,773 votes, in Outer Mission by 3,172 votes, West of Twin Peaks by 2,932. That was enough, barely, to win. She defeated Harry Britt by fewer than 4,000 votes, 36 percent to 32 percent. That made her the Democratic candidate in the runoff, for a district that was more than three-to-one Democratic.

In other words, Nancy Pelosi prevailed in her first election to Congress thanks to Republican votes.

———

There was a runoff election sixty days after the primary against the top-finishing Republican, but it would hardly matter. Nancy Pelosi scored a two-to-one landslide over Harriet Ross. In this deep blue district, winning the Democratic nomination was tantamount to election.

The day after the primary, she asked John Burton to make a pilgrimage with her.

"She wanted to go out to the cemetery to see Phillip and Sala," he told me. The couple had been buried at San Francisco National

Cemetery, their gravesite marked by a single dark granite stone inscribed with words chosen to define their public service. "His motivation was the common good / His life was service / His love was the people," the inscription below Phillip's name read. For Sala: "One must care about a world one will not see / She cared."

"Well, we went out there, and on Phillip's grave was a lit, king-sized Chesterfield cigarette, which is what he smoked," John Burton said. Decades later, sitting with me over coffee, he still wasn't sure what to make of that, whether it was just a weird coincidence or a sign from the beyond or something else. He wasn't a religious man, but he noted that his mother had been a religious woman, and so was Nancy Pelosi. "That was pretty far out," he finally said, leaving it at that.

John Burton and Nancy Pelosi returned to the gravesite again on the day after the general election. She placed a copy of that morning's newspaper on the grave of Phillip and Sala.

"Pelosi Wins House Seat," the headline across the top of the front page of the *San Francisco Chronicle* read. "I had the best endorsement possible," Pelosi had told a cheering crowd at campaign headquarters. "I had Sala, and that was the biggest factor in my campaign. I'll tell them in Washington I was sent by the people of San Francisco, and Sala Burton sent me."

# CHAPTER NINE

# EARTHQUAKE

*October 11, 1987—The National Mall*

Years later, Nancy Pelosi mocked herself for so misjudging the idea Cleve Jones was proposing. He wanted to launch a nationwide project to create a quilt that would memorialize the names of those who had died of AIDS.

"Cleve, a quilt?" she asked him dubiously. "Nobody sews. I have five children; I went to school in a convent from my earliest days. I know how to sew. I know how to darn. I know how to knit. I know how to crochet. I know how to taper. I know it all. I don't sew! I have a sewing machine. I don't sew. So if I don't sew, a mother of five, with a sewing machine and all of that knowledge, nobody sews!"

She urged him to come up with some other way to focus attention on the epidemic and all it had cost. No place in America had been hit as hard as San Francisco, a center of gay life being ravaged by the disease.

Jones was adamant. "No, this is it," he told her. "We're sticking with this." Pelosi agreed to cohost the first fund-raiser for the project at her home with two other top California Democrats, Leo McCarthy and Art Agnos. Later, she would sew one of the three-foot-by-six-foot panels herself in memory of Susan Piracci Roggio, who had been the flower girl at her wedding and who had died of AIDS. Over time, the AIDS

Memorial Quilt would become the largest community art project in the world, growing to 50,000 panels commemorating 105,000 people.

In 1987, though, the stigma was still deep for a disease associated mostly with gay men and drug addicts. Some religious fundamentalists called it God's punishment for sexual behavior they saw as aberrant. "There were people who would be offended just by the discussion of AIDS," recalled George Miller, then a California congressman and an early activist. In an interview with me years later, he parodied the hands-off horror—"Eeek!"—that just mentioning the word could provoke from some of his colleagues in Congress. At the White House, President Ronald Reagan had studiously ignored the subject, even after the Centers for Disease Control and Prevention identified the disease in 1981. Six years would pass before he would deliver his first speech on the subject, when he called it "public health enemy No. 1" and urged schoolchildren to practice abstinence to avoid contracting it.

Those attitudes toward AIDS, the acronym for acquired immunodeficiency syndrome, fueled suspicion among activists when the National Park Service rejected requests for a permit to display the AIDS quilt during the National March on Washington for Lesbian and Gay Rights, set for October 11, 1987. By then, the project had already amassed nearly two thousand panels, nearly the length of two football fields. Spreading the quilt on the National Mall, the first time it would be on public display, would be a dramatic statement. But the Park Service was balking.

"We were getting nowhere," Mike Smith, one of the organizers, told me. "The Reagan administration did not want this giant emblem of dead people, people who had died of AIDS, out on the Mall. They had fought hard to keep the March on Washington for Gay and Lesbian Rights from happening, and they'd lost that. And they were adamant that they just didn't want to have this visual symbol out there, and so we were stonewalled at every level."

Congresswoman Sala Burton, an ally, had died in February. Her successor, Nancy Pelosi, had been sworn in to office in June. Now Cleve

Jones turned to the newly minted legislator for help in convincing the agency to relent.

It would be the first big battle Representative Nancy Pelosi waged in Washington.

She summoned Park Service officials to her office. Her suite on the top floor of the Longworth House Office Building had a view of Interstate 695, cramped quarters befitting the most junior member of Congress. She and the organizers were braced for an ideological argument. "This was the Reagan administration, and everyone was thinking there was this political reason" for not issuing the permit, Stephen Morin told me. He had just joined Pelosi's staff, the first aide in Congress hired to focus specifically on the AIDS crisis.

To their surprise, the officials offered an entirely different rationale, at least officially. "They say, 'No, we've just put the seedlings down. We don't want to cover our seedlings with these mats, because then it'll kill the grass.' So this great political thing was not anything about politics. It was about the grass."

The political debate suddenly became a horticultural one.

"They say, 'Oh, yeah, we can give you a corner, a little space on the corner someplace,'" Pelosi said, re-creating their conversation. "I said, 'You're not hearing this correctly.'" She adopted the stern tone that was already familiar to her children, and in time would become familiar to many in Washington, including presidents. "That's not the 'ask.' We have a big 'ask.'" She tried to convey the perception—"earlier than maybe I should have," she acknowledged with a laugh—that she was speaking for the entire Democratic congressional caucus, even though some of them had not yet learned her name. "This was our request," she told the officials. "'No' was not a possibility. How are we going to get from here to there?"

After some back-and-forth, she came up with an idea on the spot. Volunteers could "fluff" the quilt every twenty minutes, lifting it to give the seedlings fresh air and a brief respite. That could protect the grass while also displaying the quilt. "She kind of put her reading glasses down on her nose and she looked at the gang and she said, 'You boys can fluff the quilt every once in a while, can't you, boys?' " Smith said with a grin. "And we're like, 'Oh, yes, we can.' "

She turned back to the Park Service officials. "We can handle that," she assured them. "We're not going to kill the grass. The way we handle this is we're going to get the quilt lifted up every twenty minutes." She exuded a breezy confidence, as though everything had been settled. What could possibly go wrong? "Well, you understand, I have volunteers from all over the country. That's the easiest thing in the world. We will lift up the quilt every twenty minutes, and you can check on us after."

The deal was reached. The permit was issued. The panels were unfurled, a patchwork stretching between the Washington Monument and the Capitol. Pelosi joined comedian Whoopi Goldberg, actor Robert Blake, Broadway producer Joseph Papp, Massachusetts congressmen Gerry Studds and Barney Frank, and others on the dais to read aloud the sobering toll, the names of the 1,920 people memorialized in the quilt.

Years later, Cleve Jones acknowledged that the Park Service concerns turned out to be valid. When it came to the grass, he recalled, "We killed every blade." A few days after the march, he had a bird's-eye view of the Mall as his flight took off from Washington National Airport. There was "a haunting afterimage of the grid on the lawn," he said.

———

The battle for the quilt and the issue of AIDS defined Nancy Pelosi's early days in Congress.

In 1981, the CDC had published an initial report about five healthy gay men who had been infected with pneumonia that their immune systems couldn't fight. The mysterious and terrifying disease was so firmly associated with homosexuals that officials initially called it Gay-Related Immune Deficiency, or GRID. It was dubbed the "gay plague." For years, whatever it was called, the diagnosis was considered a death sentence.

# ROOTS

The tiny Italian town of Montenerodomo, Abruzzo, was the birthplace of Nancy Pelosi's paternal grandfather, Tommaso Fedele D'Alessandro, who immigrated to the United States in 1890 at the age of twenty-two. In 1932, her father, Thomas D'Alesandro Jr., then a young man, caused a stir when he returned to visit the hilltop village, which sits on the spine of Italy. *(Elizabeth Simari, a researcher for* Madam Speaker*)*

Tombstones in Montenerodomo's cemetery show the names of Nancy D'Alesandro Pelosi's relatives from the D'Alessandro and Passalacqua families. *(Elizabeth Simari, a researcher for Madam Speaker)*

A youthful Thomas D'Alesandro Jr., the father of Nancy Pelosi, poses with his parents, Marie Antoinette Foppiano D'Alesandro and Tommaso Fedele D'Alesandro. The author found this photo and the following one in a cardboard box of memorabilia at Thomas D'Alesandro Jr.'s mayoral archives at the University of Baltimore. *(Thomas J. D'Alesandro Jr. Papers, 1927–1969; Box S4A-B2, Personal; University of Baltimore Special Collections and Archives)*

Nancy Pelosi's mother, Nancy Lombardi D'Alesandro, in her wedding dress; she was married on September 30, 1928, at St. Leo the Great Roman Catholic Church in Baltimore's Little Italy. *(Thomas J. D'Alesandro Jr. Papers, 1927–1969; Box S4A-B2, Wedding; University of Baltimore Special Collections and Archives)*

When Nancy D'Alesandro was born on March 26, 1940, the *Baltimore News-Post* ran the news in the next day's paper. The newborn was shown in the arms of her mother at St. Joseph's Hospital as her father, then a member of Congress, and five brothers look on. *(Second front page of* Baltimore News-Post, *March 27, 1940. From the collection of the Library of Congress, Newspaper & Current Periodical Reading Room.)*

Thomas D'Alesandro Jr. is sworn in as mayor of Baltimore for the first of three terms on May 20, 1947, as his seven-year-old daughter, Nancy, holds the Bible. *(Family photo)*

Big Nancy D'Alesandro helps her daughter, known as Little Nancy, with her homework in December 1947. *(Annunciata M. D'Alesandro with daughter Nancy [Pelosi], 1947, Bodine, A. Aubrey, 1906–1970, Baltimore City Life Museum Collection, Special Collections Dept., Maryland Historical Society)*

"D'Alesandro for Mayor" campaign button. *(Jack Gruber)*

This formal portrait of the D'Alesandro family was displayed for years in the living room of the D'Alesandro home at 245 Albemarle Street in Baltimore. After Nancy D'Alesandro died in 1995, it eventually was taken across the street to hang on the wall at a local restaurant, Germano's Piattini. Later, a sly sign was added: "Be careful with Nancy's painting. She will impeach you."

The "Vaporizer," a device to give steam facials, was patented and marketed by Nancy D'Alesandro, the mother of Nancy Pelosi. (Found on eBay in 2019, it was still operational.) *(Jack Gruber)*

*(Jack Gruber)*

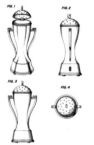

Nancy D'Alesandro filed for several patents for the "Vaporizer." *(Filing retrieved by Lillianna Byington, a researcher for Madam Speaker, from the United States Patent and Trademark Office)*

Nancy D'Alesandro was in high school in 1957 when her mother feigned illness so her sixteen-year-old daughter could accompany her father to a dinner at the Emerson Hotel in Baltimore honoring John F. Kennedy. Then a senator from Massachusetts, Kennedy was promoting his book *Profiles in Courage*. *(Family photo)*

# FAMILY

Nancy D'Alesandro's wedding portrait. She married Paul Pelosi on September 7, 1963, at the Cathedral of Mary Our Queen in Baltimore. *(Family photo)*

The five children of Nancy and Paul Pelosi in matching outfits, circa 1972. From left to right: Nancy Corinne, Christine, Jacqueline, Paul Jr., and Alexandra. *(Family photo)*

The family of Nancy and Paul Pelosi gathers for a photo on the day she was elected Speaker of the House the second time, on January 3, 2019. The Pelosis, their children, and grandchildren are standing on the balcony of the Speaker's office, with its panoramic view of the National Mall. *(Erin Schaff/The New York Times/Redux)*

Nancy and Paul Pelosi arrive at the White House for a state dinner for German chancellor Angela Merkel on June 7, 2011. *(AP Photo/Manuel Balce Ceneta)*

In 1987, her first bid for Congress, Nancy Pelosi rented campaign head-quarters at 666 Mission Street in downtown San Francisco. *(Adam Gottlieb)*

Nancy Pelosi, former chair of the California Democratic Party, was able to attract big names to campaign with her when she ran for Congress for the first time in 1987. Here she is joined by Maryland senator Barbara Mikulski (center) and New York representative Geraldine Ferraro, the Democratic vice presidential nominee in 1984. They are being introduced by former congress-man John Burton, who chaired Pelosi's campaign committee. *(Adam Gottlieb)*

On her first Election Night as a candidate, on April 8, 1987, Nancy Pelosi led a primary field of fourteen contenders for the congressional seat of the late Sala Burton. Pelosi's ubiquitous slogan, shown here, was "A Voice That Will Be Heard." *(AP Photo/Paul Sakuma)*

House Speaker Jim Wright of Texas swears in Nancy Pelosi for the cameras on June 9, 1987. Her father, Thomas D'Alesandro Jr., a former member of Congress who was then in the final months of his life, took the opportunity to lobby Wright to give his daughter a plum assignment on the Appropriations Committee. *(Family photo)*

Outgoing Democratic whip David Bonior of Michigan presents Nancy Pelosi with a black leather whip after she won the contest to succeed him, defeating Maryland representative Steny Hoyer on October 10, 2001. *(AP Photo/Joe Marquette)*

"Nancy for Whip" campaign button. *(Jack Gruber)*

At the 2004 Democratic National Convention in Boston, supporters distributed posters that portrayed Congresswoman Nancy Pelosi as the iconic Rosie the Riveter. She was then House Democratic leader, aspiring to become Speaker. *(Jack Gruber)*

Nancy Pelosi strikes the Rosie the Riveter pose at a luncheon for Emily's List, a political action committee that helps elect pro-choice Democratic women to office, in Washington on March 6, 2007. *(UPI/Newscom)*

By 1987, the year Pelosi was elected, twenty thousand Americans had died of the disease. One in ten of them were from San Francisco, a city with a vibrant and open gay community. In a ten-block radius in the Castro District, a thousand men had died by that summer. "It was one, sometimes two, funerals a day," Nancy Pelosi said as the epidemic began to crescendo, no effective treatment yet in sight.

"You would pass people on the street, emaciated and covered in Kaposi [sarcoma cancer] scars, and you would know, you were saying goodbye," Mike Smith recalled. "You were never going to see these people again."

The morning after she narrowly won the Democratic nomination for the House seat, making her election all but guaranteed, Pelosi met with reporters at her campaign headquarters downtown. The first thing she was going to do in Washington was to try to "change the attitude about AIDS," she told them. "We've got to make them understand it's an emergency situation, almost as if we've had an earthquake in San Francisco."

When she arrived in Washington, friends and family and constituents gathered to watch her being sworn in on June 9, 1987, a week after she won the general election. More than two dozen Democrats from the California delegation stood with her. So did the senators from California and from Maryland and elsewhere; she counted friends in the Senate from her stint as finance chair of the Democratic Senatorial Campaign Committee. Her father and brother, Tommy the Elder and Tommy the Younger, were with her on the House floor. So was John Burton, her campaign chairman and himself a former congressman.

Barbara Boxer, a fellow representative from the Bay Area, rose to welcome Pelosi to "a minority in this House"—that is, of women members. "We make up just five percent of this institution but we try to make our voices heard," she said. The longest welcome, as it happened, was delivered by a congressman from Maryland, Steny Hoyer, then in his fourth term. (He and Pelosi would later become rivals for a leadership post.) "Nancy and I had the opportunity of working together on Capitol Hill some five or six years ago when we were in college," Hoyer said with a smile. "Nancy probably comes to the Congress as well schooled and versed in politics and issues of our day as any member ever."

Veteran House members had prepped Pelosi on what would happen during the brief ceremony. "My colleague said to me, 'Don't say a word. When you're ready to take the oath'—it was a special election, so you were by yourself—'just raise your right hand and say, "Yes, I do solemnly swear." That's all you have to say. You don't say another word.'"

Then House Speaker Jim Wright of Texas, who was presiding, unexpectedly asked her, "Does the gentlewoman from California have anything to say in her own defense?"

She did. "Thank you, Mr. Speaker," she began. "We are very proud of the Fifth Congressional District and its leadership for peace, for environmental protection, for equal rights, for rights of individual freedom, and now we must take the leadership, of course, in the crisis of AIDS, and I look forward to working with you on that."

She concluded with this: "I told the people of the Fifth Congressional District when I got here I will tell you, 'Sala Burton sent me.'"

Some of the new colleagues standing behind her were rolling their eyes and shaking their heads. "When she wanted to speak about AIDS on the floor, there were people who discouraged her from doing that," recalled Thomas Downey, then a Democratic representative from Long Island, noting that he wasn't one of them.

But her words helped solidify her credentials in San Francisco, including among some of those who had backed Harry Britt in the primary she had won. "There was a lot of anger that she got elected, and then also a lot of skepticism," said Scott Shafer, then a young Democratic aide in San Francisco. A wealthy, straight woman who had been portrayed by her Democratic rivals as the conservative in the race had defeated a groundbreaking gay politician. "But she very, very quickly won people over, including the gay community."

"People say, 'Of course she did that; she was from San Francisco,'" recalled Hilary Rosen, a Democratic activist who was then working for the Human Rights Campaign Fund, one of the first gay and lesbian political action committees. San Francisco mayor Dianne Feinstein, Barbara Boxer, George Miller, and a few others were on the front lines of the AIDS fight at the time. But many political leaders, even liberal ones, were skittish about speaking out.

Pelosi did. "She reached out to all of the AIDS and gay activists in D.C. and said, 'I'm going to be your person,'" Rosen told me. "It wasn't a small thing for this fancy suburban lady to come in and be out there."

Her attitude toward addressing AIDS and accepting gays wasn't new. During receptions at her home leading up to the Democratic National Convention in 1984, she tried to help dispel by example some of the unfounded fears of AIDS, such as that the disease could be transmitted by casual contact. She would strategize with openly gay friends to perform a bit of instructive theater at the parties. "I'd say to a gay friend, 'Okay, let's both dip our chip in the guacamole at the same time, so they can see we are not afraid of each other.'"

At the time, standing with the gay community carried some political cost—not in San Francisco, but across the country.

Jeane Kirkpatrick, the U.S. ambassador to the United Nations in the Reagan administration, had coined the phrase "San Francisco liberals" when the 1984 Democratic convention was held in the city. GOP partisans began to attack Pelosi and other Democrats for espousing "San Francisco values." The phrase was intended to be derogatory. It was seen by many as having homophobic overtones, given the city's identification as a center of gay life. It was meant to brand someone as far left, as out of the mainstream on cultural issues.

Pelosi understood the cost. Her first political identity would be stamped as a defender of gay rights and an activist on AIDS rather than, say, as a devout Catholic or the mother of five or a daughter of Baltimore's Little Italy. Down the road, Republican attacks characterizing her as a dangerous leftist, the theme sounded in millions of dollars in television ads, would unnerve some Democratic congressional candidates from more centrist districts. It may be one reason why, even as her reputation rose in politics, Pelosi's name was almost never raised in speculation about potential presidential contenders or their running mates.

"Some say California's Nancy Pelosi might be a good pick," Charlie Cook, a nonpartisan political handicapper, wrote in *National Journal* in 1999, at a time when Democrats were searching for prospective female contenders. He called Pelosi "a titan." Even so, he assessed her odds as slim.

"It is not likely with my voting record," Pelosi told the *San Francisco Chronicle* in a story headlined "Can Pelosi's Politics Play Well in Peoria?" "It would require walking away from some of my voting record, of which I am very proud." She called it "compatible with my district, but may not be compatible with a presidential nominee."

Two years later, when she became the first woman elected House whip, she was blunter.

"When people say 'San Francisco liberal,' are they talking about protecting the environment, educating the American children, building economic success?" she demanded. "No, they are talking about gay people. Well, I was brought up to believe that all people are God's children. And the last time I checked, that included gay people."

———

Nancy Pelosi's willingness to stand up for those facing stigma at a time of life-and-death crisis may have reflected not only the demands of her district but also the lessons from her father.

Tommy D'Alesandro Jr. was such an ardent fan of FDR that he named his third son Franklin Delano Roosevelt D'Alesandro. But he broke ranks with the president during World War II over FDR's decision to rebuff pleas for the United States to admit more Jews fleeing the Nazis. D'Alesandro, then a young congressman from Baltimore, publicly endorsed the Bergson Group, a maverick Jewish political action committee that challenged Roosevelt's refugee policy and later pressed President Harry Truman to recognize Israel's independence.

The open anti-Semitism that Jews were facing may have reminded D'Alesandro of the sting of discrimination against Italians when they were the new immigrants seeking entry to America. One of the tools used to deny entry to desperate Jewish refugees, among them thousands of children, was the Johnson-Reed Act—the 1924 quota law that had been designed in part to slash the number of Italians allowed to immigrate.

What's more, Tommy D'Alesandro had long had friendships and alliances with Jewish residents of Baltimore. As a boy, he had earned spare change by working as a *Shabbos goy*, doing routine household tasks for observant Jews on the Sabbath. As a politician, he counted on Jewish voters as part of the coalition he built to win election to Congress and as mayor.

"He would get up—and he spoke Yiddish and he was a great orator—and he'd go around part of the group to have parades, rallies, and all the rest to talk about what was happening in Europe, so that he would raise awareness of it and the need for the Jewish State in Palestine," Nancy Pelosi said in an emotional speech in Jerusalem in 2020, commemorating seventy-five years since the liberation of the death camp at Auschwitz.

Her father had delivered an impassioned appeal on the House floor nearly eight decades earlier, in 1943. "Daily, hourly, the greatest crime of all time is being committed," D'Alesandro had declared. "A defenseless and innocent people is being slaughtered in a wholesale massacre of millions."

Years later, Nancy Pelosi would cite the influence that her father's support of the Bergson Group had on her. It was a factor when she decided to break with another Democratic president, Bill Clinton, on the issue of China and human rights. She was Clinton's ally on most issues but a thorn in his side on this one. She had been a little girl when World War II ended, but she remembered with pride the example her father had set. "His enthusiasm came from doing what he believed was right," she said.

———

A frail Tommy D'Alesandro Jr. had conserved his strength so he could attend his daughter's swearing-in. After a lifetime in politics, it would be the last public event he would ever attend. He assured her she didn't need to get a ticket for him; as a former member of Congress, he would be welcome on the House floor.

Two months later, he suffered a heart attack in Ocean City, Maryland, where the family had long spent their vacations. He would die two weeks later at Mercy Hospital, back in Baltimore, the city he loved and once governed. When the news broke that night, residents of Little Italy gathered on stoops and exchanged stories about Tommy the Elder.

The wake at St. Leo's, the church that had expelled him from its school at age thirteen, lasted seven hours. Governor William Donald Schaefer sent a large rectangular display of carnations in bright red, white, and green, the colors of the Italian flag. At 10 a.m. the next morning, more than four hundred mourners crowded into the church for the Mass of the Resurrection. There were politicians current and past: Governor Schaefer and former governor Harry R. Hughes, Mayor Clarence Burns and city council president Frank Gallagher, public works commissioner Francis W. Kuchta and onetime police commissioner Frank Battaglia. They told stories about Tommy as they waited outside before going in, old rivalries put aside.

The church erected two oversized speakers on the second-story porch for the overflow crowd. The steps of the row houses along Exeter Street were filled with neighbors, listening to the Mass.

Mayor Burns delivered a eulogy. "I'm going to say to my friend, 'Until we meet again,'" he said. Tommy D'Alesandro III, a former mayor now in his late fifties but still known as Tommy the Younger, spoke. So did Nancy Pelosi, who was seated with her family in the second-row pew, just behind her mother.

In her eulogy, Little Nancy talked about growing up in a family with five brothers. Tommy, Roosie, Nicholas, Hector, and Joey were all seated in the church. So were Tommy the Elder's grandchildren and great-grandchildren. The last one had been born on the day he died. "In the vitality of the city that he loved and the commitment to the people which he shared and the laughter of his grandchildren, Tommy D'Alesandro lives," she said.

She didn't need to add this: In the political career that his only daughter was now pursuing, Tommy D'Alesandro also lived.

Her father believed strongly in the two-party system, she told the congregation with a partisan smile he would have relished. "One party to govern. One to watch."

———————

The qualities that would mark Pelosi's rise and her reign as House Speaker were honed by the battles she waged on AIDS during her first days in Congress. She wasn't the most inspiring orator, on this or other subjects. She relied not on eloquence but on persistence. She made a point of mastering even the most mind-numbing details of health care legislation and regulation, as she would two decades later in pushing the Affordable Care Act through Congress. She pursued unlikely coalitions, potential allies on this issue even if they were adversaries on others. At least publicly, she dismissed political attacks, even harsh ones.

She worked the system, using every tool she could muster. Her California colleague Henry Waxman gave up one of his assignments on a health subcommittee so she could take the post. (Her first committee assignments were on Government Operations and on Banking, Finance, and Urban Affairs. She wouldn't rate a spot on the prized Appropriations Committee until her third term in office.)

Soon after being sworn in, she submitted two amendments to a pending AIDS bill. She proposed establishing two demonstration projects, one focused on developing model protocols for the clinical care of those with AIDS, another to provide mental health services. Prospects typically were dim for proposals from freshmen members of Congress, who were expected to be seen and not heard until they had gained wisdom, or at least seniority.

Pelosi showed up to make her case before the powerful Rules Committee, chaired by Representative Claude Pepper of Florida, eighty-seven years old and a political legend. And, as it happened, someone who had served in Congress with Tommy D'Alesandro Jr.

"We got to the Rules Committee, and everyone says, 'They're never going to give her [a vote on] these amendments,'" her aide Stephen Morin recalled. But when Pelosi rose to speak, Pepper perked up. "Oh, Nancy, we're so glad to see you! I knew your father so well." To the obvious surprise of others on the committee, the chairman summarily declared, "Of course we're going to give you your amendments!" The most junior member of Congress succeeded in adding provisions to a new law.

Again and again, she pressed for changes in bureaucratic rules that had been written before the AIDS epidemic, before anyone envisioned so many healthy young men being hit by a debilitating disease. The regulatory revisions often generated few headlines, but they had an enormous impact on the quality of life for AIDS victims and their families.

For example, the federal law known as COBRA guaranteed that workers who lost their jobs could buy up to eighteen months of health insurance from their previous employers, intended as a bridge until they could get health insurance elsewhere. But it took twenty-nine months to be eligible for disability benefits under Medicare. That left a gap of almost a year without access to insurance for many of those with AIDS—after COBRA had run out, and before Medicare could begin. An amendment submitted by Pelosi extended COBRA coverage for the full twenty-nine months.

She pushed the Social Security Administration to allow people with AIDS and AIDS-related diseases to qualify for its disability program, and to make federal benefits available for home care as well as hospitalization. She drafted a measure that established a procedure for cities with large AIDS populations to share data. In her first major legislative victory, in 1990, she coauthored the Housing Opportunities for Persons with AIDS bill, which provided subsidies to help low-income individuals with HIV/AIDS and their families stay in their homes. That same year, during her second term, she cosponsored the Ryan White Act. The legislation, named after an Indiana teenager who had to fight to attend his public school after he was diagnosed with AIDS, distributed $220 million to the cities hardest hit by AIDS.

After Republicans gained control of the House in the 1994 midterm elections, she found herself more on defense than offense, fighting efforts by conservatives to cut AIDS programs and to reverse protections for those diagnosed with AIDS. She was part of the successful fight against GOP proposals to slash $23 million from HIV prevention programs and $13 million from the Ryan White Act. She lost some battles, too, fueling her frustration about being in the minority. In 1998, she argued, unsuccessfully, against a Republican bill that barred federal funding for programs that distributed clean needles to drug users, an effort to reduce transmission of the disease.

During the debate, Representative Gerald Solomon, a Republican from New York and a cosponsor of the legislation, denounced needle-exchange programs as "an intolerable message to our nation's children sent by the White House that drug use is a way of life."

"You'd think we're having a meeting of the Flat Earth Society," Congresswoman Pelosi replied with exasperation.

———

In the House, Nancy Pelosi had found a home.

After a year, she told a reporter she liked the job better than she had expected, and she was better at it than almost anyone had predicted. She hadn't served in elected office before, but she had grown up in a political family, and she had led the California Democratic Party. As finance chair for the Democrat Senate Campaign Committee in 1986, she had developed personal relationships with Democratic senators that no other first-term House member had. A "seasoned newcomer," the *San Francisco Examiner* said.

Even some Republicans in Washington took notice. When Andy Card came to Washington in 1989 to join President George H. W. Bush's White House staff, he met with Margaret Heckler, a fellow Massachusetts Republican. She had served in Congress and in President Reagan's cabinet. "I remember Peggy Heckler telling me when I came to Washington, D.C., that Nancy Pelosi was somebody to pay attention to," Card told me. "It was the first time I'd ever heard the name Nancy Pelosi." (Pelosi and Card would later clash on the Iraq War when she was the House Democratic leader and he was the chief of staff for President George W. Bush.)

"I had this confidence when I came to Congress," Pelosi told *San Francisco Chronicle* reporter Larry Liebert early in her tenure, in comments that could suggest she had electoral ambitions earlier than she was willing to acknowledge. "I always believed I could do this job very well because I'm relentless in pursuit of my colleagues, and I know how to mobilize people."

She had energy and persistence. "She would corner people and they weren't going to get out of that talk without hearing her points of view and all that," Morin told me. "She would go back and she would go back until she got a vote." Some of her more senior colleagues found her presumptuous for a new member—a pushy broad. Who did she think she was? "They'd say, 'Basically, the rules around here, you're supposed to be low-key.'" She would reply, "I didn't come here to be quiet; I came here to legislate."

Not everyone took her seriously. "The institution that she came into did not have a lot of women, and none of them were in real power," Downey said. When she took office, the 100th Congress featured a grand total of twenty-five women, two of them in the Senate and twenty-three in the House. "Certainly not enough—not even close," Pelosi told the graduating class at Mount Vernon College two days before she was sworn in; the class included daughter Nancy Corinne.

Not a single committee in the House or Senate was chaired by a woman. No woman had ever reached the top ranks of the congressional leadership. Female representatives had lost every bid to rise above the job of secretary of the party caucus.

Sexual harassment, offensive jokes, and worse were routine. Judy Lemons, who worked as Sala Burton's closest aide, then as Pelosi's first chief of staff, would overhear the good ol' boys discuss and disparage their female colleagues from the back of the House chamber.

"I think Nancy became an attractive target for people simply because she is so attractive; she's an eye-stopper," Lemons said. "When she came to Congress she was in her late forties, and she just had a glamour about her and such a style that became the first impression. Then it became incumbent on her to prove herself beyond that: 'I'm not just a pretty face. I am also a serious contender.'"

Pelosi was enraged when John Jacobs wrote a profile in the *San Francisco Examiner*'s Sunday magazine about her with the headline "Not Just a Party Girl." The thrust of the article was positive. "Pelosi has shaken off the lightweight tag that dogged her early political career," it said. But the play on words in the headline "really, really upset her because she wanted to be taken seriously, and it was a sexist reference," Lemons said.

It was the same dismissive stereotype she had faced when opponents labeled her an "airhead" during her 1984 bid for Democratic national chairman, and as a "dilettante" during her congressional campaign. "There's not a lot of horsepower under that hood," one of California's senior political figures scoffed when Charlie Cook, founder of the non-partisan *Cook Political Report*, asked for his read on the new congresswoman from California. The task of getting beyond that impression, of demonstrating her stamina and her seriousness, was a "monumental" task, Lemons said. "Nancy had a longer distance to run in that regard, where men did not have to face the same challenge."

Nancy Pelosi and Barbara Boxer, congresswomen from neighboring districts, found themselves mistaken for each other so often that Pelosi sometimes stopped bothering to correct people. One evening, they attended a fund-raising event in San Francisco for the Democratic Congressional Campaign Committee, and the congressman at the podium introduced each of the other members of Congress in attendance by name. "When he got to us, he said, 'And there are the two women who represent San Francisco,'" Boxer recalled. Period. "We looked at each other and said, 'What? Do we have no identities here?'"

They were friends and allies. In Washington, Boxer introduced Pelosi to a Tuesday night dinner group of Democratic representatives. When Congress was in session, they would gather at a local Italian restaurant or someone's home for pasta, wine, and conversation. The group had started in the 1970s, often meeting at Congressman Pete Stark's Capitol Hill apartment; a millionaire banker, he had a cook. A decade later, the first women joined, Barbara Kennelly of Connecticut and Boxer.

By then, they often met at Downey's home on C Street; his wife, Chris, would cook. Two Illinois congressmen, Marty Russo and Dick Durbin, were regulars. So was New York congressman Chuck Schumer and Connecticut congressman Sam Gejdenson. The California contingent included Leon Panetta and George Miller. Anna Eshoo began to join them after she was elected in 1992.

It was a training ground for the need to speak up if you wanted to be heard.

"We had many lively debates, and one thing was clear to us: The men never turned and asked us, 'What do you think?' Never," Pelosi recalled. That was true even one night when the men began to discuss childbirth. "The first one said, 'God, when I had my first, I had the green gown on but they wouldn't let me in the room...' Next my friend Marty Russo said, 'I had a camera, but when I saw it happening, I said, "Oh, God, let me out of here."'...Another one said, 'Oh, [expletive], I thought I was going to faint.'"

None of the men turned to the women, all of them mothers, with eleven children among them.

"It was Nancy who said, 'Not to interrupt your expertise on this, but maybe you'd want to hear from actually somebody who's had children,'" Downey told me. That hadn't occurred to them. When Pelosi relayed the story sometime later, the men involved protested that it had never happened, that they couldn't possibly have behaved in that way. "They didn't even know how clueless they were," she said. "They didn't have a clue that they didn't have a clue!"

They became a core group of friends and allies for one another as they rose in politics. Barbara Boxer was elected to the Senate in 1992, Dick Durbin in 1996, Chuck Schumer in 1998. Panetta was appointed to President Clinton's cabinet in 1993 and became his White House chief of staff; he served in President Obama's cabinet as well. Kennelly left Congress to run, unsuccessfully, for governor of Connecticut in 1998. Eshoo became one of Pelosi's closest confidantes in Congress.

By the time Donald Trump was elected president in 2016, the Tuesday night dinner gang was in full charge of the Democrats. Nancy Pelosi was the Democratic leader in the House, Chuck Schumer was the Democratic leader in the Senate, and Dick Durbin was his deputy.

At the start, the group was young, ambitious, left-leaning, and impatient with the party's current leadership. They began to recognize the possibilities for Pelosi. Her ability to raise money was appreciated by her colleagues; her success in pushing legislation on AIDS had made an impression. She had gotten headlines for standing up for human rights in China since the Tiananmen Square protests in 1989.

"It was obvious to me at the time that even though she represented San Francisco, that she was very pragmatic, that she had the ability to look at both sides and get a sense of what the issues were about," Panetta, who represented a more moderate California district centered in Monterey County, told me. He credited her father's influence as mayor of Baltimore with forging her ease with power. "She wasn't bashful," he went on. "When you've got a bunch of guys who are sitting down to dinner, and some of them can be loudmouths, and she wasn't afraid to jump in. She would make her views known."

Near the beginning of Pelosi's career in Congress, Boxer recalled a conversation they had during one of their endless commercial flights across the country, heading back to their districts on the West Coast. Boxer was then a member of the House; she would be elected to the Senate later, in 1992. With Pelosi's fund-raising abilities, she could be the first woman chair of the Democratic Congressional Campaign Committee, Boxer told her. Pelosi expressed higher ambitions than that.

"She does not remember this, but I remember her saying, and this is very early on, in the '80s, 'Well, I really want to be Speaker.' And I said, 'I really want to be senator.' Each of us thought the other one was dreaming."

## CHAPTER TEN

# "I DON'T THINK THESE BOYS KNOW HOW TO WIN"

*November 8, 1994—The U.S. Capitol*

Nancy Pelosi was increasingly exasperated with the men who were leading House Democrats, and they with her.

The 1994 midterm elections were a disaster for Democrats and a turning point for American politics. Led by a brash Georgia congressman, Newt Gingrich, the so-called Republican Revolution would set the GOP on a more partisan and conservative course that would eventually fuel the rise of the Tea Party movement on Capitol Hill and the election of Donald Trump to the White House. For the first time in forty years, Republicans claimed unified control of Congress—flipping a stunning fifty-four House seats and eight Senate seats—not to mention ten governorships and state legislatures across the country.

Much of the blame for Democratic losses went to President Bill Clinton and his ill-fated proposal to overhaul the nation's health care system, dubbed "Hillarycare" by its detractors. It was so complicated and so controversial that the Democratic leadership in the House and the Senate didn't dare bring it up for a vote. That said, Pelosi thought congressional Democrats had been inept as well, failing to contain a banking scandal or to adapt to changes in the way campaigns were run.

Her scorn was no secret. Even though she was a relatively junior member of Congress who had never chaired a committee or served in the leadership, some fellow Democrats urged her to challenge Speaker Tom Foley of Washington State. That would have been an extraordinary act of insurgency. "They started asking me to run for Speaker," she told me. As a fresh face and a woman, she could represent change. They told her, "If you don't run, we're going to lose the House."

She dismissed the idea out of hand. "You want me to run for Speaker? I don't even know how long I'm staying here," she told them. "There was no way I was going to run against the Speaker, no way in a million years." Even so, word got back to Foley about a potential mutiny, and his allies warned her about the consequences of a challenge. "It's not good if people think you're running for Speaker," they cautioned her. "The Speaker could get angry."

As it turned out, that threat was moot. Voters in Foley's district dispatched him that fall. After thirty years in Congress, he was unseated by political neophyte George Nethercutt. It was the first time since before the Civil War that a sitting Speaker of the House had lost reelection.

That Election Night, Pelosi was reelected to a fifth term with 82 percent of the vote. As for Democrats nationally, she declared that they "can turn this around in two years," something almost no one believed. Her own overwhelming victory wasn't going to protect her from the consequences of her party's resounding defeat. During the previous eight years in the House, with Democrats in the majority, she had been able to help drive policy on AIDS and focus attention on human rights in China. Now she bristled at the new reality in a House controlled by Republicans and led by the combative Gingrich. "Being in the minority among moderate Republicans who share some of our values would be one thing," she said in the spring of 1996. "But being in the minority among the radical leadership we have in the House of Representatives is intolerable."

Bill Clinton adapted to the capital's changed dynamics. After working with Gingrich on issues including the federal budget and welfare policies, he easily won a second term in the White House in 1996 over Republican Bob Dole of Kansas. But Democrats regained just two seats in the House. They fell short again in the 1998 midterm elections, gaining five seats but still leaving Republicans in control.

In 2000, Pelosi thought a Democratic majority was in sight, and she offered a deal to Democratic leader Dick Gephardt of Missouri. "If you're counting on California for us to win the majority, take it to the bank—we're going to do very well here," she told him. If Democrats could regain a net of just two Republican seats in the other forty-nine states, she would flip the additional districts they needed from California alone.

Pelosi knew her state, and she understood campaigns. When she chaired the California Democratic Party, she had modernized its operations. Now she set out to recruit candidates to challenge vulnerable Republican incumbents. She raised millions of dollars. She helped organize grassroots campaigns in the GOP districts she targeted, "right down to the last blade of grass," she said. She urged candidates to focus on kitchen-table concerns.

California representative George Miller, one of Pelosi's closest friends and most trusted allies, told me that she didn't hesitate to back up her advice with threats of her own, if necessary. Her warning: "If you don't do this, there's no money for you from me or from the state party or the DCCC," the Democratic Congressional Campaign Committee.

One of the GOP incumbents in her sights was James Rogan, who had been one of the House managers in the Senate impeachment trial of President Clinton two years earlier. The 27th Congressional District, in the San Gabriel Valley east of Los Angeles, was becoming less reliably Republican. A Democratic state senator who had lost to Rogan in an earlier race for a state assembly seat was ready to challenge him again.

His name was Adam Schiff.

Their campaign would be the most fiercely contested in the country.

The two sides spent a total of more than $11 million, at the time a record for a House seat. The alliance Schiff forged with Pelosi in that race would deepen over time. Two decades later, in one of those odd coincidences, she would tap him to be the lead House manager in President Trump's impeachment trial. "It was my first introduction to her in her capacity as a political strategist and a rainmaker," Schiff told me. "She was very active in helping my campaign, not a passive supporter who sent me a check." Pelosi encouraged him not to talk about impeachment even though the topic might energize Democratic partisans. Instead, he should focus on the issues that mattered in voters' daily lives.

On Election Night, it wasn't close. Schiff beat Rogan by nine percentage points.

Pelosi also had recruited Susan Davis, a social worker from San Diego who had been elected to the state assembly, to challenge a three-term Republican. Davis shadowed Pelosi for a day at the Capitol—"to help me feel comfortable," Davis said—and Pelosi raised money for her. She would occasionally send encouraging notes: "You're doing great! Keep it up!" Davis ended up winning, too.

Pelosi fulfilled her promise to Gephardt, picking up five seats in California: Jane Harman in Palm Springs; she was reclaiming a seat she gave up when she had run for governor. Mike Honda in Alameda County. Hilda Solis in San Bernardino. Schiff and Davis. They would call the statewide sweep the California Gold Rush.

"We were ecstatic, and assumed we had taken back the majority," Pelosi recalled. She was about to address a triumphant Election Night news conference in San Francisco when a staffer pulled her aside. "Hold on," she told Pelosi. "CNN is saying the Republicans have retained control of Congress." She was incredulous. "This isn't possible, I thought." But it was possible.

She had delivered. But in the rest of the country, Democrats hadn't managed to gain a net total of two more seats. They flipped five but lost seven others, and one Democrat became an independent, for a net loss of three. Republicans, who had been in power for six years, would stay in control.

After the campaign, House Democrats held their annual retreat at a mountain resort in Farmington, Pennsylvania. In a bipartisan gesture, President George W. Bush, who had won the White House after a disputed election settled by the Supreme Court, would visit the closed-door meeting. In a decidedly partisan gesture, Pelosi addressed the group as well. She had prepared a PowerPoint presentation and brought along her team of consultants to explain why Democrats had succeeded in California while they had failed almost everywhere else.

The party needed to articulate a stronger national message and to emphasize the fundamentals of grassroots organizing on the ground, she told them; just raising money to air TV ads wasn't enough. Stop wasting money on long shots who had little chance of winning. ("I have a reptilian approach," she liked to say. "You have to be very cold-blooded in how you allocate resources.") That goes for consultants, too; stop hiring them if they don't deliver victories. She had coined a saying when she was California Democratic chair: "When you win, you work." In other words, consultants who repeatedly lost competitive campaigns didn't get hired again. But Democratic leaders elsewhere weren't demanding that sort of accountability. "People kept losing, year in and year out, and then they'd do it again, and then they'd do it again."

The Democratic leaders weren't persuaded, she said. "People thought, 'That's her way. That's not the way we do things here,'" she told Karen Tumulty of *Time* magazine. Indeed, it wasn't at all clear that they were even listening. "The leadership that was there sort of just got up at the end of the presentation and walked away," George Miller recalled. And accountability? Despite failing to lead Democrats out of the minority in three straight elections, the senior leaders remained comfortably ensconced in power. No one new had been elected to their ranks in nearly a decade. No woman had ever made it there.

"I never had any intention of running for leadership, none whatsoever. I really didn't know how long I would stay in Congress," Pelosi said. "I was not on a leadership course, but I was tired of losing. I was just really tired of losing."

Tired, and mad. She was fuming when she walked out of the room, George Miller told me. "I don't think these boys know how to win," she said to him. She already had started laying the groundwork to run for the leadership. At that point, Miller said, "The game was on."

————

She launched a campaign for House Democratic whip, number two in the leadership, at a time when the vacancy didn't exist.

She began methodically applying the political basics that she had been immersed in since childhood. Build a coalition. Keep what amounted to a "Favor File" to earn the loyalty and support of the electorate—in this case, other House Democrats. Whatever your credentials, don't expect people with power to hand it over; you had to be ready to seize it. She would run the most meticulous and the most monied campaign for the leadership that anyone in Washington could remember. It would be a training ground, too, for the skills she would later deploy as a legislative leader.

The big financial donors she had cultivated were encouraging her to demand more say in how their money was being spent. "She raised the fucking dough, she ought to be able to get something for it," said the famously profane John Burton, the former California congressman who had chaired her first congressional campaign. "My theory in life is those who pay the piper call the tune." That's why she decided to run for leadership, he said. "Because her friends are saying, 'You're raising all this money, and where are you in the picture?'"

She realized that the men in power, even those who were delighted to benefit from the funds she had raised, weren't likely to be welcoming. "By running for Whip, I would defy more than two hundred years of men following in each other's footsteps for all of the major leadership positions," she said. That was an option she didn't have. There were no footsteps for her to follow, and there were men already standing next in line. "Outside of Congress, my supporters were very energized. Inside the Congress, others were less thrilled. 'Who said she could run?' they said. *Who said she could run?* That put me into fighting mode. I did not need anyone to tell me I could or could not run."

Her polite demeanor led some to misjudge the steel in her spine. "Because she's so genteel…they keep underestimating this fucking broad," Burton said. "They didn't get how goddamn tough she would be."

For Pelosi, everything would follow from this upstart race. She was running for whip this time, but she and everyone else understood that it was only the first step toward a bigger prize. "I wouldn't rule it out," she said when asked about a future race for Speaker. Once she got on the first rung of a ladder, she would never lose her footing.

Party elders approached her with a tone-deaf offer, a dumbfounding miscalculation of the challenge she was about to pose. "We see that you have a lot of support from women," they told her. "Why don't you women give us a list of the things you want done and we will get them done for you?" Her derisive reaction, as she later told daughter Christine: "Those poor babies. I don't think so!"

After the 1998 midterm elections, Democrats reelected a leadership team that was very familiar and entirely male—the way things had always been, but a situation that was becoming harder to defend as the number of women in Congress began to rise.

More than once, Gephardt offered Pelosi the chance to lead the Democratic Congressional Campaign Committee. She rejected the offer as a stepping-stone she already had more than surpassed, a role that would tap her fund-raising abilities without giving her power over policy.

Pelosi's path was cleared by two serendipitous departures. California representative Vic Fazio, chairman of the Democratic Caucus, announced in late 1997 that he was retiring. There could have been resistance to having two Californians in leadership ranks; now that wouldn't be an issue. Then Representative Barbara Kennelly, who had hoped to rise in the leadership herself, decided to run for governor of Connecticut in 1998. That wasn't entirely a coincidence. Kennelly could see that Pelosi was on track to be the groundbreaking woman in the House. In the politics of the day, it would be hard enough to elect one woman to leadership, much less two.

In the summer of 1998, Pelosi let her inner circle know that she was ready to run. She also gave a heads-up to the person most likely to be directly affected by her decision. Representative Steny Hoyer had risen far and fast in Maryland politics while Pelosi was rearing five children in California. He was the youngest-ever president of the Maryland State Senate. Once elected to the U.S. House, he had served as chair of the Democratic Caucus, then was defeated by David Bonior of Michigan in a bid for whip. Tall, handsome, and smooth, Hoyer looked the part of a rising pol, or at least of the rising pols up until then. He was widely seen as next in line for whip, when the job was open.

"The men in the caucus said, 'You're not next,'" Pelosi recalled. "I said, 'No, we've been waiting over two hundred years; women are next.'"

She made it clear to Hoyer that she wasn't going to honor the next-in-line tradition. "It was not 'Are you running again?' or 'What would you think of my running?' or 'Would you have any objections?'" Hoyer said of her phone call. He described his reaction: "*Hurt* might be the right word, coupled with disappointment. But you know, I've been around a long time as well. I got the message."

Pelosi sent a "Dear Colleague" letter to House Democrats that expressed confidence Democrats would regain control of the House in November, an optimism that many didn't share. When they won, she wrote, she intended "to run for a leadership position in the new Congress." Gephardt would be elevated to Speaker and Bonior to majority leader, she predicted, leaving Bonior's current position as whip available. Available for her.

Some in the House saw her announcement as premature and presumptuous. "In order to buck 200 years of history, if I have to start earlier than someone else, so be it," Pelosi said, undeterred. Hoyer hadn't planned to begin lobbying for an opening that didn't yet exist, but now he had little choice. If he wanted the job, he would have to fight for it. Georgia representative John Lewis, a civil rights icon, also announced his candidacy.

An academic study of House leadership elections would call the three-year campaign that followed "a titanic battle."

———————

Representative John Murtha, Democrat of Pennsylvania, was a general in the Old Guard. The blunt-spoken former Marine, the recipient of two Purple Hearts and the first Vietnam veteran elected to Congress, had been serving in the House for a quarter century. He was a powerhouse on the Appropriations Committee, especially on military issues. In more ways than one, his district in south-central Pennsylvania, dependent on steel and coal, was as distant from San Francisco as it could be.

Yet Murtha and Pelosi somehow hit it off. When she arrived in Congress, Representative Austin Murphy of Pennsylvania, another Marine veteran who represented the district next to Murtha's, was being investigated by the Ethics Committee. He was accused of keeping a ghost employee on the payroll, of diverting government resources to his former law partner, and of letting someone else electronically cast votes for him on the House floor. Murphy protested his innocence, or at least his ignorance about what had been going on in his congressional office.

The Ethics Committee voted unanimously to recommend a reprimand. The easy vote was to support the slap on the wrist. It sailed through the House, 324 to 68. Just 56 Democrats voted against it. They included Murphy's old friend, Jack Murtha, and it included the newest member of Congress, Nancy Pelosi. She didn't think the Ethics Committee had proven its case. (She had already cast another vote that some dodged as politically problematic, supporting a pay raise for members of Congress.) Murtha walked over to her on the House floor. "Let me tell you, you got some kind of nerve for a freshman," he said with admiration. Those may have been the first words they ever exchanged.

Their friendship was later sealed when he spotted a small carved figure of a coal miner in her office. "What are you, from San Francisco, doing with a coal miner?" he asked her. It was a memento she had inherited from her father, she told him. West Virginia congressman Jennings Randolph had given it to Tommy D'Alesandro Jr. when they served together on the House Appropriations Committee, a pair of like-minded New Dealers. During an interview in the Speaker's office, she pointed out the small statue to me, still on display. "The coal miner brought us together," she told me, discussing her alliance with Murtha.

Pelosi and Murtha had more in common than it might seem. She had grown up dealing with pols like him, and Murtha saw something of a kindred spirit in her. "She's from Baltimore," Murtha once declared. "Don't think she's from San Francisco." For Murtha, that was high praise.

Still, it was a shock to Hoyer when Pelosi announced that the chairman of her leadership campaign would be Murtha. To insiders, it was a declaration of how formidable Pelosi's campaign would be, of the support she had lined up in unexpected places. Her bid would be led by a man and a moderate from a gritty industrial district, a member in good standing of the old boys' club that had long run Congress. Hoyer saw it as a betrayal, one associate said. "That was a real disappointment to him," said another, Ben Cardin, the Maryland congressman who was running Hoyer's whip operation. (Cardin, later a U.S. senator, at the time held the House seat that had once belonged to Pelosi's father.) "I think Steny thought he had Jack Murtha."

In 2008, as he was about to retire from Congress, Murtha dictated notes to an aide for a memoir he never wrote. The handwritten pages, never before reported, were filed in boxes of his papers now archived at the University of Pittsburgh. "Speaker Pelosi Book," one of them was titled—that is, notes about Pelosi for his intended book. They outlined how they met, and what he learned from her.

"Pelosi one of the premier leaders in America today," he said at one point, describing their early work on converting the Presidio in San Francisco from an Army base to a public space. "More liberal than I but she has ability to get things done and she's given a tremendous service to our Cong. & country."

In another note, he said she had as "good a political mind as I have ever seen," then detailed some of the reasons why. He praised her pragmatism. "Able to come to a practical solution. I appreciate that more than anything else. Get something that can be passed." He called her "fair + tuff" and noted, "She always lets someone else take credit." She also took care to maintain cordial relations even with foes of the moment: "You get pissed off but you have to be careful because you'll need them the next day."

"Steny was undermining her," Murtha wrote at another point, although he added that Hoyer had stopped doing that by then, around 2008. When Pelosi asked him to be her campaign manager for the leadership, he said, "some of the old guys were very hesitant to have a woman as Speaker."

At the time, Murtha's endorsement convinced some of those "old guys" to give Pelosi a second look. He also helped make sure Gephardt didn't tilt the playing field toward Hoyer, who was close to Gephardt. After the 2000 election, for instance, Pelosi wanted to chair a task force to look at election reform; Gephardt had named Hoyer instead.

Gephardt stayed out of the race even after a heated private meeting with Pelosi at the DCCC office, a session that has never before been reported. She argued that Gephardt needed her as whip, that she had proven her ability to deal with members and count votes. She noted that the donors she cultivated were contributing the money to boost Democrats. She could help make him Speaker, she told him. She deserved the post, she said, and it was in his interest as well. To her frustration, and after one of the most contentious conversations the two friends would ever have, he declined to make an endorsement.

She did have other significant backers, among them Sam Gejdenson of Connecticut, Joe Moakley of Massachusetts, David Obey of Wisconsin, Henry Waxman of California, and George Miller. For his part, Hoyer was endorsed by John Dingell of Michigan, the ranking Democrat on the powerful Energy and Commerce Committee, and Ellen Tauscher, from a California district neighboring Pelosi's. (Tauscher was the only California Democrat to openly support Hoyer, a decision Pelosi wouldn't forget.) Though John Lewis was still in the contest, Hoyer was backed by two members of the Congressional Black Caucus from Maryland, Elijah Cummings and Al Wynn. Pelosi was backed by Cynthia McKinney of Georgia and Eleanor Holmes Norton of the District of Columbia.

Behind the scenes, Pelosi was getting advice from Leo McCarthy, a mentor from California who had served as Speaker of the state assembly and lieutenant governor. Art Agnos had been McCarthy's chief of staff in the assembly; he was later elected mayor of San Francisco himself.

"I would go in his office, check in with the old boss, and there was Nancy making calls to prospective votes," Agnos told me. "There was Leo coaching her before every conversation. They would go over the profile of whoever the subject was for that particular phone call and he would give her tips about what to ask or where to take the conversation." When she called, she would already know their children's names, their electoral histories, their ambitions. For the rest of her career, she would be famous for knowing as much about politicians and their districts as they knew themselves. It was a characteristic she shared with an earlier master legislator, Senate majority leader Lyndon Johnson of Texas.

Cultivating the support of fellow politicians is different than campaigning for the public's votes. "With a citizen, you're going to talk about issues and the economy and all that," Agnos said. "Well, the politicians are going to talk about—what do they need to either get elected, stay elected, or accomplish their legislation goals and all that stuff. And what Nancy developed is a magnificent skill of starting where the incumbent is, or where the candidate is, and their needs. How can she fit what she brings to the table to help them?"

———

Democrats didn't win control of the House in 1998. Which meant Gephardt didn't become Speaker. Which meant Bonior didn't become majority leader. Which meant there was no vacancy for a new whip.

The campaign for the job that didn't yet exist continued anyway. In 1999, Texas congressman Martin Frost, who was chair of the Democratic Caucus, thought about jumping in, then reconsidered. John Lewis dropped his bid in July 2000. "The votes are simply not there for me," he said. He endorsed Hoyer. In the 2000 midterms, the one in which Pelosi managed to help flip five seats in California, the party fell just short of a majority again.

By now it was a two-person race for whip, Pelosi versus Hoyer. (The residue from their rivalry would persist for decades, becoming the source of Capitol legend.) Pelosi argued that Democrats could make history by electing the first woman to a major leadership position. Hoyer said he could be a voice for more conservative and moderate Democrats, the Blue Dogs and the New Democrat Coalition. He offered an experienced hand. She promised to be a fresh face.

Political scientists Matthew N. Green and Douglas B. Harris later published a quantitative analysis of the race in an academic study titled *Choosing the Leader: Leadership Elections in the U.S. House of Representatives.* Despite the groundbreaking nature of Pelosi's candidacy, the gender of representatives didn't have a statistically significant effect on their support, they concluded. Women were not more likely to support her over him by any significant measure.

But connections counted. Californians were inclined to vote for Pelosi, Marylanders for Hoyer, and the California delegation was much bigger. It had thirty-two Democratic members in the 107th Congress, elected in 2000; Maryland had four. Those who had served with Pelosi on the Intelligence Committee were more likely to support her. Ideology had an effect, too; the more conservative a representative was, the more likely he or she was to support Hoyer.

And money talked. Both Pelosi and Hoyer formed political action committees so they could raise money and dispense it to other members of Congress. Hoyer raised a healthy $1.5 million for Democratic candidates in 2000. Pelosi and the political action committee she created, PAC to the Future, raised double that amount and more, $3.9 million.

Of the eleven Democratic challengers who won election, Pelosi had given more money to nine; seven of those freshmen supported her, the study found. Hoyer had donated more money to two; they both supported him.

Some of the incoming members of Congress had no idea of the battle that was under way, or the depth of the rivalry. Steve Israel, a member of the Huntington Town Board on Long Island, was vying for a seat that had been held by a Republican. "I knew nothing about Steny Hoyer and Nancy Pelosi," he told me. "I just knew that I wanted to get elected." Gary Ackerman, a Democratic congressman from Queens, provided crucial help and advice. Hoyer came to his district to campaign with him, and Pelosi helped him raise money.

Once Israel won the election, he backed Hoyer for whip, in large part because Ackerman was supporting Hoyer. But when Israel arrived in Washington, Pelosi invited him to join some other freshmen members for a working dinner at her home in Georgetown, where they dissected what had happened in their elections. "The next day," he said, "I got a call from somebody saying, 'We thought you were with Steny.'"

A few months later, in May 2001, Bonior announced that he was leaving the House. Michigan had lost a congressional seat in the 2000 redistricting, and the Republican-controlled state legislature had redrawn his district. His home had landed in the new 12th Congressional District, already represented by a fellow Democrat and a friend, Sandy Levin. The redrawn 10th District had become more rural and more Republican. Bonior decided to leave Congress to run for governor instead.

Finally, there was an opening for the campaign that had begun more than three years earlier. The voting in the fall would be by secret ballot.

Many House Democrats declined to take a public position, but Pelosi and Hoyer each declared that they had the votes to win. Ninety members had signed a letter supporting Pelosi; 71 had signed a letter backing Hoyer—both shy of the 108 votes needed to prevail. The election was set for early September.

A reporter for the *Baltimore Sun* asked Hoyer what he would do if he lost. "I'll just take a deep breath and go on," he said. Asked the same question, Pelosi replied, "I have no intention of losing. I'm going to win. I'm very confident about that." She refused to even consider the possibility of defeat.

Then catastrophe delayed the vote, one last time.

---

## CHAPTER ELEVEN

# WAR

*September 11, 2001—Washington, D.C.*

Nancy Pelosi had gotten an early start on the morning that changed the world.

Both she and Steny Hoyer were assuring supporters that they had the votes to win the election scheduled a few days later for House Democratic whip. The contest for the No. 2 job on the minority party's leadership team wasn't always considered particularly newsworthy. Most Americans probably couldn't describe what the "whip" did, exactly, although in a way the title was descriptive. But this time, the battle was so heated, and Pelosi's election would be so groundbreaking, that National Public Radio made it the lead story on the *Morning Edition* broadcasts at 5:10 a.m. and 7:10 a.m., eastern time.

Steve Inskeep, then NPR's congressional correspondent, had recorded an interview with Pelosi the previous evening on Capitol Hill. The fact that she was a woman was "a giant plus," she told him. "Women across the country that campaign for other Democrats are very enthusiastic about finally breaking the barrier into the top leadership in the Congress, and why not?" she asked.

Then, at 8:46 a.m., American Airlines Flight 11 crashed into the

North Tower of the World Trade Center in New York City. Seventeen minutes later, United Airlines Flight 175 crashed into the South Tower.

By then, Pelosi was at a meeting of Democrats on the Appropriations Committee, convened in House Democratic leader Dick Gephardt's office. An aide came in and handed Gephardt a note: A plane had flown into the World Trade Center. "Of course, we all thought it was a terrible, terrible accident," she said. "We did what everybody else did in America. We turned on the TV, and we saw the second plane."

She called a longtime aide, Carolyn Bartholomew, who was on the fourth floor of the Capitol, in the quarters of the House Intelligence Committee. "Get out of the Capitol," Pelosi told her, her voice calm but firm. "The building you are in is not safe." Then she called Catherine Dodd, her district director in San Francisco, who was just pulling up to the federal building there; it wasn't yet 7 a.m. on the West Coast. "I want you to be out of that building within five minutes of the time you enter," Pelosi instructed her. The staff shouldn't come in until she had let them know there was no threat.

She had been trying to reach her daughter Alexandra, who lived in Manhattan, to make sure she was all right—akin to the frantic calls that millions of Americans were making to friends and family members in New York. "If she calls, please put her through," Pelosi told Dodd.

Nancy Pelosi was the senior Democrat on the House Intelligence Committee, but she was scrambling to get information, just like everybody else. She ended up working with dozens of other stranded members of Congress at Capitol Police headquarters, a solid stone and brick building midway between the Senate office buildings and Union Station. The Capitol had been evacuated for fear more attacks might be in the works. "It's terrifying," Pelosi told Marc Sandalow, the Washington correspondent for her hometown paper, the *San Francisco Chronicle*. The attacks had "all the earmarks and finger marks of Osama bin Laden," she said. "When we strike back, it will be fierce." Later, she would call it a "day from hell."

By now, her campaign for House whip was in its third year, extended again and again when Democrats kept failing to win back the House majority. If they did, it would have created an opening. Gephardt would become Speaker; whip David Bonior would move up to leader, and there would be space for a new whip. Now Bonior was leaving Congress to run for governor of Michigan. But the election to succeed him would be put off one more time, for just a bit longer.

The secret balloting was finally held a month later, on October 10. Nancy Pelosi won, making her the second-ranking Democrat in the House of Representatives and the highest-ranking woman in the history of Congress. "This is difficult turf to win on for anyone, but for a woman breaking ground here, it was a tough battle," she said afterward. How did she do it? She went back to basics: "Organization, organization, organization," she said. "Know your numbers. Identify your vote. Make sure it's there. Get it out."

She knew her numbers: She had predicted she would get 120 votes; she received 118. Steny Hoyer got 95. She won because she was relentless, meticulous, indefatigable. It was the most critical election she would have since the chaotic fourteen-candidate primary in the special election in San Francisco in 1987. Winning that congressional seat sent her to Washington. Fourteen years later, this victory put her on the path that led to the Speaker's chair.

Now she vowed to help Democrats retake control of the House.

But it wasn't partisan politics that shadowed and shaped Pelosi's early tenure in the leadership. It was terrorism and war, the September 11 attacks on New York and Washington and the long conflicts in Afghanistan and Iraq that would follow.

She was formally sworn in as Democratic whip a few months later, on February 6, 2002, when Bonior officially resigned. A week later, the House and Senate Intelligence committees announced a joint investigation into the terror attacks, an effort to find out what went wrong. As the ranking Democrat on the House side, Pelosi would play a key role in the inquiry. Each of the thirty-seven members of the joint committee made opening statements at their initial meeting, a session that was closed to the public and the press.

Later, Senate Intelligence chairman Bob Graham recalled Pelosi's comments as the most memorable of them all. She "eloquently reminded us that we were entrusted with a spiritual obligation to the families of the victims," Graham said, "and offered a moment of silent prayer for the dead."

———

Many members of Congress aren't eager to serve on the House Permanent Select Committee on Intelligence. It doesn't offer political plums to deliver back home, the way the Appropriations Committee could. It usually isn't a magnet for publicity, since the briefings and meetings are often held in secret. It involves a fair amount of work, reading classified documents in secure locations and digesting complicated issues that can be discussed with only a few others.

Pelosi asked to be assigned to the Intelligence Committee, though. She wanted to bolster her credentials on national security affairs, advice she would share with new female members of Congress who followed. Later, she would boast that she had logged the longest continuous service on the panel of any member in its history. At the beginning, terrorism wasn't among the committee's leading concerns. "When I first went on, in the early 1990s, it was obviously about force protection; it was about disarmament, and it was about how we balance security and privacy and civil liberties," she told me. "That was a big interest of mine."

Civil liberties in China had been a cause for Pelosi since the Tiananmen Square protests in 1989, soon after she was elected to Congress. She had pushed a proposal to waive visa requirements that required Chinese students in the United States to return home as soon as their studies were done, citing concerns about how they would be treated there. (The legislation passed Congress, but President George H. W. Bush vetoed it, and the Senate couldn't muster the two-thirds majority needed to override his veto. She would later force his hand to issue an executive order.) In 1991, she and two others in a congressional delegation visiting Beijing surreptitiously unfurled a banner in the square, reading in both Chinese and English, "To Those Who Died for Democracy in China." Chinese guards roughed up and briefly detained camera crews from three U.S. TV networks that had recorded the protest. It caused an international incident, as she knew it would.

Maintaining a balance between security and civil liberties was on her mind even on the morning after 9/11. She joined a somber news conference in the Capitol's Statuary Hall with Speaker Dennis Hastert, Democratic leader Dick Gephardt, and Intelligence Committee chairman Porter Goss. They expressed determination to find out who was behind the hijackings that had hit not only the World Trade Center but also the Pentagon; a fourth plane had crashed into a field near Shanksville, Pennsylvania. No one had any idea how high the casualty count was going to climb.

"We must insist that our civil liberties are not a casualty of the attack on our country yesterday," Pelosi said when it was her turn to speak, the last in line. She vowed that the United States would undertake "the appropriate retaliation—not vengeance, but justice, so that we can prevent this from ever, ever happening again."

Partisanship was put aside for a time as the nation reeled from the attacks themselves and the vulnerability they had exposed. "There is no space, air, or oxygen between Democrats and Republicans on the war on terrorism," Pelosi said. She defied the crowd at a memorial service in San Francisco when the Reverend Amos Brown, pastor of the Third Baptist Church and a former city supervisor, suggested U.S. foreign policy was somehow to blame. "America, is there anything you did to set up this climate?" Brown asked, citing grievances on racism, global warming, and military action in Central America. The audience at the Bill Graham Civic Auditorium cheered its approval; California governor Gray Davis and Senator Dianne Feinstein walked out as Brown was speaking.

Pelosi stood up and pushed back, breaking from her prepared remarks to deliver the only rebuttal to Brown spoken onstage that day. "With all due respect to some of the sentiments that were earlier expressed—some of which I agree with—make no mistake...the act of terrorism on September 11 put those people outside the order of civilized behavior," she said, "and we will not take responsibility for that."

A year later, President George W. Bush shifted his focus to Iraq. With that, Pelosi became the highest-ranking member of Congress to break with him.

She accepted the findings of U.S. intelligence agencies that Iraq had weapons of mass destruction—a conclusion that turned out to be infamously wrong—but she knew from her work on the Intelligence Committee that Baghdad would hardly be alone on that. Libya, Pakistan, and North Korea were all thought to have nuclear programs at one stage of development or another. What's more, there was no evidence that Iraq had the capability, the rockets, to deliver an attack on American soil. And while it was true that Iraq had ties to terrorists, fifteen of the nineteen hijackers on 9/11 were citizens of Saudi Arabia, a U.S. ally.

The president's warnings seemed to be based on "worst-case scenario upon worst-case scenario upon worst-case scenario," Pelosi protested.

She had been in the congressional leadership for only nine months. War fever was running high; Americans by more than three to one supported military action to depose Saddam Hussein. Even so, she issued a statement the next day that broke not only with Bush but also with Gephardt and Senate Democratic leader Tom Daschle. "I cannot support the administration's resolution regarding the use of force in Iraq," she declared, saying that diplomatic options hadn't been exhausted, that it would hurt the war on terrorism, that the White House hadn't shown Congress evidence that Iraq was an imminent threat.

She and Gephardt agreed they wouldn't "whip" the resolution—that is, they wouldn't lobby House Democrats to vote one way or the other as a matter of party loyalty. But they did try to make their case to their colleagues. It would be a test for both.

After all, Gephardt had backed the resolution. Both he and Vice

President Dick Cheney called Jack Murtha, the Marine veteran who had led Pelosi's whip campaign; he was an important voice on military matters, especially among Democrats. Murtha agreed to support the measure, a vote he came to regret. Pelosi was also talking to her colleagues. She never asked any of them to vote with her, she said. Instead, she would tell them, "This is why I'm voting against it. You have to make your own decision."

Some friends warned her that she was risking her political future. "People were saying to me, 'If you're not voting for this war, you'll never go any place in this party,'" Pelosi told me, contemptuous at the suggestion she might retreat as a result. "I'm like, 'Get out of here—I'm never voting for that war.'"

The conventional wisdom held that the safe political play was to back the president. Most of the Democrats who harbored presidential ambitions—Delaware senator Joe Biden, New York senator Hillary Clinton, Massachusetts senator John Kerry, North Carolina senator John Edwards, Connecticut senator Joe Lieberman among them—supported the resolution. (Notably, Senate Intelligence chairman Bob Graham joined Pelosi in opposing it, saying the administration hadn't made its case. His opinion was telling, she said. She may have been easily dismissed by some as a San Francisco liberal, she told me, but "Bob Graham of Florida—you know, he was not considered a progressive in the Congress of the United States; he had the same view of it.")

The Republican-controlled House passed the authorization, 296–133. Hours later, voting after 1 a.m., the Democratic-controlled Senate passed it as well, 77–23. Bush had prevailed, winning approval to use the armed forces "as he determines to be necessary and appropriate" to "defend the national security of the United States against the continuing threat posed by Iraq" and to "enforce all relevant Security Council resolutions regarding Iraq." It would be used to justify years of war.

But most House Democrats sided with Pelosi and voted against the resolution. Nearly two-thirds of the Democratic Caucus voted "no," 126–81. Her case had carried the day, at least among her own members, even against higher-ranking officials in their party.

In time, Pelosi's warnings against the invasion of Iraq would be seen as prescient; her opposition would become the dominant Democratic position. Her early opposition fortified her credibility on matters of war and peace and her standing among liberals. It helped propel her quick rise from whip to minority leader to Speaker.

It also demonstrated that she was willing to stand up to a president without flinching, something she had also done with a Democratic president, Bill Clinton, on the issue of China. It was a characteristic that would take on particular importance years later, when Donald Trump would win the White House.

————

Nancy Pelosi was at a dinner with other House Democrats when President Bush's national security adviser, Condoleezza Rice, called to inform her that the U.S. attack on Iraq was about to begin. It was March 19, 2003—"the Feast of Saint Joseph," Pelosi told me, a date of note in Italian American communities.

"Condoleezza Rice said, 'The president asked me to call you that we'll initiate hostilities in two hours or something into Iraq,'" Pelosi said, re-creating their exchange. "I said, 'You haven't exhausted the remedies. You haven't pursued all these other things. How could you be doing that?' She said, 'Well, we think if we do it tonight we can save lives. But that's what it's going to be.'"

Rice's language was guarded; the phone line wasn't secure. The next day, Pelosi learned why Bush had been so determined to move immediately. "They went in thinking they were going to, I think, decapitate Iraq that night"—that is, kill Saddam Hussein, she told me. "They had a human source that told them he was at this particular farm or something. The bunker busters went in. Boom! Nothing."

The "bunker busters," the bombs designed to penetrate hardened targets and underground bunkers, didn't kill Saddam Hussein that night. He wouldn't be captured for another nine months. Three years would pass before he was tried, convicted, and executed. By then, thousands of

U.S. and allied forces would be deployed in Iraq. Almost two decades later, American troops would still be deployed in Iraq despite the efforts of two subsequent presidents to withdraw them.

"They were wrong on every score, whether describing the threat of weapons of mass destruction, the reception our troops would receive, or who would pay for the war," Pelosi said later. All that would be ahead, however. The future was anything but clear on the night the U.S.-led invasion of Iraq began. The next morning, at a strategy session in the Capitol, she told her leadership team that she had felt "devastated" and unsettled by Condoleezza Rice's call. "The reality that it was happening just took the wind out of my sails."

She wondered if Democrats could have done more, and earlier, to prevent the invasion. Could the long and costly war have been averted? She called it her greatest disappointment. "It's the main issue," she said five years later. "Everything else is eclipsed by the war. All of our accomplishments are eclipsed by the war, because we didn't end the war."

By then, Gephardt had stepped down as Democratic leader as he prepared to run for president; Pelosi was elected to succeed him, swamping a challenge from Representative Harold Ford Jr. of Tennessee, 177–29. Now it was her job to hold together a divided Democratic Caucus on the war and other issues.

During her first months on the job, even a pro forma resolution to support the troops proved problematic. The Senate passed it unanimously. But she found herself shuttling between House Republicans who drafted it and Democratic liberals who objected to language that praised Bush as commander in chief and linked the invasion of Iraq to the war on terrorism. They protested that voting to support the resolution could be seen, unfairly, as indicating support for the war. She didn't disagree with them, but she was concerned that voting against the resolution could be seen, unfairly, as indicating a lack of support for the troops.

"I disagree with the policy that took us to this war," Pelosi said on the floor of the House when the resolution finally came up for a vote, no consensus reached. "I dispute some of the arguments used in favor of this resolution. But even those objections cannot overcome the pride and appreciation that I have in our troops and the message that I want them to hear tonight."

She voted "yes." Most House Democrats, 167 of them, voted with her. Eleven House Democrats voted "no." Another 21 voted "present."

––––––––

Later, Pelosi became enmeshed in a controversy involving the administration's use of "enhanced interrogation techniques"—in other words, waterboarding and other forms of torture. When a furor over the harsh measures erupted in 2009, Pelosi denied having known that they were being used. At a CIA briefing in September 2002, she had been told that the Department of Justice had concluded the use of the techniques was legal, she said, but "we were not—I repeat, were not—told that water-boarding or any of these other enhanced interrogation methods were used."

That prompted former CIA director Porter Goss to accuse Pelosi and other Democrats of "a disturbing episode of amnesia." Goss had been at the same 2002 briefing; at the time, he was the House Intelligence chair and Pelosi was the committee's ranking Democrat. "We understood what the CIA was doing," he said. In 2012, Jose Rodriguez Jr., a former CIA counterterrorism chief who was among those conducting the briefing, wrote in his memoir that he had told her that accused terrorist Abu Zubaydah had been waterboarded. "We held back nothing," he said.

––––––––

During the first months of the war, Pelosi generally tempered her public remarks. She didn't join the antiwar marches in San Francisco and elsewhere, although she spoke out in defense of the protestors. In private, she was urging Bush to change course. On May 1, 2003, Bush had landed on the deck of an aircraft carrier, the USS *Abraham Lincoln*, that was festooned with a banner that declared "Mission Accomplished." At a White House breakfast a few days later with congressional leaders, she saw an opening she advised him to take, repeating the argument that she had made when she had opposed the authorization to start the war.

"Now that we have shown our country's strength, I think it would be important to show its greatness," she told him—to "be magnanimous," to reach out to the Islamic world. Pelosi said he impatiently dismissed the idea.

Down the road, Pelosi would compare Bush favorably, even fondly, to his Republican successor, Donald Trump. But while Bush was in the White House, she was a vigorous and vocal opponent, questioning the president's judgment and even his mental health. After Bush delivered a vigorous defense of the war in his State of the Union address in 2004, she blasted his "go-it-alone foreign policy" and said he had "embraced a radical doctrine of preemptive war unprecedented in our history." In a speech to newspaper editors that spring, speaking a few hours before he would address the group, she questioned his competence. "The president's resolve may be firm, but his judgment is not sound," she told them. "It is ironic that a nation obsessed with reality television, we have a president who is increasingly divorced from reality."

Then, in May, she leveled a broadside so blistering that it brought demands from outraged Republicans for an apology. She called Bush responsible for the unnecessary deaths of American soldiers.

"The only way to improve the situation in Iraq is to elect a new president of the United States," she said in an interview with the *San Francisco Chronicle*. "He has on his shoulders the deaths of many more troops because he would not heed the advice of his own State Department."

Even her communications director, Brendan Daly, who was sitting in on the interview, was taken aback by the ferocity of her words. "She just ripped him," he told me. After the reporter had left, "I looked at her and said, 'Thanks for the heads-up you were going to do that.' And she replied, 'Well, if I told you about it in advance, you would've tried to talk me out of it.'"

At the White House, Bush himself was left "more frustrated than hostile" by her opposition, Chief of Staff Andy Card told me. The president and the House Democratic leader were increasingly estranged over the war.

Pelosi was unapologetic. If anything, at a news conference the next day, her tone was even harsher. "The emperor has no clothes," she told reporters at the Capitol. "I believe that the president's leadership in the actions taken in Iraq demonstrate an incompetence in terms of knowledge, judgment, and experience in making the decisions that would have been necessary to truly accomplish the mission without the deaths to our troops and the cost to our taxpayers."

Then she made a prediction that turned out to be quite mistaken. In the 2004 election, just six months away, she said Bush would lose. She told aides she was sure of it. "He's gone," she said. "He's so gone."

# CHAPTER TWELVE

---

# LEADER

*November 2, 2004—Washington, D.C.*

Nancy Pelosi was wrong.

President Bush won a second term in 2004, and more decisively than in his battle for a first term. Then, he lost the popular vote and carried the Electoral College only after the Supreme Court weighed in with a five-to-four decision that gave him the decisive electoral votes from Florida. This time, he carried both the Electoral College and the popular vote, and Republicans widened their majority in the House of Representatives. After a decade in the minority, House Democrats faced at least two more years of GOP dominance.

That was Pelosi's problem now. The day after the 2002 midterms, Dick Gephardt had called his second in command to say that he was stepping down as House leader. The election returns had been disappointing—Democrats lost five seats in the first election after the 9/11 attacks—and in any case he was planning to seek the party's presidential nomination in 2004. "I had to make an instant decision to run for the top spot," Pelosi said. By the end of the day, she had released a statement praising Gephardt and announcing her candidacy to succeed him.

She was ready. It was reminiscent of her protestations during high school about not being prepared for class. The yearbook at the Institute of Notre Dame had mocked her unconvincing demurrals: "I haven't opened a book yet." Now, as then, she was always looking ahead and around corners. She immediately began calling House Democrats, reaching more than 150 of them over the next twenty-four hours, asking for their support. She started with those who lived in the eastern time zone and swept west with the sun.

By the next day, when Texas congressman Martin Frost announced his candidacy for Democratic leader, Pelosi had enough commitments in her pocket to claim it. Even then, she didn't stop working to win over his natural supporters. Ben Barnes, who had served as lieutenant governor and speaker of the Texas House, was working in his Austin office one Saturday morning when Governor Ann Richards called.

"I'm going to bring someone to see you," she told Barnes, who by then was a major Democratic fund-raiser. "You're going to be for her for leader of the House." He said he'd be happy to meet Nancy Pelosi, "but, you know I'm for Martin Frost. He's from Texas. And he's a congressman. Why am I going to be with Nancy Pelosi?" After the two women had met with Barnes for an hour, Richards declared they weren't going to leave until he had switched his allegiance to Pelosi—and demanded that he call Frost to tell him.

Barnes finally agreed. He told me that Pelosi "has an ability to find out what's on a person's mind and to empathize with what they're thinking and feeling as well as any political leader I've ever seen."

After waging what may have been the longest leadership campaign ever to be elected whip, over more than three years, Pelosi had a notably short campaign to move up. A few weeks later, Frost, a realist, dropped out. Tennessee representative Harold Ford Jr. jumped in, though he had a better chance of getting media attention than winning members' support. He ended up receiving 29 votes in the secret balloting. Pelosi got 177.

Pelosi had said at the start that she decided to run for the leadership because she was tired of losing. After just two years in the minority, she declared the situation "intolerable." Now they had been out of power for a decade. Before she spoke at the 2004 Democratic National Convention in Boston, her allies distributed posters of Pelosi in the iconic Rosie the Riveter pose, sleeves rolled up and a red bandana holding back her hair, declaring, "We Can Do It!" The poster listed a website with a URL that at that point was still aspirational: speakerpelosi.com.

That November, Democrats didn't deliver a majority and make her Speaker, though. Now they needed to flip even more seats, fifteen in all, to regain control. Political prognosticators were giving them low odds of doing that in 2006. In July, the nonpartisan *Cook Political Report* rated just fourteen Republican seats as highly vulnerable. The conventional wisdom held that a good effort by Democrats might make a down payment, so the job could be finished in 2008.

Pelosi began by enlisting an unexpected lieutenant.

Rahm Emanuel had been a junior staffer at the Democratic Congressional Campaign Committee, the campaign arm for House Democrats, when Pelosi made her first bid for Congress in a special election in 1987. He gained a certain fame as a brash White House aide to President Clinton. (In the NBC series *The West Wing*, actor Bradley Whitford's character, Deputy Chief of Staff Josh Lyman, was based on him.) Then he won a congressional seat himself in 2002, representing the North Side of Chicago.

He succeeded Rod Blagojevich, a Democrat who was elected governor and would become notorious—impeached and removed from office, convicted on federal corruption charges for trying to sell Barack Obama's Senate seat, then had his sentence commuted by President Donald Trump. Emanuel eventually would leave Congress to serve as White House chief of staff for President Barack Obama, then win two terms as mayor of Chicago.

In December 2004, he was a junior member of the House, forty-five years old and just elected to his second term. In some ways, he and Pelosi were a study in contrasts. On policy, Emanuel was a more centrist Democrat than the liberal Pelosi, on issues including trade policy and the Iraq War. In personality, she was precise and polite; he was restless and often rude. She was rarely heard uttering a word of profanity; sometimes it seemed rare for him to be able to finish a sentence without dropping the f-bomb.

But the qualities about Emanuel that others often found offputting—his intensity, obstinacy, arrogance—were ones Pelosi found appealing, at least for the task at hand. He would be as obsessed with winning as she was, and she had never had any problem dealing with pugnacious men. After all, she had grown up in a boisterous household with five older brothers. "I love people who are operational," Pelosi said of Emanuel. "They're there to get the job done." "Operational" was high praise in Pelosi's vocabulary; it was the word Sala Burton had used when she was persuading her skeptical brother-in-law, John Burton, to support Pelosi for Congress.

Both Pelosi and Emanuel could be ruthless about making hard calls, and neither anguished over creating enemies if that was necessary to get them where they wanted to go. She would tell associates that they needed to be "two-ventricled." The anatomical reference was a bit obscure—it referred to the fact that the ventricle in a reptile's heart is at least partially partitioned into two chambers—but the political meaning was clear. They had to be cold-blooded.

A month after the 2004 midterms, Pelosi asked Emanuel to chair the Democratic Congressional Campaign Committee.

For the next two years, Pelosi and Rahm would be a relentless team, usually in concert and occasionally in conflict. He sometimes complained that she was too slow to make decisions, Naftali Bendavid reported in *The Thumpin'*, an account of Emanuel and the 2006 midterms; she sometimes complained that he was too quick to claim credit that she deserved to share. They would call each other several times a day, conducting rapid-fire conversations in political shorthand. They calculated which Republican-held districts to target. He used persuasion and pressure to recruit Democratic challengers, including a fair number of political neophytes; she would often call to seal the deal. She raised an astonishing amount of money for candidates, more than $50 million.

She also made sure that Republican incumbents, especially those in swing districts, weren't able to burnish their bipartisan credentials by cosponsoring legislation with Democrats. She would call House Democrats and forbid them from doing that, even with a Republican partner they had worked with in the past on an issue. That was a sign of her political acumen, perhaps, but it also reinforced the hyperpartisanship that was already making it hard to do almost anything across party lines.

Pelosi once again enlisted Pennsylvania representative John Murtha, the Marine veteran from coal country who had led her campaign for the leadership. He had voted to give Bush the authority to go invade Iraq in 2002, but three years later he had decided it was time to bring the troops home. His opposition could provide political cover to other House Democrats who had fewer military credentials. Murtha was no San Francisco dove; he was a decorated Vietnam veteran and a leading voice on defense policy. He called the war "a flawed policy wrapped in illusion."

His comments were a sign of how much unease in Congress was growing. Deaths in the Iraq War were rising, while the justification the president had given for the U.S.-led invasion—the assertion that Saddam Hussein had weapons of mass destruction—was proven false. Republicans were having other problems as well. The Bush administration botched the response to Hurricane Katrina, one of the deadliest hurricanes ever to hit the United States. The House GOP had to deal with a late-breaking scandal involving Florida congressman Mark Foley, who resigned amid disclosures that he had sent sexually explicit messages to teenage boys who had been congressional pages.

All that helped boost Democratic candidates in the 2006 midterm elections. When the votes were counted, they didn't just pick up the fifteen seats they needed to take control. They gained thirty-one.

It was a victory of historic dimensions, and a political turning point. The Democratic sweep, gaining control of both houses of Congress, helped set the stage for the groundbreaking campaign two years later that would put Barack Obama in the White House.

After a dozen years in the minority, House Democrats were back in control, and Nancy Pelosi was poised to become the Speaker of the House. She would be the first woman, the first Italian American, the first Californian ever to hold the job. She had been the irresistible force—targeting districts, recruiting challengers, raising money, blasting Republicans, and shaping the Democrats' message.

She would stand at center stage.

At the Democratic victory party that night at the Hyatt Regency hotel, a few blocks from the Capitol, Emanuel spoke first as Pelosi waited in the wings. He called her "a tireless campaigner, a heroic fundraiser." The crowd in the ballroom chanted, "Nancy! Nancy!" When she walked on, they switched to "Speaker! Speaker!"

Even at that celebratory moment, the topic she talked about most was the war. "We cannot continue down this catastrophic path," she declared. "So we say to the president, 'Mr. President, we need a new direction in Iraq.'"

Two days later, President Bush invited Pelosi to lunch in a private dining room off the Oval Office. Steny Hoyer, who was about to rise from House whip to majority leader, was there. So was a stone-faced Vice President Dick Cheney. "It's the George and Nancy Show. Episode One: Grin and Bear It," a flip New York *Daily News* headline read. The story described Bush as "humbled" and Pelosi's smile as "icy."

Bush was gracious. Cheney was not. "Obviously, they had suffered a bad defeat, and Cheney was just so grumpy and miserable and didn't say anything," not even feigning politeness, Pelosi aide Brendan Daly told me. "And Bush was telling stories and being charming. I remember coming home to my wife and saying, 'I hate to say it, but I like George Bush.'"

In San Francisco that day, Art Agnos and Leo McCarthy were reveling in the moment as they watched coverage on cable TV; they could see Pelosi as she emerged from the West Wing to the White House driveway. McCarthy had been Pelosi's mentor from her early days in San Francisco. Now he was in the hospital, dying.

"The phone rings in the hospital room," Agnos told me, "and it's Nancy saying, 'Leo, I just had my first meeting with the president of the United States as the Speaker of the United States House of Representatives, and you are the one who helped me make it possible.'"

––––––––

Presidents and House Speakers can be ideological comrades-in-arms, like the legendary Sam Rayburn with fellow Democrats John Kennedy and Lyndon Johnson. They can be respectful rivals, negotiating across party lines, like Tip O'Neill and Ronald Reagan. They can become partners of necessity, like Newt Gingrich and Bill Clinton after Republicans won control of Congress and the Democratic president adjusted his strategy to get things done.

Or they can be unyielding adversaries, as Nancy Pelosi and George W. Bush proved to be—at least until the final months of his second term, when they joined forces to contain a financial catastrophe. During most of the time he was leading the executive branch and she was leading the House, they were at war over the war in Iraq. "Speaker Pelosi has no relationship with the president of the United States," said Rich Bond, a former Republican national chairman with ties to the Bush family. He blamed Pelosi's attitude for that, though partisans on her side would blame Bush's policies. "It's toxic and that really doesn't serve either side."

Bush and Pelosi were from opposition parties, of course, but it seemed possible that they would have a friendly working relationship despite conflicts over policy—something like the cordiality Reagan and O'Neill took pains to project. Both had grown up in big political families, the children of successful officeholders. Pelosi admired the elder George H. W. Bush and especially liked Barbara Bush; she appreciated the older woman's blunt and down-to-earth humor. Pelosi's daughter Alexandra had made her first documentary after covering the younger

Bush's 2000 campaign for NBC, a well-received film called *Journeys with George.*

Some significant bipartisan legislation would be passed on their watch: An energy bill that included the first increase in vehicle fuel standards in more than three decades. A rise in the minimum wage for the first time in a decade. Increases in aid for college tuition and for veterans.

But the Iraq War would define and haunt their relationship, over-shadowing everything else.

They spent the 2006 midterm campaign targeting each other. At Republican fund-raisers, Bush would quote Pelosi as saying, "We love tax cuts," then use various punch lines after that setup. "Given her record, she must be a secret admirer," he told donors in Macon, Georgia, to laughter. At a Chicago fund-raiser a few days later, he joked, "If this is the Democrats' idea of love, I don't want to see what hate looks like." In GOP ads, Pelosi was demonized as a loony liberal—pro-abortion, anti-gun, soft on national security.

Her rhetoric toward him was harsher. Pelosi described Bush as an incompetent president who had mortgaged the future of America's children and offered only hot air to address climate change. She accused him of misleading the nation into a costly war, one she had opposed from the start, and one that had been based on a lie.

Opposition to the war was rising, including among Democrats who had been war hawks. The invasion had not been followed by the easy victory that Vice President Cheney and Defense Secretary Donald Rumsfeld had predicted at the start, and the justification the administration had used to command support in the United Nations and among the American public had fallen apart when no weapons of mass destruction had been found.

The day after the 2006 election, Bush acknowledged that voters had sent a message about the Iraq War; he called the results "a thumpin'." He announced the departure of Rumsfeld, a lightning rod who had taken a lead in shaping war policy.

That day, Pelosi expressed hope that the election returns might persuade Bush to change course. "We must not continue on this catastrophic path, and so hopefully we can work with the president for a new direction, one that solves the problem in Iraq," she said.

In January, at the State of the Union address, there was a moment of comity between them, though it would be short-lived. President Bush acknowledged the history of the moment with the first woman sitting in the Speaker's chair behind him, the first Madam Speaker. He mentioned her father, a former congressman who in his time had sat in the chamber for State of the Union addresses. Bush was now facing a new Congress, one that was controlled by opposition Democrats. His gracious tone was deliberate, adviser Andrew Card told me, and one that carried some cost for him among angry, battered Republicans.

"He was not afraid to say, 'This was the result of the election; I respect the results of the election and I'm going to work to make sure that this works,'" Card, who had been White House chief of staff for Bush until mid-2006, said. "So I thought he was reaching his hand out. I'm not sure that I ever felt that she reciprocated by reaching her hand out."

She called ending the war "my highest priority as Speaker," and she believed that the president would now have little choice but to agree. "This war needs to come to an end," she said on her second day as Speaker. "The president is going to have to step back."

But Bush didn't step back. Instead, a few days later, he announced the deployment of more than twenty thousand additional troops, a surge that would double down on winning the war, not withdrawing from it.

Pelosi was outraged. She called the president's war strategy "a desperate cause" and "a failure." White House spokeswoman Dana Perino responded by labeling those comments "poisonous."

At a White House meeting, reported by Bob Woodward in *The War Within: A Secret White House History*, she again urged Bush to change course. He had ordered at least four troop increases in the previous three years, she noted, mostly for additional security during Iraqi elections.

None of them had worked in bringing about any sort of long-term solution. "Mr. President, we've had surges," she told him. "What makes you think this one is going to work?"

Bush replied, "Because I told them it had to."

"Well, why didn't you tell them before?" she pressed.

Afterward, she told top aides, "I'm very, very worried about the state of mind of a person who has decided to stay in a war without the public support."

She tried every legislative maneuver she could think of to oppose the war. Nothing they did dissuaded the president. He ignored a nonbinding resolution, then vetoed a measure passed in March 2007 that would have required all U.S. combat forces to leave Iraq by September 2008.

On the day of the Senate vote on that bill, Pelosi and Bush held a private meeting in Pelosi's office. They were waiting to speak at a ceremony under the Capitol Rotunda to honor the Tuskegee Airmen of World War II. "Mr. President, we owe it to the public to try to reach some consensus," she told him. She offered to support legislation that simply set a troop drawdown as a goal, not a mandate. Bush rejected the idea: "My views are well known," he said. "I've made myself clear."

"My views are well known, too," Pelosi replied. "But that's not the point. The point is we owe it to the public to try to find some common ground."

Bush later told Woodward he didn't remember the exchange but said that Pelosi's idea of compromise would have been unacceptable once he had decided to order the surge in forces.

They would not find common ground on the war—not then, not ever.

Pelosi thought Bush was in a state of denial, refusing to recognize how poorly the war was going and how much opposition was building among Americans. In the four years since the Iraq War was launched, he had enjoyed a compliant Congress, controlled by Republicans. Now Democrats controlled Congress. They opposed the war. But they were unwilling to take the most drastic step—cutting off funds for the troops—and were unable to convince the commander in chief to bring them home.

"The president has a tin ear to the voice of the American people," Pelosi complained, returning to the harsher rhetoric of the campaign. "They spoke. He didn't care. He has a blind eye to what's happening on the ground in Iraq. He's got his head in the sand."

Again and again, the House passed bills setting a timetable for troop withdrawals, only to see them fail in the Senate. Democratic senators and their two independent allies had a narrow majority there, 51–49, but not a margin wide enough to muster the sixty votes needed to overcome a filibuster.

At the end of her first year as Speaker, there were more troops in Iraq than there had been at the beginning. The House's final vote on legislation in 2007 gave Bush another $70 billion for the wars in Iraq and Afghanistan with no deadlines set for a troop withdrawal. "The war in Iraq is the biggest disappointment for us—I mean, the inability to stop the war in Iraq," Pelosi told a year-end roundtable with congressional reporters. The headline on the Associated Press analysis: "Pelosi's First Year Full of Frustration."

A decade later, in an interview in the Speaker's office, Pelosi told me that the consequences of the war had been catastrophic, just as she had feared from the first. The setting was pensive—out the window, a late afternoon sun could be seen striking the Washington Monument—but her tone was as fierce as ever.

"It's one of the biggest mistakes in American history, the Iraq War," she said. The war had been based on a lie, an exploitation of the tragedy of 9/11. "That was a terrible thing, and that war caused so many problems. The biggest mistake, I think, our country has ever made. Ever made."

---

Despite her heated criticism of President Bush on Iraq, Pelosi rebuffed calls by some Democrats to impeach him for misleading the American people into a long and costly war.

"Democrats are not about getting even," she said the day after the 2006 midterms returned Democrats to power. "Democrats are about helping the American people get ahead, and that's what our agenda is about. So while some people are excited about prospects that they have in terms of their priorities, they are not our priorities. I have said, and I say again, that impeachment is off the table."

For a time, her stance against impeachment made her the unlikely target of antiwar liberals who had for so long seen her as a champion. The group Code Pink propped up a giant papier-mâché statue of Mahatma Gandhi outside her home in the tony Pacific Heights section of San Francisco. (The Pelosi family had moved there from the Presidio during the 1987 campaign to be inside the boundaries of the Fifth Congressional District.) Activist Cindy Sheehan, who had been maintaining a vigil outside Bush's ranch in Crawford, Texas, filed a third-party challenge to Pelosi's reelection in San Francisco. Pelosi sailed to another term with 72 percent of the vote; Sheehan finished second in a seven-candidate field, with 16 percent.

"I believe that Nancy Pelosi committed treason when she took impeachment off the table," said Sheehan, whose son Casey had been killed in Iraq. She accused congressional Democrats of "caving in" to the president by supporting continued funding for the war.

A decade later, Pelosi would hold back Democratic demands to impeach another president, Donald Trump, though her views on that would change over time. Then, she described the parallels with her decision to block calls to impeach President Bush.

"When I was Speaker the first time, thousands of people said, 'Impeach George Bush for the war in Iraq,'" she told me. "What could be worse than the war in Iraq? Probably the biggest mistake that has ever been made in our country's history." But she worried about the consequences of impeaching a president, whether it was Bush or Trump. The House had impeached President Bill Clinton. "Now we impeach Bush, we impeach the next. That's just not, it's not unifying. If there's one part of the oath of office to protect and defend the Constitution that I honor, it's the spirit that our Founders gave us, their guidance: *e pluribus unum*, 'from many, one.' They couldn't possibly imagine how many we would be or how different we would be from each other, but they knew we had to be one, and that oneness is a responsibility."

One reality-TV star endorsed the idea of impeaching Bush, a position that would later take on a certain irony.

"I think she's a very impressive person. I like her a lot," Donald Trump, then a real estate mogul and host of NBC's *The Apprentice*, said of Pelosi in an interview with CNN's Wolf Blitzer in October 2008. "But I was surprised that she didn't do more in terms of Bush and going after Bush. It was almost—it just seemed like she was going to really look to impeach Bush and get him out of office, which personally I think would've been a wonderful thing."

"Impeaching him?" Blitzer asked.

"Absolutely," Trump responded. "For the war. For the war."

By then, though, Pelosi was suddenly immersed in frantic efforts to rescue the nation's economy, and with it the final months of Bush's presidency.

# CHAPTER THIRTEEN

---

# MELTDOWN

*September 18, 2008—Speaker's conference room, the U.S. Capitol*

It was late afternoon when Nancy Pelosi called Henry Paulson Jr. She asked the treasury secretary to come to her office the next morning to brief the House leadership about what was going on in the troubled markets.

"Madam Speaker, tomorrow morning will be too late," he told her.

*What?* "If things are this bad, why aren't you calling me?" she demanded.

At that moment, Paulson was on his way to the White House for yet another emergency meeting. He and Federal Reserve chairman Ben Bernanke and others who gathered in the Roosevelt Room advised President George W. Bush that a massive intervention in the American financial system was imperative. Bush agreed. "Go tell Congress we're fixing to have a meltdown," he told Paulson.

Pelosi suspected that the administration had been deliberately keeping Capitol Hill in the dark about the depth of the nation's financial crisis as officials scrambled to avert a debacle. Paulson disputed that to me, saying he had kept congressional leaders informed. In any case, now he was ready to fill in Pelosi on their dire conclusions. "You're the Speaker of the House; I'm the secretary of the treasury," he told her. "You're asking me, so I'm telling you what's needed." Pelosi remembered a slightly different version of this quote. "You're asking me, so I'm telling you what's *happening*."

What was happening was the worst economic crisis since the Great Depression. Following that phone conversation were sixteen days of frantic maneuvering to pass unprecedented legislation to prevent the American financial system, and the global one, from falling off a cliff. Pelosi would be at the center of it, in the end the key player who pushed through a bailout nobody liked but almost everyone argued was critical to avoid a cataclysm.

It would be a case study in her strengths and her weaknesses. It spotlighted her ability to negotiate the details of complex policy, to win over and hold wary Democrats, to persist in the face of setback. But it also underscored her failure to forge friendly and functional relationships with Republicans. President Bush and House Republican Leader John Boehner complained to others that they had been more willing than she was to moderate partisan rhetoric, to try to reach out across the aisle, however tentatively.

But the childhood lessons in politics she had learned didn't have much to do with reaching across party lines. Baltimore was dominated by Democrats; the bigger political imperative was to hold together the party's disparate and often warring factions. In San Francisco, too, Democrats ruled, while Republicans risked being politically irrelevant. Until she came to Washington, she had little need to build relationships with the GOP.

Even in Washington, a relentless partisanship had been hardening since well before she was elected to lead House Democrats. The increasing polarization of Congress and American politics was hardly Pelosi's fault. But during her tenure, almost every battle had sharpened those divisions.

That partisan landscape would make it harder for political leaders to respond to a crisis that demanded action, and quickly.

Pelosi and Bush hadn't spoken for months. Given their fraught relationship, strained by differences over the Iraq War, Bush had told advisers that his personal involvement now would probably just make things more difficult. But Paulson developed a working partnership with her. She would be one of the central figures responsible for rescuing the nation's economy, and with it the remaining days of Bush's presidency.

The nation's economic news was spiraling downward. With Election Day approaching, members of Congress were hearing from panicked constituents facing foreclosure. They saw their homes and their savings and their futures slipping away.

Problems with subprime mortgages had started to ricochet through the financial system more than a year earlier, stoking anxiety and uncertainty about the economy. In January, Congress had passed a bipartisan stimulus package that was backed by the Bush administration. In July, Pelosi had pushed through the administration's plan to rescue mortgage giants Fannie Mae and Freddie Mac over the opposition of some congressional Republicans. Now the housing meltdown was spreading to the banking system and beyond.

In recent days, some of the most prominent financial brands in the country had encountered calamity. Investment bank Lehman Brothers had filed for bankruptcy, the biggest in U.S. history. Brokerage firm Merrill Lynch had been rescued from collapse by being sold to Bank of America. Insurance giant AIG survived only after getting a bailout from the Federal Reserve.

As Speaker, Pelosi regularly received briefings from the treasury secretary on the state of the markets and the financial system. For the past two years, those had been handled by Paulson. The respected and well-liked former Goldman Sachs CEO had been appointed to the Treasury post during sunnier times. As clouds gathered over sixteen crucial days, their consultations would become more frequent, almost around the clock, and increasingly urgent.

*Thursday, September 18*

Paulson sounded frantic on the phone.

"Nothing we say will calm the situation until we come up with a policy that is overwhelming force!" he told Pelosi. When they hung up, she called Bernanke; his message was just as dire. That afternoon, the Fed had released the routine accounting of its balance sheet, statistics that rarely warranted much attention. This time, it sparked headlines: Lending to securities brokers had reached a record $60 billion, up from zero the previous week. There was no time to wait. Pelosi agreed to convene a meeting that evening with Paulson and Bernanke and congressional leaders from both parties, and from both the House and the Senate.

No one was sure what was going to happen next, but everyone understood that the deliberations would be historic. Pelosi's chief of staff, John Lawrence, kept contemporaneous notes on legal pads, now archived at the Library of Congress, which he used a decade later to write an account in the *Atlantic*. Paulson and Bernanke and other key participants would write memoirs portraying events from their perspectives.

Before he left the Treasury Department for the meeting, Paulson strategized with his chief of staff, James Wilkinson, who had started his career working on Capitol Hill for Texas representative Dick Armey. Wilkinson told me he sent Paulson off with a warning. "This is only going to work if you scare the shit out of them," he advised.

Paulson had no problem delivering that message. Unnerved by the meltdown in markets, the venue in which he had made his name and fortune, he believed it was true.

Bernanke noticed that the sun was setting when they arrived at the small conference room adjacent to Pelosi's office. The west-facing windows offered a spectacular view of the National Mall at the end of a summer day—not that anyone was in a state of mind to enjoy it. He and Paulson and Christopher Cox, chair of the Securities and Exchange

Commission, sat on one side of the long table, across from Pelosi and Senate majority leader Harry Reid. Around the table were a dozen congressional leaders, among them Senate Republican leader Mitch McConnell and John Boehner as well as the leaders of key committees. Bernanke, a professorial sort not given to hyperbole, stunned the room when he warned that a global financial disaster was looming. "If we do not act immediately," he said, "we will not have an economy by Monday."

The Federal Reserve already had done everything it could do to maintain stability, Bernanke told them. The only remedy left was for Congress to authorize the Treasury to make massive purchases of the toxic assets that were dragging down the financial institutions. (The legislation would be dubbed TARP, for Troubled Asset Relief Program.) They were facing a crisis unlike any of them had ever seen, Paulson said, "once in 100 years." Without it, Bernanke warned, the country was poised to plunge into a long, deep recession. He had the credentials to know: He had spent his academic career studying the Great Depression.

Boehner noticed something that alarmed him more than the words he was hearing. "We're all listening to Paulson, but I glanced over at Bernanke and I saw his lips quivering," he told me. "That's when I knew we were in big trouble."

Everyone was "flabbergasted," Pelosi would recall.

Paulson "then put forth his break-the-glass solution which they said they were saving for the next President," she said in her account of the meeting. That would surely have been an unwelcome surprise for Democrat Barack Obama, who would defeat Republican John McCain for the White House seven weeks later. (Paulson's account of this differed from Pelosi's. He told me that the administration wasn't "saving it" for the next president but rather had calculated that Congress wouldn't act until a crisis loomed. He also said that wasn't the question Pelosi raised in the meeting. "How do we make this look like a stimulus?" she asked—that is, help for voters, not for bankers.)

Reid asked how much buying the toxic assets would cost. A hundred billion dollars? No. Two hundred billion? No. Four hundred billion? Paulson told the senator that he was getting warmer.

Paulson already had a number in mind—five hundred billion dollars—but he wasn't ready to tell them, not yet, and just a day later even half a trillion dollars would be too small an amount to manage the crisis at hand. One of his senior aides, Michele Davis, had cautioned him beforehand not to give Congress a number at the first meeting because its size would "spook them before they got started."

Pelosi's frustration was clear. She blamed the Bush administration for pursuing regulatory and other policies that contributed to the crisis. What's more, congressional Republicans had resisted a more robust response. Senior Democrats saw GOP representatives as recalcitrant and administration officials, however brilliant they may have been in business or academics, as politically naïve. They didn't seem to have a clue about how difficult it would be to get Congress to act, especially on such a tight timeline.

Regardless of how the nation had gotten to this crossroads of catastrophe, though, Democrats now controlled Congress. The two parties would have to work together to take the unpalatable steps ahead. It was one of those times—like raising the debt ceiling or approving a congressional pay raise—when few wanted to be recorded voting for a difficult measure but just about everybody wanted it to pass. In cases like that, congressional leaders often would agree to share the pain. Each side would provide support from half of its members to reach the minimum needed for passage. This time, that meant 118 House Democrats and 100 House Republicans.

The package would have to include provisions to bail out regular folks as well as Wall Street, Pelosi said—for instance, to create jobs and extend unemployment insurance. Representative Barney Frank, the blunt-spoken Massachusetts liberal who chaired the House Financial Services Committee, said that executive pay would have to be restricted to win Democratic votes.

Congressional Republicans objected to all those ideas. They went back and forth for nearly two hours. It was dark outside when the meeting finally ended. "I can't tell you the bill will pass" unless the incentives that Democrats demanded were included, Frank cautioned. Reid called that "political reality."

After a moment, Paulson glumly responded, "Then God help us."

Reporters had been staking out the hallway outside the Speaker's suite, waiting for the meeting to break up. The officials all went to the cameras together—Pelosi, Reid, Boehner, and McConnell, plus Paulson and Bernanke—presenting a rare unified front. Congress had to act, they said. But the details hadn't been negotiated yet. The deal wasn't done, and it wouldn't be easy.

"History was sort of hanging over it, like this was a moment," New York senator Chuck Schumer said the next morning. He called it "a brave new world," and a perilous one. Without quick action to open credit lines, "the economy will just head south at a rapid rate," he warned. He made the gesture of a bird plummeting from the sky. "You know, we'd be lucky…" His voice trailed off. "Well, I'll leave it at that."

*Friday, September 19*

The day after that first meeting, Nancy Pelosi called President Bush to discuss what she would need in the bailout to convince congressional Democrats, not to mention the American people, to support it.

She was unsparing. The crisis was a consequence of his lack of leadership—of the "cowboy capitalism" in the financial industry and the "anything goes" style of regulation in his administration, she told him. The country was in this fix "because no one has been watching the store." The signs of trouble had been there. Mortgage-related fraud had exploded during his tenure, and he had failed to rein in the abuses that had now undermined the nation's financial institutions.

"Let's get it done," Bush responded, citing the need for a "simple and lean" approach. She gave no ground. "We need to get as much as we can," she replied.

At midnight, Paulson finally sent the administration's three-page proposal to Congress. He was ready to put a number on the amount the Treasury Department would need to buy toxic securities, with no guarantee that the government would be able to recover the money. It was a jaw-dropping amount.

Seven hundred billion dollars.

*Wednesday, September 24*

John Boehner gave Nancy Pelosi a heads-up. The two leaders had a respectful working relationship, friendlier and more functional than she would have with his successors as Republican leader, Paul Ryan and Kevin McCarthy.

He was having trouble lining up the hundred Republican votes he had promised for the bill, which was still being negotiated. "My people are looking for a reason not to support it," he told her. Bush wasn't helping; the president seemed to be in hiding. Even some of Boehner's lieutenants in the House leadership were breaking ranks. Virginia congressman Eric Cantor, who as the GOP's chief deputy whip was supposed to help sell the deal, was instead working on an alternative plan that Paulson already had dismissed as "ridiculous."

Arizona senator John McCain, in the final weeks of his campaign for the White House, was inclined to oppose the bill, too. McCain, a maverick often willing to support bipartisan compromises when other Republicans balked, called Pelosi to complain that the negotiations were moving too slowly. "We are making progress," she replied sharply. "It's not accurate to say otherwise." She knew their exchange was a sign of trouble.

That afternoon, McCain made a dramatic proposal of his own: Suspend the presidential campaign and convene a bipartisan White House summit.

That was a political stunt, Pelosi raged, and one that was more likely to delay a deal than reach one. When White House chief of staff Josh Bolten called to invite her to attend, she reproached him for capitulating to McCain. "Tell the president to lead!" she said. "I will not allow Congress to look like it's in disarray!" Obama was skeptical that the summit would achieve anything. But he was also worried that rejecting the invitation would set an unhelpful precedent if and when he was in the White House and invited Republicans to meet with him.

The Democrats accepted the president's invitation.

*Thursday, September 25*

To the surprise of no one, the White House meeting called to seal a deal instead imploded.

The president opened the session in the Cabinet Room with a plea for quick action and a warning about the consequences of failure. Then Bush turned to his right and recognized Pelosi, as protocol required.

"Senator Obama will be speaking for the Democrats," she replied. Pelosi and Reid and Obama had agreed beforehand that the party's presidential nominee would take the lead. Their message: We are united. Unlike the GOP.

Obama outlined the proposal that had been in the works. Boehner floated an alternative approach. Alabama congressman Spencer Bachus, the ranking Republican on the Financial Services Committee, said House Republicans weren't ready to endorse the deal but they did deserve credit for including taxpayer protections in it. That incensed Pelosi; she jumped in, saying House Democrats were responsible for those protections. Voices were raised, loud enough to be heard out in the hallway.

McCain, who had called for the summit in the first place, still hadn't spoken. Obama finally turned to his presidential rival. "We need to hear from John," he said. McCain seemed unprepared. He rambled, thanking Bush for convening the meeting and saying he shared the various concerns that other Republicans had raised. Obama snapped, "That's not an answer!" Barney Frank began to bait McCain. "So you came all the way back, you canceled your campaign, you don't have any ideas," he said tauntingly. "What are your ideas? Why don't you give us your ideas?"

Bush seemed to agree with the Democrats. "I don't know what the hell they are!" he said as Frank needled McCain. Vice President Dick Cheney began to laugh at the chaos.

The president leaned over to Pelosi and whispered in her ear: "I told you you'd miss me when I am gone," he said. She responded dryly, "No, I won't." (Her view on that would soften after Donald Trump was elected to the White House in 2016.)

After a moment more, Bush abruptly stood up. "Well, I've clearly lost control of this meeting," he said. "It's over."

The Democrats clustered in the narrow corridor outside the Oval Office, then ducked into the Roosevelt Room across the hall to confer in private. Pelosi, Reid, Obama, and a few others were discussing what to say to the reporters waiting in the White House driveway. Robert Gibbs, the communications director for Obama's campaign, began to sketch out talking points.

Suddenly, the door opened. Paulson strode in and headed to Pelosi. He was alarmed and disheartened, he would recall later; people seemed to be further apart than ever. He worried that Democrats would say something so inflammatory to the news media that no deal could ever be reached.

To the astonishment of everyone, Paulson fell to one knee, a dramatic gesture by the six-foot-two-inch man, balding and sixty-two years old. He was "genuflecting at the altar of the Speaker of the House," he would later explain, a joke and yet not a joke. "Nancy—" he began.

"Why, Hank, I didn't know you were Catholic," she replied, trying to lighten the mood.

"Please don't blow this up," he begged her.

"We're not," she replied. "We're not the ones that are blowing it up."

Nancy Pelosi and Bono, the Irish singer-songwriter, after a news conference on Capitol Hill on September 21, 2000, urging Third World debt relief. *(Photo By Bill Clark/Roll Call/ Getty Images)*

Nancy Pelosi and the Dalai Lama, on November 13, 2005, after she introduced him for a lecture at the MCI Center in Washington. *(AP Photo/Kevin Wolf)*

Nancy Pelosi takes a selfie in her office with Supreme Court justices Elena Kagan, Ruth Bader Ginsburg, and Sonia Sotomayor, before a Women's History Month reception on March 18, 2015. Pelosi deputy chief of staff Drew Hammill is helping. *(Photo By Tom Williams/CQ Roll Call/Getty Images)*

Speaker Pelosi Book.
- good a political mind as I have ever seen
- taking her to Kuwait before the war
- able to come to a practical solution
    - I appreciate that more than anything else
    - get something that can be passed
- amazing ability to comprehend something

- first real interaction when Boxer and her came to him about a base in San Francisco that was Braced ("Persato")

- asked JPM to help her get on Approps.
    - he picked Kapter cause she was in the zone
- she's portrayed as fair + tuff
- she always lets someone else take credit

- "come up with a policy the Democrats can live with"
    - she told him before speaking out

Representative John Murtha, Democrat of Pennsylvania, a member of Congress's Old Guard, led Nancy Pelosi's insurgent leadership campaign. Near the end of his life, he dictated observations about her for a memoir he never wrote; he died in 2010. He called her as "good a political mind as I have ever seen *(John P. Murtha Congressional Papers 1974–2010, AIS.2010.04, Archives & Special Collections, University of Pittsburgh Library System)*

Jubilant Democrats celebrate Election Night on November 7, 2006, when they regained control of the House and the Senate. Nancy Pelosi, then poised to become Speaker, stands with Illinois congressman Rahm Emanuel, left, who chaired the Democratic Congressional Campaign Committee; Senate Democratic Leader Harry Reid of Nevada; and Senator Chuck Schumer of New York, who chaired the Democratic Senatorial Campaign Committee. *(Photo by Chip Somodevilla/Getty Images)*

When Nancy Pelosi was sworn in as Speaker of the House on January 4, 2007, a groundbreaking moment, she invited her grandchildren and other children in the chamber to the dais. The gavel she used would be displayed at the Smithsonian's National Museum of American History in an exhibition marking the centennial of women's suffrage. *(Bill Clark/CQ Roll Call via AP Images)*

President George W. Bush acknowledges the historic nature of Nancy Pelosi as the first female Speaker of the House at the beginning of his State of the Union address on January 23, 2007. *(AP Photo/ Charles Dharapak, File)*

Speaker Nancy Pelosi announces a tentative deal after cliffhanger negotiations for legislation to address the financial crisis on September 28, 2008. She is standing between Senate majority leader Harry Reid of Nevada (left) and Treasury Secretary Henry Paulson. *(AP Photo/ Lauren Victoria Burke)*

President Barack Obama signs the landmark Affordable Care Act on March 23, 2010. Speaker Nancy Pelosi, the crucial figure in pushing it through Congress, stands just behind. *(AP Photo/Charles Dharapak, File)*

Representative Steve Cohen, Democrat of Tennessee, passed out buttons to his congressional colleagues commemorating the opening of the Affordable Care Act exchanges on October 1, 2013. He dubbed the landmark legislation "PelosiCare." *(Courtesy of Steve Cohen. Photo: Bart Sullivan.)*

The Republican National Committee dispatched a "Fire Pelosi" bus on a cross-country tour during the fall of 2010. Steve Wayte, a member of the Central Valley Tea Party, gestures toward the bus at this stop in Fresno, California, on October 5, 2010. *(Photo by Gary Kazanjian/Fresno Bee/Tribune News Service via Getty Images)*

Nancy Pelosi can't hide her distress at an Election Night rally in Washington on November 2, 2010. Democrats lost control of the House, and she lost the Speakership. *(AP Photo/ Alex Brandon)*

Nancy Pelosi is elected Speaker of the House a second time, on January 3, 2019. *(Photo by Olivier Douliery/ Abaca/Sipa USA [Sipa via AP Images])*

In the Oval Office on December 11, 2018, President Trump and House Democratic leader Nancy Pelosi spar at their first meeting after Democrats won control of the House in the midterm elections. The meeting also included Vice President Mike Pence and Senate Democratic leader Chuck Schumer of New York. *(AP Photo/ Evan Vucci)*

Outside the White House after the meeting with President Trump on December 11, 2018, as Nancy Pelosi and Chuck Schumer emerge from the West Wing to talk to reporters. The confident image of Pelosi would become iconic. *(AP Photo/Andrew Harnik)*

At the State of the Union address on February 5, 2019, Speaker Nancy Pelosi applauds conciliatory rhetoric by President Trump with an exaggerated clap that seems more mocking than congratulatory. *(Doug Mills/The New York Times/Redux. This photograph Doug Mills won the 2020 Award for Excellence in Presidential News Coverage by Visual Journalists, presented by the White House Correspondents Association.)*

A White House meeting on October 16, 2019, after the House of Representatives had begun an impeachment inquiry of President Trump, ends with an angry exchange between Speaker Pelosi and President Trump. She led Democratic congressional leaders in a walkout. *(Official White House Photo by Shealah Craighead via AP)*

After President Trump finishes delivering the State of the Union address on February 4, 2020, Speaker Nancy Pelosi stands up and shreds the text of his speech in a show of defiance. *(Jarrad Henderson/USA TODAY)*

Waiting twenty-eight days after the House of Representatives voted to approve two articles of impeachment against President Trump, Speaker Nancy Pelosi announces on January 15, 2020, the names of the House managers for the Senate impeachment trial of President Trump. Left to right: Representatives Hakeem Jeffries, Sylvia Garcia, Jerry Nadler, Nancy Pelosi, Adam Schiff, Val Demings, Zoe Lofgren, and Jason Crow. *(Photo by Caroline Brehman/CQ Roll Call via AP Images)*

Nancy Pelosi briefs reporters on Capitol Hill as Majority Leader Steny Hoyer (second from right) and others watch during the debate over a coronavirus relief bill on March 13, 2020. *(Photo by Alex Wong/Getty Images)*

Nancy Pelosi wears a protective mask at the Capitol on April 23, 2020, the day the House passed the first of a series of relief bills in the COVID-19 pandemic. *(AP Photo/ Andrew Harnik, File)*

Nancy Pelosi meets with reporters on November 6, 2020, to discuss the election returns. Democrat Joe Biden defeated President Trump, but House Democrats unexpectedly lost seats. *(AP Photo/J. Scott Applewhite)*

# Couples

This book belongs to:
Roma Francis

# Couples

EXPLORING AND

UNDERSTANDING

THE CYCLES

OF INTIMATE

RELATIONSHIPS

Barry Dym, Ph.D., and
Michael L. Glenn, M.D.

HarperCollins*Publishers*

HarperCollins books may be purchased for educational, business, or sales promotional use. For information please write: Special Markets Department, HarperCollins Publishers, Inc., 10 East 53rd Street, New York, NY 10022.

FIRST EDITION

*Designed by George J. McKeon*

Library of Congress Cataloging-in-Publication Data

Dym, Barry, 1942–
    Couples : exploring and understanding the cycles of intimate relationships / Barry Dym and Michael L. Glenn.—1st ed.
        p.      cm.
    Includes bibliographical references and index.
    ISBN 0-06-016713-0
    1. Marriage—United States. 2. Unmarried couples—United States. 3. Interpersonal relations. 4. Intimacy (Psychology) I. Glenn, Michael L. (Michael Lyon), 1938– . II. Title.
HQ734.D985 1993
306.8—dc20                              92-53375

93 94 95 96 97 ❖ /HC 10 9 8 7 6 5 4 3 2 1

*To our wives,*
*Fran Jacobs*
*and*
*Susan Jhirad*

# CONTENTS

# ACKNOWLEDGMENTS

Every book, every idea, has many roots. We would like to acknowledge a few.

I, Barry, would like first and foremost to thank my wife, Fran Jacobs. She has provided the constant and virtually unconditional support that has made my participation in this project possible. She has buoyed me when I got down on myself and enjoyed with me the triumphs along the way. She has read and provided invaluable criticism for each page of each draft. And, as my partner, she has helped provide a model for so much of what I believe is good in relationships.

My children, Jessica and Gabriel, have not only tolerated the reclusiveness demanded by the writing, but have read parts of the manuscript and offered their warm support and insight and enough teasing to bring laughter and tears to my eyes.

My mother, Rhoda Kirsch, has supported so many of my projects for fifty years. My appreciation for relationships and whatever good sense I have developed about them comes directly from her.

My father, Norman Dym, always wanted to write books. He was stopped by poverty and uncertainty, but he passed the wish on to me. It has taken me twenty-four years since his death in 1968 to finally comply with his wish and, thereby, to feel a great fulfillment. In the deepest sense, then, this is a book that he helped to write.

My brother, Kenneth Dym, read the book and offered more supportive criticism than a once competitive sibling should be able to do.

My sister, Jackie Ertischek, and I form a mutual and very supportive Fan Club as both of us in our middle years have finally begun to pursue our own creative muses.

Carter Umbarger, friend, confidant, and backpacking buddy, lent a sympathetic ear as we walked together along the streets of Cambridge and the trails of West Texas.

Finally, I want to thank my students in the Couple Therapy Training Program at the Family Institute of Cambridge who have provided a wonderful, critical audience, and many of their own ideas for this project; and Deborah Haynor, whose enthusiastic suppport and application of the ideas contained in this book have continued to open ideas and buoy my own enthusiasm when it waned.

I, Michael, want to thank my wife, Susan Jhirad, for her patience and understanding while this book was being written. I also appreciate the interest, curiosity, and warm support shown in the project by my children, Jason, Ezra, and Cathy, and by my stepson Raj.

Finally, together, we wish to thank a few other people. Our literary agent, Sallie Gouverneur, smoothed the way for us. Our editor Janet Goldstein's good sense kept us on track, and her finely tuned editorial skills taught us a lot about constructing a book. David Kantor was important to both of us in the early years of our work with couples and families. Allyssa McCabe came to our rescue early on when we were wondering how to find a publisher. Amy Stromsten and Michael Aronson helped us find our agent. Finally, we wish to thank our friends, whose relationships have been an endless source of marvel and inspiration for us, and our clients whose experience has helped inform this work.

# Preface

Not so long ago, a simple story stated that a couple began when a man and a woman fell in love. They would then marry and form a family. The woman would take care of the home and children; the man would support them by toiling in the heartless world. They would both sacrifice their individual goals to the greater good of the family. Their romance would gradually melt into affection and partnership. The man would be the acknowledged leader, following law and custom, but the woman would rule in most domestic matters.

Not every couple followed this prescription—far from it. Forms of coupling varied from couple to couple and from community to community. But each couple, whatever it did, had to contend with this story, this Cultural Narrative.* Some adopted it with relative ease; some twisted and changed themselves in order to accommodate; others were defiant, but their very defiance proved the story's continued vitality; and each individual might invoke it as an authority against a partner who failed to play the assigned role. The same is true today, albeit in response to a different Cultural Narrative.

The contemporary couple is changing rapidly, responding to shifts in where and how people live, in the economics of employment,

---

*The Cultural Narrative is the sum of a society's images and messages about how people should and do behave. We discuss the concept in depth in Chapter 2.

in the different kinds of power women and men wield, in beliefs about how things are supposed to be between the sexes, and in the nature of the family. As couples change, so does the Cultural Narrative about them.

Fascination with couples fills today's media and shapes our popular imagination. The romantically engaged couple is the icon of our time, a major focus of movies, television, books, and music. Most people devote tremendous energy to trying to find the perfect partner. And yet the couple is an isolated and fragile form, caught between great expectations and decreasing resources. It is supposed to be the cure for all that ails us. But the couple falls apart almost as easily as it comes together: half of all marriages end in divorce; early love often fades into domestic boredom. Contemporary couples must develop in the shadow of their potential demise.

The development of couples is neither linear nor singular; there have always been many different kinds of couples: "just living together" couples, gay and lesbian couples, childless couples, interracial couples, postdivorce couples, couples of vastly different age, and so on. The life course of real couples varies widely: few march in a straight line past every predictable milepost, from the first romantic attachment to the birth of children, to the empty-nest syndrome, and finally into retirement together.

Because different kinds of couples are continually being assimilated into the prevailing culture, several differing stories of "the way couples are supposed to be" may exist together at any one time. But *certain* stories regularly prevail. Against them, social diversity continues to build, often in unexpected ways (as by the impact of new immigrant families).

The contemporary couple has been evolving over the last few centuries. First nuclear families pulled away from those extended families and communities that had supported and constrained them. Then, gradually, the couple became more autonomous within the family, assuming greater and greater importance in the lives of its partners. This winnowing process has continued to our day. Since late in the nineteenth century, the solitary individual has been viewed as the basic unit in society: the brave figure of the Western movie who fills American mythology, struggling alone for meaning and survival; the alienated man out for himself in a bleak, unsympathetic urban landscape; the woman out to define her own story; the immigrant, the entrepreneur, the artist, the athlete.

While most people now agree that both women and men have a right to pursue their own self-development, there is a growing insistence that it should not be at the expense of others. In recent decades, society's fascination with the individual has been branded a narcissistic, "masculine" vision. The self-centeredness of the 1980s has worn thin. Americans are turning more than ever toward the couple as the vessel for forming their central identity. It is as though the historical movement away from family and community has gone too far, denying the universal desire for connectedness. The renewed focus on couples is one counterbalancing response.

One summer night in 1988 we sat on Barry Dym's porch, sharing our amazement at the drama of relationships over time, especially our own. We had both read jeremiads like Lasch's *Culture of Narcissism*[1] and Bellah et al.'s *Habits of the Heart*,[2] books noting the increasing social and moral bankruptcy of contemporary couples, driven by the pursuit of individual rather than collective ends. But we found ourselves far more interested in what allowed couples like us to *survive* in such chaotic times. If half of all first marriages end in divorce (as did ours) how did the other half do it?

Clearly, it takes a lot of stamina, luck, and determination for a couple to survive in an often unsupportive world. In our professional lives, we have been moved by the hopes people pour into their couple relationships; and we know from personal experience how much effort it takes for a couple to endure, how much dedication for a relationship to fulfill even a modest proportion of its early promises. And yet, we reflected, not much has been written about this struggle.

Childhood has long been mapped through developmental stages.[3] And over the last few decades, this developmental sensibility has expanded to include adults in books such as *The Seasons of a Man's Life*[4] and *Passages*,[5] which have helped many people see individual developmental crises as essential transitions along the longer road of life. Such a developmental view makes our difficulties seem more "normal," thus letting us hope we can move beyond them.

Intimate couple relationships are also filled with painful and confusing passages, and we need a comparable map to understand their complex journey. Yet most of the language used to describe couple development comes from writings on individuals or families. To do justice to couples, we need new language, new concepts, and new metaphors. With that in mind, we decided to write a book on the development of couples.

Each of us had independently concluded that couples pass through recognizable stages, and that these stages, even more than individual personalities, form the identity, the *character* of couples.

We felt that people—psychotherapists included—often participate in, theorize about, and try to fix ailing couples without a clear sense of how a couple functions or an understanding of how it has developed. This is like trying to treat the heart or lungs without knowing something about their normal functioning. Couples today have only the most rudimentary map of the territory through which life takes them. They are in a psychological and moral wilderness. Self-help books and psychotherapists try to help but often fail. The former are often superficial, while the latter often turn the people they describe into "patients." We wanted to discuss normal couples, not psychopathology, to create a living narrative—a map of couples in our time.

We focused our thinking on a simple observation: so many people seem disappointed in their relationships. What is the disappointment all about? Psychotherapists look for the roots of disappointment in unresolved childhood conflicts; philosophers and psychologists note its origins in our attachments to specific goals and material comfort. But the more we thought, the more a simpler answer emerged: relationships are disappointing because they do not seem to fulfill their early promise.

Our culture asks so much of couple relationships—romance and passion, partnership, friendship and nurturance—that disappointment is inevitable. The expansive promise of new beginnings often comes to seem like a youthful illusion, at best—a cruel hoax, at worst. The implicit contracts people make with each other, the deals they strike that are based more on potential than on past performance, come tumbling down. Partners break promises; individuals break their own resolutions. Husbands and wives are forever noting, "This is not the person I thought I had married" or, "I really thought that he was different from the rest, but ..." and, "If I had known then what I know today, I never would have married her." These statements are not simply sour grapes or the distorted complaints of dissatisfied individuals. They reflect the truth of broken promises.

As we discussed what contemporary couples experience, we understood that people's disappointment was more than an intellectual issue for us. It was intense and personal. There have been times, when our own prior marriages collapsed, when we questioned not just ourselves and our spouses, but the validity of marriage—or even couples—as a social institution. And, like others, we blamed ourselves, became obsessed with our "failures," and imagined that others were much better at relationships than we.

In trying to understand this sense of disappointment and betrayal, Barry began systematically asking couples about their original promises. What was it they had originally pledged to each other, what *contract* had they tacitly made? And how did this contract affect the dissolution or reconciliation that followed their sense of betrayal? Further, how did couples move *beyond* their outrage? How did the resolution of their disappointment affect how they subsequently thought of themselves—both as individuals and as a couple? Out of these questions arose our notion of a recurring three-stage cycle. It was a surprisingly simple idea, but the more we turned it over and measured it against our experience, the more it seemed to fit.

Our basic idea was that couples initially pass through three recognizable stages: Expansion and Promise; Contraction and Betrayal; Resolution. The early expansiveness of relationships expresses our desire for romance, our yearnings to burst through the walls of our isolation and alienation in order to connect with another person, and our longings to be more than insignificant beings on this "little" planet.

Later in relationships we contract and pull back into our skin. This contraction demonstrates our pessimism, our cynicism, our capacity to see ourselves as victims, and our lack of vision and enduring discipline. It expresses our belief that men and women are not natural allies, but naturally at war, and our conviction that we were fools for believing in romance.

When we bring these two opposing currents together, when we struggle past our pessimism with a sense of perspective and compromise, there is a period of resolution, a time of calm and apparent stability. But new challenges, like the birth of a child, the loss of a job, or one partner's press toward self-fulfillment and growth, often threaten and topple these stable places. No couple can stay at a point of resolution forever; they must always adjust. The character of couples is thus constantly evolving.

\* \* \*

This notion offered us a surprisingly simple schema to approach the confusing terrain of couples relationships. Barry presented the framework to a seminar on couples' therapy at the Family Institute of Cambridge in 1988–89. The responses of participants in that seminar helped clarify the strengths and weaknesses of the concept.

Several participants objected to the notion of *any* developmental scheme, believing that all such schemes are inevitably judgmental and prescriptive. A lesbian woman worried that the theory was inexplicably bound to gender issues inherent to heterosexual issues and therefore not applicable to gay and lesbian couples. People without children wondered if we were implying they had "failed" to pass some "normal" stage of development. People in couples outside marriage wondered if we were talking to them.

Others wondered if our scheme was purely chronological or if it hid some kind of hierarchical view—i.e., that couples get more and more mature as they pass through the stages, or that the more stages or cycles a couple passes through, the better off it is. Stage-oriented schemas frequently exclude large numbers of people from the norm by implying that the stages form a ladder, and that those who have reached the top are somehow more mature, more successful, and more normal than others.[6]

We set to work on the schema, trying to avoid these pitfalls, prepared to look at our own biases. We are both middle-aged, divorced and remarried, heterosexual white males, psychotherapists by profession, with mainly white middle-class practices. In talking about couples, we cannot claim to explore or define all two-person relationships. Our focus is principally on people who have selected each other as partners-in-life, romantic or otherwise, for brief times or longer ones. The most common form this takes—and the form we mainly discuss—is the heterosexual male-female couple, usually but not always oriented toward marriage and children.

Neither of us is an expert on gay or lesbian couples, African-American, Hispanic, or Asian couples, although we have in fact known and treated many. For this reason we leave the more comprehensive discussion of the particular issues faced by different kinds of couples to writers who more fully understand their experience. We invite people from diverse cultures to consider, as they read this book, how different and/or similar their experience is from the cycles described in this book.

In spite of this disclaimer, however, we feel that couples follow dynamic and developmental patterns that hold true across a very wide range. Even though particular differences exist between one couple and another, even though the universe of couples is very wide, and factors of nation, race, and class may be critical in any particular couple's life at a given time, we feel our observations describe the basic issues most couples face. We hope all couples find our observations useful.

We also struggled over how to describe gender-related issues, for we wanted to avoid any implication that that gender was a biologically determined category. Our view is that much of what society regards as masculine and feminine is socially constructed.

Gradually we elaborated our notion of the diversity of forms and paths couples today take, our sense of how the character of a couple is basically formed early in the relationship, and then honed and reworked as they endlessly cycle through the stages again. The schema was becoming more coherent.

This is not an entirely comfortable book. We make no effort to shave the sharp edges of anxiety and betrayal, and we portray difficult times as inevitable and essential aspects of getting on in life. We have little to say about how to fix troubled relationships, but we do describe how other, "normal" couples have moved through such difficulties. We have no wish to absolve individuals of responsibility for their own dilemmas; just because crises are inevitable does not mean that we cannot influence their shape, duration or resolution. Finally, we are not interested in providing formulas or moral prescriptions for all couples to stay together "no matter what." Rather, we want to clarify the life course of couples so partners can make more informed decisions about each other.

In exploring the life of couples today, we realize we are mapping a large uncharted territory. We have tried to create a portrait of the couple with some complexity, with an appreciation of couples' spunkiness, their drama, and their sense of triumph and heroism: a portrait worthy of human beings. Our approach is descriptive and speculative—not a research essay, an attempt to be all-inclusive, or a self-help manual.

*Couples* reflects our personal and professional experience, for we are participants ourselves in the process we describe. We have a large personal stake in the fate of couple relationships, and are unashamed, if bemused, advocates for them. In spite of this position, we have tried to be good observers, and to remain curious about the fate of couples in these fast-changing times. As we see it, the couple is a flawed but fascinating solution to the dilemma of relatedness in today's alienated society, a solution worthy of our closest attention. We hope the reader will find this exploration useful for understanding his or her own relationships, both past and present.

# 1

---

# A PERFECTLY NORMAL
# COUPLE

---

Let's start with a story ...

Jonathan and Marie met on a date arranged by a friend. She thought they'd be a perfect match: Both were hard-working, bright, and attractive people, with good values. Each "deserved" a decent relationship. Marie was twenty-five, Jonathan twenty-seven. She was in her third year of medical school. He was working sixty hours a week with a downtown law firm.

They were immediately attracted to each other. He loved her smile and sense of humor; she loved his eyes and the way he shifted his shoulders when he spoke. They couldn't stop talking. They spent that first evening in a restaurant, at an Italian café, and then just walking until 2:00 A.M.

Jonathan called her the next day, and they went out again that night. He called again the following evening, and they talked for three hours; by the following weekend they were inseparable. It was hard for them to manage it—them both being so busy—but they found ways of getting together all the time. They talked on the phone, stole a half hour for coffee, went on walks. They made each other feel comfortable. And each felt a sexual energy they wanted to explore further. It was gentle and loving, not "electric," but satisfying. They could talk so easily, it was easy to warm up physically, too.

Jonathan was tall and slender, a whimsical guy from New York.

1

His father, dynamic and tempestuous, ran a small wholesale appliance business; his mother stayed home, and busied herself with volunteer work. Jonathan was the only son; his sister Diane, five years younger, was just finishing college.

Marie was also tall: dark-haired, vivacious, and very outgoing. She came from an Italian family north of Boston. Her father worked in construction; her mother had remained home with Marie and her four younger siblings. Marie had been an academic whiz in school, but she was also popular and active in sports and clubs. She'd been her high school valedictorian and "Most Likely to Succeed." Her parents had urged her to take a scholarship to a local college—which she'd accepted—and they were pleased when she later decided to stay in Boston for medical school.

At first, Marie had been reluctant to get so involved with Jonathan—or with anyone at that point in her life. Her last relationship, ended just three months earlier, had been horrible. Mark had been tight, withdrawn, and arrogant; and Marie hated to think of herself helplessly chasing a man. She knew she didn't want to spend a lot of time brooding; that wasn't her style. But still she was surprised to find herself sliding so easily into a relationship with Jonathan.

She liked his wry humor. She found him sexy. She caught herself daydreaming about him almost from the start. His enthusiasm was contagious, and she liked how interested he was in her work, and how he wanted her. So she put aside her reservations about men and relationships and yielded to his courtship.

For his part, Jonathan was all eagerness. He'd been dying for a real relationship for a long time. Sure, he'd have to be more outgoing this time, more engaging than before: but it felt easy with Marie. Jonathan felt his problem with women had been that he hung back too much. He could assert himself as a lawyer, but not in relationships. Marie drew him out. She was the kind of woman he'd always wanted: sensual, accomplished, and smart—an independent partner who'd be there when needed but who would never drag him down. He thought the two of them were like other legendary couples: Paul Newman and Joanne Woodward, Marie and Pierre Curie.

At first, Jonathan's image seemed to fit them well. They opened up to each other—with long confessions, stories of past hurts and triumphs (some of which they'd never shared with anyone else), catalogues of their dreams—and marveled at how alike they were. They each liked the Stones, Fellini movies, Mozart, peanut butter, and long bike rides. And they each hated long novels, musical comedies, bananas, and Barry Manilow. They even appreciated their differences: Jonathan's stoicism under pressure made Marie feel secure, and her sparkling personality made him feel more alive.

They said they were "compatible." Each felt "better" in the other's company—more deeply known, more likable as a person, able to be kinder, more generous, and simply "themselves." They didn't even mind being vulnerable with each other. Soon they began talking about the future. Fueled by the other's appreciation, each felt expansive and expanding, larger than life.

After a few months, though, they began to quarrel—usually when Marie felt Jonathan pulling back. Once he canceled a date because he had to work, and she got angry at him and wanted to discuss it, but he said he just couldn't talk then. Another time she wanted to see a movie, and he said he was too tired to go out, and she said she should be able to say what to do sometimes and have him go along with it, and this night she *really* wanted to go out and see the movie—and he got very quiet. Marie felt that he resented her, but she couldn't understand why; and Jonathan felt she was trying to control him, but he couldn't understand why. They began to fight over which of them was in charge.

For several months, they rationalized their arguments as anomalies, accidents stemming from differences in their personalities or from differences between men and women. The spats didn't last long; they weren't nearly so bad as the knockdown fights they'd had in past relationships; and making up was fun. So they even painted their arguments in a bright light—nothing to worry about. They had improved over their past selves. Coping well, they felt pleased with themselves, and remained hopeful.

One day, however, the fight got out of hand. They were in a café, talking, and Marie felt that Jonathan wasn't listening. "Where *are* you?" she snapped, stopping in mid-sentence. "Umm, I was *listening*," he said. "No, you *weren't*," she insisted, and she asked him why. He became angry and defensive. "But I *was* listening!" he cried. "And even if I wasn't, so what? I don't have to hang on your every *word*, do I?"

"You don't have to listen to me at *all!*" she cried. "You don't have to go *out* with me, either. Be by yourself and do whatever you damn please!" And she picked up her purse and stalked out of the café, and refused to pick up her phone for the next twenty-four hours.

Jonathan was devastated. He blamed himself, kept calling to apologize. Finally Marie answered and heard him out, but she said she wouldn't accept his apology, because it didn't sound to her like he really meant it. Jonathan pulled back and clammed up into himself. He felt Marie had been "out of control." Why, he asked himself, were even the best-educated women so irrational? He began to think about going out with someone else. Marie was also distant. To her, Jonathan suddenly looked a lot like Mark and other men she'd known.

That week their whole world seemed to shift—not a lot, but enough so that everything was different. When he finally called her (and he did) to apologize again, he felt conflicted. Why was *he* always the one to call? Why not she? He felt humiliated. And Marie felt he'd taken an awfully long time to realize how insulting he'd been. She missed him horribly, but she still couldn't forget his angry tone. After a long talk together they made up; but, afterwards, Marie sometimes felt Jonathan's stoicism as withholding, even punitive; and she felt his openness and intimacy as sometimes misleading, even exploitative— especially when they only led to sex.

Jonathan started feeling Marie's effervescence as a little loud sometimes—even pushy. He worried that her constant talk about old hurts reflected a bottomless, unfillable pit. Also, she seemed to *demand* his attention more than before. Although they moved in together a few months later, they argued more often; and these argu- ments, once so innocuous, seemed to define their relationship more accurately now than did the warm and expansive feelings.

The fight ushered in a confusing few years in which happy times alternated with bad ones. There were marvelous days of studying hard together, taking long walks, making love in the afternoon, going to movies and Celtics games. But there were also more fights. Some- times one felt the other was "too" close. Sometimes Jonathan wor- ried about feeling attracted to other women, especially to one secre- tary at work.

Each wondered whether to end the relationship or go on. Unable to decide, they teetered. Loyal and somewhat afraid, they kept their difficulties largely private. One day, though, an argument over com- mitment got out of hand. They shouted, blamed, and blurted out all their fears: "I don't think you really love me!" Jonathan cried. "You just want me to do what you say." "I don't think you love me either," Marie answered. "Or else you'd want to be with me more." Feeling alone, Marie went back to her parents for a few days.

Jonathan missed her and was desperate by the time she returned. He told her he couldn't do without her, never wanted to be apart again, and wanted to get married. Pleading with her, he suggested asking their friends for help, and they spoke to the friend, Harriet, who had first introduced them.

Harriet provided them with a safety net. In her presence they expressed their unspoken hurt and anger, as well as their yearnings for each other and their hopes that the relationship could be saved. After a tempestuous evening they returned to their apartment, made love more passionately than ever before, and agreed to stay together. Soon afterwards, they were married. Jonathan was thirty; Marie, twenty-eight.

Marriage opened up new hope and excitement. Both plunged into their careers with renewed energy, but they felt their time together as special and delicious. Jonathan advanced in his law firm. Marie entered a pediatric residency. They decided to wait on having children. But their separate careers demanded more and more from them, and the distance between them grew.

They felt they had few illusions about themselves now; they could struggle through whatever conflicts might arise. They drew strength from their friends' support, their own shared wish for children, and a sense that there was light at the end of the tunnel. They continued to blame each other at times, but they also found they'd built up some basic trust along the way and had become better friends. When Marie's dad had a heart attack, Jonathan visited him at the hospital every day. And when Jonathan's sister floundered in her small business, Marie invited her to Boston for a few days. Involvement with each other's families brought them closer together.

After residency, Marie started working at a community health center. Jonathan was even busier. Each absorbed in his or her own work, they began keeping secrets, and divisions grew: his world, her world. When they were together, they sometimes rubbed each other the wrong way. She felt him sounding like a typical lawyer: cold and logical. He felt her sounding "mushy" and sentimental, but acting hard and pushy toward him. At the same time, Marie began having problems with her male clinic administrator. She got together with two other women physicians, and all three of them began talking about women's issues in medicine.

Just then, Jonathan again raised the question of having children. Marie was ambivalent: she was moving ahead in her career and didn't want to have to stop; she felt having a child was a duty, for him and for her parents. But, deep down, she really wanted a child, too. When she reached thirty, she gave in and soon became pregnant. They had a baby girl, Beth. Jonathan was ecstatic. Their problems seemed to be working themselves out ...

Then the bottom fell out. Marie discovered that Jonathan had been having an affair with a woman in his office. Angrier than ever before in her life, and feeling totally betrayed, she told him their marriage was over. She wanted him to move out within the week.

This time both their families intervened. Jonathan's parents took Marie's side and confronted him sharply: "Family is the most important thing," they said. What did he think he was doing? His sister Diane also advised him to straighten up his act. Marie's parents urged her to give Jonathan a chance to admit his problems and get some help.

Surprisingly, each seemed to soften then. Jonathan opened up and tearfully confessed he'd felt distant and alone. Things hadn't been going well for him at work, either. He took full blame for the problem and begged Marie to stay. They saw a marital counselor together for several weeks, and after that Jonathan continued on his own. Issues they'd kept under wraps now surfaced. They resolved to keep the marriage going.

Marie found she couldn't completely let go of her resentment. She became almost completely unavailable sexually, and—albeit promising each other they'd try harder—they plunged back into their careers.

Having a child brought them closer and made them realize they were part of something larger and sturdier than their rickety couple relationship. Good times again appeared, mingling with the bad; distance and closeness alternated inexplicably; the old fights reappeared but no longer seemed to define their relationship completely.

Taking care of Beth, they were reminded of their original dreams and once again noticed the traits in each other they'd ao admired before. Slowly the relationship took an upturn. They wondered about buying a house, fantasized about redecorating rooms. Talking to each other more, they discovered new areas of generosity and support. For example, Jonathan said he'd change his schedule so he could be home two afternoons a week with the baby, and Marie said she'd take a less desirable but better-paying clinic position, which would let her work less and be home more.

The crisis passed. Jonathan had given up the affair a few weeks before Beth's birth, but Marie remained suspicious. She watched him carefully for several months; then, convinced he genuinely regretted breaking her trust, she forgave him.

Over the next several years, their relationship continued to oscillate back and forth in cycles that felt arbitrary and beyond their control. Major events could buffet them about. Some, like the births of their second and third children, brought out the best in them, and they once again became expansive, warm, and hopeful. At other times, quibbling prevailed, their "old fight" seemed to dominate, and they grew increasingly bitter. They fought about issues of commitment and closeness over and over again. This was especially true after unforeseen events occurred, like Jonathan losing his job and having to find a new one, or their second child becoming ill, and their blaming each other for it.

Up until a few years ago, Jonathan and Marie had a hard time getting a handle on their life together. Things were always changing for them, and none of their solutions seemed to endure. Each time they thought they had gotten their relationship in shape, some unexpected event would start them off in another phase of grumbling and feeling misunderstood. Then they would fall back, avoid one another, and stew in their angry fantasies, until—finally falling back on their most fundamental ways for solving serious problems—they would eventually stagger past the bad feelings, reach another accommodation, and begin all over. Each new beginning would give them hope; each crisis would make them sad and resentful again.

They had friends who divorced when they couldn't resolve their squabbling, and yet they themselves stuck together. Considering this, they admit having been dissatisfied enough themselves at moments to wonder what would have happened if they had acted differently. Jonathan wonders what would have happened if he had "taken a stand earlier." Marie wonders what would have happened if she had "taken charge of my own life, instead of getting tied down" when she did. Both have wondered if the other was really the "right" person for them.

Six years ago, when Jonathan was thirty-nine and Marie thirty-seven, they entered a prolonged period of unhappiness and disappointment, whose ultimate resolution two years ago profoundly changed their life. During this period, they came closer to divorcing than ever before in their lives. To resolve it, they finally had to admit to themselves that their relationship was less than they had originally hoped, that they had never fully healed their old wounds nor fully accepted the loss of their old hopes. And yet the transformation wrought by the shared experience of their coming through this difficult time together has given their relationship a new sense of optimism and purpose.*

Now they feel more at ease with each other and with themselves. They believe that getting older together means having to give up some expectations, and accepting some limits in order to be happy. They deeply appreciate the companionship, love, and family they share today; and, indeed, they have many values in common, and are entwined in a network of supportive friends and family. Marie and Jonathan have changed over the years, but they can still recall the hopes and dreams they shared years ago; they still feel the love and trust that first kindled their relationship. Their relationship has endured and endured well.

*This experience will be described in Chapters 12 and 13.

# 2

---

# COUPLES IN OUR TIME

---

Couples do not grow in a straight line the way an acorn becomes an oak. Nor do they develop apart from others in their society. Couples are profoundly influenced by their social and historical surroundings. Throughout the years, the partners weave their couple relationship out of different threads of their own lives, strands of their families' stories, and the fabric of beliefs and expectations of other groups to which they belong—all in relation to the prevailing Cultural Narrative, a vast tapestry that presents the sum of society's messages about how people are supposed to do things. Each step of the way, the couple reacts to one factor after another, defies it or accepts it, steps aside or strides ahead. The partners make choices, take risks, move closer or further apart, stick together or break up.

Jonathan and Marie are a fortunate couple, a privileged pair moving through life with the advantages of education, position, and money. Neither is particularly "neurotic" or "dysfunctional." They appear to like and respect each other much of the time, and they work hard to make things come out right. Yet, talented and successful as they are, they go through the same painful cycles as every other couple. We chose to write about them precisely *because* they represent our culture's ideal of who should succeed in love and marriage.

Despite their advantages, their life is characterized as much by

9

bitter conflict and impasses as it is by satisfaction and success. Their "normality" lies in the way they oscillate between problems and possibilities, between good times and bad. Like all other couples, they cycle from optimistic expansiveness to defensive contraction and back. Stretched by the inherent conflicts of their lives—the desire for sturdy friendship as well as passionate romance, the wish to succeed at work but still carefully nurture their children—their relationship is rarely stable. Each time they resolve a conflict, the solution eventually disintegrates, and they must start all over. What is true for Jonathan and Marie is true for most couples today: instead of having orderly, stable lives, they regularly move from one cycle of conflict and resolution into another.

This chapter explores how recent social changes have shaped couple development in our time and then introduces our notion of the three-stage cycle of couple development.

## Cycles of Conflict and Resolution

The character of couples is forged through regular cycles of conflict and resolution. Conflict is not an aberration that can be ignored or cured; it is inherent in couples' lives. It stems from real dilemmas that couples must acknowledge and resolve. In relationships, conflict often appears as a choice: individual versus collective good; women's rights versus male entitlement; one partner's style of upbringing versus the other's.

Most contemporary couples follow this pattern. As with Marie and Jonathan, courtship is an expansive time. Couples evaluate their success and failure in terms of the immense potential they actually feel, and they compare this to their expectations. Their optimism is usually counterbalanced by their experience of everything that can be upsetting in relationships, the "fall" from a good place, the hurt that comes with vulnerability, the knowledge that early promises can be betrayed.

Couples struggle for a perspective that can embrace both the good and the bad and help them move ahead. But the perspectives they reach, and the solutions they attain, are always partial: they resolve enough so they can move on, but they rarely resolve disputes completely. Core conflicts hang around, serving as sources of new antagonisms.

Virtually every couple moves through the same cycles as Marie and Jonathan. We all begin with a growing sense of elation and expansion, a sense of promise that seems bigger than life. And sooner or later we all stumble. We start arguing, see our life together as *less* than it originally seemed, and enter a time of Contraction. In this stage, which follows every period of Expansion, each partner feels let down, hurt and misunderstood. If we stay together, however, negotiating, compromising, settling, we will arrive at a new point of departure, a Stage of Resolution, which tends to regenerate some of our original hopes and optimism.

Yet, just as we feel we have resolved a conflict about sex, money, or children, our solution unravels or another problem appears. The lack of clarity in men and women's roles opens opportunities for growth, but it also increases the chance of conflict. Partners need to negotiate everything, from how to structure child care to how and when to make love—and who should initiate it. Couples must find their own way amid the chaos of their newfound freedom. In times of rapid social change, people move back and forth between old and new, between hope and fear, between a sense of expansiveness and the need to contract into old or defensive places.

Couples will be frustrated if they expect to solve their conflicts once and for all. But if they learn to recognize their cycles of conflict and resolution and adapt to them, they may survive the hard times, grow together, and thrive. Later in this book, we will explore each of the three stages in turn and see how a couple's character forms from their cycling constantly through them. First we'd like to describe the social context that has led to this form of couple development.

## The Urgency of Couple Relationships

Every culture promotes distinctive ways for couples to start and develop relationships. Forty years ago, for instance, men were expected to earn a living and contribute minimally to domestic family life, while women were supposed to stay home, care for the children, and maintain the house. But the rules, images, and expectations that shaped our parents' relationships do not fit couples today. They do not fit the college-educated women who pursue careers and expect to work outside the home, the men who expect to share more fully in domestic chores and child care, or the many people in their twenties who now think that assigning social role by gender is archaic.

Ours is an age of rapid transition and great urgency; and this holds for relations between women and men as well. Old images exist beside new ones. Freed of many traditional constraints, we have become more confused, yet more self-conscious. Wide swings between expectations and disappointments characterize many couples' lives today.

Men and women have always been drawn together, but in the United States today, the quest for the right mate has taken on a mythic, even frantic quality. Coupling has become a world unto itself—no longer a brief prelude to family life. The couple has replaced the individual as the cultural icon of our times.

Images of romantic love fill the media. The romantically-engaged couple is the object of endless public fascination and concern. Most of us take it on faith that we will one day separate from our parents, dedicate ourselves to another person, and *not* stay married just for the children's sake. The structure of coupling supports this separatist ideology: many couples live together for years before marrying or having children; some wonder *whether* to have children or not; many adults spend years between divorce and remarriage, contemplating and nurturing new relationships. Others spend years alone after their children leave home—and years before that contemplating the empty nest.

Coupling in America is supposed to be romantic at heart, but it rarely lives up to these expectations. Confused, we anxiously seek answers outside of ourselves.

The couple has never before been burdened with such enormous expectations. It's seen as a panacea, a cure-all. If we're lonely, the couple will fill the void. If we feel powerless, it will support us. If we need a friend, a lover, a confidant, a family, we're supposed to find them all through our couple relationship.

These relationships are so important, and we are so vulnerable to the wounds of rejection and abandonment, that we experience many of our greatest risks and joys in life through being a part of a couple. This might be all right if someone could tell us how to go about it, but contemporary couples have to navigate these stormy seas without reliable models or guidance. In such an uncertain atmosphere, the possibililty of divorce hovers as a punishment for failure—as well as a final relief for the suffering. Romantic beginnings and bitter divorces provide bookends to half the marriages in this society, and all new couples today must approach the future knowing their road ahead is tortuous and uncertain.

## A Revolutionary Time for Couples

As the intensity of contemporary coupling has grown, many of society's greatest dramas focus within the couple. For example, since the time of the troubadours, romantic love and marriage have been considered opposites, even enemies.[1] Love is seen as hot, emotionally compelling, and outside society's rules; marriage is cool and domesticated, a partnership formed to carry on daily business, bring children into the world, and pass on social values.[2] Now the two are supposed to coexist in harmony. A couple's partners are supposed to be able to switch from lawn-mowing and diapers to torrid sex at the drop of a hat; from long hours at work to sweet moments in the sun.

At any moment one partner in a couple can stand for romance, the other for getting things done; but these roles often rigidify, leaving each partner frozen into half a self. Skeptics have long warned that the introduction of romantic love into marriage created a degree of unreality and instability that threatened the family's very existence.[3] Today the effort to keep love and marriage both alive at the same time creates an inherent tension in many long-term relationships.

Today's heterosexual relationships have also become battlegrounds in women's struggle for equality; in the process, the urgency around them has increased. This struggle is played out in a million households, in a thousand different ways, every day. Men and women fight over who should care for the children, take on the chores, earn money, make decisions, and even how to make love. Partners try to bolster their positions by invoking the wisdom of friends, teachers, TV gurus, and therapists. As partners' positions become polarized, emotions run high; every move, every kiss, every refusal to wash the dishes takes on great significance.

Large-scale changes in our economy, in the family, and in the ways we think about gender have made the domestic world of the couple undergo great shifts and variations. One result of this is that both women and men tend to overestimate the power the *other* sex wields in intimate relations today. Both feel like victims in the war between the sexes. The general view is that women are increasingly winning more (but not fast enough), while men are losing ground. Some argue that, in the long run, any male loss of power over women is a good thing, because it can help men focus on the value of intimacy and cooperation. Others are dismayed by the loss of any predictable pattern.

It is difficult to be a man and difficult to be a woman today. Men feel themselves fighting a rearguard action: attacked, even when they agree with many of the things women are saying. Women are perpetually wary—and rightly so—of being mistreated, abused, conned, and patronized, even when they really like being with a man.

Because of this, the interior landscape of the couple has turned into a wilderness. Yet it is here that we meet one another to create relationships. Old images of what women and men should be and do hover around us, dogging our every step. New attitudes and new images spring up on every side. A contentious intermingling of old, new, and even newer images makes every couple's journey today problematic.

Take a couple determined to maintain their equality. They will each work, share their income, and split up their chores. It seems effective, but after a while each of them may start feeling nervous or deprived: she turns out to be too assertive, for example; and perhaps he isn't protective enough.

Another couple might be more traditional. The man comes home from work, expecting his wife to fix dinner and take care of the children. The woman, even if she has a job herself, accepts the view that the home is *her* bailiwick. And yet, even with such a clear division of labor, they may still argue furiously about money, the discipline of their children, and the rules that guide their domestic, social, and sexual lives. The man, for example, may want his wife to be a bit less independent; and she may want him to follow more of the respectful virtues in which her family excelled.

Many women find themselves working outside of the home *and* doing most of the child care and housework; yet they feel uneasy with the resentment and rage this brings about. Many men who work hard at their jobs and take care of children when they're at home resent their wives for treating them as if they're not doing enough; yet they feel ashamed of begrudging their wives the least favor.

Any two-person system presents major problems: there's no third deciding vote to resolve differences; and a decision to leave (or even considering such a decision) threatens the life of the unit. The struggle for consensus can be long and hard; it often includes coercive strategies such as withdrawing affection or bullying. An inability to come to resolution can threaten the whole relationship. The struggle for control between the two partners, played out as it is against the backdrop of a "War between the Sexes," has become a central motif in the lives of contemporary couples.[4]

In the midst of these struggles over love and power, couples must also manage their domestic households, which present them with all the problems of a small- to medium-sized organization. Consider how we live our lives. We have to handle children—schools, day care, babysitters; maintain our houses or apartments; work our jobs; and participate in the complex web of our community. For many of us, our lives are strung so tight, we have little room for adjustment. We do well when things go according to plan, but when the plumbing breaks or a child gets sick, we argue over who's going to stay home from work, and our carefully orchestrated systems feel vulnerable to collapse.

In spite of all this difficulty, nothing has dimmed the ardor with which we seek relationships. While the divorce rate has risen to one in two, the rate of remarriage matches it.[5] No one really blames "relationships"—just the one they're in. In times of trouble we always believe a better relationship is just around the corner. The flowering of self-help books, audiotapes and television programs fans this hope by suggesting that, through a combination of hard work and "getting it right" this time, we can overcome any difference, and even despair.

Our commitment to the inner life of relationships has grown as our commitment to the larger society recedes. We feel powerless to influence the world events that parade before us on TV like Nintendo games. We move from community to community and often live far from our families. We seem starved for authentic engagement and support. Society prescribes the couple as a solution to such feelings of alienation and loneliness. So we concentrate our yearnings for connection onto one little relationship, with one other person.

History may understand the contemporary couple as an evolutionary solution to an immense dilemma. What we need is a social group that performs the functions once provided by the family, extended family, and community. It must be mobile, fast-forming, and capable of dissolving quickly. It must compensate for childhood's wounds and relieve the loneliness of the present. It must provide stability and continuity, food, shelter, and child care (if there are children). Friends and neighbors aren't always available. That is the couple's mission today.

## Negotiation and Other Ways of Resolving Conflicts

Themes of power and control are increasingly central to today's couples. Almost every couple that comes to therapy bemoans their prolonged and unresolved struggles over control, struggles that touch every area of their lives—financial, sexual, domestic. Trivial questions like what movie to see or what color bathroom towel to buy can turn into mammoth battles. Men and women no longer subscribe to the idea of separate domains—his and hers—which means that neither partner gets to play out their own vision or style without an argument somewhere along the line. In this contentious atmosphere, simple feedback is turned into "Criticism!" and simple difference can be a source of extended conflict.

Conflicts are difficult to resolve. Each partner invokes a different set of rules, hoping to carry the day. "This is how my family disciplined children," says one; and the other retorts: "Well it didn't work so well, as far as I can see. Why don't we at least look at this book on child development together." We haul out rules from our childhood or from books, try to combine thoughtful introspection with the advice we've gotten from others. But generally the invocation of separate rules or the suggestion of new problem-solving methods just adds fuel to the fire. It seems like another attempt to gain the upper hand.

The quintessential modern method for resolving conflicts is negotiation. This has become as true for couples as for diplomats or corporate executives. To negotiate well, each participant has to assume that the other has a valid point of view, that compromise is possible, and that flat-out winning is not good if it causes too much resentment. Instead, the idea is to satisfy both participants without making either give in too much. "Win-win" is the operative phrase, which has come to represent an ethical stance as well as a procedural skill.

But negotiation—however valuable a skill it is—cannot solve every problem. It is no substitute for a generous, harmonious fit. And it often overlooks the depth of psychological attachment we each have to our positions. The truth is, we are often deeply committed to how we do things and we do not want to compromise them. We feel it as a self-betrayal to negotiate away freedoms we fought for years ago, or to abandon beliefs about child-rearing that we—and our parents, and their parents before them—have always held strongly. *Having* to negotiate rather than being able to relax in the comfort of a genuinely shared belief exhausts us. It demands more of our scarce time, and it violates an ideal of marriage many of us carry deep inside, an ideal which emphasizes shared tastes and values rather than the ability to bargain.

It just seems *wrong* to us to have to negotiate everything. As one man said, "I don't want to negotiate whether the sun is going to come up and the earth will be under my feet. I want to assume some basic things between us."

Some partners try to resolve conflicts by seizing control of how the couple's money is spent. A couple can discuss buying a new sofa, taking a vacation to Disneyland versus the Poconos, or when to pay off their credit card debt; but if one partner controls the money, all the talk may be in vain.

Historically, men controlled the couple's finances and all the choices that went with it—unless the woman had independent wealth. They worked while women stayed home.[6] In our time, many women work, but men still have a greater earning capacity. This reinforces their claiming the upper hand in financial matters. Dominating the finances is one technique men use to impose their will on women. Many women have been infantilized, for instance, by receiving household "allowances."

Nowadays, however, this inequity is changing. As women enter the work force in record numbers, they bring home a substantial income. Women are the sole wage-earner in many families. And even though women frequently earn less than men for comparable work, they are nonetheless the main wage-earners in many couples. In couples, women take care of all the financial tasks: they write the checks and pay the bills. These changes have heated up the struggle. Today neither partner is automatically in charge, and every financial issue can be an additional source of tension.

The situation can become even more chaotic and confused. In Barry Dym's current practice, about one-third of the women earn more than their husbands. Each of these husbands feels threatened. They are too "modern" of course—and need the money too much—to propose that their wives earn less, but they feel less manly because of it and admit to doing little things to "get back at" their wives and reassert their masculinity.

These women are proud of being successful. But they are also angry. They feel unprotected in the world and unappreciated at

home. In spite of their making more money, they still take on most of
the child-rearing and housework, and they feel exploited because of
it. They want to be taken care of, too. They argue that their men
want it all: mother and wife as well as breadwinner. But the men
argue that *they* want it all: equal power, the right to succeed, and permission to be furious at the men who "let" them do so.

Other conflicts focus on intimacy, a domain in which women have
long been acknowledged to have the upper hand. Barbara Ehrenreich and others have described how the "feminization of sex" has
spread through our culture.[7] Over the past two or three decades,
women's feelings and women's experience have come to characterize our concept of love. We now feel that, to be acceptable, love has
to include—if not emphasize—conversation and self-revelation.
This may work as a guideline in the early phases of relationship;
but, with time, the female call to conversation and feelings can
become a red flag to her companion. "Let's talk," she says; and he
replies: "Do we have to, right now?" She feels abandoned and
grows urgent: "We *have* to talk," she says, feeling demeaned at having to persuade him. He feels invaded. "All you *ever* want to do is
talk. Leave me alone!" If she does leave him alone, of course, he
feels hurt and abandoned (but she rarely does that, because women
are the keepers of our intimate domain). If she doesn't, he feels even
more jammed. This dance of pursuit and distance often makes our
search for intimacy more frustrating than satisfying.[8]

A further extension of the "feminization of sex" is that contemporary women claim fuller citizenship in the sexual arena. Women
have the right to initiate; they have the right to say no; they have a
right to say what they want and what they don't. In some circles,
focus on women's total-body sensuality has supplanted the older
forms of more male-oriented sex, which emphasized genital sex and
rapid climax.

But if today's sexual encounters may be more mutual, they are
also more self-conscious. We boast of believing that sex is natural,
just a simple good-natured expression of affection, pleasure, lust, or
desire; but we often fear we're not doing it right.

The domain of intimacy makes us negotiate with each other, talk
about embarrassing things, learn about our partners and—what is
often more difficult—about our own sexual appetites and prefer-

ences. Typically, women want to make love after an intimate atmosphere has been created, while men insist that sex itself creates that mood for them. They may argue about which comes first, she feeling pawed and invaded, he feeling controlled and deprived. In good times they may compromise or alternate; in bad times the sexual difference becomes entangled with other issues of control.

"He's always hovering around me; I feel caged," she says. He answers, "She knows how important sex is to me but she never invites it; I don't believe she really cares about me." In sex, men still generally pursue women, just as in conversation women generally pursue men. The somewhat theoretical "liberation" of women to pursue men has released an avalanche of complex feelings in which men may feel objectified, teased, chased, ignored ... but frequently still dominant.

All this makes us even more insecure. As we venture into new domains of man- and womanhood, we leave behind the safety of old definitions and open ourselves to criticism. We rarely know our own threshold for change, that point at which we've moved too far beyond the gendered imagery of our childhood. Nor do we know when we'll surpass our partner's limits. Just as we think we're being generous, we're told we're patronizing. Just as we think we're anticipating our partner's needs, we're told we're controlling. Just at the point we pull back to give our partner's needs priority, we're told we're passive and withholding.

Everyone wonders if he or she is man or woman enough. This insecurity makes it hard to support the changes we call for in our partners. If we lose our sense of being on a wilderness adventure together, we can feel pushed or harassed: our mate is pushing us too far and too fast, and judging us as lacking because we're changing too slowly, too awkwardly, or too much. Even when the couple relationship supports change, friends and relatives may not. "Don't you think it's wrong for Edie to go back to work so fast after having a baby?" Mama says. Their questions can divide even the most together couples.

No new model of relationship has arisen to replace the old ones, and so many couples live in a twilight zone, straddled between traditional roles and expectations and those they invent on their own or adapt from the media. In stable times, we can move through life in patterned ways, without thinking much about the hows or whys. In

times of change we ask more questions. Refreshing as it is to live by
our own choice and creation, it may still feel less solid than living by
the wisdom and customs of generations past.

Until we have forged a new tradition, based on equality between
the genders and a new agreement about what is inherent, and what
must be created, we will continue to be anxious and self-conscious in
relationships.

## Contradictions

In times of change, contradictions sharpen. This process marks the
lives of contemporary couples, making both partners tense and
excited. We can point out three basic conflicts with which couples
today must cope.

1. *The clash between great expectations and limited resources.*

According to our Cultural Narrative, the romantically engaged
couple is an answer for everything. We want more from our partners,
but we're less and less able to give, ourselves. Our partners must be
passionate lovers as well as loyal confidants, willing to join us
intensely when we want, but leaving us alone when we need "private
space." We ask for romance in our quiet moments, but want a sturdy
partner to help with the tasks of raising children, maintaining a
household, and coordinating schedules. These activities interfere with
one another, and our expectations don't mix.

The couple is supposed to be a stable haven in a cool, hostile,
unpredictable world. In the past, women had the role of maintaining
domestic relationships, but now that two incomes are often required
to get by, in more and more couples both partners work. Many couples, even without children, return home each day spent and
exhausted. No one stands at the threshold to welcome and soothe
their return.

At the same time, couples are more isolated than ever from the
resources that used to sustain them, such as extended families and
communities. We all have friends, but fewer of us live close to our
families. Who can we depend on, no questions asked, to take care of
the kids when we are in a pinch? Who will support us through the
hard times and offer us wisdom? Most couples are jammed for time,
for emotional energy, and for patience. "I just need a minute to
myself" has become our modern litany. Our partner's company some-

times drains us more than it enhances us. We probably do more for one another these days, but we expect so much that we're still often disappointed.

2. *The clash between the individual and the couple.*

We always marvel at those selfless individuals who place others' needs and comforts first, for in an age such as ours, individual pleasures, development, and fulfillment often come first. The contemporary concern with self—the "me generation"—intensifies the basic tension between our allegiance to the relationship and our allegiance to ourselves.

In couple relationships this tension is often polarized: women have tended to stand for relationship, connection, and mutual dependence; men have tended to stand for individualism and independence. Such polarization, where it exists, exaggerates and distorts and leads to dramatic confrontations, such as those in which women feel abandoned while men feel controlled. This is probably the most common dilemma presented to couple therapists today, and can be seen as the archetypal struggle of the modern couple.

But there is a growing trend to dissolve this simple division-by-gender. Women are also concerned with their own development, with being independent and respected partners, capable of pursuing their own goals outside of the relationship. The question then arises: just *who* in the couple is committed to the relationship?

In other historical eras, romantic love centered on the partner.[9] "What can I do to win you?" was a burning question. These days we look for partners who can bring out the best in ourselves. "What can you do for *me?*" we ask. The ideal partner today is a cross between a psychotherapist and a good parent. Even generosity, we are told, proceeds best from self-fulfillment: only if we feel good about ourselves will we be good to our partners.[10] But when we feel bad about ourselves, and our partners are not filling our needs, we may soon lose our commitment to the relationship. We and our partner then become two islands in an unfriendly sea.

3. *The clash between staying together and splitting up, marriage and divorce.*

Many relationships last a short time. We discard our partners—or they discard us—and we move on. Even longer relationships have a way of fizzling out after a year or so: they just don't seem right anymore; nasty arguments turn us sour; our involvement fades away. Even those relationships that lead to marriage have trouble holding fast. And yet we keep starting relationships again, keep remarrying, hoping each time we'll find the right partner—or at least take a more realistic attitude toward them.

We seem less angry, less disillusioned with relationships or marriage than with ourselves or our current partner. As difficulties in a relationship mount, we often persist because we have so much "invested" in it; but eventually we wonder if it makes sense to put any more into such a losing relationship.

Most of us become less willing to accept a stale relationship. As breakup and divorce have become easier, so has our dream of the good partner. We imagine anew that they will save us from loneliness, redeem us as individuals, and help us avoid the problems that destroyed our last relationship.

We're vividly aware that breakup and divorce are possible. Such awareness can take the edge off our own commitment: it is like an escape clause, a skepticism built into contemporary relationships. We react to this skepticism by nervously maintaining a safer distance, withholding a part of ourselves, and trying to let go of some of our romantic intensity. As we struggle to avoid breaking up, we often distort the very relationships we are trying to preserve.

## Stages of Couple Development

Without guidelines, without a map to help them understand what's happening, couples often blame themselves and each other for their difficulties. This book is intended to provide such a navigational map, which can help couples weather the bad times and linger a bit less warily when things are good.

In order for a couple to endure, the partners must resolve the problems that emerge in their relationship. No couple does this by moving in a straight line; instead all pass through series after series of endlessly spiraling three-stage cycles. The three stages are Expansion and Promise, Contraction and Betrayal, and Resolution.

Couples first move through times of positive hopes and experiences, then through times of trouble and disappointment—perhaps the positive experiences were not deep enough, perhaps they did not last long enough; then into some middle ground between the two opposing conditions. Each cycle reflects their effort to recognize and reconcile a conflict: the freedom and promise of the early relationship versus the crushing defeat that invariably follows; the value of individual development versus the collective needs of couples and families.

Initially, two people first come together enough to form a lasting relationship. This is the task of the first Expansive Stage. According to today's Cultural Narrative, couples should begin in a burst of romance, exploration, and sexual attraction. But not every couple, and not every partner, falls in love. Instead, couples commonly begin with a shared experience of expansiveness and promise, which may include romantic love, but which may also arise from a warm and respectful friendship.

In this stage, individuals feel somehow larger, more witty and charming; stronger yet more vulnerable—in short, closer to their ideal selves than ever before or after. The developmental trajectories of men and women converge for a moment, so that men take time to talk and understand, while women appear more independent. Each partner's appreciation spurs the other to expand his or her capacities. Early relationships lack the constricting patterns that eventually emerge. They are spacious instead, encouraging both exploration and experimentation.

The Expansive Stage is one of the few times when we tell our whole story to another person, who bears witness to it and helps shape it further. The two individual narratives are then woven into a couple narrative, which takes on a life, an identity, of its own. People will say, "This is how we do things," and "That is just how we are." In this way, individual identity becomes inextricably bound to the character of the couple.

But couples must also find a way to include the fears and insecurities, the ineptness and even the cruelty that figures prominently in their lives. Introducing this material into the relationship is the task of the Stage of Contraction and Betrayal.

This second stage begins when one partner pulls back to routine and familiar ways. The withdrawal may be neutral, not angry; but the person who is left inevitably feels abandoned and betrayed. When she—it is almost always the woman who stays connected longer—objects, he may feel controlled and withdraw further; she may then be both frightened and furious, insistently asking that the person she had gotten to know reemerge. In response, he may build his shell thicker, and so the sequence grows.

This nightmarish cycle makes caricatures of the two partners. The great potential of the Expansive Stage, when men and women shared "male" and "female" attributes, dissolves into cruel stereotypes. Each partner feels trapped, diminished, and betrayed—not only by the other but also by himself or herself. More than anything, people wish to remain the person they were in the Expansive Stage, the person they had striven to be through years of dreaming and preparing. Now they feel immensely let down by their own failures. They blame both self and other, and a mood of accusation permeates this stage. Just as the Expansive Stage brings us closer to our ego ideal, so the Stage of Contraction confronts us with our greatest fears and our poorest self-image.

During this stage, distinctive, repetitive struggles form and consolidate. They seem to define the whole relationship. The struggles are so distressing, the couple may draw someone, like a child or parent, or something, like alcohol or excessive work, into the relationship to buffer the conflict. Patterns of "triangulation," "complementarity," and many others become integral parts of the couple's moments together.[11] These patterns recur throughout the life of the couple; they become as familiar and distinctive as the implicit promises of Expansion.

In order for the couple to move on, it must climb out of the Stage of Contraction without entirely excluding its messages. It must at least partially reconcile the first two stages. This is the task of the third stage, the Stage of Resolution.

This is a stage of compromise, negotiation, accommodation, and integration. The partners struggle to be reasonable and maintain perspective, to affirm complexity and to handle difficult situations with competence and maturity. In contrast to the intense, narrow focus on one another that characterized the first two stages, the couple now opens up more to family and community. Having a child, for example, may serve as a bridge of common concern to repair long-strained relationships with parents; it may become a rite of passage into a more durable adulthood.

The early desire for fusion in the Expansive Stage gives way to close, bitter struggles in the Stage of Contraction. Paradoxically, the blaming and rejection may eventually lead to a sense of perspective. For example, a statement uttered in close, angry combat, like "I'm not at all like you," may usher in a realization of genuine difference:

"We really are different." With this realization comes first alienation, then at least toleration and possibly acceptance, followed by a flood of relief. For a moment the struggle seems over. What had seemed mean in one's partner now seems tolerable. Relief follows, and renewed optimism often comes in its wake. At this point the couple frequently moves forward into another Expansive Stage; but just as quickly, they can be thrown back into Contraction, with each partner feeling disappointed, as if the whole experience had been an illusion or a setup.

This moment of increased perspective represents a "foray" into Resolution (the concept of forays will be further explored in Chapter 11). The accumulation of these moments of realization, these forays from Contraction into Resolution, puts the couple past a threshold that consolidates their transition. As the forays overwhelm the experience of contraction—which comes to seem like such a crabby, limited view—the couple move ahead to the next stage.

Couples try to hold onto their new perspective and onto the optimism and expansiveness that follow, but they invariably fail. The progression of Expansion, Contraction, and Resolution is a spiral through time: stages cascade one after the other. The character of the couple, as distinguished from the character of the individual partners, is shaped more by the overall cycles than by any single stage. (This concept of couple character will be elaborated in Chapters 8 and 10.) Cycles can be precipitated by a wide number of crises and events.

At first, the promise of the Expansive Stage and the fears of the Stage of Contraction remain relatively separate; but with each turn of the cycle, they become more integrated. Each revolution brings new information into the couple's domain. One partner's terrible and characteristic rages, for example, may suddenly emerge after years of life together, and eventually become acknowledged and worked into their ways of being together. Memories of childhood trauma, long repressed, may surface after a particularly difficult time sexually; and this, too, will gradually be integrated into the couple's shared identity. So, too, with many positive traits, such as capacities that only emerge in response to dangerous or tragic situations.

For those couples who survive many turnings of the cycle, the Stage of Resolution tends to broaden in content and lengthen in time. Couples spend more and more time in it, and its qualities of tolerance and accommodation increasingly come to define their character.

The character of couples is shaped as much by the rhythm of the cycles as by the content of their stages. In this, couples vary greatly. Some couples, for example, move through wild swings: everything's great, then everything's awful; then there is a brief moment of reconciliation, after which everything's better (or worse) than ever. For others, the stages pass more subtly, and their cycles are relatively smooth. Some couples move very slowly out of one stage into another; others seem to be cycling all the time.

Every couple has a Home Base, a stage in which they generally reside. This habitual stage represents both its public persona (how others perceive them) and its evolved self-image, but not, as we have implied, its full character. Those who reside on Contraction, for instance, think of themselves as conflicted and troubled, even though they have moments in Expansion and Resolution. Once a couple has settled into a stage as its Home Base, its cycles will tend to begin and end there. The couple in Contraction might climb out through one compromise or another, relax momentarily in Resolution, which feels good enough to revive some old romantic feelings reminiscent of Expansion, but with its first minor disappointment, fall back to their familiar Home Base in Contraction.

After the first few cycles the stages in each couple's repertoire become more like different states of being. The couple can enter them, know them as familiar, and then move off. In this sense the stages become a relatively constant, autonomous reality in the relationship.

A couple's characteristic patterns usually stem from their first time through the cycle. For example, we develop our characteristic ways of loving and being loved, of being warm and affectionate, in our first time through Expansion. Subsequent expansive moments will usually bring back the memory and flavor of these patterns. Similarly, the fights we had in our first cycle usually recur over and over again through our relationship. They become our characteristic fight. No new fight seems all that new, but looks like a variation on the old one. Later, in our first passage through Resolution, we develop our characteristic ways of solving problems—our distinctive ways of talking, negotiating, tolerating, and accepting.

## Turning Points and Transformations

At some point, almost all couples find themselves in a profoundly disturbing and immovable impasse. No matter what they do, they cannot escape; there are no more areas of conversation to open up, no more strategies to try, no more activities to limit. They feel totally stuck. Many couples separate at this point. Many others, perhaps only through inertia or devotion to children or to the idea of marriage, stay together. Most couples simply endure, emerging diminished but essentially unchanged after their ordeal.

But some couples are transformed by these terrifying crises. Instead of simply enduring, the partners manage to give up their blaming and bitterness, but remain in the relationship. They realize they cannot get what they want by demanding, by manipulating, or even by negotiating. In despair and exhaustion, they finally stop trying to change their partner, and stop trying to make themselves over as well. Giving up this fight has a paradoxical effect. For a moment, the partners may experience each other in a new, fresh, and undefined way.

This experience is so dramatic it often takes on a spiritual dimension. The partners feel individually enhanced—better known and accepted for who they are, joined anew. They feel as if they have awakened, as if they are seeing a new truth. Beyond the conflict—and their own, selfish version of what's right—they can sense a deeper meaning of their relationship. This awakening becomes a great divide in the history of their relationship, separating a time of truth from one of ignorance. The partners can then return emotionally to each other and share the wisdom and inner strength they've now gained.

Not every couple goes through this trying time of transformation. Nor can the experience be taken on willfully; it has to emerge through the pain of life as lived. Still, these couples who survive and thrive through today's arduous journey strike us as having accomplished something astonishing. There is something heroic about people who have the capacity to sustain crushing disappointment, undergo repeated tests of their relationship, and still feel enhanced by their commitment to each other.

We are strongly moved and deeply impressed by the energy and courage of couples who refuse their own dissolution and who seek instead to explore the potential for fulfillment in their relationship.

# 3

# THE CHANGING CULTURAL
# NARRATIVE

Every couple's development is influenced by the themes of the society in which they live. At every point in their life together, the partners must engage their culture's expectations of how to behave.

Couples judge themselves by the standards set by the larger culture. These standards are articulated as contemporary parables in films, television, fiction, and popular psychology, as well as in stories told and examples set by parents, teachers, friends, and relatives. Taken all together, these accounts form a Cultural Narrative that presents couples with the conventional wisdom about the right and wrong ways to start out; whether to marry, when, and whom; who in a couple should take the lead in financial matters or in sexual encounters; who should deal with friends and family; how the partners should resolve disputes; and so on.[1]

Couples engage the Cultural Narrative in many ways. Some follow it slavishly; others loosely; some rebel and defy; some try to change themselves in order to fit. Others try to do everything at once. Some succeed in their tasks, and feel comfortable in their degree of (or lack of) fit with the Cultural Narrative. Others wear their accommodation like ill-fitting clothes. Still others fail completely, and are torn apart by the conflict over being like everyone else. In any case, all couples, as they struggle with the Cultural Narrative, weave its themes into the tapestry of their own relationships.

* * *

Take Steve and Charlene, a recently married couple. Each of them works and plays hard, and they make sure they have time for aerobic workouts three times a week. Each owns a car, maintains a separate bank account, and has separate charge cards. They like to keep things straight. They have no children yet, but will soon try for one, then a second. They stay busy in their separate worlds during the week, and their daily contact consists of anecdotes about their day, checking in with each other, and negotiating around weekend activities, household chores (which they share equally), and future plans.

Steve and Charlene had fallen in love when they met. Now, three years later, their spark is a little dulled, and they feel and behave more like good partners. They can revive the romantic feelings with a weekend away, but they worry about having changed. They read pop psychology books and even discuss them together to figure out what to do. Their friends have told them that this is what happens to couples after marriage, and so—knowing they feel deeply and warmly about each other—they accept the subtle shifts in their relationship.

Charlene and Steve conform closely to the contemporary Cultural Narrative. They check each move out against the imagery they see all around. They are so good at approximating the norm that they do not have to spend excessive energy worrying and making adjustments, but their vigilant efforts to be "with it" still create a certain brittleness.

Didi and Chuck are a hardworking couple in their late twenties, with three young children. Chuck, an electrician, has been out of work several times in their seven years together, and during these times he did whatever he could to support the family. Didi holds down a part-time job at the local grocery store, but she mainly stays home and takes care of the kids. If it weren't for their families in the same neighborhood, they feel, they wouldn't have gotten through the hard times; and they are deeply appreciative of the help they received.

Didi and Chuck are proud of their family and proud of their kids, and they are proud to adhere to traditional family values. Their best friends are their relatives—siblings, in-laws, cousins—and other people they grew up and went to high school with.

Didi and Chuck also fit well with the Cultural Narrative. They see themselves in most boy-meets-girl stories on TV or in the movies, and feel many people like themselves depicted in the culture that surrounds them. They laugh at having been high school sweethearts, and feel they are doing well as a couple now. Didi and Chuck are in fact living lives much like others in their family and community. They don't spend a lot of time worrying about their "relationship." TV sitcoms and popular movies suit them fine, and popular songs often express the feelings they have for each other as well as the feelings they have in the secret corners of their hearts. They're a bit wary of all the new changes they perceive in society, don't much trust people who are different from themselves. But they have an optimistic view of the future, and unbounded confidence in their ability to make things work out well for themselves.

Lil and Harry are different. She earns most of the money and is very much a woman of the world, while he is a homebody, who likes to read, listen to classical music, and cook. Harry is often out of work, which was fine when they had young children, because he could take care of them, but they thought of it then as a temporary arrangement. Lil's parents frequently wonder how she is doing with this arrangement, and her friends openly oppose it. Even when Lil is content, they maintain that she is being exploited. Maybe if they had been left alone, Lil and Harry would have lived easily with their arrangement, but they haven't. As they often say, they are not "Mr. and Mrs. Mainstream."

This affects them in three dramatic ways. First, despite assuring outsiders that they like their arrangement, they frequently fight about Harry's "failure" to work, sometimes to the point where Lil threatens divorce. Second, the internal and external doubts raised by their role reversal wound up amplifying some other, earlier, feelings of personal failure; and, for a time, they experienced difficulties in their sexual life together. Third, in order to cope with the judgment of others, they have isolated themselves a good deal—which brings them closer, in love and in conflict, but which also makes them miss the comfort of family and friends.

Susan and Judith are a lesbian couple, "out" within the safer confines of the lesbian community but still "not out" at work and to Susan's family. They have had none of the ritual markers, like weddings and family gatherings, which help formalize and sustain a relationship. They have struggled with cultural stigma and with their own internalized versions of it. This need for struggle has been explicit, prolonged, and productive. With the help of friends and therapists, they have come both to accept their difference and to understand that their relationship is not so "different" as others might think. As Judith sometimes quips, "We are pretty good candidates for Yuppie heaven, what with our two good jobs, two cars, bank accounts, and Caribbean vacations." For reasons they do not really wish to explore, they are relieved at how regular they are.

Gail and Grant are older. They have invested a lot of time and energy in their marriage, and have stuck together through both the hard times and the good. Their children are now grown, and live scattered around the country, coming back home only for family events like Thanksgiving or Christmas, birthdays or anniversaries.

They have several other friends like themselves. They worry when their friends have problems, and they are pleased when they manage to "work things out." Together they feel that the country has strayed far from the values of their own upbringing. They do not recognize themselves or their experience in the half-hour evening programs they watch on TV. Watching the latest advertisements for perfume, beer, or jeans, they shake their heads and think wistfully of the songs and stories of their own era. They remain loyal to the values of their own youth: fidelity, commitment, marriage, hard work. To them, the youth of today has simply abandoned everything that might hold a family together.

Each of these couples has an immediate, personal relationship to the Cultural Narrative. They are not simply influenced by broad sociological "trends." They interact directly with prevailing ideas about men, women, and couples, sometimes consciously, sometimes not. Struggling against its standards or trying hard to meet them shapes their lives. The Cultural Narrative is a third presence in the relationship, setting one partner against another, praising and criticizing, calming and instigating conflict.

A couple's relationship with the Cultural Narrative is probably strongest at the beginning, when the partners evaluate both each other and the relationship to decide if they are right. But it continues throughout their lives together, raising its voice at critical junctures, like anniversaries and Valentine's Day ("Does she love me?" "Why aren't we more romantic?" "Why didn't he get me a gift?"). When change occurs, the Cultural Narrative pushes forth. When a woman who has been primarily an at-home mother returns to a job outside the home, the couple will ask, "Is this right?" When couples must make adjustments because of illness or lost jobs, affairs, retirement, or geographical moves, they will renew their relationship with the Cultural Narrative. At every turning of the road, they ask, "Should we be doing things *this* way?" and they think of the stories they have heard and the resolves they have made.

## Patti and Marshall

Patti and Marshall met in a supermarket late one afternoon, shopping for groceries. Wheeling her cart rapidly down one of the aisles, with her four-year-old son, Simon, riding in the child seat, Patti ran smack into Marshall. He was absentmindedly entering the aisle from the corridor to the right, a red plastic shopping basket in one hand and a pile of books in the other. Patti's cart knocked Marshall down, and his books went flying in every direction. Simon started laughing, but Patti's first impulse was to get angry.

"Hey, why don't you watch where you're going?" she cried, her heart pounding. "Someone could have gotten hurt." Marshall looked up at her, a bemused expression on his face. "I guess so," he said, brushing off his pants. "But I'm all right."

"My son could have gotten hurt," she insisted.

Marshall got to his feet and drifted over to Patti's cart. He peered at Simon, who was giggling in the cart, then grinned. "I guess he's okay, too. Hey, I'm sorry. I guess I was thinking of something else instead of where I was going." He pushed his glasses back on his nose and began gathering the books up off the floor.

When she saw Simon giggling, Patti couldn't help smiling herself. She bent down to help Marshall pick up the books. "You really okay?" she said.

"Mm-hmm. Yeah," he answered.

"I guess I was going pretty fast?" she said.

"Oh, I don't know," he said. "But you do pack a mean wallop in that cart."

They continued talking. He was entranced by her face, by her funny way of speaking out of the corner of her mouth; he also liked the sparkle in her eyes. He told her he was a biology teacher at the high school. She said she was living with her son, not working now, but taking a photography course. He seemed so easygoing to her, so laid back, so friendly, that she wound up asking him over for potluck dinner. "Maybe it's fate," she said, laughing. "We shouldn't miss the chance." He'd agreed, and the two of them had spent a wonderful evening "just talking."

If the truth be told, it was love at first sight for Marshall. Patti, so full of energy and excitement, so fetching, made him feel alive. Patti liked Marshall, too; she found him more of a "really nice man" than anything else but he calmed and comforted her. She was used to moving in a faster lane than she thought he'd be comfortable with and she wasn't ready for a relationship: she had too much to do to get back on her feet, take care of Simon, pass her photography course, begin supporting herself now that her parents had limited the money they could send her. Still, she felt good about herself when she was with him; at his invitation, and without her thinking too much about it, they started seeing each other more.

Patti came from a strict, traditional family in northern Wisconsin. Her father was an insurance broker; her mother taught elementary school. She had an older sister and a younger brother, but was critical of them both for remaining "too close" to their parents. She herself had wanted to move as far away as possible. For the past few years she'd had to remain financially dependent on her parents, which galled her no end, for she was resentful of their moralizing and critical intrusiveness. The only family member she admired was her aunt Belle, an independent, free-spirited woman who had never married. Aunt Belle lived in Madison, Wisconsin, where she worked in the university library and filled her life with exciting friends, creative pastimes, and fascinating vacations.

Marshall came from a religious southern family. His father had died suddenly in an accident when he was seven. His mother had always worked odd jobs to support him and his older brother: waitress, cashier, file clerk in the courthouse. She was an attractive, intelligent woman who never remarried. Alternatively cloying and distant, she had undergone several bouts of depression since Marshall's father died. Most of her ambition seemed to spill over onto Marshall's brother, a fledgling broker; but she had pressed Marshall to read more, to study hard, and to go to church.

Marshall was a dreamy kid. He hadn't gone to church, but he had read, and he was interested in the outdoors, sports, and nature. He'd been a good student in high school, and had won an out-of-state scholarship to the University of Wisconsin. He liked the area and remained around afterwards, teaching in the public high school in a town near Madison. After four years he was well-liked, a successful teacher, and especially popular with the kids.

Patti had gone to the University of Wisconsin, too. In her junior year, she'd gotten romantically involved with one of the graduate students, Bill, the instructor in her art class. They'd had a stormy relationship, involving drugs and a lot of drinking, and Patti had become pregnant. She and Bill found an apartment off-campus and moved in together, and she dropped out of school and had the child. But when Simon was only two months old, Bill left, claiming that she "wasn't the same anymore." He claimed she loved the baby more than him, and he resented her being "turned off" sexually. Besides, he said, he was too young to be a father. Patti felt furious at being abandoned. She applied for welfare, borrowed money from her parents, and started planning how she could get back on track again.

Patti and Marshall's relationship moved ahead quickly. They seemed to click together, and, as the days went on, Patti responded to Marshall's innocent humor and charm. She was impressed by how good he was with Simon, and by how much Simon liked him. She believed that every boy should have a father figure in his life; and, if Marshall was to be the one for Simon, his lack of machismo and his willingness to help out with domestic chores made him a better male image than most. For his part, Marshall enjoyed having an "instant family." He loved kids, and he loved spending time with Simon. Most importantly, he was passionately drawn to Patti and determined to be with her.

One day Marshall proposed and Patti accepted. She got off welfare and began working afternoons as a receptionist in an orthopedic surgeon's office. At the same time, she started taking courses to complete her college degree, and also volunteered a few hours a week as a photographer for a local weekly newspaper. Simon went to nursery school, then kindergarten. Domestic life became routine for them. They split up the chores and enjoyed easy time together. Sometimes, though, especially on weekend evenings after they'd had a few drinks, Patti and Marshall would fight.

The fights often involved sex, which Marshall seemed to want more than she. But he also sometimes criticized her for being too flighty, for not wanting to settle down, and for trying too many things at once. If he implied that this was bad for Simon—echoing criticisms she'd already heard on that subject from both her parents—she would respond loudly and dramatically. She might shout and stamp her feet, or throw things. Marshall would try to stay emotionally above it all; but when things would get to him he would withdraw, sleep on the couch, and feel sorry for himself. If the fight was really serious, they might not make up for a day or two; and then they would walk around the house coldly, not talking to each other, and exchanging messages only through Simon.

After they'd been married for close to a year, the question of their having a child together was in the air, hanging over them like a fog. Marshall felt it would be good for Simon to have a brother or a sister. And he felt it would be a sign of Patti's love for him for her to make a baby with him. But Patti saw another child as a curse: she'd *never* be able to get her career on track then. She'd always be stuck with diapers and dinners, just like her mom.

## Patti, Marshall, and the Cultural Narrative

Patti and Marshall have an uneven fit with the Cultural Narrative. As individuals, they are defiant. Patti has had a child out of wedlock and has placed her career on a more-than-equal footing with motherhood. She is brash and sometimes abrasive, not always showing the soft, supportive qualities that are traditionally esteemed in women. Marshall is softer at times, quicker to cry or make up, more domestic in his orientation. Although he is comfortably settled in his job, he is actually less ambitious than Patti. Some people might accuse Patti of being "unwomanly," even though she is very much in keeping with contemporary trends for women; and some might say that Marshall is "not manly enough," even though he holds down a steady job, and likes sports, sex, and canoeing.

Patti and Marshall began their relationship by falling madly in love. This was "as it should be," although the seeds of discontent were already present: Patti was wary from the start about depending too much on a man. Marshall mistrusted overcontrolling women, but he earnestly courted Patti and, despite her reservations, she loved it. Their sex life was romantic, passionate, and reciprocal; they exulted in the way it "completed" them.

They also enjoyed how they complemented each other: She was the fiery core, the "energy of my life," according to Marshall. He was the "rock" from which she could launch her career in photography. Since he held a steady job, his support of her more erratic, artistic career fit well within the traditional boundaries of male-female relationships. However much they might feel like misfits as individuals, their couple relationship fit within the bounds of the Cultural Narrative, and Patti and Marshall found this reassuring: it permitted them to have their cake and eat it, too.

They were proud of being different, she with her ambition and he with his apparently uncomplicated domesticity, both informed by contemporary feminist ideology. For a few years, conformity and deviation melded well, but they began to pull apart when Marshall pushed Patti to have a second child. Besides worrying that Marshall would favor a new child over her son, Patti worried that a new baby would interfere with her education and developing career. Marshall accused her of thinking only of herself; he argued that Simon would profit by having a sibling, and that a child would deepen their marriage.

The more Marshall argued for child and family and pressed closer, the more Patti insisted on being able to finish up her degree and begin pursuing her own career. He felt that she was pulling back from the relationship. The claims of the two individuals thus clashed against those of the couple. When Marshall became confused and depressed and withdrew his support, Patti became frightened and furious. She called him inconsistent, and a wimp. He called her selfish, and a bitch. In their minds, they believed each other's accusations and wondered whether their marriage could last.

Patti mused morosely that you couldn't have a man and a career at the same time; she felt she'd been a fool to let her guard down. Marshall had said he'd be glad to do the lion's share of caring for the new baby, but Patti knew better than to believe that of a man. Besides, deep down, she found it hard to give up the idea that if anyone should take care of the baby, it should be her. Patti never said this directly, for it contradicted her beliefs, but the way she acted implied it.

Marshall painfully remembered his conviction that women, like his mother, would never believe in him and would always try to take control of his life. Early in their relationship, then, divorce loomed ominously. They didn't know where to turn. They had isolated themselves from their families, and most of their friends didn't know how to manage any better than they did. Thrown back on their own resources, they had to confess they really didn't know how to make this new kind of relationship work.

After two years of classes, Patti got her degree. She continued working part-time at the doctor's office, but now began taking art and photography classes, and spending more time trying to do freelance photography. It was hard, but she felt she was gaining a toehold with the local press, and her confidence was building. Suddenly, the orthopedist informed her he was expanding his office work: she would have to put in more time or lose her job. She was thrown into conflict. She wanted to be a photographer, not a full-time receptionist. Marshall's job was steady; so she quit.

For the next few months, though, she found it hard to create the kind of photography she wanted to do, and she hit a roadblock in terms of selling her work. She felt stuck and began doubting her talent. Depressed, angry, and feeling like a failure, she gave in to Marshall and agreed to have another child. She quickly became pregnant. He was elated. The two of them began making plans ... and then she miscarried. Seeing the whole experience as a mistake and a failure, she turned her wrath on Marshall, and the two of them spiraled downward into Contraction. (This part of their lives will be dealt with in later chapters.)

Several years later, after their relationship had survived this and other crises, Patti would become pregnant again, and this time her pregnancy would go to term. Like Jonathan and Marie, though, this couple would go through several periods of hard times during their life together. They would have to deal with Marshall's developing diabetes; and several years later, after Patti had had the child Marshall had always wanted, Patti would have to cope with the death of her Aunt Belle, who had been her model and inspiration.

Patti and Marshall were living out the themes of their generation: the growing autonomy of the couple; the influence of the women's movement; the impact of imminent divorce; the claims of selfishness; the difficulty of enduring relationships. But they often saw themselves as abnormal failures during this period. The Cultural Narrative may acknowledge conflict, but it leaves little room for prolonged discord and unresolvable dilemmas.

In fact, Patti and Marshall are following several paths at once, but each path contains its opposite. Patti's ambition is consistent with contemporary ideals of gender equality, but to pursue this path she abandons the emphasis on relatedness that is both a traditional and contemporary feminine value. Marshall's nurturance and domesticity suit the "new age" man but jeopardize his sense of traditional manhood. These contradictions make it hard for them to accept themselves, and they end up careening among various relationships to the Cultural Narrative, including accommodation and defiance, self-affirmation and self-condemnation.

Patti and Marshall have a volatile relationship to the Cultural Narrative. When they are down on each other, as they are in the Stage of Contraction and Betrayal, they see themselves unable to meet its demands. Their response is either to intensify their defiance or to sink into despair at their inability to fit in. In the Stage of Expansion and Promise, they interpret themselves as keeping more closely with their own version of a modern Cultural Narrative. Patti's failure as a traditional woman, for example, becomes recast as an integral part of her effort to become a new kind of woman. Marshall's domesticity is called courageous. Together, they believe they are forging a new model of relationship. When they finally arrive at a Stage of Resolution, they can live more comfortably with the contradictions and the complexity of their relationship.

If Patti and Marshall deviate too far from the Cultural Narrative, they stretch their capacity for self-affirmation. Then they get nervous and feel off balance. Such disequilibrium sometimes precipitates a shift from one stage to another: when they are too expansive, they contract; when they are contracted, fearing the loss of their relationship, they pull together. Patti's next pregnancy, for example, threw them into a mutual depression—she because she feared the end of her independence, he because he felt blamed and criticized for the way things were turning out.

The actual birth of their baby, however, catapulted them back into Expansion. The new child was marvelous, and she brought them together, making them feel more like a family. And it did seem good for Simon. Patti remembered fondly that one of the main reasons she had been attracted to Marshall in the first place was that he seemed like such a good father. This almost-forgotten trait now moved into the foreground. It was like a new beginning. When Patti saw Marshall sprawled on the floor with the two children, it reminded her of their first meeting in the supermarket.

Deviation from the Cultural Narrative may thus precipitate developmental shifts in the couple, and developmental shifts may help the couple reinterpret their fit with the Cultural Narrative. The relationship between couples and the Cultural Narrative is dynamic and ongoing.

## What Is the Cultural Narrative?

The Cultural Narrative is the sum of society's messages about how people are supposed to do things. In our time, the Cultural Narrative about couples begins with a very simple story. A couple consists of a man and a woman who meet, fall in love, and remain together for life. They solve all their problems, keep their love alive, live independently of their families, encourage each other's personal development, have healthy and happy children, and endure as partners and friends. It is rare for couples to follow this script perfectly to a "T," but for most Americans the idea of the forever couple remains a compelling ideal.

The Cultural Narrative presents couples with the conventional wisdom about the right and wrong ways to start out, how and when they should or shouldn't live together, when (if heterosexual) they should marry, how they should handle arguments, who should take the lead in matters of daily living, how they should deal with friends and family, and how they should look at disputes. It presents a composite portrait of the preferred rites, routes, and routines that couples should follow and serves as a filter through which they will weigh both their experience and that of their friends.

The Cultural Narrative thus anchors universal themes like love and heroism, sex, courtship, marriage, and gender to the particular imagery of a given society. It also brings archetypal characters into specific cultural focus. For example, the hero in search of his or her destiny today might be cast as an entrepreneur who begins with an idea, develops it with a few close friends in a basement laboratory, and transforms the idea into a major software company. Or it might appear as the "working girl" struggling against all odds for respect and independence.

The Cultural Narrative is more than just a "perspective." It is the actual means by which a culture puts forth, promotes, and imposes its standards on its members, particularly the young. Those who fit well with its story are more comfortable in society and, perhaps, with themselves. Those who do not fit must struggle. They are punished: internally, through discomfort and shame; and externally, by the representatives of society—employers, parents, the in crowd, etc.

In transitional historical periods, the Cultural Narrative generally presents both sides of important issues. Movies like *Working Girl* and *Prince of Tides* promote images of career-minded women whose ambition is considered reasonable in its own right and because the women are sexy, attractive, and yield to men. A film like *Terms of Endearment* or *Parenthood* reinforces the conventional wisdom that women should be concerned mainly with relationships.

## Jonathan, Marie, and the Cultural Narrative

While couples have complex relationships to the Cultural Narrative, these relationships generally consist of several basic responses. Let us describe some of these with respect to our first couple, Jonathan and Marie.

*Defiance.* Like most couples of their generation, Jonathan and Marie believed their lives would be different from those of their parents—that is, from the Cultural Narrative of their parents' time. Marie was not going to stay home and "just" raise children. Her mother had passed on a more ambitious, more ambivalent message: "Be like me but better." "Better" meant: Be more independent so you can achieve things. Marie absorbed this message, but—believing herself a liberated woman—buried its first part for many years. When she married, her mother, who now wanted a daughter-companion who could validate her life, pressed Marie to stay home and have children.

Marie felt betrayed by her mother's turnaround, and she became contemptuous and defiant. Since she was a medical resident during this period, it was easy for her to turn to work with a vengeance. Jonathan supported her choice because his view of marriage included having an independent, working wife with whom he would share domestic tasks and child rearing. He was damned if *he* was going to be distant and autocratic like his father (who had left his care almost entirely to his mother). Jonathan knew that his parents would have liked him to marry someone like his high school sweetheart, a smart-enough "girl" who would support his career and raise his children, but, by choosing Marie, he rejected that idea.

*Compliance.* Compliance can be eager, urgent, placid, or ironic. Jonathan and Marie found themselves in an ironic compliance with the contemporary Cultural Narrative. They joked with themselves and with friends about how they had two careers, two cars, two children, a dog, a cat, and a house in the suburbs. They dressed stylishly, went to the "right" movies, read the right books, and—except when it became important for their children's education—pursued very little religious observance. Jonathan in particular felt this to be a sad irony. He had been "different" as a kid, too smart and interested in politics to fit into his hometown crowd, a loner in high school who took refuge in Greenwich Village with its motley array of folk singers, beatniks, and political radicals. Through much internal effort, he had turned his fear of exclusion into a mark of pride. Later, he and Marie felt themselves very much part of the cultural ferment of the sixties. Now it was deflating for them to see themselves like everybody else, and, worse, to have little energy to fight it.

*Accommodation.* Many individuals and couples judge themselves as defective according to the Cultural Narrative. As a result, people spend a lot of time and energy either regretting their failure or trying to make up for it in a variety of ways—like being "Super Mom," working full-time while taking care of children and household almost single-handedly, and making love often and passionately "enough," or "Macho Man," performing dazzling professional feats while ritually working out every day at 5:00 A.M., coaching children's sports teams, renovating houses on the weekend, and claiming to have an endless sexual hunger.

Individuals are forever trying to be thinner, smarter, stronger. Couples, following society's prescriptions, are forever trying to be more sexual, more communicative, closer yet more independent. If one partner wants to try, but the other resists, their effort to accommodate to the Cultural Narrative becomes a major bone of contention.

Jonathan and Marie were disappointed that their relationship was not more romantic nor their sexual life more passionate. True, they were good friends and partners, but each felt cheated by the lack of passion. He emphasized the need for sex, she longed for romance.

They also believed in an intermingling of roles. With the birth of their first child, Marie took a two-month maternity leave, while Jonathan only took two weeks—even so, a brave move considering the dinosaurs who ran his law firm. Within six months, though, they were sharing child care equally. This felt right but not necessarily good to them. In fact, they each held deep, old-fashioned imagery about children; and, in some sense, each wanted Marie to stay home, Jonathan to "provide," and for them as a couple to greet each other at the end of the day just as their parents had done in their best moments. Their accommodation to the Cultural Narrative cheated them of following their more deeply held imagery.

After several small fights, when Marie implied that she wanted Jonathan to admire her as a mother (as her father had admired her mother), they admitted what they jokingly called their "reactionary sentiments." They then decided to risk the wrath of their friends. After their second child, Marie stopped working for nine months. Jonathan worked harder to earn more money, and they tried to live on less. Those were among the best months of their lives together. To be sure, Marie had already put in over ten years of work and was by then both well-established in her career and less impressed by success. She was also far enough from resenting her mother's self-sacrifice to yield to her own desire for family.

There are many other experiences of the Cultural Narrative. For example, virtually any couple from a subculture *resents* the prevailing picture of happy, affluent, "white-bread" couples. Some working-class couples find it aggravating to see such affluent couples on TV. Gay and lesbian couples rarely see themselves reflected—let alone positively represented—in the Cultural Narrative. But resentment is not limited to minority groups. Every couple who has tried to be perfect and failed bears some resentment toward others who appear to have fit the bill better. Most couples at least *envy* others who they think have attained the cultural stereotypes better than they. Yet, as we have suggested, most couples have a distinctive mix of all these responses.

## Multiple Cultural Narratives

At any one time the Cultural Narrative contains at least three elements: reworked archetypal images, images particular to a certain culture or country, and images particular to a certain historical era.

The Cultural Narrative offers a blend of coexisting stories. It is itself a fabric of many threads. Each generation grows up with its own predominant Cultural Narrative and communicates its story to the next generation, which, in turn, communicates stories to the next. Because of this, several generations of the Cultural Narrative are always residual in each person, always ready to influence him or her.

The Cultural Narrative continually evolves. Changes in society, shifts in cultural attitudes, economic conditions, national boundaries: all affect it. It grows out of historical traditions, contains residues from the past, and yet develops its unique identity each generation.

The prevailing image of couple life, for example, has shifted decade by decade in our lifetime. The fifties largely upheld the monogamous, sex-role-stereotyped twosome. Sex was to be postponed until marriage. Wives would not work. Movies ended happily, with romance and marriage, while straying husbands returned to their wives, and evildoers were punished. Togetherness was the ideal.

The generation of the late sixties—at least the vocal, avant-garde element—challenged whatever forms they had been handed: the nuclear family, monogamy, the acceptance of racist attitudes and institutions. Relationships were suddenly seen again as an aspect of community. After the civil rights and antiwar movements, women made their move for "liberation." Women were encouraged to work outside the home. Premarital sex was permitted, and often encouraged, if the partners loved each other. In the seventies, women seized much of the cultural agenda. Men were asked to confront issues of child care and domestic equality. Premarital sex was everyone's prerogative and a regular part of dating.

In the eighties, attention shifted to ideals of self-interest and self-fulfillment and retreated from the benign view of human nature that had informed the sixties. The increasing public awareness of domestic violence, incest, and drug and alcohol abuse, among other crimes perpetuated within the home, made people, particularly women, more cautious. And in the eighties, women established themselves, like the suffragettes of the nineteenth century, as the moral arbiters of couple relationships. Feeling defensive, men tended to withdraw from this bid for moral supremacy or else to fight back. Thus the 1950s story about coupling, which persists to the present day in our remembered hopes, lives side by side with the reemergent story about the battle of the sexes.

The media tend to homogenize cultural experience, but neighborhood, family, and class forces diversify it. Gay and lesbian communities, for example, are increasingly public in their insistence upon the validity of their own life-styles. The constant influx of new, different people through immigration has promoted a growing sense of national, cultural, and class differentiation. Each ethnic or racial group has its own particular Cultural Narratives about family life, marriage, gender roles, and the place of children. Couples whose partners are from different subgroups have to contend with the conflict between society's dominant Cultural Narrative, which is distinct from their own and different still from their experience. The "second generation" of immigrant families tends toward greater assimilation; they are caught between their loyalty to their family's narrative and their wish to approximate more closely the narrative of the dominant, white culture. Furthermore, it would not be much of an exaggeration to say that women and men in our society adhere to different "cultures"—certainly, to rather different interpretations of the dominant Cultural Narrative.

The Cultural Narratives of subgroups mediate between couples and the dominant narrative. Gays and lesbians, for example, create their own cultural narratives about relationships, sexuality, fidelity, gender, and attractiveness. Members of minority groups must know the majority culture as a matter of survival. They can describe it, imitate it, and state how it is different from their own. This knowledge, expressed, for example, in the humor or songs it spawns, reduces the shame and confusion they might otherwise feel for falling short of the prescriptions in the Cultural Narrative. Since almost all couples are more or less part of racial, ethnic, regional, or just community subgroups, it is fair to say that each of us experiences the Cultural Narrative through subcultural filters.

## An Interweave of Narratives

All of us organize our individual experience into stories or narratives, which lend shape to the events of our lives. In repeating our story, we come to know ourselves and shape our identity. Throughout the book we will refer to this story-as-identity as an Individual Narrative. Of course, whatever stories we tell about ourselves are limited by the Cultural Narrative, which shapes and influences how we experience ourselves and others.

Members of every couple organize their experience together into a common story. This does not have to be a conscious process; it just happens. Over time, they build up a common repertoire that lets them say, "We are like this, but not like that." Or, "We are solid and staid, not the life of the party." As with the Individual Narratives, this Couple Narrative changes with new experience. It is both continuous and adaptive, providing couples with an ongoing sense of identity.[2]

The interplay of Individual, Couple, and Cultural Narratives is continual and dynamic. Consider how relationships begin. We tend to choose people who support the positive threads of our Individual Narratives and with whom we are most likely to create an ideal relationship, as selected from the Cultural Narrative. But this initial situation does not last in its pristine form. One day we behave so badly that our partner cannot keep supporting the "better" view we've chosen in our Individual Narrative. This threatens and enrages us, so we blame and demean our partner. Paradise is lost. But we still need a story that makes sense of this fall from Paradise. We will find one out of all those available in the Cultural Narrative. We might, for example, decide that this crisis represents an opportunity for growth, that such a challenge will enlarge our vision. Or, if we are more influenced by the more traditional Cultural Narrative of our parents' day, we might acknowledge that such difficulties happen but we will eventually "adjust" to them.

Each major change in the partners or the partnership makes us check in with the Cultural Narrative. For instance, the birth of a child, a major professional advance, or a woman's return to work outside the home can create an "identity crisis." When a woman goes out to work, her partner may wonder if this means he is not manly enough to support the whole family. At the same time, he may be deeply grateful for the needed income. If a man's job requires a move that would wrench a woman from her family, friends, and (perhaps) her job, she may well be resentful: but will she then also criticize herself for not being a good woman to her man?

Each threat to one partner's Individual Narrative reverberates in the couple. For instance, the man who is threatened by his wife's working might withdraw into himself, avoid sex, or, alternatively, insist on more sex to compensate for his loss of dignity. In the first instance, the woman may feel unloved or unattractive, reinforcing the belief that work makes a woman less desirable. In the second instance, she may feel invaded and controlled. Both situations can make the couple question their relationship. This questioning will take place against the backdrop of the Cultural Narrative, within whose parameters the couple will seek solutions. Most couples in this situation will not make the connection between their sexual or work-related dilemmas and the threat to their Individual Narratives, but they will question their relationship. Is it as strong as they thought? Has the spark gone forever? Have they made the right choice? Are they inadequate, according to the Cultural Narrative?

The relationship between couples and the Cultural Narrative remains dynamic because partners are attuned to different aspects of life. Men and women approach things differently, and may emphasize different aspects of the "same" experience. Women's interpretations are filtered through their experience as women—and also by the burgeoning feminist literature, which has clarified women's particular ways of seeing and thinking about the world.[3] Men tend to be more isolated in their thinking; they try to work things out by themselves. Their interpretation of the Cultural Narrative is often inarticulate and defensive: they feel they are losing or have lost their power in the relationship.

Either partner at any time may cite the Cultural Narrative to bolster his or her position. This can be to remind their mate of some social amenity—opening the door for them, not opposing what they say in public. It may be a way of gently scolding them for some gauche act or word: "Don't chew with your mouth open." "Horace, we just can't sleep together in my parents' house before we're married." Or it may be a way of more strongly bringing them into line for inappropriate behavior: "It's not right to shout like that at someone you love. Do it again, and I'm walking out!" The Cultural Narrative may be hauled in to "prove a point" in an argument and show that the mate is wrong: "Everyone knows that happily married women aren't *supposed* to flirt with single men at a party."

At times, bringing in the Cultural Narrative may simply add fuel to a smoldering fire. What follows is more like a courtroom debate (for example, who should cook dinner on a night they both work late) than a discussion between partners. But a couple can also resolve arguments within the parameters of the Cultural Narrative. If both partners accept its conventions, it can act as a guide to their behavior. The Cultural Narrative, for example, holds that it's good for couples who disagree to compromise—a position that helps many couples move ahead in the Stage of Resolution.

The active interplay of couples and the Cultural Narrative continues through each of the three stages. Couples refer to the Cultural Narrative to gauge their joy in Expansion, their misery in Contraction, and their problem-solving in Resolution. They will return to the tenets of Cultural Narrative as they cycle through the stages again: "Uh-oh, here we go, back into the muck again," they may say, recognizing a turn into Contraction. Or, "I can't take another round of this arguing. It nearly killed me last time. Count me out."

In sum, the Cultural Narrative structures the *social* world in which couples live. Now let us explore how each of the partners has structured his or her own inner, *psychological* world in preparation for their first meeting, long before it has ever occurred.

# 4

---

## SETTING THE STAGE

---

Many powerful influences converge upon each individual, setting the stage for the partners to come together.

Some influences, like the biological urge to reproduce the species, are universal and "hard-wired" in our genes. Others, like the need for connection and closeness, seem rooted in the experience of all primates. We have already discussed in the previous chapter ways in which the Cultural Narrative shapes how we court and negotiate with each other.

Other factors that might draw the partners toward each other at this particular time reflect the partners' own individual experience and character. Before the partners ever set eyes on each other, each has developed a unique style and personality, as well as complex expectations about what will and what should happen in a relationship. These *strictly personal* elements involve inner images that we carry with us our whole life long.

## Internal Images

We filter information about our relationships through internal images or mental templates.[1] These act like transparencies, permitting some information in, blocking other information out, distorting it all in some way. Imagine two women, for example, looking at the same man. One sees his straightforward way of speaking as assertive and feels therefore assured; the other sees it as aggressive and feels endangered. Taken all together, these templates form a cognitive map that shapes and organizes the information we receive every day.

These templates represent our general premises, the sum of what any particular person feels is true about life: good deeds will come back around; people must be married to find fulfillment; a woman must have nice legs to be sexy; if someone tries hard enough, he or she will succeed; people are generally reliable, unselfish (or the opposite). These templates are not objective facts, but they *feel* objective. They describe reality as we ourselves believe it: how things are, and how things ought to be; who we think we are, and who we want to be; how we think others see us, and how we want them to see us. And each person's inner reality is distinct.

The templates that most directly concern couples are internalized images of relationships: you can trust a man who is nice to children; women who smile make good mates; people who lose their tempers are dangerous; it isn't love if you don't do everything together. Experiences with our mother, father, siblings, and others form powerful impressions, like engravings on some inner wall of our psyche, which become the standards against which all other relationships are measured. These templates become our givens. We work and rework them all our lives, and they constantly influence how we feel and act in the world.

With repeated experience, for example, one child learns he can trust his mother when something worries him. Later in life, he may continue to trust women with his secrets. Another child has a different experience: whenever he tells his mother what worries him, she listens briefly and then changes the subject. He winds up feeling betrayed and inadequate, and later in life may find himself reluctant to share his feelings with his wife.

Repeated trauma, such as physical or sexual abuse, leaves profound self-shattering impressions. Even single traumatic incidents can leave indelible internal images (and the need to defend against recurrence). Many women incest survivors, for example, find it impossible to believe that their husbands, no matter how gentle and reliable they are, are *not* abusive people, too, or about to become so.

These templates are so strong, they often prevail long after new events contradict them. In one couple, for example, an ordinarily assertive woman lost both her job and mother at the same time, and became increasingly needy for attention and commitment. Her husband, who believed that men can never "really" satisfy women, could only experience her tears and pleas as demands. Nothing, not even others' observations, could persuade him that she really did need his love.

Templates are also shaped by other important relationships—our first love, revered teachers, close friends, even a business partner. The intensity, for example, with which ten-year-old "best friends" engage each other builds a model that often influences the yearnings, expectations, and fears in later friendships, marriage partners, and professional relations.

While these images are usually not conscious, few are so embedded in dark, inaccessible places that they cannot be teased out with a little reflection. Ask a woman, for example, how men respond to criticism, praise, or tenderness, and she will tell you. She might hesitate, say it depends on *what* man, but she will then express her inner conviction about the matter. Ask a man what would happen if he and a woman had a task to do together—a jigsaw puzzle, paying the month's bills, going shopping—and he, too, will impose the major outlines of his templates onto the situation. Most of us can play out entire scenes with potential partners long before the scenes ever take place. Our accumulated images are like open-ended scripts: they provide a base for improvising in almost any situation we might meet.

Unconsciously, we project these images onto the external world like moving pictures onto a screen.[2] Then we see them everywhere and react to them as if they did indeed exist "out there." We experience our projections as perceptions. Our mental templates set the stage for and contextualize all our relationships.

Of course, no partner acts exactly like an image, and this can present a problem. We try to solve that problem by *inducing* our partners to act more like the image we project onto them. Again, this process is mostly unconscious, and it only comes briefly to consciousness if the lack of fit between template and partner prods us into some recognition of what is going on. If, for example, I cast the image of a rejecting person onto you and then act as if you were indeed rejecting me, you might pull away, be critical, or otherwise treat me rejectingly. The closer your actions mirror my projections, the more my beliefs about who you are are confirmed. Suppose that earlier in our relationship you were more accepting toward me. Even though I might like to hold onto this "accepting" person, I gradually come to see it as a "cover," a pretense that hides your true rejecting self.

This is not a static process, however, and our images do change. Induction is imperfect. If you continue to behave in ways that don't fit my images of you, then—unless I am rigidly closed to experience—my images will have to change. Not only will I revise my image of you, but the powerful mental templates that shape my ideas of relationships in general may also shift.

The formation, projection, and reflection of templates are a normal and natural process. Projection is characteristic of all human interaction. Our partners often do a good deal to draw forth our images, and the projection of images is interactional. I may project images onto you and induce you to behave in certain ways, but your actions also tend to selectively draw forth certain projections of mine. At the same time the reverse is happening, with your projecting images onto me, inducing my behavior, and so on. Over time these reciprocal processes become patterned so that some of our images become more central to the relationship while others become peripheral.

This is what makes couples so complex. Internal templates always mediate each partner's relation with the other. Even when they think they are on the same stage, the partners are often acting out their own separate dramas that overlap in varying ways. This is one reason they argue so frequently about whose "reality" is correct, feel hurt when the other does not validate their sense of reality, and are relieved when they reach a common vision.

Many people (and most psychotherapists) characterize such fighting as a struggle for control, and, indeed, they are struggles: but they arise because each partner perceives "reality" differently.

We constantly filter feedback from our partners through our templates. In the process, some of what they tell us reaches us so deeply that it can even change the templates. Because we know ourselves through our own templates, such changes can alter our sense of ourselves as well. This is what happens through new events and new relationships. A loving relationship can thus help make an insecure person more secure; a steady, honest relationship can heal the hurts of an abusive childhood.

Relationships are not so much a meeting of "objective" realities as a mutual encountering of two people's layered images and perceptions. Our identities, to which we look for a sense of stability, depend on the coherence of our templates. While we are loath to change them substantially or to let others challenge them, we can nonetheless amend them under the influence of powerful new experiences.

Let's illustrate some of these points. Helen had an extraordinarily steady and supportive father. She believes that all the men she likes are also steady and supportive (at least at heart), and she will usually explain their behavior, even when it contradicts this image, by her belief. During the expansive phase of a relationship, she need not rationalize how good things feel. When her relationships finally move into Contraction, however, she feels cruelly betrayed; and she bitterly attacks her partner for falling so far short of the person he had promised (and pretended!) to be.

Larry's father was inaccessible and withdrawn; his mother was overinvolved with his life. Larry always chooses responsive, needy women. In Expansion, they shower him with affection and approval, and this seems to repair the injury caused by his father's absence; later, though, these same women always seem to demand more of Larry than he is prepared to give. Then he complains that they are just like his mother.

Mary was raised in a highly critical and abusive home. Even though she is trying to get beyond her early experience, part of her still believes she deserved the abuse, because deep down she is bad. She forms tentative relationships with gentle, somewhat superficial men, hoping that they will fail to see the depths of her evil nature. But the men always seem to have an angry, critical side, whose emergence never surprises her. Their criticism proves what she had always known. During Expansion, she holds her breath, loving the good feelings but distrusting them. When Contraction arrives, she feels it was inevitable, even overdue.

## The Myth of the Perfect Partner

Romantic myth holds that each of us harbors one ideal, one template, and that we spend our lives searching for someone who fits it.

Settling for anyone else is a compromise. Conventional wisdom holds that we all carry one narrow set of images exclusively derived from our parents, and are thus fated to a script shaped by our unresolved issues with them. Whether we get stuck in one such relationship or compulsively enter upon *many* such relationships, this view holds that we will inevitably get together with someone just like our mother or father. In other words, we unconsciously choose our mate as a ticket to redemption. (I look for a woman like my mean mother while I act out a cleaned-up version of my dad.[3] You look for a man like your adoring father while you act out a tougher version of your mom.) It's as though we have a "couple script" waiting inside us and need only find the partner willing to play the complementary role.

In fact, we carry not one but *many* images with us into later life—images from relationships with relatives, friends, and teachers; images of relationships we have observed from without; images in combination. For example, we might absorb parts of our relationship with both parents. Imagine, for instance, that each time we got close to one parent, the other moved in and claimed him or her, leaving us feeling abandoned. Later in life, we might very well be nervous when third parties, even if they were our own children, moved between us and our partners. Alternatively, one parent might have preferred us to the other, leaving us vulnerable to the latter's anger. These are two versions of the Oedipal triangle; there are many others.

Not all mental templates are equally charged. One may be hot, passionate, and dangerous, while another is safe and friendly. Over the course of our lives, one may be more appropriate than another at a given time; and, over time, we may be guided by different templates according to the needs of the moment or to who is available. Mary, for instance, married a gentle, somewhat weak man, the opposite of her powerful, intrusive father, and actually quite like her accommodating mother. After divorcing him, she had a steamy affair with a man who reminded her of her father; and now she finds herself with a third man, who feels most like a peer, almost like her brother. We are often "ready" to meet a person who resonates to a particular set of imagery that then becomes dominant.

This process parallels what Gestalt psychologists call figure and ground.[4] In the *ground* of our psyche are many *figures,* images that can respond potentially to different men and women. Some images become dominant in response to certain people and in certain situations. Certain people evoke certain responses in us. On the other hand, at some times in our lives, one set of images is supreme and we take as partners only people who fit it. This is what happened to Mary when she married her very gentle man. At the time, she could not possibly tolerate the thought of going out with anyone who was overtly assertive. And yet she was equally unprepared for encountering her husband's harsh, critical side, which he had always tried to cover up.

Angry relationships correspond to the pull of our inner images just as much as happy ones. We may be drawn into different patterns or into the same recurrent pattern as our lives go on. The universe of our inner images continues to affect us. This is one reason why relationships change, why partners may drift off toward other people as time goes on, why some people keep falling into the same wretched situation.

We haul our whole repertoire of scripts with us in our search for partners. At any given time, and for whatever reason, one model leaps out of the background and becomes figural. When we are just becoming absorbed in work, for example, our relationship with our siblings may be the most central image, and we will tend to attract and be attracted to sibling-like relationships. If we are obsessed with our relationship to our boss, then parent-child images might become figural. A woman may find herself attracted to a series of relationships like the one she had with her older brother; a man may encounter a woman who reminds him of his first girlfriend in the tenth grade. Alternatively, a strong attraction to one person may precede the script. The other person may have a clearer sense of what he or she wants than we do; and so, acting in a somewhat passive, willing manner, we permit the other to "draw out" (induce) from us a particular model of a couple's relationship. This is an example of the other person's "shaping," "selecting," and "inducing" one response from us from among the wealth of possible responses we possess.

Different partners are fully capable of drawing forth different internal images from us. One partner may elicit childish responses, another parental ones, and still another, reminding us of our best childhood friend, may bring out friendship modes. Most partners in long relationships will bring out more than one of our internal scripts.

## Jonathan and Marie

Let's return to Marie and Jonathan for a moment. Marie's father worked long, hard days and she missed him very much growing up. When he was around, he provided her with intelligent companionship, which she couldn't get from her mother. He was like a pal, and the two of them did everything together: they played games, talked about her school projects, and took "research" trips to factories, forests, museums, and even baseball stadiums. Later, in her married life, while she sometimes regretted Jonathan's devotion to his legal practice, she never resented it. Besides, she was a physician who worked long hours, too, and she had come to expect these separations. During their courtship and early marriage years, she and Jonathan were close when they were home together. Even without a huge amount of time, they could create a magical time together which she savored, just as she had the times with her dad.

The arrival of children further limited their time together. Marie was surprised and then resentful when Jonathan stopped taking advantage of their rare moments alone to seek her out. Now he was acting like the other boyfriends she had refused to marry, not like the man who appeared so ardent during their courtship. This created dissension and discussion. Even when Marie resigned herself to Jonathan's disengagement, she still resented his unwillingness to play enthusiastically with their children, as her father had done.

Jonathan's parents had lived fairly separate lives, each in their own domain. His mother spent all her time with domestic chores, children and parents, reading and volunteer organizations. His father lived for his appliance store, local politics, and TV sports. On weekends, there were ritual gatherings of the extended family and lots of time alone. No one complained. Jonathan expected the same in his marriage, simply assuming that this was how the world was. Previously, he had run from any date who seemed too demanding. When he was courting Marie, she was very much into her work, and Jonathan loved their intense, infrequent times together. He also loved when they studied together, not talking much, but feeling each other's presence and occasionally stopping to make love. Eventually he discovered that Marie liked to talk more than he'd originally thought and he resented it. He felt tricked. His resentment resurfaced around the children's demands for time. Jonathan felt they should play on their own more. He saw their "need" for more time as unnecessary. In his mind, Marie was encouraging their dependence for her own needs, not theirs.

## Patti and Marshall

Inner images helped Marshall and Patti feel right about each other, too. Remember that Marshall's dad had died when he was seven, and he had missed having a father as he was growing up. This loss left him with a wish to be a good father himself. This meant he needed to find a woman who had or could have children, and who understood the importance of nurturing kids. In being a kind father, he would be able to enjoy the pleasure of parenting, but he would also be able to identify with his children, who were receiving the kind of love he'd longed for himself.

Marshall respected women who worked outside the house, like his mother, but he did not like them to exercise any control over his own life. Although he had respected his mother, her inconsistency had caused him to suffer. She'd been distant when he wanted her to be close, close when he wanted her to stay away. In this respect, Patti was perfect for him. He appreciated her constant emotion: "I always know where you *are*," he would say. He adored her warmth and energy. And he appreciated her love for her son, her openness and her honesty.

He didn't even mind her wish to be independent—in fact, he appreciated her courage and energy, so long as it didn't wind up undermining his own schedule. He was secure enough himself in his work and other relationships to be able to give a little and be tolerant. If Patti arbitrarily put her own agenda first, simply expecting him to fit in, though, he bristled. He wanted to be consulted in the matter, wanted to be asked. His resentment of a controlling woman, on whom he was emotionally "dependent," could pull him down into quarrels, spats, and total funks.

For her part, Patti had recoiled in distaste from her cold, strict parents. She wanted a man who had *feelings,* who could be flexible and warm, humorous and supportive. But the man she chose had to accept her desire for being independent. He had to be kind and loving, but also back off when she wanted her own space. In this respect,

Marshall had seemed perfect for her. He was anything but the image of her rigid, unyielding father. Of course, when he seemed cloying to her, she felt trapped. "Back off! Jesus, you're just like your *mother!*" she'd cry. And when he demanded sex, she'd feel furious: "Stop it!" she'd say. "You're just like Bill!"

## Rehearsals

New experience modifies our templates. Consider our originals as dramatic scripts. We improvise on them, depending on the circumstances and on who we're with. Thus, over time, our templates are constantly changing and deepening. A relationship between childhood sweethearts will then proceed differently from one between people who meet in their late twenties. A relationship begun when partners are desperate will be different than one they might begin if they were more independent. If we are nestled in a supportive network of friends and family, our relationships evolve more measuredly than if we are isolated and the relationship is everything.

An original template may develop out of a relationship with a brother or sister, a parent, or even a childhood friend. During the first few times through, we may play its script out unconsciously. But with repetition, we become aware of the patterned quality of these relationships. "I always have to have one—and only one—best friend," a woman reported. "This is what makes me feel secure and good about myself. But I always get *so* involved. My friend becomes too important and I stop seeing everyone else. Then I become clingy, my friend gets mad, we fight, and it falls apart."

Each time we begin a new relationship, a number of our templates stand ready. One may seem more applicable than the others, and we gravitate toward it. Its script, once chosen, continually colors and narrows our understanding, both of our partners and of ourselves. Over time our repertoire narrows, and we find ourselves repeatedly choosing from a few well-rehearsed options.

In this sense, each significant relationship is like a rehearsal for all subsequent ones, and for the relationship that we hope will last. At times we may try to shift our prevailing script. "I used to like quiet men," one woman said, "but I got tired of chasing them; lately I've been going out with guys who talk more." Even explicit efforts to buck our templates and form different kinds of relationships may serve as rehearsals; they help us define the parameters of our taste and set the limits of our capacity to stretch. It's a little like trying out a new role that challenges us to tap into different aspects of our personality.

Rehearsals provide opportunities for practice and experimentation. Through them, we try to consolidate the qualities we like and eliminate those that are painful. We want to be more independent, more engaged, more assertive, kinder, gentler, stronger, less defensive, and to control our anger, cry less, and stay close even when we panic and want to run.

And so we try out different models. One man who constantly chose extremely responsive—but combative—women tried out a more self-contained woman. It was like switching from a marriage with his charismatic but critical father to one with his sweetly distant mother. One woman who tended to go out with very "laid-back, intellectual men" tried a hard-driving, competitive businessman for a change. She did not like it for long but she thought she ought to try someone more like her father before settling down.

Not all experimentation is intentional. But we do constantly try to improve ourselves or our selections, often telling ourselves that, in the process, we are moving steadily closer to attaining our ideal. We make fierce promises to ourselves and sometimes to others:

"I'm never going out with another drunk!"

"I'm going to hang in this time, even if it means going to therapy."

"I'm going to choose someone who respects me this time, and if he doesn't I won't wait around so long."

Each rehearsal provides us with another chance to repair old wounds, correct mistakes, fulfill our dreams, and be our better selves. It is a self-correcting process: like archers focused on their target, we keep changing our aim by reflecting on how our last arrows went off course.

Frequently, we change relationships to keep ourselves and/or our self-images stable. We may try to choose a partner who will help us continue to feel good about ourselves or help us feel more assertive, alive, or flexible. We also try to change ourselves in order to keep our ideal of relationship stable. That is, we try to fit ourselves to the picture we see when we envision the positive side of the templates that we have carried since childhood.

In between relationships, we try to figure out what went wrong and, to a lesser extent, what went right. Our most recent serious relationship represents our most important rehearsal, our latest effort to find and refine our "type." These rehearsals can be successful by helping us distinguish the templates that offer us more chance of satisfaction from those that keep getting us in trouble. Making new adjustments based on past experience can lead to a better fit the next time around. And yet, because so many deep-set images are always contending within us, no search for a "perfect partner" is immune from disappointment.

## Beginnings

Now that the stage has been set, the partners enter the scene. For some time they may not even be aware of each other's presence. Some people fall in love immediately, in what the French call a *coup de foudre*, the thunderbolt of love; but many more take time before noticing one another as possible partners.

The partners may play out the first few steps of their drama separately, each gradually developing a sense of the other until, some conviction having crystallized, they finally notice each other in a more personal way. Up until then, they have been two separate people in the world, with separate histories, separate personalities, separate tastes and expectations.

But now something has attracted them to each other. Perhaps the feeling is mutual; perhaps not. Perhaps the other will "come around" over time. Perhaps mutual attraction will build so gradually that neither partner is sure exactly *when* he or she first became aware of it. Perhaps the relationship will proceed like a seesaw: first one pursues the other and then retreats, and then the other begins to chase and court instead.

Couples' actual beginnings vary tremendously, with varying degrees of readiness and urgency; experience moves us in different rhythms. What initially attracts can be a small detail: the cut of clothing, the scent of cologne or perfume, the way people walk, their posture, a gesture. We can be captivated by their position in life, by their friends, by their families. What attracts may seem totally random, yet it frequently surges up from our core images. It can be the expression in someone's face (like the Good Parent), their gaze, their touch (Sexually Accepting), a word, a sympathetic expression, a shared experience, a gradual realization that crystallizes. Whatever it is, a connection is made. One person has noticed the other and now looks upon him or her *differently*. Pursuit and courting have begun.

Here are some examples:

## Marcia and Sam

Marcia and Sam met during the Depression. Sam, from a large hardworking family, was two years older. When he was seven, he had a newspaper route in his neighborhood, and by the time he was nine, he had organized a grocery delivery service. He worked hard as he was growing up, and had very little time for girls. Besides, they intimidated him. Marcia's father owned a store, and she remembered, as a girl, seeing Sam trudging up and down the streets on his rounds. But she was shy and hadn't talked to him then. Her family moved away, and she didn't see Sam for years.

One night, when Sam and Marcia were in their early twenties, they met at a dance at a social club. Sam sensed something familiar about Marcia, and went over and asked her to dance. She was surprised to see him again. He seemed "older and more mature than most of the other young men in the hall." They danced once or twice, and then Sam was amazed to find himself pouring out his hopes and ambitions to this woman he barely knew; and yet she was listening to every word, which made him feel important. For her part, Marcia was thrilled that Sam would confide in her. He seemed to be hardworking, responsible, and mature, with his life's plan already worked out. He was someone who could take care of her. But she also felt an emptiness in him, a need for companionship. She felt special when she thought that this man who could conquer the world might actually need her. Sam was deeply moved by Marcia's enthusiasm and support. She made him feel that he could do anything. "I'd never met anyone so ... well, so **warm** in my life," he said. "I guess that's when I knew I was going to stay with her the rest of my life."

Over the next few weeks, they saw a lot more of each other. Sam realized that Marcia's natural intelligence might be useful some day, say, if he started his own business. The two of them perfectly complemented each other's abilities. And they each seemed to be "family" people: when Sam's sister was hurt in an accident, for example, Marcia helped find a good doctor for her and seemed genuinely concerned. Sam spent a lot of time in Marcia's house and talked with Marcia's father, who was having financial problems. The father approved of "this fine young man." While they were not physically intimate or even openly affectionate with each other (each was shy), Sam and Marcia felt comfortable together. Each thought the other was "good for them." When friends asked if they were "serious," they smiled and said they supposed they were. Sometimes Marcia had fleeting regrets about the absence of romance; she wondered if she was really "in love." But when the two of them were together, planning their future together, those questions seemed foolish, and she succeeded in putting them out of her mind. In fact, they spent most of their free time planning together because it made them both feel hopeful, competent, and a little larger than life.

## Jim and Janet

Jim and Janet were both sophomores in college. They'd been introduced by Janet's friend Nan, who thought they were "so much like each other, it was weird." Twenty minutes after they met, they couldn't believe it. "It was like looking in the mirror," Janet said. "She's just like me!" Jim exclaimed. They found they both liked the same movies, listened to the same music. They were each interested in the arts—Jim wanted to be an architect, Janet was a literature major. It seemed they shared a secret language: each instinctively seemed to know what the other one was thinking and feeling. It was an incredible "fit." Jim loved the way Janet's hair blew in the wind and how she hunched her shoulders when she giggled, and Janet kept thinking about the silly pout Jim made when she teased him. It was a match made in heaven.

They saw each other every day for lunch, studied together, went to parties together, spent every weekend together. After a few weeks, they had a little argument: Jim wanted to spend some extra time on a paper, and Janet felt "excluded," but they worked it out. One day Jim grumbled about how much time Janet was spending with Nan, who was having boyfriend problems, but that, too, passed. After several months, they felt they were still "cut from the same cloth," and could accept the fact that they might have subtle differences. Still, they believed that each fulfilled the other. They could share things together they'd never shared with anyone else. The relationship brought things out of them they'd never even known existed. Janet wanted Jim to meet her folks, and they planned a four-day weekend for just that purpose.

## Brad and Mark

Brad was a newcomer in town when he first met Mark. He had left a rural community where he felt odd and unwanted, and was hoping to find a relationship in the urbane world of advertising. Mark was more of an old hand: respected by others in the office, he took a kindly though jaunty interest in Brad's arrival and offered to show him around. The two men hit it off instantly. Brad's earnest, country quality appealed to Mark, and Mark's sophistication seemed just what Brad had been seeking to develop in himself.

The two began spending more and more time together—socially as well as professionally—and then went away for a weekend together. The emotional intensity of those two days was so strong that Brad moved in with Mark the following week.

## Susan and Andy

Susan and Andy hadn't planned to fall in love. Andy was Susan's husband Walt's best friend. Neither Susan nor Walt came from successful families—each had a father who drank—and after a few years of marriage they had big problems: she thought he was seeing other women; she knew he was drinking too much. One afternoon she happened to ask Andy if he knew anything about Walt that she should know, and he looked embarrassed and blushed. That was how they started talking together. Andy kept a respectful distance, though, and tried not to get in the middle of the marital dispute. But one night she and Walt had a huge fight: Walt threw his clothes in a suitcase and left, and Susan had no one to turn to. In a panic, she called Andy, who came over and stayed with her, talking to her for hours. He seemed calm and supportive, "so much kinder than Walt had ever been." She felt a great surge of gratitude for this man who had helped her when she was vulnerable and not "at her best." Andy felt amazed that his friend could have treated a woman as pretty and kind as Susan the way he had. Didn't he know a good woman when he saw her? Tender feelings soon brought them into bed together—a surprisingly profound experience for them both. Susan felt she'd never experienced sex as deeply before.

Between the conversation and the sexual excitement, she felt for the first time like the woman she had dreamed of being. And Andy, her loving guide, felt as heroic and fulfilled as he had ever been. Before they knew what had happened, they were living together and Susan's depression had gone. They wanted to get married as soon as Susan could get a divorce.

We have long been told that finding a mate and falling in love are the great experiences of life. These expectations have become part of our deepest images, shaping our hopes and fantasies. Parents have told us that we need a husband or wife to feel complete, to feel good about ourselves and to feel safe; and they have helped us worry: "If you dress like that, Rita, you'll be an old maid the rest of your life." Or: "Once you find the right person, you'll know what I'm talking about, Bernie."

Friends and peer groups have pushed to get us involved as well: teenagers are pressured to fulfill their group's standards; singles of any age are urged to "find someone compatible"; the newly divorced are set up with new partners; even the recently widowed find their well-meaning friends eager to introduce them to new "prospects" who can "take care of you now."

Now that all the elements are in place for a couple to begin, let us consider the initial stage of relationships, the Stage of Expansion.

# 5

---

# THE STAGE OF EXPANSION
# AND PROMISE

---

The Expansive Stage, established early in a relationship, is a time of excitement and great promise. Its promises are so compelling that they take on the character of a contract between the partners and become the standards against which the couple will measure all their future experience.

The essential quality of early relationships is expansiveness: expansiveness in ourselves, expansiveness in the perception of our partner, and expansiveness in the relationship as a whole. We feel more capable and more available. In the enthusiastic gaze of our new partner, we are likely to feel more witty, more charming, and more animated than ever before. We feel vulnerable, yet strangely strong. We are expressive, bold, and open. We are in touch with images and yearnings from childhood as well as with hopes and expectations for our future. Our unfolding couple relationship feels encouraging, flexible. Possibility and potentiality abound. There is space here for being awkward, for being funny, for starting and stopping, for fumbling about, for being passionate and sexual, and for making discoveries. Time slows down as we linger with our new partner, but it also rushes by, and we find there are never enough minutes in the day for everything we want to do.

While the Cultural Narrative suggests that couples should begin by falling in love, there are actually many different ways to begin, many forms of expansiveness. A large number of couples do begin with a burst of romance and sexual passion. Others begin and remain mostly friends. Some couples resemble business partnerships, taking pleasure in cooperation, negotiation, and mature discussion. Others are tempestuous and sexual but never develop a sense of respect or equality. In yet others, partners offer one another the gift of the comfort of their families, but downplay the importance of passion and intimacy. Some partners are "symmetrical," matching passion with passion, friendship with friendship. Others are "complementary," trading security for romance, strength for gentleness.[1] One partner might get the intense attention she's always desired while her partner is rewarded with her sturdy, if unemotional, family—something he's always yearned for.

Everyone diverges from our culture's prescribed romantic path in some way; we all have to come to terms with how we are different.* Often, we try to accommodate outwardly to the cultural prescriptions, but we feel differently inside. We might act as if we are in love, perhaps even convince ourselves of it; or we may deal with a lack of ardor by trying to get our partners to be more romantic.

If our real feelings are less torrid than our expectations, we may have to give up the fantasy of being more passionately in love. If our partner falls a bit short of our dreams, we may have to grieve the lost ideal. But these compromises are easy to make. The overwhelming euphoria of the Expansive Stage makes us feel unbelievably better than before. We can still be genuinely in love, even if it is not with the dashing artist, the successful lawyer, the all-giving woman, or the ever-competent man we had always imagined.

However they may start, though, virtually all relationships of substance and duration begin in an expanded state. Both persons (and the relationship as a whole) feel larger, more bounteous, more open, and more connected than they may ever feel again.

Expansiveness is encouraged by the crisis of new beginnings, a period when two autonomous individuals, with all the images, habits, values, and expectations of their past, must fit themselves to each other. They flex and expand and transform themselves into a new unit: the couple.

Beginnings create genuine crises in people's lives. They disrupt

---

*Other factors affect couples who differ from the cultural norm. Gay and lesbian couples always must contend with the social stigma of their choice. Interracial couples may have to handle two conflicting sets of cultural expectations. The ways in which couples accommodate, defy, and adjust to the Cultural Narrative create their particular character.

our old routines and alter our sense of time, space, and energy. In crisis, some moments stretch into eternities, while others pass in the blink of an eye: a person may feel boundless enthusiasm on Monday, but terminal lethargy on Tuesday. The closeness we feel is both exciting and frightening; our loss of control may be soothing at one moment and terrifying the next. Our schedules, life-styles, and attitudes all seem up for negotiation with our new partners. Events take on altered significance. Our senses and understandings are heightened, sharpened, challenged—and sometimes even satisfied.

As the couple forms, both individuals and their couple relationship are unstable. During this crisis, yearnings from early childhood for love and attention break through our carefully constructed defenses, overwhelming our best efforts to be reasonable and mature. Very little remains the same. We are delighted, we are ecstatic, we are unstoppable. And yet everything is in flux. We cannot be as we had been in the past, but we have not yet found a stable shore either within ourselves or with our partners.

Each of us has a different explanation for the expansiveness. Some feel "completed" by the other and therefore, as one woman put it, "more than I ever imagined I could be." Some feel "reconnected," as if reunited with a parent who loves unconditionally and rarely criticizes. With such reunions, we finally feel secure enough to venture forth with greater confidence. Others feel "calmed and contained" because their nervous search for a partner has finally been resolved, thus freeing up energy for their own vital projects.

During the expansive phase, we come closer to being the person we wish to be, our ideal selves, than at almost any other time in life. We can be more generous and forthcoming, not because we are on good behavior or because it is demanded of us, but because it seems right; it flows from inside, because it is a source of internal satisfaction. We feel impelled to kindness and consideration in ways we have often wished to be or in ways we only vaguely remember from parental examples and parental lectures. We find ourselves wittier and more charming, experience ourselves as wise and clearheaded. It is as though the clouds of the past had lifted and the true meaning of life had appeared. We feel strong, yet open and sensitive: an often elusive combination.

The constraints, the miscalculations, and the dead ends of the past seem past. We appear free to create ourselves in the present and the future. This is a heady experience.

We can be more available emotionally. Those of us who usually rush are able to linger. Those who lack energy now seem to find it. Timid people are bolder. Some people take on qualities of romantic heroes and heroines, and a few even manage to capture the whole picture. But we do not all expand equally or in the same way.

There is variation and a continuum of expansiveness. Constrained or inhibited people still act in relatively constrained ways during this period. People who seem alienated from their own good feelings might wonder if they are really in love at all, or they may express their doubts in judgmental form. But still, they manage to express what, for them, is the most open, generous, responsive, and euphoric personality of which they are capable. The internal experience of even the most constrained people in this stage is expansive.

The relationship gains strength from a powerful synergy: each partner's appreciation spurs the other to expand his or her capacities, and a spaciousness, an absence of constricting patterns, emerges and makes exploration and experimentation possible more than at any later time.

## Sex

Sex—both the anticipation and the experience of it—fills the air between new partners with electricity and heightens their sensibilities. It gives increasing charge and significance to each touch, glance, gesture, and phrase. The delights that accompany sexual feelings are a key contribution to the magic of the expansive moment. Of course, not all sexual feeling or anticipation is sweet and untroubled: fear and anxiety, deriving from social taboos and unhappy earlier experience, may play as vibrant a role in this moment as lust and tenderness. From the start, sexual encounters mingle desire and inhibition, dominance and submission, sharing and cooperation. The immediacy of the moment mixes with powerful expectations built on the recent and ancient past.

## Internal Experience

Expansiveness feels like an internal and an external experience at the same time. Our partners' goals mirror our own. We feel so responsive, we believe that our enhanced capabilities flow from our partners' encouragement as much as from our own hopes and abilities. Our partners make us more generous and expressive. Their acceptance helps us transcend our ordinary capabilities.

Many relationships are built on possibilities. We base our marriages as much on the hope that our partners will improve as on the qualities we see in them now. We imagine that passive men will become assertive, frantic women will become calm. According to this view, each of us is a "diamond in the rough," waiting to be polished by the right partner. Later, the call for improvement will be taken as a lack of acceptance—"Why can't you just love me the way I am?" But during Expansion, these requests reflect our own best hopes for ourselves.

We ask—even insist—that our partners encourage us to change. We know we need their help. Men want their partners to point out when they're not being kind enough to their family, not open enough about their feelings. Women want their partners to be interested in them as *people,* to support their desires to be both strong and nurturing, and to accept them even when they are neither.

During Expansion, boundaries come down—both within ourselves and between us and our partners. As a result individuals experience themselves in broader, more complex ways than at most other times. We may feel witty and sophisticated in our partner's eyes, but also naïve, innocent, and awkward. One moment we are reasonable and in control; the next, we may feel drunken and swept away beyond reason. We may be as happy as children, but we can also feel terrible sadness.

Indeed, in this period we are more in touch with *all sides* of ourselves: the frightening as well as the familiar. Bursts of sexual feeling may be scary; the intensity of a feeling may unleash unwanted anger and jealousy. Yet even the pain we feel can be affirming. Even sadness can be cherished as a sign that the relationship is so special.

The Expansive Stage is much more than a happy time, although memory sometimes sanitizes it in this way. It is best characterized as a time of deep, rich, and far-ranging experience.

It has become fashionable to demean this wonderful time.[2] Some "experts" in relationships call it neurotic: a momentary madness, regression, and illusion. Put off by its manic energy, they cannot join its intense feeling and idealization, and they deride its "acting out" of desires and fantasies as so much self-absorption. But expansiveness is a *real* experience, no more a distortion than the painful, or "realistic," periods in couples' lives.

Expansion does, in fact, include regression. We may act in childlike ways. We want to depend on our partner, to be stroked and held and assured. We may "act out" with a lover as though he or she were a parent who had failed us in some important way. We may idealize ourselves, our partner, our relationship. We may feel a sense of oneness and wholeness akin to a religious experience. Since outsiders do not share this experience, they cannot define it, for they—family, community, experts—enter the relationship later. The partners themselves best understand the crisis of new beginnings. Our "regression" is one way of bringing our past into the present: reviving old memories, reenthroning earlier images, reconnecting to what has been meaningful for us. It makes the beginning relationship deeper and rounder than our usual existence. It lets us gain access to our primitive feelings of dependency and attachment, and brings forth a wealth of imagery from all stages of life. Dreams and fantasies add dimension to this extraordinary period, so that we experience ourselves in the fullness of our beings.

This is a key moment. The intense and sustained contact of past and present, rational and irrational, old imagery and new dreams, old models of relationship and new partners—this dramatic mixture produces a transformational experience. As we pass through it, we feel like different people, and we are. Going through the Expansive Stage is a rite of passage, a developmental milestone in the lives of most contemporary individuals.

## Male and Female

Traditionally rigid boundaries between masculinity and femininity break down during the Expansive Stage. Men and women's developmental paths converge, and both seem freer to express all sides of themselves—anima as well as animus—more fully.[3] This leads to some surprises in gender-linked behavior. Men, for example, may take time to linger, talk, and understand; women may take more initiative and appear more independent.

Usually, in our society, women talk more; they seek intimacy through chatting and sharing feelings, and often feel abandoned by their less verbal partners. Men usually prefer to "do things" together;

they move toward intimacy through activities and sexual engagement, and often feel intruded upon by their verbal mates. In this stereotypical standoff, men appear flat and inexpressive to women, and women seem intrusive and histrionic to men.

During the Expansive Stage these trajectories come together. Men often act and feel more open, more connected than usual; women, more independent, even standoffish, and more wary than they usually do. Men are typically more talkative, more emotionally vulnerable in the Expansive Stage than at any other period of their lives. They seek connection, especially while courting, and do not run from it as they often do later in relationships. In Expansion, women are thrilled with these men. They feel that they have found a different kind of man than the withholding and critical men they had to deal with previously, both in their families and in their earlier relationships. And, for the moment, they are right.

Women tend to be more aware of the risks of intimacy. Remembering the difficulties of fusion, dependency, and loss in past relationships, they tend to be more reserved at a new beginning. They can play "hard to get." They are afraid to give too much away, are slower to respond, and maintain their boundaries and their autonomy a little longer. At this stage, they are pleased to feel more autonomous, more at home with boundaries and independence, more open to adventure and spirited interaction. Where, later, they become the pursuers in the domain of intimacy, here, at this stage, they are pursued.

This is fine with a majority of men. They enjoy being involved with a woman seemingly so unlike the devouring creatures of their nightmares, a woman who *doesn't* want to control them. Where women are cautioned by their last relationship, men seem to put it out of mind faster and begin again in much the same style.

For a time, then, both ease up on restrictive gender-typed behavior. Both partners experience themselves as fuller. Each rejoices at finding such a fullness in the other and supports it strongly. The "androgyny" of Expansion emerges, permitting a much wider range of behaviors and expression. Men and women seem to have an equal potential. Some men begin to express a softer "feminine" side; and some women, encouraged by their partners' acceptance, feel freer to express what society typically views as their "masculine" aspects—their boldness, initiative, self-sufficiency, and sassiness. Sexual exploration is more open; sexual response less inhibited. Both may worry a bit about these role reversals, but they manage to put it aside in order to revel in the delightful expansiveness of it all.[4]

Encouraged by our partners' responsiveness, our sexual feelings tend to be more intense during this first stage than ever again. Expansion tends to be the most sexually absorbing and involving stage in the life of a couple. The experience is deeply satisfying for those men whose way of feeling close is largely nonverbal. Perhaps more than any other experience, it opens men to the gentle, vulnerable (and private) selves that they hide for so much of their lives. The mixture of storytelling, reminiscences, idle chatter, and sexual play that emerges in Expansion is deeply satisfying for women, too, for it builds trust and assures them that the disappointments and exploitations they experienced in the past will not exist in this new relationship.

## Encountering an Expanded Partner

When we first encounter our partners, we are both in an expansive state. Thus we experience them, like ourselves, as more open and available, more capable and charming, more generous than usual. Actually, we don't yet know what is "usual" for them: what we see is usual to us.

Conventional wisdom says that, in the grip of strong emotions, all of us tend to idealize our lovers. Romantic poetry and psychology support this notion as well. But we do not *idealize* our partners in Expansion so much as actually *encounter* them as more or less ideal partners, and believe our experience. Early in relationships, we are both at our best. We have truly expansive feelings, and we genuinely love and esteem our partner whose affection has brought us into this state. Even when we are told to take our feelings with a grain of salt, we still believe what we see—both because the evidence in front of us is so convincing and because we want to believe it.

But ours is an unsettling historical time, and we sometimes qualify our feelings. We are often afraid to idealize our partners. Because of the underlying belief that ours is a small world with only so many resources to go around, we fear disappointment even before it happens. Someone else's gain may be our loss: if I idealize you, I may diminish myself.

Men often fear that idealizing a woman obligates them to be

attentive and giving in ways that will make them captive. In olden days, it was fine for partners to say "I am nothing, except to please you." Now we fear that praising another person unconditionally may point to our own deficiencies, and nothing in our contemporary Cultural Narrative will give us satisfaction if we are less than our partners.

So we play it safe and hedge. We prefer to say "You are wonderful to the extent that you please me, and I am wonderful to the extent that I please you," and we build up a portrait of all the ways we please each other. This is not as enduring a portrait as the one that values us for our own intrinsic qualities—beyond what we do for the relationship. Lacking independent strength, the new portrait will waver with the vicissitudes of the relationship. Through the years, we retain this image of our partners as facilitators and as good parents to our ideal self, but the image gains strength only insofar as our partner's character gains independence—both in reality and in our eyes—and divorces itself from our focus on what they can do for us.

Withal, the Expansive Stage also includes moments of great doubt. Conscious of the need to remain better than we ordinarily are, we go through moments of feeling intensely jammed and inadequate. How can we match our partner's love and generosity? How can we plumb the depths as deeply as is required? Won't our partner sense that, deep down, we are not really so marvelous as they think? The suspicion that we are only acting out a more idealized version of ourselves unsettles us, serving as a basis for the arguments that appear like thunderstorms, and that will resurface in subsequent stages, with deeper, darker consequences.

In this stage we also go through some of our greatest self-doubt and torment, even though the self-doubt does not dominate. We ask friends—and, more than ever again, we ask our lovers—"Am I good enough?" We ask about the other: "Is he [she] good enough, stable enough, handsome enough?" This stage is characterized not by the absence of doubt but by an appreciation of the *totality* of our feelings and by our capacity to make the optimistic view predominate.

## Synergy in the Couple

Expansiveness goes beyond the two individuals' opening up. It is a synergistic ongoing process that becomes an integral part of the whole relationship: we feed off each other's energy. Synergy creates upward, expanding spirals in relationships. One partner, for instance, may be greatly encouraged by the other's appreciation, which in turn helps him be more forthright, humorous, and playful, thus drawing forth even more playfulness from her. Early in the relationship, synergy absorbs many themes into its orbit—kindness, consideration, a heroic act, a self-revelation. One partner's telling a fearful secret in Expansion often elicits long-hidden information from the other; what once was humiliating and distancing can now bring the partners together.

The more you see me as wonderful, the better I feel about myself; the better I feel, the better I perform; the better I perform, the more I confirm your affirmative perceptions; and so the synergy builds. Seeing you in special ways, I spur you to greater heights. Feeling more capable, both of us dare to stretch beyond normal limits and inhibitions.

The more we stretch, the more eager we are for our partner's feedback. A circle of positive, sometimes giddy, feedback builds. Generosity of action and spirit breeds generosity of action and spirit, and our relationship ascends to its highest point. Finding ourselves in a spacious, unpredictable terrain, we reach further and further out. Neither our patterns of behavior, nor our images of self and other, nor our expectations have yet grown rigid. We are still distinct from our roles as breadwinner, mother, father, housewife, soother, placater, initiator, pursuer, distancer, or fighter. The character of the couple is still unformed, which leaves room for experimentation.

The synergistic process does not always go without hitches. At times it can feel overwhelming and out of control. Another's love can frighten us. We can be startled by the implications of an impulsive forward gesture that raises the specter of commitment. Even the most positive feedback can misfire: missing the message, we may misinterpret encouragement, affection, sexual desire, and simple enjoyment as demands. Responding to our own anxiety, we may lash out in anger, cry, and distort reality. For a while, we may have to get off the synergistic circle, sometimes at length or permanently. During Expansion, however, we tend to emerge intact from these defensive reactions and be able to continue stretching a bit further.

Over time, we develop fairly fixed ideas of our mates. We develop patterns that encourage certain aspects of their character and discourage others. In effect, these patterns serve to define both our own and our partner's character within our particular couple. After all, we are different with *this* partner than we have been with other partners, in other couples. These particular patterns of behavior create our character in this particular couple and keep it in place. Our images of each other lead to a matrix of expectations: if we only do this, all will be well; if we dare do that, trouble will start. *Image and behavior reinforce each other and come to define each couple's character.*

Before the linkages of image and behavior are established, our relationship is more flexible, more experimental. Experimentation, in fact, characterizes Expansion. We experiment because there's room to do so: we have a new partner, and our relationship is not clear-cut. Trying to compensate for past wounds and deficiencies, we struggle to learn what to do more of and what to do less of. These experiments extend our capacities for intimacy and independence within a relationship, and expand our range of experience. Indeed, we cannot avoid experimentation. The very act of accommodating to another person automatically stretches us. We each try out a variety of positions before settling on a common style.

All this experimentation is encouraged by our culture. Our Cultural Narrative scorns conservatism and prescribes expansiveness in the initial phases. It requires that we come together in romantic love, be sexually attracted to each other, a little crazy perhaps, impractical, lost in each other to the fullest. We should linger with each other, touch and explore, move naturally and spontaneously from one activity to another. We should be open and vulnerable, involved, chatty, even capable of flaunting convention. There will be plenty of time later, says our conventional wisdom, to settle into more of a routine.


## Patti and Marshall

Patti and Marshall's first few months together closely fit this description of the Expansive Stage. Following their unexpected meeting in the supermarket, they made an instant connection with each other, as though each was the person the other had always been looking for. Patti was a source of light and life for Marshall: her passionate nature made him come alive. He was stable, a rock of support to her: his calm and unconditional affection made Patti feel accepted for the first time in her life.

Their early weeks together encouraged and confirmed their

hopes. Each was understanding, empathic, and loving; their sexual life was exciting and liberating; and they laughed a lot. They talked for hours at a time, amazed at how alike they were, even though they had come from such different places. They spent endless hours listening to each other tell stories about when they were young, about past relationships—real and fantasied, and about their wishes for the future. They took romantic drives in the country, cooked exotic dishes, went to the movies on Sunday afternoon. With Patti's son Simon in tow, they imagined themselves a new kind of family.

As they trusted each other more, they were able to take more risks in what they revealed. Opening up, they found that the other could accept parts of themselves they had always had trouble revealing. They could admit their failings and still be loved.

This expansive experience became the *foundation* of Patti and Marshall's relationship. Later, in times of difficulty, they could remember how close together they had been these first few months, could recall aspects of each other's personality that attracted them initially, could get in touch with the deep love they felt for each other at the core—even though they might be angry at the time.

## Individual and Couple Narratives

There are only a few times in life when we have a chance to tell another person our whole story. The Expansive Stage is one. As we reveal ourselves to our partner, we revisit and reshape our past. The telling transforms us. Disclosing our inner selves, we hear our own stories with a sense of discovery. The process fills us with insight and wonder, and we become even more enthusiastic when we hear our partner's revelations and find how closely, how intricately they match our own.

All history is written to serve the present; all stories are told with a listener in mind. Our personal narrative, which we periodically update when our lives are shaken up, is a vivid example of these maxims. Our stories are not fabrications: they are efforts to tell the truth about who we are. The sum of these stories at any one time defines us: how we portray ourselves to others and to ourselves. In the expansive moment, we narrate ourselves into being.[5]

The partner who hears our narrative helps shape it. Our listener's responses make us share some stories and hold back others. We shade our accounts one way or another, focus them toward a happy ending or tragic conclusion. We tell how deliriously happy we were with a previous lover, or how we have *never* been able to find anyone who undertood us; how our parents forbade us from consummating a forbidden romance when we were still under their control, or how the greatest love of our life walked away and chose someone else. The story we share is a collaborative creation, an effort to fit the bare facts of our past to the needs, goals, and mood of the present and our new partner.

With our partner as both coauthor and audience, we narrate ourselves into becoming the new people we are together. Our intertwined stories become the basis for a new story: us as a couple. This common fabric now takes on a life, an identity of its own. Facing a choice or a dilemma, we refer back to it. "*This* is how we do things," we say, "we talk things over first," or "That's just how we are: if it doesn't feel right, we don't do it." We tell certain stories over and over again—about the moment we knew we were right for each other, about how a certain movie perfectly captures how we are as a couple, about a magical time when we each *knew* just what the other was thinking.

The new narrative encodes the rules of our burgeoning relationship. It indicates what is open for discussion and what is not. It sets the parameters for independence and intimacy. It contains the stories about how we first met, about our first fight and how we got past it, about how we may have rescued each other from our families, about how we intend to raise our own children differently. We tell these stories not only to each other, but also to friends and acquaintances. With each telling, our character as a couple in its expansive phase becomes more established.

Through this process, we reach a shared reality. During Expansion we may suppress negative and dissonant material about ourselves, reframing who we are and often idealizing ourselves and our partners. For example, a woman may think, "Such a cool person is perfect to balance my impulsiveness," while her partner feels, "I love the way her spontaneity brings me out." Later his coolness may prove infuriating and her spontaneity may seem disorganized, but for now the complementarity works.

The Couple Narrative does not include all the material of our Individual Narratives. We think we know our partner ... yet we know there is more to *us* than we have put into the relationship. The same is true of them. Much in us still remains unsaid, separate, and unintegrated: it is too upsetting to share; it is forgotten; it does not fit the mood and style of our relationship. Through the years, however, this material about ourselves has to come out; we will eventually bring it forth and weave it into the Couple Narrative. Sometimes, this will happen in the next stage, the Stage of Contraction, when the darker side of ourselves and our partners emerges and takes on more prominence. Sometimes, this will happen in later moments of expansion, when we feel able to deepen the story we have shared so far.

There is an ongoing interaction between Individual and Couple Narratives: each supplements and adapts to the other; each limits the other. With time, they may grow hard to separate, because our identity tends to become so embedded in our couple relationship.

## Arrival: The First Contract

A relationship in its initial Expansive Stage is so compelling, so responsive to deep and powerful yearnings, that we hope it will last forever. The implicit and explicit promises we make to each other take on the binding quality of a contract.[6] It is not a written or a logical contract. It is more like a composite picture, a model of feeling and function by which we try to live, that becomes the standard against which we will measure all our future experience. Through the years we'll refer back to this contract:

"When I married you, this was what I expected."

"You are not the man I married!"

"This is how I remember you."

"This is how I always thought it would be."

The contract is less a set of rules than a series of images, but our feelings about these images are very strong and become prescriptive:

"I will be steady for you; you will enliven my life."

"I will take care of money; you deal with our social life."

"Together we can deal with all those phonies out there."

"We are all the support we will ever need."

Remember, our own identity develops along with the developing identity of the couple. If our relationship is threatened, so is our sense of ourselves. As a result we try to build safeguards against any threat to our couple's stability in the "contract" we form. We say, in effect, "Here's how I promise to be, and here's how you promise to be."

The first contract we form, then, is the promise that the way we have come together in Expansion will remain forever. It is a composite picture of images and behavioral patterns, including the explicit and implicit promises we make to each other during this initial Expansive Stage—the sum total of sorting out universal, cultural, and personal predispositions, the sum of explorations, the sum of our capacity to make things work during courtship. These then assume the quality of a binding contract.

While some of this picture and some of the promises we make are not wholly conscious, we do have a consciousness about this period. We know we have arrived at a stable place, a place where we can rest for a while, a place of common identity.

By the end of this phase, the couple has developed a sense of itself as a collective entity, a "we" that is more than two individuals, an identity as a couple. It is a moment when we say, in effect, "Look at us. We've really done something, become something, and we're different than other couples."

With this arrival, this settling into an identity, comes the creation and acknowledgment of regular feelings, patterns of behavior and meanings that characterize us as a couple. The acknowledgment emerges through the anecdotes and stories we love to tell, through the rituals we develop around saying hello and good-bye, through our repeated moments of getting up together and going to sleep, through the way we find special names for each other, special ways of talking, special gestures, and maybe even a special language.

We have created a culture of two. It is a moment in couple development a little like the seventh day of creation. In the act of naming our creation, we have, in a way, created ourselves. At this point in the Expansive Stage, we too rest on the seventh (or seventieth day) and say, "This is good."

## Cycling Through the Expansive Stage over Time

The organization of the Expansive Stage is established early, but it appears again repeatedly throughout a couple's life. Couple development is cyclical. The Stage of Contraction and Betrayal follows that of Expansion and Promise, and the resolution of these opposites eventually leads the couple into a Stage of Resolution. Later on, propelled by the momentum of their success, the couple moves again into

Expansion, and a more optimistic action and imagery again dominate their experience. Sometime later, of course, another Contraction will follow, and then another Stage of Resolution. Later, the couple will settle into yet another Stage of Expansion, their third time in this stage.

Expansion comes around again many times for long-lasting couples. Each time they move into this stage, they reexperience some of their favorite expansive qualities, savor once again the synergy and optimism of their early days, and may even revive some of the magic they originally felt together. But subsequent passages through Expansion differ from the first time through in some important ways. First, the partners' experience in all subsequent passages through Expansion reflects their having gone through all three stages. Theirs is no longer just an expansive vocabulary, for they have now seen each other's darker sides. Knowing each other better, their portraits of each other and of themselves become ever more complex, ever more rounded each time. Second, a couple's experience in subsequent Stages of Expansion may differ in quality or degree from the first time through: the couple may spend a good deal more, or a good deal less time in the stage. They may display new qualities, new images that were not available in previous passages. Their expansive experience may focus on one particular part of their relationship—say, communication, sex, or the discovery of a new pastime together—in one cycle, and on another aspect in another.

Each time through, the original expansiveness reappears. It may be modified, augmented, restricted, deepened, or thinned out. Perhaps it will be bolstered by greater sensuality, greater relief, joy, or a more spiritual feeling. Perhaps it will be accompanied by the revelation of secrets not known in earlier passages. Complementary couples, for instance, may feel enhanced in each new Expansion by their partner's qualities and therefore less threatened by the limitations they feel in themselves. For others, the unhappy dance of pursuit and distance in Contraction yields happily to the pleasures of another expansive pursuit and responsiveness: those who pursue do so with confidence; those who respond take pleasure in the greater mingling with their partner. Many couples experience a sense of "returning home" when they pass through the Stage of Expansion for a second or third time.

Here is a more elaborate example. When Charlie and Ruth met, they felt like a prince and princess. He was charming and successful;

she was beautiful and lively, successful in her own work as well. Charlie loved to imagine himself going off to work like a crusader going off to fight the foe, and for a while, Ruth even enjoyed his fantasy. She spent a lot of effort preparing candlelight dinners for him when he returned. But Ruth was a talented, capable woman, and she grew tired of playing a supporting role in his play. After considerable conflict and disillusionment they worked out a more equal and symmetrical relationship: two professionals who would treat each other with respect, negotiate and divide domestic chores, and discuss differences with mature perspective.

Then they decided to have a child. Ruth got pregnant. They were pleased, but something was missing. "This should be one of the great experiences of our life, but it's just hard," she said. It remained disappointing until she proposed to Charlie that—instead of sharing child care equally—she would not return to work as they had originally planned, and he would support them while she made a home for their family. Charlie worried that Ruth might not be happy in the role she wanted, but he agreed. Their subsequent experience with the birth and infancy of their first child was exhilarating for them both.

Eventually they fought about the growing inequities of this "awfully traditional" arrangement and returned to their more symmetrical ways. But they had found an important key: whenever they faced a great trouble in their lives, they could return to the original organization of their Expansive Stage—sometimes intentionally, sometimes by accident. It made them feel more together, more romantic and secure with each other than the individualistic and democratic way in which they lived their daily lives.

Through the years, the quality of a new Expansive Stage depends on what happened in the previous cycle. If a couple has spent a lot of energy in Resolution trying to reconcile their bitterness and anger, their subsequent surge into Expansion can be tremendously exciting. And their joy may be all the more poignant because it is so close to the sadness of their Stage of Contraction. When a couple's climb out of Contraction into Resolution is relatively easy, their next Expansive Stage may be rather bland. When the climb is steep and dramatic, the next Expansive Stage may rival the liveliness and excitement of the initial one. Even though it changes with the input of each new cycle, the Expansive Stage still retains much of its original organization and flavor. Each time it comes around, the couple can reexperience some of what they felt in their beginnings.

## Moving Out of the Expansive Stage

The Expansive Stage is not all ease and happiness. The seeds of its passing are present from the start. It always includes change and instability. Anxieties from past failures burst forth at odd moments. Betrayals born of ignorance are rampant—we often learn about our partners' sensitivities only by violating them. Commitment frightens us: some partners temporarily depart; many more express their ambivalence. We feel smothered and controlled—frightened about being left and frightened about being imprisoned by the wrong choice. Our partners turn out to be different than we expected, so we feel a need to adjust, as well as a developing sense that we've been deceived. Disappointments trigger fights, foreshadowing the later phase of Contraction.

When difficulties surface, there may be a quick "mini-cycle" through all three stages. Satisfaction changes to anguish: for a moment the relationship seems lost, but the problems are then rapidly dismissed—sometimes denied, sometimes optimistically integrated into the expansive narrative. Partners may downplay the importance of a fight, for example, and crow about how they handled it. The capacity to weather the storm and handle new information helps them feel closer. They feel they can grow in the face of difficulties. "This relationship is different, more mature, more resilient than our last one," they say.

Throughout the early days, the mini-cycles of Expansion, Contraction, and Resolution turn more than once. Couples who stay together feel emboldened by the way they handle conflict. Contractions and small betrayals don't yet overthrow their expansive mood. The couple's ability to handle previously insurmountable difficulties adds to their delight. With each solution, the individuals become more invested in one another.

Still, no Expansive Stage lasts forever. Its effervescence eventually yields to the pressures of everyday life. Quarrels and differences accumulate. Having resolved some fights, we feel both good and a bit wary. We know that the struggles have brought real albeit less admired aspects of ourselves to the surface. One partner, for example, may not yet have expressed how much she likes being alone and reading; another may not have expressed how close he is to his parents; another, how much she hates the kind of conventional social customs her partner seems to covet. Work, family, and other obligations pull on the partners' time and allegiance. Personality traits, such as temper, moodiness, compulsivity, and indecisiveness may become more prominent, souring our hope of finding a "perfect mate."

Differences emerge that can be neither overlooked nor well-integrated. These can cover a wide range: differences of temperament, religion, or political persuasion. One partner may need to go to sleep early, while the other is a "night person." One may like to party and the other is a homebody. One turns out to have a temper while the other was traumatized during childhood by her family's rage.

We begin to acknowledge our differences and disappointments. We argue more, carp at each other and acknowledge that we feel deceived and betrayed. As our anxieties grow, we increase our efforts to change our partners, which makes them feel less accepted and more defensive. Their defensiveness confirms our need to change them, and negative feedback cycles begin to replace the positive cycles that had characterized the Expansive Stage. The more critical we are, the worse our partners seem to behave; the worse they behave, the more critical we feel.

Eventually we believe that our partners have violated the most basic terms of the Expansive Contract. Instead of getting what we thought we had bargained for, we fear that we have gotten something else. And that, above all else, is what drives us out of the Stage of Expansion and Promise.

Let us return to Jonathan and Marie to illustrate this point. Their contract can be stated as two related agreements: (1) *He* would be more outgoing, loving, and conversational. He would extend himself, would not compete or be arrogant, would support her stoically ... if only she would draw him out, accept him, be responsive, and give him "a real relationship." (2) *She* would be easy, sensual, happy, and challenging, a true partner for him ... if only he would pursue her and not withdraw, be loving, not arrogant or chilly, tell her what he thinks, really need her, yet respect her independence.

Gradually the contract begins to erode. Contract or no contract, Jonathan withdraws when he is threatened, and he isn't always "there" for her. Marie is threatened, then angry at what she sees as his aloofness, and she cannot sustain her loving attitude. She snaps at him when she feels wronged, and grows critical. He doesn't tell her what he thinks because he's afraid of her reaction. In the midst of these struggles, their sexual life diminishes to a trickle. They hold onto their optimism with difficulty, worrying more and more that this relationship is like all the others, the ones that did not work out.

The erosion of their original deal represents an abrogation of the Expansive Contract, leaving Jonathan and Marie lost, angry, and confused. They do not know where to turn and find themselves in genuine crisis.

In the early days of Expansion, couples resolve or contain their difficulties and feel enhanced for doing so. After a while, however, the struggles go deeper. Soon there are more forays into Contraction, and the forays begin to define the relationship more than does the sense of expansiveness. The optimistic mood is overwhelmed. But that is the story for our next chapter.

# 6

---

# THE STAGE OF CONTRACTION
# AND BETRAYAL

---

The Stage of Contraction and Betrayal ruptures the Expansive Contract, threatening both the relationship and our sense of ourselves. Its essential quality is contraction: contraction into ourselves, contraction in the picture of our mate, contraction of the relationship as a whole. It is like a pulling back into our skin. We are less impressed with our partners and find them less enamored, less infatuated with us.

In Contraction, the relationship that had opened and transformed us now closes us down. We are thrust back into ourselves. Old limitations and problems resurface. We feel regressed when we are with our partners, but we are more our adult selves at work and in other relationships with family and friends. In these other settings we feel freer, but we become bitterly constrained with our partners.

We feel alienated from our partners and less capable as individuals: more aware of our fears and disappointments than the hopes and yearnings of the Expansive Stage. This is the dark underside of couple life, the reversal of the synergy of the Expansive Stage. In Contraction, aspects of each partner's character that had hitherto been kept out of the relationship now spill pell-mell into it. The relationship that once endlessly encouraged now breeds failure and despair: menaced, we show our worst selves. It is every couple's nightmare come true.

Each couple experiences this nightmare differently. Just as there is a broad range of ways couples can experience expansiveness, so there is a gamut of styles and patterns through which couples experience Contraction. Some couples are dramatic, like those in *Who's Afraid of Virginia Woolf?* or *Fatal Attraction.* Some permit themselves to feel only the slightest disappointment before proceeding with well-ordered lives. And there is a broad spectrum of experience in between.

## The Move into Contraction

The Expansive experience is transient. After a period of time every couple begins to contract. This may take anywhere from a few days to a few years. The demands of daily life, the pull of regular roles, the safety of routine, and the call of character all combine to lure us back to our familiar selves. One partner's job seems more demanding than before, and he has to stay later at the office. Another partner may feel taken for granted. Yet another person worries because his mate is more fastidious than he had thought. After a hiatus of months, one partner suddenly needs her morning run—but at just the hour they had been making love. Each person reverts back to their "thing"— old friends, old activities, family.

In many ways this is a relief. Expansiveness is exciting but exhausting. Some people (or some part of each person) want the Expansive Stage to last forever. But we also feel exposed and pressured by the need to be constantly pleasing. Perhaps it is disappointing to experience ourselves in a lesser, diminished mode, but the return to familiar ways can feel refreshing.

It is easy to be cynical in Contraction. We see our partners returning to their "true colors," as though the Expansive Stage had been a temporary delusion or deception. Initially, though, Contraction need not be angry or distorted. It is primarily a declaration that we have limitations, an effort to regain balance after the excitement of our expansive beginning.

In a living relationship, the partners move freely between being engaged and being separate. Comfortable with themselves, they can tolerate difference in their partners. The intense engagement of Expansion, though, leaves little room for separation. As a result, Contraction comes as a shock and feels like a betrayal of the promised intimacy.

The move from Expansion to Contraction can begin in many ways. Often, it is precipitated by a developmental event, such as getting married, or by suddenly being faced with the need to care for an elderly parent. It may be triggered by situational crises, such as the onset of an illness or the inability to become pregnant. It may happen gradually, as difficulties slowly build up until they define the relationship; or all at once, as when one's loss of a job bursts a couple's expansive bubble.

Take the situation where one partner takes on a new, promising job. After having initially been enthusiastic, the couple finds problems emerging they had not considered. Suddenly, he is not around as much as before. There's a lot of extra work, and neither of them is getting enough sleep. They get cranky and start finding fault with each other. Different attitudes about work now emerge. She may feel threatened by his new colleagues and sense of importance, and may move closer to establish more intimate contact again. But this may make him feel hemmed in and controlled. Perhaps early in their relationship this couple had celebrated their perfect fit: his independence and perspective gave her more expressive personality an anchor. Her warmth pierced his shell, relieving his loneliness. Now this complementarity divides them.

Contraction feels like a betrayal of the Expansive Contract and brings grave disappointment, both with our partners and ourselves. We feel self-doubt and deprecation, rage, blame and confusion. "Is this really the person I married?" we ask. Much as we try to be mature and make adjustments, we still feel that a deep promise has been violated.

The partner who first expresses a sense of loss is the one who has remained connected and vulnerable longer. This is usually a woman, whose partner attributes her shocked and angry reaction to her gender. She is called needy and hysterical, a bitch or ball-buster. Both partners, however, deeply experience the sense of betrayal, and each has a slew of names to hurl at the other. If the man feels most betrayed, he is called weak, a wimp, or a crybaby. Whichever partner first pulls back and then becomes defensive is called withdrawn, aloof, "up-tight," immature, an unfeeling bastard, controlling. Each accuses the other of starting the problem.

Contraction unleashes a series of conflicts; each one is the flip side of some valued feature of the Expansive Stage. The conflicts begin with disappointment over the failure of the Expansive contract, but they soon spread and generalize. Partners blame each other for their own long-standing problems that Expansion had temporarily eased. They struggle to change and improve each other, and push hard for the return of "the person I fell in love with in the first place" and for being recognized themselves as the same fine person who began the relationship.

When we urge our partners to return to the persons they were in Expansion, they feel attacked and criticized, not supported. They want us to like the imperfect persons who have gradually emerged, and when we talk glowingly about their former "better selves" they grow distrustful. Arguments become confused. On the one hand we insist we are *still* that marvelous expansive person; on the other hand, we demand to be loved no matter what, just as we are.

The fight to change our partners externalizes our own insecurities. Blaming them for everything becomes a bitter routine, that—with time—takes up more and more of the relationship. The couple finally believes that this constant blaming reflects a deeper truth than what they knew before.

## Preparation

However painful, the Stage of Contraction is not entirely surprising. We have been prepared for its arrival since childhood. We have been repeatedly told that a fall from grace is inevitable, and that love and romance are invariably followed by strife and boredom. From adolescence on, we spend as much time defending against rejection as we do looking for romance. For every dream of love, we harbor nightmares about its betrayal.

The Stage of Contraction and Betrayal is a rite of passage, a time in the desert when we are tested and forced to endure pain. We may ultimately pass through its bitterness and confusion, affirming both the relationship and ourselves; but—since fifty percent of all marriages and a much larger percentage of all relationships break up—we also may not survive the trip.

Contraction is the stage most familiar to therapists. If Expansion represents the couple's positive ideal, Contraction crystallizes their deepest fears. Its images become the basis of an entirely different way of organizing the couple's experience, and this, too, will become a central marker in their development: a second contract in their repertoire. Feelings of disappointment and betrayal become an organized image of how a particular couple thinks, feels, and behaves when the partners are struggling and at their worst. Throughout the years the partners will pass through this form of organization again and again. They may even learn to see it coming: "Oh, no, here we go again," they will say. And many couples spend much of their lives in the Stage of Contraction.

Before exploring the Stage of Contraction and Betrayal in greater depth, we have two stories to tell. One is about Christine and Mike. The other is about Jonathan and Marie.

## Christine and Mike

It is jarring to see Mike cowering by the far wall as Christine shakes her finger at him. He is six feet five inches tall, with broad shoulders, immense wide hands, and a jaw that seems to jut an inch farther forward than his nose. She is barely five feet two: petite, with medium-length black hair, cool, perceptive blue eyes and, on the rare occasions when she lets down her guard, a smile that lights the room. Christine does most of the talking for the two of them.

When they met, Christine was very happy. She thought Mike was an Adonis. His gentle manner and modest ways contrasted starkly to her father's bombast and her brothers' drunken brawling. Mike listened respectfully to what she said, and she felt an easy acceptance in his presence. He liked her softness best, and the respect she gave him. His mother had ruled his family with a determined martyrdom; she'd had a masterful capacity to humiliate her husband and all seven children. Mike was determined to have a wife who was different, and Christine was. Both of them were proud that he wasn't a serious drinker.

The rest of their story is disheartening. Bit by bit, Mike began spending more time with some buddies from his old neighborhood: after work, after softball games, anytime on the weekends. And that meant drinking.

"Just a few beers," he argued. But Christine didn't believe a few meant two or three.

"Mikey, when do you think I was born?" she'd say.

"Why the hell can't you trust me? I'm not your goddamned father!"

"You could fool me," she'd say.

"The hell with you," Mike would say, and he'd head out to the bar where his buddies were waiting.

They'd never fought like this during their first two years. Even when Mike had drunk too much, they both treated it like a mistake and sighed with relief that it was not an ingrained part of their life. But once the fighting began, it became regular and frequent, like the waves of an angry sea. The weight of their fighting crushed their fragile dreams, and they couldn't stop. The fighting felt ancient, as though the Christine and Mike who had met years earlier had left and had been replaced by her father and his mother. The shrew and the drunken brawler angrily confronted each other, wondering if it was meant to turn out this way all along.

## Jonathan and Marie

A couple's move from Expansion into Contraction is often based on one of two issues: (1) one partner's sense that the Expansive Contract has been betrayed, (2) one partner's apparent withdrawal from the couple. Both were true for Jonathan and Marie. Each time they moved into Contraction, it was around the issue of commitment versus withdrawal.

As a young professional couple, Jonathan and Marie had to organize their time closely: they needed time to work, time to be together, and time to spend with friends. In order to do this, they had to trust each other's love and commitment. Frequently, though, Jonathan resented Marie's time apart. Why was she always busy when he needed her? At times, he responded by becoming more absorbed in his own work, thus unavailable when she wanted him. Then Marie would become peevish, angry, and Jonathan would move even further away. When this interactional sequence was coupled with the need to make difficult decisions, bad feelings would emerge, and they would begin a slide into Contraction.

Jonathan would become absorbed in work; Marie, feeling neglected, would angrily withdraw. They might describe this process differently to friends: she was troubled, but he was unresponsive; she was pushy, and he withdrew to avoid being controlled; he was too intellectual, she too emotional.

Three years after they met, this struggle flared up. They were living together, and found themselves bickering about marriage and commitment. When either asked the other about making a deeper commitment, the latter would hem and haw, talk about not being fully settled into his or her career yet, and seem to be putting the first one off. Either of them could ask, and either could put the other off.

Out of sync, each felt unloved and rejected. Marie began to see Jonathan as more aloof than she had first thought, more selfish, more like the other men from whom she'd broken away. She wondered if he even had the strength to make a commitment to her: he seemed only to want her when he needed her sexually, or to help him "blow off steam." She found his lapsing into guilt particularly obnoxious, and wondered if—underneath it all—he was just a baby. She hated him when he acted this way, and she contrasted him with her dad, who could laugh off troubles and seem to support *her* no matter what she might say or do.

For his part, Jonathan was tiring of what he felt were Marie's demands. He found her less fanciful, more rigid and opinionated. Now he saw her as downright moody, and as demanding as all the other women he had dated and distrusted: eager to take time off for herself when *she* needed to, but quick to pressure him to spend time with her if she felt lonely—even if he had mountains of work to do. But then, he told himself, she was spoiled. Hadn't her father called her his "little princess"? He felt so angry that at times he had to go off by himself. How could he be expected to get married when he felt like that?

His little ways of organizing his personal things began to drive her crazy: "You're so *neurotic!*" she'd scream. He felt her scorn, and hated her for it. He also hated how she kept forgetting to replace the toilet paper or how she'd finish the mayonnaise and not buy a new jar. He hated "having to apologize all the time for everything."

Just then, Jonathan found himself attracted to a secretary from work: she was cute, much less "pushy" than Marie, and she treated him like God. Marie sensed something going on and kept questioning him, but he denied everything. Finally, faced with her persistent queries, he admitted the attraction, but advised her not to worry. Marie was not reassured. She'd been struggling with her clinic administrator, and her antennae were fine-tuned to empty words. She was furious when she heard that Jonathan was "turned on by that bimbo." Fearing her rejection, Jonathan moved into his placating mode, but now she refused to listen and rejected all his apologies.

He had no idea how to proceed. He was afraid that his own foolish behavior had done him in; he was going to lose the only woman who'd been able to tolerate him, the only woman with whom he'd been able to be himself. In a state of demoralization and confusion, he began to strike back on his own—criticizing, making sarcastic comments, coming home late.

As this flare-up grew, each felt their hold on the relationship ebbing. Each day they would privately resolve to stop fighting, but they couldn't. They seemed to be addicted to it. Nothing they tried helped. They couldn't let things drop and they couldn't talk things out. In this atmosphere, it became too hard to even raise the question of marriage.

One day, when Marie once again told him not to drop his socks on the floor, Jonathan turned and yelled at her, "I *know* what I'm doing. I was just going to pick them up, if you'd only give me a *chance!*" And he stalked out of the bedroom and slammed the door. "*Don't* you slam that *door!*" she cried, chasing after him. When she caught him in the kitchen, she let out a torrent of abuse, calling him selfish, ignorant, arrogant, rude, abusive, and chauvinist. Then she packed her bags, stalked out of their apartment, and stayed with her parents for a week.

This brought the crisis to a head.

Jonathan desperately missed her. He asked their friend Harriet to intercede, and she did. Marie really did miss Jonathan, and when she finally listened to him she felt he was genuinely apologetic; and so she returned. Over the ensuing weeks, they felt good about resolving this fight, and, soon afterwards, decided to get married.

But we are getting ahead of ourselves. For now, let us note that Jonathan's resentment at having to placate Marie did not disappear, but went underground, as did Marie's anger at having had to walk out to get Jonathan's attention. Not that they intentionally held in their negative feelings. If you had asked them, they'd have said they felt mostly free of doubt and resentment. But their angry, irritable patterns lay dormant, ready to emerge again later, when they entered an even deeper period of Contraction. Later we will investigate more in depth what happened here.

## Internal Experience

In Contraction, we feel that our partners have betrayed their promises to support and love us, to bring out the best in us, to let us make mistakes without coming down on us, to forego retribution. Contraction brings a sense of loss: the loss of our ideal partner, a perfectly loving friend, a concerned mentor. Our partner's requests for change no longer feel supportive. Instead, they make us feel judged and controlled.

During this stage partners frequently adopt roles of "parent" and "child," and each partner may assume either role in turn. The "parent" partner becomes scolding; the childlike partner must protect him or herself through withdrawing or rebelling. Both feel misunderstood and unappreciated, off balance, needy, and frustrated. If the childlike partner withdraws, the other may become shrill and bullying.

This is the context in which much domestic violence and abuse occur.* Partners may misread each other's behavior. One may approach to establish contact, but the other takes it as aggressiveness or control, and lashes out angrily. One partner withdraws to be safe, but the other angrily pursues her, losing his temper in the rage of feeling misunderstood, ignored, or abandoned. When one or both partners cannot hold back from expressing these feelings physically, the results are all too familiar.

In Contraction, though, we feel betrayed and disappointed by ourselves as well. We have not sustained the loving generosity, independence, or perspective of the Expansive Stage. We had promised ourselves that "this time we would keep it up," but we could not carry it off. We have to admit that much of our expansiveness depended on the support of our partner, not just on our own efforts. Our capacities, which for a while seemed enhanced and expanded, now seem more diminished than ever before. We thought we had reached beyond the petty quarreling, the nasty rage, the loss of per-

---

*By describing this interactional process which may lead to violence, we neither condone violence nor imply that battered women share equal blame with men who batter. There is no justification for one partner hitting another and even less when one is much stronger. Nor do we think that the interaction which we describe is the only or even the prototypical form taken by domestic violence. Many men batter women in drunken, impotent rages. Others hit or maintain the potential for violence in order to bully and contain women. There are many motives and forms for domestic violence, most of which support an imbalance of power in relationships.

We do mean that a common form of domestic violence includes an angry, escalating buildup in which, before the violence itself, both partners participate.

spective that fills us during this stage, but now we are right back in it.

Everything we try seems to fail, and we feel trapped. The harder we try to climb out of conflict, the deeper we sink into it. Talking is supposed to help, but it is often like pouring gasoline on a fire. Being quiet is seen as judgmental. Wishing to talk is interpreted as controlling. This stage is characterized by double binds: "If I ask for what I want, he thinks I'm demanding and pulls back. But if I *don't* speak up, I can't get what I want, either." Or: "I always feel I'm doing what *she* wants. Even when she doesn't say it directly, I know what she expects. And if I don't do it she gets mad and makes my life miserable."

We may feel like caricatures of ourselves now. Men appear flat and unexpressive, sullen or enraged; women, overly dramatic and demanding, depressed or needy. We fall back into roles we played out with our parents or enacted in our last unsuccessful relationship. Our partners describe us harshly, which we believe is unfair—but then our actions support their every word.

Regressions in this stage are the flip side of those encountered in Expansion. Partners whine and blame, rarely taking responsibility for their own actions and feelings. They defend themselves against their partner as they did against their parents: screaming when the other leaves or arrives late; cowering as if the other were gigantic and menacing; refusing advice as if the other were nasty or devouring.

Now we come face-to-face with our night thoughts, our shadows, our shame. We revisit the pain we have always dreaded: the time our father said we would never amount to anything; the time, at thirteen, when that person we had a crush on joked about our acne; all the times when we feared we were not good enough, pretty enough, strong, smart, or interesting enough. As this portrait grew, whenever we felt unhappy and even when we did not, we feared that this was our real, our deeper self: frightened, defensive, selfish, angry, and nasty.

Since we tend to push this pessimistic portrait underground as much as possible, it seems darker and less civilized than our cheerier side. It is not the portrait we want our friends and lovers to see, nor the person around whom we want to build relationships. Unrefined through open interaction with others, this portrait feels primitive. Since we haven't dealt as openly with it, and since it has been lurking beneath the surface, we often take this darker self to be a truer representation of ourselves. In a perverse way we trust it more than our expansive portrait.

When our partners accuse us of being this diminished, shameful self, we believe them. We may deny it, but in our hearts we believe that we have been discovered, that the real "us" has been unearthed, exposed for the phony we really are, despite what now seems like the charade of Expansion. It feels at last as if we have pierced the false ideals of that earlier stage and moved toward a deeper reality. Our wounded partners, defending themselves, do little to dispel this notion, because it gives them a momentary advantage in the competition over who is more to blame.

This exposure can be terrible and terrifying. We spend a great deal of psychic energy guarding against its occurrence. Once it has taken place, much of our life's strategy focuses on pushing the revelations back underground. But during the first passage through the Stage of Contraction, such a cover-up seems impossible, like trying to stuff an immense, shameful secret into a small, transparent bag. It feels impossible partly because the person who first exposed the humiliating secrets is the person we had most trusted, the person with whom we are still locked in close relationship. We cannot escape the other's gaze. Day after day, we are forced to live with the very person who sees our weaknesses, our fall from grace most clearly. We huddle against them, both relieved and infuriated that only they know our most shameful secrets.

Many relationships never recover from this crushing period. The seeds of their dissolution are sown in that dreadful moment when each partner too vividly feels the long vulnerable sores without comfort or respite from the other's view. Dating as well as married relationships frequently break up during this period. Partners want to escape the humiliation of living with a partner who sees their weaknesses so clearly but who cannot be trusted to be safe or kind.

## Two Kinds of Contraction

Because so much is expected of couples in our culture, the Stage of Contraction is a major trauma and challenge. Our Expansive Contract has been betrayed, and we are devastated. How severe the stage will be depends on how much the previous Expansive Stage had been counted on to heal past wounds, on what early injuries the Stage of Betrayal revives, and on how each partner responds.

Contraction has two somewhat different modes of organization. At first, the partners are in a state of shock, and their feelings are raw and bitter. But as the stage continues, the couple begins to organize itself in a more routine, less cataclysmic way. Patterns of behavior emerge that take the edge off the rawness and let the partners carry out their daily chores and duties. Their more bitter feelings and angry impulses are kept under wraps; and a grinding, distant, pessimistic mode of interaction sets in.

This second, more grinding mode of organization may come to characterize the Stage of Contraction in later cycles. In fact, its gloomy, distancing features become built into the defensive structure of many couples, as "the" way they experience their repeated times in Contraction.

## The Couple

In Contraction, the themes around which the couple is organized shift. The happier themes that first brought the partners together no longer play figural roles. Instead, their lives are dominated by themes of alienation and antagonism. Much of the intensity is now robed in conflict.

"I never knew you were such a *workaholic*," one man tells his lover.

"You didn't tell me that you wanted to see your son [from another marriage] so much," a woman says to her new mate.

The themes run from significant to petty: "If I had known that you pick your nose like that, I'm not sure I would have married you."

Those couples who do not separate do not move far apart. They have little perspective in this stage. It's as if they were stuck together. Their actions become increasingly limited and predictable, a painful, endlessly repetitive dance. He demands; she resists. She inquires; he withdraws. He seduces; she is turned off. She talks on the phone; he works harder.

In place of the upward cycles of the Expansive Stage, a downward cycle now unfolds. Here, each partner's move inward is followed by the other's also pulling in. Ever more narrow interpretations of the other's actions and character follow, and the partners protect themselves by gaining distance through mood, silence, work, alcohol, other relationships, or power plays. For example, one partner may claim the importance of being true to himself. Another may seize the moral high ground by playing the helpless victim. The more one partner pursues one strategy, the more the other monomaniacally pursues its counterpart. These strategies may be "symmetrical," as when each tries to bully the other or claim moral superiority; or they may be "complementary," as when one's bullying consistently elicits a victim-like response from the other. Sequences of moves become patterned. Negative feedback begets negative feedback.

## Male and Female

Instead of magically converging as they did before, men's and women's paths now diverge. Both partners revert to type (and stereotype); pouting withdrawn men battle critical women. Bullying men struggle with women who won't say what they need. At this point, the apparent convergence of the Expansive Stage appears like an error in judgment. A type of gender war defines the relationship, and, in place of the androgyny that flourished earlier, an inflexible role division emerges. Gay and lesbian couples in this stage often divide up in similar ways, as one member plays out a stereotyped male and the other a stereotyped female role.

Partners shut down and close off qualities that they had joyfully but tentatively expressed: it is too dangerous to be different from their norm, and they feel vulnerable. Instead, they attack each other for "typical" male or female behavior.

As they fall back into their most contracted selves, men close off their "feminine" sides, often feeling "set up" because their partner now seems contemptuous or disinterested in their vulnerability; women regret their own vulnerability because men seem disinterested or cruel in response, and they "know" that experiments in assertiveness have driven men off.

Men, experiencing themselves as oppressed by "irrationally critical" women, respond in a closed, tight-lipped, rational manner. Women react emotionally, pursuing and complaining about their walled-off mates. Disillusioned, both claim they are only acting this way in response to the other, whom they see in generic terms: he or she is "just like" other men or women they have known: they have *failed* to find the exception. The mate is discovered to embody either all the traits of that gender the partner has most feared and despised, or none of those traits the partner has admired. Each is too much or not enough. Men now seek out the company of other men, usually at work; women seek out other women. Friends and family applaud old Charlie, resuscitate old Peg. Reinforced by their old buddies, each partner revives long-abandoned behaviors. Friends may imply that their partners influenced them too much: he was too "soft" and yielding to her ways; she lost herself in her man instead of retaining her independence.

Now we insist that our partners accept us as we really are—not exactly what we had promised to be, but "warts and all." We are not some projection of their own wishes. This demand is difficult, because it acknowledges how far we've fallen, and because we hurl it defensively and angrily, and give our partners little chance to comply.

Women often pursue men to repair the relationship. They try to be accommodating; they propose conversation, perhaps therapy. But the more they pursue, the more men perceive them as demanding. In response men alternately try to accept their partners' advances and withdraw into punitive silence or bullying eruptions. This downward spiral of anxious pursuit and frightened withdrawal fails to solve their problems and makes them even less secure.

The constriction that follows affects every area of their life. Sex becomes more routine, predictable, and infrequent, and once again intertwined with power and control. Fun and experimentation decrease. The partners want to have sex so they can reach orgasm, because they need to feel close, or because they are tense. Hugging, cuddling, and foreplay fall away; the capacity for expressiveness, closeness, autonomy, and adventure diminishes; and the partners fall into more mechanical, genitally focused sex.

The sexual reversal creates even more distance. During Contraction, sex often becomes the domain of one partner, usually the man but often enough the woman. He wants it. He complains about its infrequency. He initiates it. But the more he initiates, the more she pulls back. Her own independent desire seems to be slipping away. Sometimes sex can be satisfying to her, and she responds to his initiative. Sometimes she pretends to respond, hoping to get him off her case. Occasionally, at this time, she may confess she never really liked sex and gave in to it only to please him. Often she reacts negatively, shutting him off as he tries to open her up.

He feels abandoned and deprived of what he had felt to be one of Expansion's main promises. Physical contact is the door to intimacy for him, and now he cannot achieve it. He may now fantasize about other women, while she—feeling hassled and unloved—may simply turn herself off in order to cope better. This is the counterpoint to what goes on in conversation, as women initiate but feel abandoned while men pull back, feeling pushed.

Coercive male physical power may replace shared assent. As men act out rituals of sexual dominance, women recoil. The emergence of a pattern of rapid, impersonal sexual encounters disgusts many women: they become convinced that it was a mistake to have so opened themselves in the earlier stage of the relationship. They miss the lingering and talk, being related to as a person, not an object. The decline of mutuality makes men feel deprived of the easy closeness and acceptance they had earlier experienced. The relationship no longer feels special.

In Contraction, aspects of both partners' personalities that no longer seem to fit into the couple relationship become pushed down, split off, and suppressed. They now form the basis for fantasies about other people, for obsessive ruminations and affairs. (Maybe *that* person over there will be soft and gentle, yet understanding, dynamic in expressing him- /or herself, capable of wild sensuality ...) Instead of giving up their fantasies, the partners squirrel them away from the ever-more-constricted relationship. Both partners thus alienate themselves from each other and withhold their better, fuller selves in self-preservation.

## Encountering a Contracted Partner

During the Stage of Contraction our partners shrink before our eyes. They appear to be less capable and less charming. Good qualities are transformed into flaws: what has seemed feisty now seems anxious and pushy; what had seemed quiet now seems withholding and depressed. Observing these transformations, we feel surprised or foolish. Why hadn't we seen the flaws earlier? Why had they seemed so limited and manageable? We rarely take responsibility for these changes in our partners. We do not want to know that our anxiety about her forthrightness threw her off balance and gave her that anxious edge. We do not want to know that our anxiety about his shyness frightened him into a more icy retreat.

We only see that our partners have become more like those former lovers and parents whom we had tried to avoid encountering again. We become convinced that our mates lack goodwill, consideration, and ordinary human kindness. The more we see them turn into the persons with whom we have had so much trouble, the more we recoil and try to protect ourselves. Why, we ask, should we spend so much effort on a person who makes us feel so bad? We look for others who still bring out our best.

A more shodowy, stingier side now seems to dominate their personalities. They pull back and tell us that we had been mistaken, that it is unfair to hold them to such high standards, and that they need room to mess up, to be bad. All true, we think, but so disappointing. And we feel foolish as well.

In protecting ourselves, we again engage the Cultural Narrative. Now we pay attention to the songs and stories about love's betrayal. We hear the blues with new ears, and listen to other people's tales of failure. We try to accommodate to the cynical views about what happens to relationships after their romantic beginnings—that routine replaces romance, quarrels interfere with sex, and coping supplants excitement. As we struggle between our dreams and what we take to be a more realistic attitude, we try to gain wisdom and maturity.

As our mates diminish, something happens inside us as well. Our sense of our own potential begins to shrink. Doubts about our own abilities, our own wonderfulness surge up and take on new life. Like ugly balloons, these fears swell, distorting our self-image and undermining our confidence. Deep down, our partner's diminished view of *us* has hit a truth we knew was there all the time. The more we demean our partner, the worse we feel about ourselves.

## Depleted Energy

Just as an increasing flow of energy between partners—positive, synergistic, and enabling—characterized the Expansive Stage, so the Stage of Contraction is marked by a decreasing flow of energy.

Instead of "upward, expanding spirals," Contraction traps both partners in "downward, contracting spirals." My critical attitude brings you down, and yours brings out the worst in me. Your stinginess makes me stingy, too. My lethargy makes you tired. When I want everything neat, you won't help. The neater I want things, the sloppier you seem to get. I grow obsessive; you, neglectful. At every turn, the downward cycles distort and undermine what we like in ourselves and our partners. Happiness, energy, confidence, and hope are all sucked into the pit from which, it seems, there is no return.

Time together becomes exhausting. Friendly comments are "misinterpreted" as attacks; warmth is seen as deceptive. Instead of encouraging self-revelation, partners flee into themselves. They keep secrets, hide their most personal feelings, and feel they must *defend*, not expose, their inner selves. As we cease to replenish ourselves through our partners, we have less energy for them and they for us.

Within these safe confines partners oppose change, take on narrower roles that they can play without much effort, and move stiffly through life together. A sexual advance is angrily rejected; a request to "pass the sugar" at the table is met with an insult; an idle comment about a friend is stuffed into the middle of a day-old fight about the differences between men and women; an invitation to take a walk is mockingly recast as a manipulative move. Trust breaks down. Kindness is wooden. The partners keep their energy within.

Feeling vulnerable, each partner falls back to earlier defensive patterns. They *regress* to conventional ideas about the "right" ways of settling disputes, or the right ways women and men should act with each other. Suddenly they feel the redemption of acting as their mothers or fathers acted; they demand the same respect as their parents enjoyed: they cloak themselves in the garb of past models.

Experimentation now takes new forms. First, the partners begin to keep more distance. Second, they try new approaches to restore affection, love, and respect. These attempts will be tentative and represent forays into the realm of Resolution; they require courage because the partners are still in a fighting mode and may see any momentary "opening" as a sign of weakness.

## Updating the Narratives

Early in relationships we tell our life's story to our future partners. By listening sympathetically, they become trusted custodians of our past, and help move our story in promising directions. We are thrilled with the identity mutually woven in the Expansive Stage. Later, our less savory qualities emerge: we have always known they were integral to our story; now our partners angrily weave them in, crafting a new story about us without our willing collaboration, drawn primarily from the underside of our identity and colored by their own anxieties. The new story feels somehow more real, more ancient and enduring. We fight it, but fear that a careful reading will confirm the portrait. Our identity is in crisis, and we writhe in indignation and self-doubt.

Now we turn to other activities and roles, hoping to rebuild a sustaining narrative for ourselves. The new narratives may emphasize our roles as parents or community participants. But the season for coupling seems over. This is partly practical and realistic: there is much to do in life, which the intense early focus on one's relationship impedes. We return to the "rest of our lives," and turn our backs on our partner because our identity within the couple has become intolerable, and we need to sow the seeds of a separate, free-standing identity.

We completely revise our Couple Narrative during the Stage of Contraction. We tell our story more to outsiders, because they listen less defensively and more compassionately. The tone varies according to the teller and the listener. A moderate person talks of disappointment and the need for adjustment. A more dramatic one emphasizes shock and devastation: "I never thought we'd have so much trouble: I couldn't *believe* what started happening! Now we've got to pick up the pieces and start all over again."

The narrative takes on a tragic quality, adding themes of inevitability, fatal flaws, bitter blindness, and sad victims. It is as though we always knew it would come to this, but were helpless to stop it. During the second telling, we may portray the Expansive Stage as a sentimental but necessary beginning. In this way, we may defend ourselves against disappointment by minimizing Expansion's importance.

Both partners struggle to reorient themselves during Contraction. They have to cope with what they discover about themselves, have to make meaning of their painful experience. If they try to maintain the story they created during Expansion and treat the discoveries as aberrations, they will delude and lose touch with themselves. If they make the discoveries into the whole story, they will probably become despondent and break up. Integrating the discoveries of Contraction with the story of Expansion can enrich them both, adding depth and authenticity to their story.

Indeed, the narrative of Contraction is as compelling as the narrative of Expansion. It, too, becomes a marker in the life of a couple. The former represents our positive image of our relationship; the latter, our negative one. A couple usually travels between the two.

## The Contract of Contraction and Betrayal

The troublesome experience of the second stage forms the basis for a new contract, a set of expectations about what happens when couples are at their worst:

"Whenever I'm unhappy, all you want to do is get away."

"Whenever I say the least critical thing, you have a fit that lasts a week."

Couples grow very accustomed to the predictable experiences of Contraction.

"If you did not throw a fit when I criticized you I might feel confused and—to check out my sense of reality—might criticize you again, perhaps a little more harshly this time."

"If you stayed around and did not leave when I was unhappy, I might feel crowded and humiliated at your seeing me at my worst. So, instead of letting you comfort me, which I really want, I might crankily try to chase you away."

In this way, we develop very stable patterns of behavior that are reinforced by the stable negative images we have carried from as far back as childhood. This weave of behaviors and images organizes our fears and insecurities. Curiously enough, although the patterns do not eliminate or protect us from our fears, they bind them up somehow and keep them from getting out of control.

This is what the new contract is about. It acts to keep the worst of the Stage of Contraction within tolerable limits. It lets us know the worst but still remain together. If partners survive the first experience of Contraction, or the first few, they will refer back to this contract as well as to that of their Expansive Stage. This second contract represents the nadir of their relationship, the lowest point to which they can sink and still remain together.

Like the Expansive Contract, it is less a set of rules than a series of images and feelings.

Couples pass through Contraction many times. Each passage threatens their relationship, and they must continually find ways of controlling their own destructive power. So each time around, they let themselves be guided by the Second Contract.

The paradoxical quality of this second contract is that it offers the partners some comfort, since it stops them this side of disaster. Because of this, they are reluctant to let it go. But it also keeps them from changing the rules and trying something new—something that might pull them out. They measure their experience against it: If the experience fits the pattern, it is tolerable. If it does not, it is too threatening and is therefore dismissed. Many efforts to break out of Contraction are thus dismissed. The couple may try to impose more intimacy than they can tolerate in the face of Contraction's mistrust, or attempt more independence than the partners' insecurities permit—even though being together is painful.

Unable to tolerate some of their best efforts to change, couples may remain longer in Contraction. The Second Contract helps them by keeping difficulties within limits but hinders them by inhibiting change.

This bitter identity includes its own particular grim anecdotes and stories. These, too, will be told many times again, and may act as deterrents to further injury. The "culture of two" has been further developed.

## Patti and Marshall

Patti and Marshall fell into their first arguments over questions of love and independence. Patti had begun to feel that Marshall was holding her back, inhibiting her development as a photographer, and jealously keeping her from expressing the creative spark she felt was her *essence* and that he so much claimed to love. She felt him strangling the very part of her that could love and create. So she pulled back. Angry, she reasserted her right to live her own life and make her own choices. If he wanted to be with her, fine: but he had to accept her control over her own life.

Marshall felt Patti's pulling away as a rejection. He felt he had been "giving" as much as he could. All he asked in return was her love and affection, and some degree of sexual contact. But sexual contact was one thing Patti took away from him when she withdrew.

She stopped hugging and kissing him, touching his arm, or even *smiling* at him. The sense of coldness made him feel bereft; he entered a state of panic.

Now, insisting on her freedom to do what she wanted, she began to demean Marshall's way of life, implying that while *she* was indeed wild and creative, *he* was weak, unsure, and vacillating. He felt abandoned and attacked. For her part, she felt weighed down, as if by another clingy child. She rejected his ideas, his complaints:

"Don't tell me what to do," she challenged. "I'll make my *own* decisions. If you're so hot to tell people what to do, why don't you get your *own* life in shape? Go do something with your*self* and get off *my* back!"

Unable to take what he felt as continual abuse, Marshall became furious. He felt like a fool. Patti was no different from other women: she was domineering, selfish, controlling, and volatile. Her energy was focused around herself. Instead of being loving and tolerant, she was spiteful and critical. How could he have been so mistaken? He withdrew even further, became depressed, sniped at her from a distance, felt sorry for himself ...

The more Marshall withdrew, the angrier Patti got. She saw him as frightened, like her father, and she grew troubled. How could she have misjudged Marshall so? Instead of being her "rock," he was really jelly: and now he was expecting her to support him. It infuriated her. How could she realize her ambitions if she had to take care of Marshall, Simon, and everyone else? Where would she find the man who could care for *her*?

The more she attacked, the more he withdrew, until finally—self-esteem crumbling—he began to lash out angrily:

"You don't think I'm a man? Is that it? After all I've done for you? Goddamn you!"

"Don't threaten me!"

And they were off into a fight that ended only when one of them fled the house.

Just as they reexperience the expansive, sunny images of their first time through the Expansive Stage each time they pass into Expansion, so Marshall and Patti revive and reexperience the bitter, desperate images of this, their first time through the Stage of Contraction and Betrayal each time they pass into Contraction. When they slip into their Stage of Contraction, Patti and Marshall reexperience their worst fears and nightmares. The other's angry taunts painfully echo their *own* inner feelings of inadequacy. Their sense of failure in choosing the "right" mate undercuts their fragile self-esteem. Angrily projecting their own feelings of weakness and bitterness onto their mate, they then launch into a bitter, furious attack, which only serves to drive them further apart. Each feels betrayed and undermined. The traits they so esteemed in the other now seem like a cruel travesty, a caricature, a hoax. They have been misled. They are trapped.

Patti and Marshall first experienced feelings of Contraction a few months into their relationship, when they argued about love and affection (his issues) and independence (her issue). The next time they slid into Contraction was after they got married; then, their arguments focused on the questions of having another child and advancing Patti's career. Two years later, Patti got pregnant and miscarried, and they fell into another period of bitter, desperate Contraction, blaming each other and themselves. This crisis was resolved by their deciding to stay together and relocate for her work.

If we followed Patti and Marshall through their life together, we would witness their undergoing other periods of Contraction. For example, at one point Marshall became seriously ill, which required Patti to take on more caretaking functions, and she had to make some unplanned sacrifices in her career. Another Contraction emerged after Patti's Aunt Belle died. Later yet, Patti and Marshall entered a period of Contraction after Patti's son, Simon, began having serious problems in school.

Each time they entered Contraction, the same arguments revived. Dilemmas that had seemed settled reappeared, still alive, still thorny, bristling, and devastating.

## The Importance of Contraction

Even though it is a difficult time, the Stage of Contraction is essential to couples' development. Unless partners can bring their wounds and uncertainties into the relationship they will feel neither real nor whole, and the vigilance required to protect themselves will make them guarded and superficial. In Contraction, critical themes and images from the partners' past enter the couple's experience, further deepening its character. In this sense, Contraction should not be seen as just a "negative" stage, the unwanted counterpart of Expansion's happy times. It is as necessary for couples to go through as the other stages.

For we confront ourselves honestly in Contraction's harsh light, telling the truth about our limitations and those of our partners. We may perceive grim realities in such a time, and may reach insights about ourselves and our loved ones that we would "rather not know" but that are crucial for us to deal with. These may not be truer than the realities of Expansion, but they are *also* true and must be folded into the relationship. Eventually, these themes may be seen not as some alternative to Expansion but as a supplement and balance to it.

Contraction permits the partners to be open about unpleasant things. Secrets, fears, obsessions, distortions, jealousies, and other awful but true aspects of ourselves emerge. In this gutting of self and partner couples may find an antidote to the sometimes Pollyanna-ish world of Expansion. Without Contraction, we would feel unknown in our relationships: hidden, secret, and unauthentic, left alone to grapple with our rage and pain.

Couples who endure this stage and remain together will look back on this as a rite of passage, a time when they were tested and triumphed.

## Moving Out of Contraction

To survive, couples must move out of Contraction and reach Resolution. Over the course of a long relationship, they do this again and again. Each time, they must find ways of holding their difficulties at bay or at least of placing them in enough perspective for the stuff of Expansion to enter and balance the disappointment of Contraction.

Couples remain in Contraction for varying lengths of time. Some stay there most of their time together, escaping into Resolution or Expansion for only brief moments. For others, the only way out is to dissolve the relationship, and this is what finally happens. For still others, there is no way out; but they feel so afraid of being alone, so dependent on the financial or social support of their partner, that they cannot face splitting up. Children keep some antagonistic couples together. Religious belief is a glue for others. Other couples avoid Contraction at all costs, and will even skate on the surface most of the time if it keeps conflict to a minimum.

Most couples pass regularly in and out of Contraction, but the length of time they spend there may vary: they may take brief passages; they may take lengthy stays that threaten to last forever or end the relationship.

Each couple develops distinctive ways to break out of Contraction. Some escape through intense fights. They yell and blame and let out all their pent-up frustration. But when they are done, they admit how lonely they have been, how unloved they have felt, and how much they want to be close, and they come together again. Others extricate themselves bit by bit. One small reconciliation may lead to a brief compromise; even if this falls apart, it still serves as the basis for a second compromise ... which might establish a broader basis for agreement; and so on. Eventually the couple passes a threshold, and their goodwill endures: they feel sufficiently redeemed and respected to believe that Contraction is only a stage, not the whole relationship.

There are false starts during Contraction, too—brief moments when the pain and struggle seem forgiven and the couple experiences a temporary return to the good feelings of the first stage. When the mood of Contraction retains its hold, these moments seem like cruel jokes. But when the moment proves to be one of several in a redeeming chain, the couple moves ahead. The accumulation of these moments can break the sequence and give rise to a new organization, which ushers the couple into the Stage of Resolution.

Sometimes couples cordon off a problem in order to get out of Contraction. They may agree not to discuss an inflammatory topic or avoid activities that bring out the worst in them. They might eliminate activities that feel threatening to one partner: visits to the in-laws, some forms of sexual interaction, socializing with certain acquaintances, trying to discipline the children together. When they are successful the negotiated walls can provide them with the time and space they need to resuscitate their expansive times. Of course, no wall is impregnable: cordoned-off difficulties will probably break through again later, thrusting the partners back into another stage of Contraction. To some extent the recurrence of Contraction depends on how much the wall can hold back, or on whether the difficulties can be resolved in more lasting ways.

At times couples do more than cordon off their difficulties: they actually move to resolve them. (This will be taken up in the next chapter, on the Stage of Resolution.) Resolving problems so the couple can break out of Contraction is their main goal at this time. Cordoning off problems is like putting on a bandage. Some last a long time. Some do not. But whether the solution offers temporary or permanent relief is a secondary issue. Later on, the couple may return to their old problematic ways. But this will be something for them to worry about *then*.

Couples are always trying things out, making small forays into new domains. Even in the bleakest Contraction, they make momentary excursions into compromise, attempt to negotiate, or experience a return of feelings of togetherness. Sex may provide an occasion for this lessening of tension; but so may hobbies like dancing, going to movies, having dinner out, visiting friends or parents, or taking a vacation or holiday weekend. Almost anything that *interrupts* a downward cycle can provide a spark to change, an impetus to move upward and together again.

In Contraction, partners often feel so isolated and unappreciated that they start living in their own minds. A few kind words, a respectful gesture, a smile, a warm touch, a gift, an afternoon of talking and being together—any of these can provide the spark for a couple's beginning to move out of Contraction. What matters is that the partners sense a potential to be different. If they can see some relief from the fighting, from the isolation, even some partial resolution, some kind of truce, they may agree to try again. They need their partners to love and respect them. They need to see glimmers of the old partner they fell in love with. They need to feel themselves esteemed, if only for a moment, in the other's eyes.

As Theodore Roethke has written, "In a dark time, the eye begins to see."[1] In the days of Contraction, even though they are angry, self-righteous, and withdrawn, each partner is usually also looking for a way out. Each partner is usually on the alert for a sign, a signal that things can change. The random appearance of any such signal can be a catalyst that moves the couple toward the succeeding stage, the Stage of Resolution. And the steady accumulation of such signs and signals will lead to the development of new patterns of feeling and acting toward each other that enable them to move out of the pits and swamps into which Contraction has thrust them, and back onto solid ground again.

# 7

## THE STAGE
## OF RESOLUTION

Couples in Contraction have three basic options. They can break up. They can remain stuck in Contraction. Or they can move into a new stage, Resolution, which at least partially resolves the conflict between Expansion and Contraction.

The pain of Contraction so overwhelms and demoralizes couples that many end their relationships then and there. Others remain in Contraction because they fear that their efforts to resolve their problems will lead to divorce. Still others, frustrated by their attempts to escape, settle into Contraction for long periods; they find ways to avoid their angriest confrontations and build defensive walls around themselves to limit their feelings of rejection, abandonment, and unworthiness. Their attempts to resolve problems become mostly ritualistic.

This chapter focuses on those couples who contain or resolve enough problems to move into the Stage of Resolution.

### The Essential Character of Resolution

Resolution marks a new beginning. It is characterized by a new spirit: a feel for accommodation, a capacity for seeing the complexity of things; and a tendency to elevate affection and partnership over romance and passion. In Resolution we put our cranky, blaming feelings aside and let hope and commitment flourish once more. It is a more sober time than Expansion, more of a time to work together than to linger in each other's embrace.

This is a stage of compromise and negotiation. Partners strive to be reasonable, to maintain a sense of perspective, and to take responsibility for themselves. If Expansion stretches our capacities in optimistic ways, and Contraction in pessimistic ways, Resolution establishes a new sense of balance and solidity. At last we feel we have our feet on the ground: we know what we are doing, and are in control of our lives.

Resolution often leads into a new phase of expansive feelings, reviving the optimism, shared dreams, and sense of mutuality we once enjoyed. Early in a relationship, this optimism may lead couples quickly into a new Stage of Expansion and the beginning of a second or third cycle. Later in their relationship, couples may pull the reins in on moving too quickly toward Expansion. They may prefer to remain as long as they can in Resolution, because its solid attributes feel more reassuring and more stabilizing than the exciting but regressive pulls of Expansion. After all, a new Stage of Expansion may last only a little while, and the couple may end up too quickly ushered into another stage of disappointments.

Couples' experience in their first passage through Resolution falls along a broad spectrum. Some achieve a dramatic shift from pitched battle into free-flowing cooperation and mutuality. Others move doggedly forward, with an emphasis on solving problems and restricting conflict; these achieve a companionable, if guarded, intimacy—more like friendship than romance. Still others approach Resolution with a spiritual perspective, accepting their limitations and those of their partners in a more philosophical, less tormented way. For them, Resolution means letting go of long-powerful but unrealized, "unrealistic" hopes in exchange for a calmer, quieter life together.

Since couples spiral through many cycles of Expansion, Contraction, and Resolution in their life together, their behavior in any one Stage of Resolution may differ from that in another. This way, some couples become familiar with a wide spectrum of styles for this stage. Usually, though, each couple will find its own distinctive style of Resolution and follow it again and again.

* * *

Resolution accomplishes several tasks. First, it brings us out of Contraction. Second, it helps us integrate the feelings and images of Contraction with those of our earlier Expansive Stage. Third, it brings out images and feelings of friendship, maturity, and partnership that had not been prominent in the other stages. Cautiously, we sift through our ideas of who we are, what we want, and how to get it; and we experiment with new ways of expressing ourselves. Then, gradually, we organize these new ways into a common vision born, not of romance, but of more realistic assessment.

The stage of Resolution feels pluralistic, democratic. Disparate feelings can coexist here. Divergent images seem like different sides of the same coin—not as mutually exclusive. Instead of dividing us, they bring us together in conversation. We talk of both/and, not either/or.

We are as prepared for this stage as for those which preceded it. Parents, grandparents, teachers, and mentors have all taught us that toleration and compromise are the stuff of adulthood. In the long run, they say, love, passion, and the idealism of youth run their course. When we stop blaming or leaning too much on others and begin taking responsibility for our own lives, we will be able to stay the course.

The Stage of Resolution has an ideology all its own, similar to that of being a good citizen. It makes us more generous in opinion and action, more flexible, more capable of making adjustments. We maintain a better sense of perspective, and try to remain aloof from petty resentments. We recognize and accept differences among people. Resolution celebrates complexity, good judgment, decisive action, and the capacity to handle ambiguity. It is the voice of experience.

Resolution ushers in a new contract. Whereas the Expansive Contract represents the promise of relationship, and Contraction represents our defensive fortress, the contract of Resolution focuses on working things out. If we assess our relationship at the deepest levels by the hopes of the Expansive Contract, we measure it most explicitly by the arrangement we worked out in Resolution. This is a more conscious contract. It contains the compromises and accommodations we negotiate with ourselves and with each other.

## Mixed Views of Resolution

The ideology of Resolution fits uneasily with the Cultural Narrative of our time. On one hand, the Cultural Narrative tells us that compromise is the hallmark of mature individuals. On the other, it warns that compromise means giving in and giving up. In our society, women have come to feel an imbalance in carrying the burden of compromise, for they are usually the ones asked to do the compromising. Increasingly today, women insist that any compromise must be symmetrical, with equal power and respect. Similarly, Twelve-Step programs like Alcoholics Anonymous equate compromise with the enabling of addictive behavior. Such cultural ambivalence about compromise reflects our own personal ambivalence about how much to insist on our own values and desires.

These conflicting attitudes jeopardize the balance we try to achieve in Resolution. How should we solve problems when we are not clear which weighs more: the good of the individual or the good of the couple or family? What happens when partners disagree—not only about an issue, but about the relative importance of individual needs versus the survival of the relationship? Men and women today prefer to negotiate from a position of strength and toward clearly defined goals—"If you want that from me, this is what I expect from you." This modern form of enlightened self-interest enables partners to negotiate more adroitly, accommodate to new situations better, and tolerate differences without sacrificing our principles. According to this view, which many psychotherapists hold, greater self-development leads to a bolstered internal sense of security, which can then sustain us in acting more generously.

Resolution is not, however, the crowning achievement of couple development; it is not even every couple's goal. For some, it feels stiff and formal: what you do at work but not at home. But Resolution does provide a route out of Contraction and toward Expansion. And it focuses our experience by containing the passions and knowledge of the other stages. Many of us wish we could stay longer in Expansion but, knowing we cannot, we choose Resolution. With time, most of us strive to remain in Resolution as much as possible.

Resolution never lasts. The accumulation of happy moments will move us ahead into Expansion; the reappearance of disaster or grinding disagreement will push us back into Contraction. Couple development rests on an integrated experience of all three stages, and on their continual cycling. Each Resolution is followed by Expansion, Expansion by Contraction. The cycles spiral throughout a couple's lifetime.

## Jonathan and Marie

Jonathan and Marie feel two ways in Resolution. Initially, they are tremendously relieved. They feel successful, supported, and loved once again. Their individual ambitions no longer seem in complete conflict with their relationship. This feeling fits their ideal self-image. So they grow closer and begin again to think about their future together.

But their renewed closeness makes them anxious. In Contraction, they built defenses to protect themselves against further harm. They grew distant and formal, fortifying themselves with caricatured views of each other. Contraction had its advantages: it released them to return to their work. As hard-driving people, work felt natural to them. They enjoyed their autonomy and felt enhanced by the positive feedback they got from colleagues. It was their relationships, they felt, that were problematic. Now they had to open up again, let go of their caricatured views of each other, share, and compromise. This was hard.

Let's go back to the time before Marie and Jonathan decided to get married, when they were deep in the throes of their first Contraction. They were still apprentices in their careers, each working long days and wanting support from their relationship for staying on their chosen paths. Fighting over closeness and commitment, Marie found herself angrily pursuing a withholding Jonathan, and he felt her to be demanding and intrusive.

Eventually Marie herself drew back, and threw herself into work and friendships instead. At first, this was a relief to them both. But Jonathan soon grew lonely and insecure. He worried that Marie was bored with him and didn't love him any more. She appeared so competent, he thought, she didn't need him. For a long time he worried and watched. From the safety of distance, he eventually saw that, in spite of her incredible competence, Marie sometimes really *did* seem to need him or, at least, want to be with him.

At this safe distance, he was less afraid of being engulfed by her and was more willing to spend ordinary time together. So he let down his guard a little. For a few days, Marie urged herself to be calm and clear as well, because she saw that Jonathan was trying. This new mood was not exactly to her liking, but it beat the futility of pursuing Jonathan. This way, they experienced some brief forays into the stage of Resolution, even while remaining primarily in Contraction.

Remember that after one of their bitter fights, Marie had stormed off to her parents' house. After she left, Jonathan felt relieved for about five minutes, then missed her terribly. Afraid she would never come back, he begged her to return. She refused.

Jonathan then asked their friend Harriet to intercede. The three of them spent a long evening together, drinking wine, and venting their complaints and injuries. Marie admitted that she had missed Jonathan, too. Watching her talk so animatedly, Jonathan could remember how marvelous she was, and how he enjoyed being with her. Each admitted not having lived up either to their own or to the other's expectations. Each promised to try harder. Jonathan said he would stop treating Marie like some kind of "devouring monster," especially if she would give him a little room when he first came home. Marie said she would support Jonathan's need for "down time," providing he sought her out enough for her to feel sure of his affection.

This was when they felt so good about resolving their conflict that, a few weeks later, they decided to get married. Marriage consolidated their shift into Resolution: it reassured Marie about Jonathan's commitment, and it helped Jonathan feel like an adult once more. They still worked hard but felt more supported by each other. They saw themselves as a talented pair who could work as hard as necessary to succeed.

At the same time, Marie saw Jonathan as more available: among other things, he had begun to seek her company in the small ways that she liked—walking and talking together, hanging out with books and music in the evening, sharing the day's triumphs and insults— and not just for sex. He shared the dilemmas at the office and asked about her days. When they were comfortable together, he might lean against her, rub her back, and make gallant little moves that had been absent for some time. Sex took on a more companionable quality, without the pressure and obligation Marie had come to expect.

Marie found herself being charmed—not so much that Jonathan could see it; she was still a little guarded, but mostly in the privacy of her thoughts. As the months went on, she recognized that Jonathan's desire to be alone had limits. He seemed less aloof, and, at least some of the time, she did not feel his periodic withdrawals as a personal rejection, but rather saw them as a need for time and space that was independent of his feelings for her. Jonathan also developed a sense about the importance of Marie's work for her, and he sometimes understood that her emotional pressure that so frightened him was a simple emanation of her personality—free-flowing, and not a malevolent force. To Jonathan, this felt like a release from prison; without her pursuit, he could more easily tap into his need for her.

This pattern was typical for them. The defensive organization of Contraction would open up to brief forays into Resolution and Expansion. But these forays could not hold, and the promise they held out made any return to Contraction even more painful. The couple's bitterness would finally prove intolerable and, invariably, Marie would explode—usually by leaving or threatening to end the relationship. But the couple's forays into Resolution had laid a groundwork for that new stage to take over, and this is what happens after they resolve the fight Marie precipitates.

## Foreshadowings of Resolution

The Stage of Resolution is never entirely new to couples. It is always foreshadowed, for instance, during the Stage of Expansion. In that first stage couples also fight, resolve their fights, and feel reassured that they can do so—it usually seems different than in their previous relationships or in their families.

Jonathan and Marie had such a fight during their first year together, when they were still in their first Stage of Expansion. The way they resolved it prefigured how they would resolve difficulties later on. At the time, Marie had been furious at Jonathan's obsession with work. He said it was out of his control and barked at her for being "immature." She threatened to leave rather than be treated in this way—and she did withdraw. Jonathan quickly understood that Marie could tolerate this kind of angry distance much better than he could, and he pursued her with apologies and flowers. After keeping her distance for a few more days, she accepted his apologies and explanations about what it was like to be a junior member of a law firm.

The whole struggle took a few weeks, not the months and years that later transitions from Contraction to Resolution would take, but it set the pattern they would continue to follow.

That early resolution depended on Jonathan's pursuing Marie to accept his apology, just as he had pursued her to win her during courtship. Feeling him come closer, Marie accepted his apology. His career did leave him little room to maneuver. She was not happy about it, but she could live with it and be supportive. And she felt pleased at being able to get beyond her own insecurities and "tantrums." For his part, Jonathan felt pleased at being able to rise above his fear of being controlled. He could say he was sorry, be reasonable, and help repair the relationship, because deep down he loved Marie and understood that she really loved him, too.

Early in their relationship, Marie and Jonathan did not remain very long in Resolution. Like most couples, their initial relief in escaping Contraction gave way to elation. They enjoyed the easing of tension they found in Resolution, and fairly quickly moved forward into a new period of Expansion: happy, but somewhat more restrained, sharing their hopes and dreams much as they had in their first months together.

Their particular brand of Expansion, however, was fairly close to Resolution, since they prided themselves on their capacity to talk things through and be mature companions to each other. In later cycles they would learn to hold their more extravagant desires in check in favor of the moderation of Resolution.

## Jonathan and Marie's Pattern

Each time they moved into Resolution, the stereotypes by which Jonathan and Marie had come to characterize each other in Contraction gave way to a more multifaceted appreciation of each other. They were able to enjoy each other's quirkiness and difference, and they enjoyed their newfound identity as a successful couple.

To be sure, each was still wary, anxious that they might return to their fighting, or that the mutual support of careers might not last. But they enjoyed being reasonable. It meant they could plan for the future, could manage problems so they did not get out of hand, could avoid debilitating arguments and incidents that might leave them anxious or afraid. And another thing happened: affection sometimes replaced sex in their repertoire of great things to do. They felt happier together, took care of each other a great deal, and enjoyed both loving and being loved. It was a quieter good time than in Expansion, but it had its richness. Their lives were intertwined: neither was as wholly independent as he or she might have thought, and this was all right. Being guarded did not necessarily prevent being close. They were proud of themselves.

They were proud of the open way they now handled their anxiety. In their hearts, they were still nervous about the renewed intimacy: each was afraid to be let down again, and each felt nervous about the extra time it took from work. They feared that the bitterness would come back to haunt them. But for now, their ability to handle anxiety and tensions by admitting and discussing them was reason to celebrate.

Marie and Jonathan have gone through similar times in other cycles. Several years into their relationship, in the depth of a bitter period of Contraction, Jonathan pulled away and began an affair while Marie was pregnant. When she found out about it, Marie exploded. Jonathan, chastened and apologetic, pursued her. He apologized, asking their parents to intervene and offering to get into therapy. This was the closest they have ever been to breaking up.

When things finally settled down, Jonathan took the major responsibility for what had happened, and said he would change. Marie sensed that Jonathan was great at his work, but not so great at relationships. In part, he was still a child; he couldn't cope with her anger or withdrawal without acting out.

Marie also reflected that Jonathan had been her friend over the years before the affair. He knew her better than anyone else; he had given her steady emotional support with her problems at work, and that counted for a lot with her. Now he said he wanted to be there for her again. Even in the wake of his betrayal, Marie felt that Jonathan genuinely cared for her, and that he wanted to be with her as a person.

Jonathan, for his part, sensed that Marie sometimes seemed rejecting, when she wasn't. He realized that all her life she had been eager to succeed, did not want to repeat her mother's experience, and had the temper to go with her wishes. So he learned to ease up a bit, ask what was really happening when he felt rejected, and not leap to negative conclusions. The more he recognized Marie's complexity, the less alienated he felt from her.

Some of Marie's friends urged her to get rid of Jonathan and make a new life for herself, but she felt unwilling to do that. It seemed extreme to her. She took comfort in friends and family members who urged forgiveness. Jonathan did tend to be selfish and insensitive: but she wanted to take him back, tarnished as he was, because she believed he wanted to change, and because she genuinely wanted his renewed love, support, and companionship.

Jonathan entered this period of Resolution with the understanding, perhaps for the first time in his whole life, that the sun did not rise and set just for him: he finally "got it" that he wasn't the prince of the family, but instead was one of four people, all of whose needs had to be considered. That would have to be enough. He knew he'd acted badly and he wanted a second chance. He didn't want to lose his wife and family over what now seemed like a foolish act. Therapy was helping him see his patterns more clearly, and he was enthusiastic about that. He felt that his tendency to be spoiled and peevish had a lot to do with his being the son and first child in his family, and he wanted to change.

The pattern that developed over the years goes like this: They begin resolving their problems in Contraction when Marie, responding to Jonathan's withdrawal, makes a dramatic, noncontingent move—blowing up and threatening to leave. The explosion frightens Jonathan, who then takes much of the blame on himself and finally apologizes for the ways he has in fact wronged her. After a period of wrangling, Marie accepts the apology, then accepts a little of the blame herself. They both feel relieved, proud they can rise above their insecurities, anger, and bitterness. A period of Resolution develops.

Over time, Jonathan and Marie tend to reside more and more in the Stage of Resolution; their cycles begin and end there. Their resolutions—like those of many other couples—are not always rosy and "sweet"; and, through the years, they have preserved few illusions about each other: they know that Jonathan is weaker, less secure, and more dependent than he first seemed, and that Marie can become irrational, lose her self-control, and act wildly when she feels threatened. Neither is so self-contained as he or she had first seemed. And yet they both have also come to value their strengths—the ability to hang in, their gutsiness and intelligence, their humor, the deep sense of love and connection, and the fit they feel with each other. They have both grown more interdependent, more tolerant, and ultimately more accepting of each other, and their defects matter less as time goes on.

## A Forward-Looking Experience

Resolution is the only stage that does not build on our primitive yearnings or early defenses. Both Expansion and Contraction contain strong regressive tendencies. In the first, our dependence, our wish for total, uncritical acceptance, and our delight in simple pleasures all play a major role. In the second, we revisit the injuries and losses of childhood. Resolution, by contrast, is forward-looking. It helps us let go of youth's anguish, joys, and all-or-nothing dreams. In exchange, we reach a saner, more practical way of handling life. We plan for the future, make choices, and feel some conscious control over the way our time is spent.

Our primitive feelings stay under wraps during this period. The raw excitement of our initial stages is protected and contained. Now we expose and carefully nurture our partners' feelings. Many couples work out their own languages, including "baby talk," to modulate or circumvent conflict. Sex and affection become more routine, more regular in time and place. Attentiveness replaces passion. Conscious efforts to change may build on one another and lead to break-throughs in the couple's way of being together at this time. The couple develops caretaking rituals, such as one partner's serving break-fast in bed each Sunday morning; and they define caretaking roles, such as breadwinner, housewife, and career counselor. They explore less and settle in more; they build more partnership, as in managing projects and raising children, and less direct engagement.

The first two stages of couple development provide a living labo-ratory in which our hopes, fears, and vulnerabilities are exposed. Sometimes this is intentional, as when people set out to be more open in a new relationship. Sometimes it is unintentional, as when we reveal more about ourselves than we wish, or when the sudden inten-sity of a hurt forces us to act differently.

In Resolution, we already know the preliminary outcomes of these earlier experiments. Each partner has decided how much to trust the other with a vulnerable feeling or a wound. We learn to tame, to modulate the intensity of earlier times. We get more organized, no longer trusting the unorganized expansiveness of the first stage and fearing the loss of control in the second. We return to our more "civilized" selves and are, consequently, more contained and more balanced during this period. Now we can approach subjects that were too threatening earlier.

## Patti and Marshall

Life has not been easy for Patti and Marshall; yet they constantly manage to pull out of Contraction and reach Resolution again. How do they do it? Where do they find the strength and resources?

When Patti and Marshall are in a period of Contraction, both feel unloved and distant. Patti feels hemmed in—by Simon, by Marshall, and by life. She feels drained and misunderstood, squeezed by taking care of everybody else without having time for herself, and she resents it. She is convinced that she could succeed if she were only left alone, but that's not possible. Her life seems like a series of mistakes. She becomes bitter, furious at Marshall, and down on herself.

Marshall feels unappreciated and abandoned, lonely, rudderless, and helpless: the best he can do has not been enough, and he is once again in danger of falling short. His usual equanimity and air of calm assurance break down. He feels in danger of losing Patti, the only light in his life, the woman who "makes everything happen" for him. He twists and turns, but doesn't know what to do. Everything he tries turns bad.

The two of them fight and call each other names. Neither feels respected. Each feels like a failure.

When they move out of Contraction, Patti and Marshall follow a sequence like this:

Patti, exhausted from the struggle to succeed, and tired of blaming Marshall and herself, finally starts talking to him. She holds his attention, touches him, expresses what they have both been feeling, cries.

Marshall, even though he has been feeling like a failure, tentatively moves toward her. She is so distraught, so frazzled, she no longer seems to be a threat. He touches her, consoles her, allows himself to be consoled.

Patti feels less alone, less guilty, she responds by becoming more affectionate—hugging Marshall, caressing him, or just saying something kind.

Marshall, relying on his strength as a negotiator, suggests a way of resolving their dispute.

What he proposes seems rational and intelligent. Patti is once again in awe at how sensible a man he is, how strong and supportive. He offers a way of solving their dilemma, and in a way that affirms what she has said, that recognizes the Patti she *wishes* she could be all the time. She is warmed by his love of her "better half" and resolves to stop being so cutting, and to meet him halfway.

Loving the feel of her affection and respect, he becomes bold enough to assert that their problems can really be solved. He seems cheery and optimistic, just when she needs this most.

In Resolution, then, Patti and Marshall are filled with a sense of mutual appreciation and wonder. Each feeds off the other's strength. Marshall's practicality clarifies things for them both; Patti's drive gives them both energy. Marshall's easy optimism makes them confident that their plans can succeed. Patti's vision makes them each feel creative: they sense they are "really growing" as a couple. For them, Resolution means a happier partnership, as each helps push the relationship forward in the way they know best.

The first time they moved into Resolution was soon after they were married. Patti was then insisting on her right to take courses, try out whatever job she wanted, meet people, and pursue her ambitions. Her insistence threatened Marshall, who felt Patti might meet someone else and leave him. Although she told him she depended on him for support and couldn't do what she was trying to do without his help, his old insecurities undermined his ability to tell her to go ahead. He threw up a hundred objections: what about Simon, what about their time together, what about money, what about the difficulties she'd encounter, what about waiting? He'd do anything to make her happy, but deep down he was afraid of losing her.

Their first bitter argument over this ended with Patti's shouting, throwing dishes around their apartment, and retreating into their room. Marshall didn't know what to do. He lay about the house, saying nothing. If Patti came into the room, he avoided her eyes. He went to work, stayed out late, drove around the countryside, then came home and talked only to Simon. His heart was breaking, but he couldn't open up. He left it to Patti to initiate any resolution.

Patti felt helpless as well. Here she was, married to a man she hoped would always "be there" for her, ready to back her up and give her his love and support ... and he was acting threatened and angry. He seemed too devastated by the conflict to be any help in solving it.

About a week after the big fight, Patti sat down next to Marshall and said, "Honey, look ... this is no good. We're married. We're adults. We've got to resolve this thing." She talked. He listened. She said she was sorry if she upset him, but she *did* tend to get emotional at times. He shouldn't take it as a personal attack. She still loved him, but he had to understand who she was. He confessed how bad he'd been feeling; she said she didn't *want* him to be upset, but she had to do what she had to do. She needed his help. He said he felt afraid. She reassured him. He clung to her. They hugged each other, talked softly, made love. He felt calmed down, his fears assuaged, his desperation washed away in the tide of physical closeness. The next day he felt better. He knew they could work things out, and now he proposed some options. He addressed the problems one by one, proposed solutions.

Patti felt pleased that they could come to an agreement. And she felt pleased that *she* had taken the lead. In addition, she felt good that Marshall let her do most of the talking at first, and that he responded openly to her.

They would repeat this pattern again and again over the years. For example, their next major crisis came at the end of a stage of Contraction marked by Patti's experiencing more and more setbacks trying to get her career started. Without a job, feeling inadequate, she retreated to the house for a period of several weeks and let Marshall persuade her to try to have a child of their own. She got pregnant, but miscarried. Despair breaking upon her full force, she blamed Marshall for all their troubles. He responded by becoming deeply depressed himself: he withdrew, began drinking. The two of them fought constantly. Their marriage appeared close to collapse.

At this point Patti's father invited Marshall to spend a weekend with him. Marshall did. The older man gave him a lot of support and encouragement; the following Monday he phoned Patti and urged her to trust in her marriage. He said Marshall was a "good man" who loved her. Moved by this intervention, Patti initiated a talk with Marshall in which they again shared how desperately sad and overwhelmed they'd each been feeling. Marshall felt he could reach out to Patti again, could "be strong" for her, and he was. Once again they moved ahead together.

* * *

Marshall and Patti spend very little time in Resolution once they reach it. They enjoy the feelings of consensus and harmony, and they enjoy the sense of growth. But they tend to move on. If things are going well for them, they move quickly into Expansion. When things are going badly, they sink into Contraction. As a couple, they tend to act more dramatically than rationally. This is an aspect of their *character* as a couple, a topic we will consider in depth in Chapter 11.

Sometimes a couple cannot move into Resolution, no matter how hard it tries, and no matter how much it reenacts the strategies that worked before. When Marshall developed diabetes, a few years after Patti's miscarriage, he felt his life was over. He was convinced he wouldn't be able to meet Patti's needs, and again feared she'd leave him: he withdrew into himself, began drinking—which exacerbated his illness—and then developed a potency problem. The desire for another child was now a cruel reminder of how impaired he'd become.

Patti responded by being more warm and supportive than she'd been in years. Marshall said he appreciated her kindness and attention, but that the change in her behavior couldn't change his attitude. He only felt more of a burden. Frustrated with what she took as his chronic pessimism, she pulled away. Her kindness had not brought them back together, and they were frozen in a Contraction as painful as any they'd experienced before.

This time they moved more slowly into Resolution, based on the accumulation of small events. As Patti became more and more successful as a free-lance photographer, she felt more confident about herself, and began to be cheerier around the house. Marshall felt he had nothing to lose any more—he couldn't be worse than he was—so he began taking on more chores, cracking a few jokes, and loosening up. His humor and enthusiasm returned. The layering of small bits and pieces of such forays into Resolution eventually brought Patti and Marshall into that stage again.

## Male and Female

Gender issues lend complexity to the stage of Resolution. Earlier, in Expansion, gender development appears to converge; similarities

flourish between the partners, and they tend either to ignore stereotypes or to enjoy them. If a man likes to cook, it is good that he is different. If a woman likes to cook, it is good that she can nurture and
be nurtured. Later, in Contraction, divergence returns. Stereotypical
conflicts reappear; similarities seem to have vanished, and differences
mainly aggravate the couple's problems.

In Resolution, each couple works out its own blend of elements
from the first two stages. Stereotyped roles may coexist with creative
compromises. Men may deal with lawns and carpentry while women
manage the kitchen, but the partners may care for the children in
equal and shared ways—such as one taking mornings and evenings,
the other afternoons. The total shared labor may be more equal. To
be sure, women are still likely to want more intimate conversation,
and men to counter with requests to "do" more things together. But
the couple may have so relaxed into some stereotyped roles that the
angry edge of Contraction is gone. In Resolution men and women are
more settled into their own gender identity than at any other time
and therefore feel less threatened.

Three more open aspects of the partners' attitudes about gender
can help the partners change:

- The relaxation of tension around difference
- The depoliticization of gender issues
- The grudging acceptance that some stereotyped differences
  exist

The stage of Resolution recurs many times in the course of a
couple's life. After the first several times, the partners tend to gravitate more toward their own particular preferences and away from
stereotypes. This is particularly true as couples reach middle age,
when women are frequently eager to be out of the home, and are
excited about work and outside commitments to which they have
only recently been able to devote their full energies. At the same
time, men's careers may be leveling off: finding that they have few
friends and lack an intimate sense of family, they may begin to shift
their center of gravity homeward and become interested in the
"female" activities they had long ignored. They cook and clean
more and want to talk. The traditional gender roles may be reversed
in these couples.

## Issues of Difference

Greater differentiation in the couple during Resolution is paralleled by greater individuation in the partners. During Expansion, the partners had been accepting and curious about difference. They tended to ignore or deny potentially threatening differences, to emphasize complementary differences, and to focus on similarities and connection. Contraction made differences a source of fighting and blame. Instead of feeling curious or enhanced by them, partners felt betrayed and struggled to bring the differences under control.

The emphasis in Resolution is more pluralistic and laissez-faire. Individualism and difference may not be celebrated, but they are far more accepted than before. The forms of acceptance vary from person to person and from couple to couple. They may sound like this: "Thank God, George is such a stick in the mud. I have fought with him about it, but he sure has provided some security for me over the years." Or: "Well, you know Sally. That's just the way she is." Or: "She's always protecting me, and sometimes it drives me crazy, but to tell you the truth, I've come to realize it also holds me together." Or: "I don't much like his Sunday football games, but I've learned to live with them, and I probably wouldn't know what to do with him if he were available after all these years." And it can be celebrative: "She is just so smart and alive and attractive to others that I have a social life which I otherwise would not have!"

The accommodating character of Resolution feels somehow learned. Whereas the first two stages seem to derive from our deep, inner feelings and impulses, the third stage seems to emerge from our making sense of experience. Resolution is not overwhelming, not primarily reactive. Yet what we learn often seems ancient, eternal— oddly universal. Even though this period emphasizes distinctiveness, the accepting of differences seems to create in us a more mellow cast of mind. Resolution may be our first brush with wisdom; people in Resolution often describe their experiences in philosophical phrases, and may even quote religious texts.

Our accommodation to each other during Resolution is part of a broader pattern of accommodating to the world. Resolution generally takes place when we are making commitments, having children, buying homes. These commitments—in particular, the emergence of children—often help end old, bitter disputes with parents beginning as far back as adolescence, perhaps abating for a time, and then flaring up again as we struggled for independence and spurned our parents' advice and affection. Children are for two generations of couples to share. They permit the generations to identify with each other. The older generation's experience becomes valued. Parents know about residential mortgages and household appliances. Perhaps not up on the latest child-rearing practices, they nevertheless know how to appreciate grandchildren, and nothing is closer to parents' hearts than seeing their children valued.

## Resolution as a Rite of Passage

This closer connection between the generations is a frequent feature of a couple's move into Resolution. During the first two stages, common parental values of moderation, perspective, and negotiation seem old and staid—a frank rejection of youth's adventuresome spirit. But as the young couple moves to take on work, children, and household, the parental attitudes that had earlier separated the generations now join them together. Many couples in Resolution actually seek out parental approval. They feel they are finally doing something right. Having a child or buying a house or settling down to a job or emerging intact from a horrible fight is "doing something right." The focus on these "adult" tasks forms so compelling a bridge, it can melt the thick ice formed over years between parents and children. At this stage, for example, a number of gay and lesbian couples who have been estranged from their families find that their parents can finally accept them for who they are.

The young couple's desire to be mature is often aimed partly at impressing their parents. The lifelong desire for parental approval, forsaken but not forgotten, leads some to a reaffirmation of parental values. But this is no one-way street. Parents, supposedly mature enough to tolerate and even enjoy youth's rebellions, have also felt painfully rejected. They suffer from their children's alienation, and feel a sense of failure at the rejection of family values, life-style, and affection. Given the chance, they often fall gratefully back into relationship.

This is one of the first times the young partners find support for themselves as a functioning couple—something beyond adulation at how "attractive" they are together. They feel parents, relatives, and friends perceiving them positively as they take on their new responsibilities. Now the partners emerge from intense focus on each other and open themselves more to others. These others, less invested in the couple's struggles, tend to treat each partner as an individual, thus supporting individuation within the couple. Except for those who are helplessly ensnarled, couples respond positively to these interactions.

Resolution represents a rite of passage for the couple. Both the couple and the individual partners now enter the community of adults. As they emerge from their ordeal in Contraction, they will be initiated into the ways of adulthood. They will begin to use its special language, words emphasizing accommodation, compromise, calm, and rationality. Elders now feel they have some traditional knowledge to impart; and we, often for the first time since adolescence, believe there is reason to listen.

Now, for the second time, the partners can approach their ideal selves: not the romantic lovers of Expansion, but the mature, loving adults of Resolution. We put our ideal into practice through the repeated experience (more than once and perhaps with more than one partner) of moving from Expansion through Contraction and into the stage of Resolution. As we do, we revive memories of how our parents were with us and with each other when we were children. People whose childhood experience was primarily painful revive fantasy images from daydreams, books, and movies. If the ideal of Expansion is the passionate lover, then the ideal of Resolution is the problem-solver, the flexible companion. If the first took pleasure in being rapt, driven, and intense, the latter prefers balance, ease, and perspective.

## There Are Many Resolutions

Couple development does not follow a chronological order, with each stage representing an advance on the one before. Expansion is not confined to our youth; nor does Resolution represent the wisdom of age. Often enough, for instance, couples who come through a long period of contraction and crisis can return to a prolonged period of expansiveness. Young couples may remain as stuck in Contraction or as determinedly fixed in Resolution as any seasoned couple. Forty-year marriages can founder and break on the horns of a shocking revelation.

Through the years, there will be many Resolutions. No one Resolution holds forever. For a while marriage may resolve our concerns about commitment, but intense involvement at work, with extended family, or with our own children may soon challenge our sense of coupleness and togetherness. We may find ways to negotiate our responsibilities and routines, but each change in circumstances may threaten our arrangement. Or one of us may come to feel that the deal we struck is unfair. This may renew the struggles that eventually return us to Contraction, until we find a new Resolution. And so the cycle goes.

The Stage of Resolution may be ushered in by particular resolutions to particular problems, but these build and accumulate over the years, like sedimentary rock being layered on a foundation. Early events may explode with symbolic meaning before being fully integrated into both the individual and couple narratives. One partner may get sick, and the other might take care of her in what feels like the most cursory way. The sick person feels that she could not possibly spend the rest of her life with such a callous person. To the cursory caretaker, who was taught in childhood that sick people prefer to huddle by themselves, both his partner's request for help and her angry reaction to his response feel threatening. The couple goes into a tailspin until the partners realize they come from different backgrounds; they will have to intentionally and explicitly negotiate how to deal with illness together. This conclusion, however early and unsturdy, can be thrilling in its promise: the potential to include both partners' styles forms the Resolution and is incorporated into the next Expansive Stage.

Some couples dwell mainly in Resolution throughout their relationship. Others rarely achieve its reasonable shores—some through incapacity, others because it seems so pale compared to Expansion; still others because its rational light seems so revealing that they prefer both the embrace of Expansion and the intense struggles of Contraction. Over the years, resolutions broaden in content and expand in time. It is a cumulative process. It may take years, for example, to work out a relationship with parents, to settle on a viable division of labor, to know how much religious or political difference can be discussed before conflict breaks out. Over the years more and more intimacy may be absorbed into the partnerships common to the Stage of Resolution. Little irritations—the way he chews his food, the way she clutters up the bathroom—may also take time to resolve. But eventually couples in the Stage of Resolution work out a pretty smooth modus operandi.

Major Resolutions can take place early on, and a few may happen later; intermittent Resolutions of moderate importance may take place all through the couple's life together.

Resolution can never include all the material from prior stages. Some themes are always hidden: too loathsome, perhaps too explosive to integrate at any particular moment. The couple may quarantine this material, make it out of bounds for discussion, perhaps even push it out of consciousness. The quarantine may involve content: the couple refuses to talk about sex or money or their parents or retirement. Or it may involve process. They may put a cap on any discussions that get heated: perhaps one partner routinely walks away; perhaps a child is recruited to deflect the fight by getting into trouble as soon as it gets out of hand or by somehow having an attack of a chronic illness, such as when parental tension stimulates wheezing in an asthmatic child. These strategies keep threatening material from the field of interaction, and therefore prevent it from being integrated into Resolution.

The broadening character of Resolution increasingly makes that stage define the character of couples. Again, this does not happen chronologically or linearly, but couples tend toward Resolution. Each turn of the cycle makes Resolution a bit broader, and it does the same to Expansion and Contraction. The Expansive Stage is likely to become more relaxed and less intense because it has been influenced by the accommodations of Resolution and by the remembered disappointments of Contraction.

With Resolution such a welcome experience, couples may wish to remain there, to hold firm and never permit themselves to sink into the morass of Contraction again. But they do not have this option. No one can stay put. Relentlessly, they will be swept ahead into the cycle that lies ahead. To be sure, couples may learn to spend longer and longer amounts of time in Resolution; or they may manage to let Contraction upset them less than it used to do. But they cannot hold back the dialectical press of the stages that roll forth as naturally as the rhythm of breathing in and breathing out that it so resembles.

# 8

# THE COUPLE'S
# CHARACTER FORMS

All couples develop a character of their own: unique, idiosyncratic, and distinct from the character of either individual partner. Even though couples may change over time, they still retain this basic character. It becomes their trademark, their style—the identity by which they are recognized by themselves and others. In time, every couple's character becomes as distinctive as a fingerprint.

What do we mean by a couple's character? It is like an individual person's character: an "aggregate of distinctive qualities," their "main or essential nature."[1] A couple's character is made up of regular, enduring patterns of thinking and feeling, acting and reacting.

Each partner plays a role in his or her couple's character, even though one partner may carry more weight. Some partners dominate their relationship; others seem almost absent. Some play a necessary but harmonious second fiddle, others the requisite counterpoint. Whatever the blend or balance, each couple is an entity in itself, developing its character in accord with its own particular history and concordance of partners.

Some couples are fun to be with; others are difficult and socially awkward, even if the individual partners are enjoyable by themselves. Some couples focus on their children; others are always competing with each other; still others carp and grumble all the time. Some fight in public, but are marvelous when they are alone; others fight when they are alone but present a seamless façade in public. Some are excellent planners, others atrocious bunglers. Some are lively, others boring; some energetic, others depressed; some relaxed, others tight and jumpy. Some couples seem collectively smart and never make stupid mistakes, while others appear dumb and klutzy and are always in a jam. There are couples who seem to go from one crisis to the next, always frenzied and involving everyone else; and others who move smoothly along life's path, calm and unharmed, while their friends are alternately jealous and judgmental about their "easy" life.

Couples vary greatly in their social and public presentations, and their character is very complex and complicated. For example, some couples are reflective and whimsical with close friends, but more outgoing in larger social groups. Others are chatty with close friends, but quiet in larger groups. Some couples are at their best with relatives; others, with colleagues or a handful of close friends.

A couple forms the core of its character in its initial three-stage cycle. By the time the partners have completed their first few passages through Expansion, Contraction, and Resolution, most of their basic issues will have emerged, and their essential patterns and sequences will have taken shape. A couple's first time through Resolution punctuates the themes, meanings, and interactional patterns by which they will know themselves for years to come. Subsequent cycles may modify and constrict or expand and transform their character, but, just as the adult is recognizable in the child, so a couple's character is formed by the end of their first cycle.

## Brief Portraits

To illustrate the notion of a couple's character, let us present some portraits of couples we have known. Each has its own unique and characteristic style. Once you get to know them, you realize that the character of a couple is more than the sum of its parts.

Nell and Peter are always involved with kids. They have two children of their own, and are also raising Peter's son and daughter from his previous marriage to Paige, an alcoholic. Peter works two jobs. Nell works part-time. Although money is tight, their house is always filled with neighborhood kids playing games, watching TV, hanging out in the den. Peter is happy and gruff, thirty pounds overweight, almost always dressed in flannel shirts and jeans. Nell is a vigorous, fast-talking woman with a high-pitched voice and a wild sense of humor. She always has some "latest" story to tell, some recent embarrassment to laugh about. The kids in the neighborhood say they're like two bears, awkward, rough, but good-humored. Nell and Peter don't pressure anyone, but are always "there" when you need them.

When Arlene and Sam married, each in their early forties, each already had well-worn styles and long-established goals. They spoke about these on their first date and carefully managed to guard their separate lives even during the height of early romance. Their ability to work as each wished was sacrosanct, the cornerstone of their relationship, and they each respected it. Sam would never make a social engagement without checking to see if it fit with Arlene's plans; and Arlene did the same. They were vigilant about equality, too, whether in household chores, speaking time in public, or financial contribution to their bank account. If one earned more than the other, it went into that person's separate account. Sam and Arlene had few friends—although earlier they had had more—because they seemed too nervous about taking precious time from each other or from their free time together. Friends and relatives walked carefully around them, nervous about intruding or upsetting their balance.

Lena and Bill met while they were in high school and are now in their early twenties. They seem happy with each other, but spend very little time together alone. They seem always busy—especially with their relatives. They have an apartment in the same three-decker as Lena's parents and younger brother. Lena's sister lives just down the street; Bill's parents live two blocks away. After high school, Lena worked as a waitress, but now she stays home with their two young children. Bill is an electrician at one of the nearby plants, and also works at whatever odd job he can get. His ambition is to start a contracting business with two of his brothers.

Lena and Bill's relationship seems immersed in their families. They spend a lot of time at family birthday parties, holiday dinners, and weekend cookouts. Bill goes bowling with his buddies on Thursday nights, and Lena spends time with her high school friends and their small children, her mom, and her sister. Bill is always willing to help a friend or relative with some odd chore; Lena seems always up for a chat. They don't talk much about their relationship, but if you asked them, they'd say it feels fine.

Orrin is a sculptor, Dave a teacher. They met in their mid-twenties and are still together a decade later. Orrin had dated a number of women in adolescence, but he had never felt satisfied in these relationships. At twenty, he developed a passionate relationship with an art teacher and realized he was gay. Dave has always been attracted only to men.

The two of them live in a sun-filled apartment in a neighborhood frequented by artists and other gay men. They are deeply absorbed in their work, but the major focus of their life has always been their relationship. Orrin is wry, witty, and frenetic, Dave, more laid-back. They enjoy spending free evenings with a couple of friends, a huge bowl of popcorn, and an old movie. They also go off for weekends at country inns, where they can hike or cross-country ski.

Often, Orrin and Dave find themselves thinking and feeling the same things, but sometimes the closeness gets claustrophobic for Orrin, and he pulls away. Dave might then feel hurt, and the two of them might start a round of fighting that lasts for weeks. They often wind up drawing their friends into the middle of these fights to help them make up, but—since great understandings and even greater intimacy usually result—their friends do not mind it at all.

Rebecca and Nathan met sixty years ago when a friend who thought they'd be perfect together introduced them. Rebecca was friendly and pretty. She liked to dance the Lindy Bop and discuss current events. Nathan was tall, very thin, and dark, sometimes brooding but always brilliant. He needed someone to listen to him. And Rebecca did. He thought she was the liveliest person he had ever met and, although she was "no genius," was sure he could teach her enough about art and literature for her to be a good companion. For her part, she told her friends that Nathan was a diamond in the rough: a little brusque, a bit crazy, but with a heart of gold; with time, she'd bring out the best in him.

Throughout their lives together, they were each other's main projects. During good times, they were like trainers and promoters. He would casually mention to a friend, "Rebecca just finished *Anna Karenina*, and, you know what, she has some interesting things to say about it." She would tell her friends how nice Nathan was to the kids and to his second cousin, Hannah. In bad times, she found him disrespectful and implored him to take her more seriously.

They were perfect for each other. But they were difficult with others. They found their projects so engrossing that they had little need for others—including their children, who later talked about having been an audience to the "Nathan and Rebecca Show." Still, the kids could also feel a bit bemused: their parents might be somewhat self-centered, but they didn't harm anyone, and they sure kept themselves busy.

When Nathan died, Rebecca painted his portrait from memory in order to remember him forever, but she was not satisfied with her rendition. Nathan had had a slight scowl on his angular face. In the following years she painted many more portraits, but even though some were more kindly and others more scowly she felt she never got the likeness quite right.

## Elements of Character

The character of couples is a complex weave of elements. It is the way partners talk with each other; how they make decisions, manage households, and raise children; how they play, fight, and make (or do not make) love. It is in their shared values, goals, and ideas, and their routines for smoothing ruffled feathers. Nell and Peter laugh off their problems or do some project together. Arlene and Sam seek out carefully negotiated solutions. Dave and Orrin feel very much part of a supportive community. Bill and Lena speak to their parents or siblings about their problems. Rebecca and Nathan maintained their privacy from others for fifty years, but opened up deeply to each other.

A couple's character embraces differences and conflict. You and I may have different styles and values; our couple's character comes out in how we handle these differences. Will we fight over issues of closeness and distance, affection and privacy? Or will we reach some "golden mean" between our two positions? While we may reconcile some contradictions, others may persist, emerging sharply at stressful times.

Self-definition and self-recognition are essential qualities of a couple's character; they are central to the creation of a stable identity. Nell and Peter would roar with laughter if anyone suggested they read the *New York Times* instead of their tabloid. Orrin and Dave are closer to each other because they understand the tension each feels in the "straight" world. Lena and Bill define themselves through their families' values.

But character is not unitary. Partners emphasize different elements in their relationship, and they often tell such divergent stories that an outsider can hardly recognize them as the same couple. This is like the phenomenon depicted in the movie *Rashomon*. So we say that the character of couples includes the *ways* they recognize themselves.

Character is both conscious and unconscious. Many couples may be unaware of even their most characteristic patterns, their most obvious assumptions, but they can see them once an outsider points them out or once they run into difficulty. When we struggle with each other over differences, we become more aware of who we are—both together and as ourselves.

Take, for instance, the importance of religion. This may be a non-issue for young couples. But when they get older and have children who approach the age for possible religious education, the partners have to define their positions. When they do, surprising differences may emerge. Couples from different backgrounds, different cultures, or different classes may do well until some dilemma like this occurs; then they realize how much they had assumed attitudes in their partner that the latter did not share, and they have to work out some kind of compromise.

As transitions from stage to stage, and from cycle to cycle, make us more aware of our patterns, more aspects of our couple's character will become conscious. The first time around, each stage can bring us tremendous surprises. The second and third times around, we may still be surprised, but the surprises are already nestled among the familiar and the *déjà vu*.

## The Independence of Couple Character

People commonly think that couples take their character from the individuals they comprise, but a couple's character exists apart from, and often strongly shapes, how the individual partners appear and behave. Consider how every couple brings forth certain traits from each of the partners' repertoires, but leaves others untapped. This can be called the *organizing* effect of a couple on the individual partners' own styles. As the couple's particular character develops during its first three-stage cycle, the partners pour themselves into the relationship. They share many images, memories, needs, and hopes, and apply many skills they have learned so far in life. But at the same time, they squirrel other aspects of themselves away.

This is the basis for the common observation that people are different in one couple relationship than in another, and different when they are with their partner than when they are alone. We all know people who are very talkative by themselves, but who clam up when they are out in public with their spouse; and we all know people who acted distant and gloomy in a previous relationship, but who are now much more engaging, with a different partner. These are results of the couple's organizing effect on the partners.

Years before he met Arlene, for instance, Sam (from the portraits above) had formed a relationship with Beverly, a shy, insecure woman who withdrew deep into herself whenever he became in the slightest bit assertive. At first, he tried to reassure her and cajole her to return to him. But eventually her withdrawals drove him into angry frenzies, bringing out an aggressiveness he had kept under wraps—but which she had always claimed to see. Anyone who met Sam during this period, especially if they knew him primarily in Beverly's presence, would have thought of him as a wild man, insistent and domineering. Yet this is the same Sam who is now so calm and collaborative with Arlene.

In previous relationships, Orrin had felt tense around the issue of independence. He felt his partners were threatened by his interest in his work, which led to fights and eventually to the ending of these relationships. By contrast, Dave encourages his independence. This is one way Orrin feels Dave is supportive. For his part, in his previous relationships, Dave had felt under great pressure to "be a star," to shine and excel in his own work. With Orrin, he feels he can simply relax and let himself become domestic. The complementarity in their relationship, in contrast to the competitiveness with previous lovers, "works" better for them both.

The character of couples tends to persist even as the character of the individual partners changes. For instance, Nell and Peter's relationship sustains the active community of children and friends who pass through their home, and people say that Nell and Peter's constant warmth draws them there. But Peter has not always been the happy bear of a man he seems right now. Early in the relationship he was anxious and vigilant, fearful for the well-being of a son who still lived with his alcoholic ex-wife. During another period, when he had been laid off from his job, Peter brooded a great deal; and Nell, knowing him well, gave him room and did not try to reassure him. Yet throughout these times, they continued to relate to each other as if they were partners in the creation of the neighborhood center.

The remarkable thing is that our roles are often reversible. Everyone knows a story about when the "steady" member of a couple had a crisis, and the "irresponsible" partner took over. Tough parents become tender, and tender ones become tough in the other's absence. It is as though we all have a broad-enough range of character traits to assume either role, but are inclined toward one. When roles are reversible, the character of a couple can maintain much of its shape even while the individual partners shift back and forth.

A couple's character appears in a wide variety of events—the humdrum, everyday things couples do over and over, the special milestone moments in every couple's life, the extraordinary moments of crisis.

## Character in the First Cycle

In their first passage through the entire cycle, couples develop different aspects of their character in each stage. Schematically put, in Expansion we develop patterns that correspond to our experience when things are hopeful and going well; in Contraction, patterns that organize our experience when things are going poorly; in Resolution, patterns that correspond to a time of solving problems. What develops is what we can summarily call the couple's characteristic way of being happy together, their characteristic fights, and their characteristic way of solving problems.

Character begins with the essential "deals" couples make with each other in the Stage of Expansion. For example, Jonathan agreed to be strong and steady while Marie would be animated and interesting; Patti would be passionate and loving while Marshall would support her career. The deals are then elaborated into a complex set of mutual rules and expectations. Together, these make up the Expansive Contract. As couples develop behaviors that reflect their contract, their character takes shape.

Contracts set the terms for assessing success or failure. If, for example, Marshall is supposed to support Patti's career, his actions will be interpreted as supportive or unsupportive, but not something different. Suppose that one day, when Patti has been feeling insecure for a while, Marshall happens to be very involved in a project of his own. Supporting her at that moment is not a major part of his consciousness; and, for a while, he is essentially unaware of Patti's concerns. If then Patti comes up to him with an important story about something that happened to her, he may fail to respond enthusiastically enough. In her eyes—and later, to an extent, in his—he has therefore failed to be supportive and betrayed their Expansive Contract.

## Character and the Stage of Expansion

In order to illustrate how couples form their basic character, let us follow two new couples through their first cycle.

Gerry and Sharon live in a big city. Gerry runs a catering business, Sharon works as a middle-level manager in a large corporation. When they met, each was looking for equality and sharing, and they immediately made these the central features of their relationship. Early on, in their first period of Expansion, they felt enhanced by how these qualities pervaded their talk, their lovemaking, and even their career-planning. They felt smooth and efficient together like a well-oiled machine.

Many expectations we have for our partners can be understood as condensed images of childhood experiences. Sharon, for example, bitterly told Gerry how her father treated her mother like a servant, and how she promised herself never to be in her mother's situation. Gerry told Sharon how close he felt to his mother, how alienated from his autocratic father; he promised himself never to be cruel like his father. Their shared recital of hurts built their sense of connection: each was fleeing a family controlled by a domineering man. Sharing their stories felt like putting a balm on their still-open wounds and consolidated their early relationship.

The powerful injunction against male domination became one of their central themes, alerting them to Gerry's potential to do harm.

Vigilant, they worked together to curb the slightest signs of his anger, even simple assertiveness. When Gerry is kind, gentle, and collaborative, they do well. But when he oversteps the bounds, or when Sharon just *thinks* he does, mistrust develops; they begin to feel anxious and frightened.

We cannot always tell each other all the implications of our stories in this early phase of Expansion. Sharon knew she hated hierarchies and wanted an *equal* relationship, but she was less aware of the fear a man's anger created in her. Long ago she taught herself to ignore her fear and help her mother by standing up to her father. Yet this fear continues to inform her narrative in some way; in concert with the pleasure she finds in an egalitarian relationship, it anchors her tie to Gerry.

In Expansion, so long as their basic contract is observed, Sharon and Gerry are hardworking and optimistic about their future. The basis of their character in Expansion revolves around mutual trust, sharing, and equality.

Byron and Carrie both grew up in small midwestern towns. When they met, they were both unsatisfied with their lives. Carrie, twenty-eight, had been unsuccessful in finding a career, and she felt herself drifting through a series of pointless positions. Byron, thirty-six, had begun, developed, and sold a small business. Now he had a well-paying job as regional sales manager for a large corporation, but he still felt unfulfilled. For him, the only thing that made life worth living was passion, and his life lacked it.

They met at a party and instantly clung together. Carrie felt Byron to be intense and compelling, a large man whose big stubby fingers and broad face showed he could mold the world. To Byron, Carrie was a lost waif waiting for him to sweep her up. He stunned her by his knowledge of art and music, by his ebullient manner, by his hunger for life. She excited him with her absolute attentiveness.

Carrie's dad had been an indiscreet and ambitious social climber. Her mother had been ineffectual. Raised to have whatever she wanted, Carrie never quite figured out what that was. She was sent to fine boarding schools but felt out of place there, and escaped into dreamy novels, folk songs, and hippie clothes. Growing up, Carrie felt ignored by her charismatic father. Later, she always seemed to be attracted to self-centered men like him, who first drew her in and then ignored her.

Byron was raised in another part of the state. He had barely known his father, who would disappear for years on end. His mother was a pale, unhappy, critical woman, whose chronic depression left him to fend for himself. He had worked hard to get an education and was proud of what he accomplished. He regarded himself as a self-made man.

The one thing Byron needed was someone to love and admire him. When Carrie responded to him, he courted her like a queen. They came together like two magnets, seemingly drawn by forces beyond themselves—passionate, reveling in each other's attention. Even their early titanic fights seemed all right because afterwards they made even greater promises to each other and carried on daylong bouts of romantic lovemaking.

In essence, Carrie was looking for meaning and fulfillment through love. So she chose Byron, a man who needed a woman to appreciate him and support his ambitious career plans. Without exactly saying it, the two made a deal. Byron would provide an exuberant link to the outside world and a steady (if preoccupied) presence at home; Carrie would listen enthusiastically to his plans and stories and provide a warm and orderly home base from which he could launch himself.

In their early days together, Carrie felt bountiful and calm at being part of Byron's plans. Byron felt reborn. They managed to remain in Expansion for several years. He worked hard, Carrie basked in his success, and they were fanatastically romantic together. There were weekends at distant inns, unexpected boxes of roses, dinners by candlelight at fancy restaurants, theater evenings by limousine with a marvelous play followed by late-night dancing. To be sure, Carrie felt some strain around Byron's being so busy, but Byron was so caught up in his own sense of romance and adventure that he seemed to make it up to her.

When he felt expansive, Byron would expound his ideas and gesticulate broadly; Carrie, despite her stillness, could radiate a softness that touched him to the core of his being. And they were passionate sexual partners. Byron no longer needed friends or family. It was Carrie, himself, and his projects against the world. That was all either of them asked for. They imagined their home as a well-ordered castle, complete with a moat, with Byron as king and she as queen.

Their relationship was organized in Expansion with both partners focused on Byron as their weather vane of success. The major themes of their relationship are the importance of Byron's work, the necessity of Carrie's nurture and support, and the vision of them both against the world. In Expansion, Carrie's focus on Byron both fills her own emptiness and helps him feel on top of the world.

The rules of the Expansive Contract begin from the first contact. Sharon, for example, insisted on paying for her own dinner during their first date. Gerry gladly accepted, and that interaction's meaning was clear to them both.

Carrie could hardly believe how consistently passionate and loving Byron was, and after trying to pick a fight with him and failing, she came to expect his romantic responses, even when she was forgetful and distracted. All she had to do was continue loving him.

Some rules emerge fully formed, such as Sharon and Gerry's egalitarianism. Others must be negotiated or fought for. Some rules develop out of experimentation. With time, the rules cover most aspects of a couple's relationship, all the while (in Expansion) resting on the promise that each partner will continue acting in as ideal a style as possible. If Byron needs admiration, for example, Carrie's affection won't do; nor will pleasantness, distractedness, or enjoyment. She must *admire* him or the contract is violated.

By regulating which aspects of each partner are welcome and which are not, the Expansive Contract sets the stage for the feelings of betrayal that later inevitably appear. It is hard to restrain prohibited traits for long. Sooner or later, these unwanted parts of ourselves emerge, often urgent and insistent, and intrude upon the relationship. "This is *me*, goddamn it!" the partners say. "I can't hold it back any longer. You'll just have to *accept* me now."

Some of these traits—one partner's depression, another's angry outbursts; one partner's sexual appetites, another's wish to be alone much of the time; one partner's fastidiousness, another's histrionics when threatened—will eventually be integrated into the relationship. Others will not. If our partners refuse to take them in, they will either remain suppressed in the relationship or have to find expression elsewhere.

While still in Expansion, many couples run into rigidity, doubt, and inconsistency. They uncover fears of intimacy, commitment, and control, even when the predominant mood is expansive. These early problems may lead the couple into full, rapid *mini-cycles* that prefigure the full cycle's more comprehensive presentation of the couple's character. Resolving these fights helps couples maintain their optimistic spirit and minimize the fears and ambivalence that momentarily surface.

Sharon and Gerry squabbled about equal sharing of household chores. Carrie grew frightened by a sense of Byron's irritability. These early struggles remind couples that problems can and will arise. In any case, though, the couple now has a clearer sense of itself, and its character is developing through the handling of these minor setbacks.

The particular character each couple has in Expansion influences its transition to Contraction. Couples who have had a great romance, like Byron and Carrie, tend to experience dramatic falls and terrible betrayals. Those, like Sharon and Gerry, who exult in cooperation and negotiation may find the transition more confusing than anything else.

## Character and the Stage of Contraction

There are many ways of sliding into Contraction. Sometimes a couple sinks disheartedly after a series of minor but bitter disappointments— persistent quarrels, repeated failures to live up to promises, increasing accusations and blame. Sometimes they plunge into a profound Contraction after a major betrayal by one or both partners: an affair, an angry drunken evening, a fight in which they act as never before— with nasty threats, insults, and shouting. Sometimes they simply contract, slowly drawing into themselves and disengaging in small, almost imperceptible steps.

Whatever pattern they follow, *the partners eventually pass a threshold of disappointment and have to revise their sense of who they are as a couple.* Early on, they may have tried to cordon off this disappointment by somehow interpreting their failures in an optimistic light ("Well, at least it's good we can bring this up with each other"), or by trying to avoid them, say, by making a mutual decision not to discuss certain subjects. But each violation of the Expansive Contract proclaims its failure. The couple's character as it appeared in Expansion no longer seems authentic.

This process brings new aspects of each partner's personality into the couple relationship. Each partner has to cope with the other's being *less than* he or she had expected. And each has to deal with his or her own diminished self, which has emerged as well. The result is to introduce a sense of limit and failure.

Gerry and Sharon's first slide into Contraction came close on the heels of their first serious fight in which Gerry lost his temper—not much by many people's standards, but too much for them. Sharon was frightened and dismayed; Gerry felt horrible for having betrayed both Sharon and himself. The emergence of his anger so shocked them that they slipped rapidly into the defensive organization of Contraction.

Here is how Sharon and Gerry adapted to their disappointment. Their search for equality through the creation of a well-oiled machine turned into a rigidly organized system, with the creation of separate bank accounts and little warm companionship. Their tasks became strictly assigned and monitored, and they set out to live parallel lives, reacting strongly whenever one invaded the other's territory or failed to live up to a prior obligation.

Their discussions became mainly contractual—who would do what when: "If you agree to do the laundry on Friday, then I can depend on clean clothes on Saturday, so it's not fair if you change it to Monday." Since every act requires negotiation, business language pervades their relationship.

In Contraction they each feel deeply hurt and humiliated, with no chance of redemption. Sharon feels she has been a fool ever to believe that any man could be different. Gerry feels like an emotional failure, suited only to carry out tasks. Their relationship truly *contracts*, as their free-flowing collaboration is transformed into a wary two-person bureaucracy. Their characteristic fight is over style, not content: about Gerry's being unable to control his anger.

In Expansion, Carrie's focus on Byron had filled her own emptiness and made him feel on top of the world. But in Contraction, Carrie feels slighted and left out by Byron's absence and egocentricity, and Byron feels controlled and diminished by Carrie's mothering.

In Contraction, Carrie's kind mothering becomes domineering. Byron's gentle protectiveness turns into angry bullying. Each makes statements the other feels are "hostile," but then denies any hostile intent. The sense of magical fit evaporates, and they are filled with mistrust. Byron feels Carrie prying into his mind all the time, while Carrie knows that Byron is angry but just won't admit it. Caught in their nightmare, Byron pushes Carrie away in order to get some distance (but then feels incredibly lonely), while Carrie feels abused and ignored.

The first time they moved into Contraction, Carrie and Byron fought after Byron stayed out late for business meetings four nights in a row and Carrie felt abandoned. He became indignant at her failure to understand how important these meetings were for him. Of course, he said, he'd have been home if he could. Her reaction made him feel like a dog between two masters, Carrie and his boss. He felt betrayed by her no longer responding enthusiastically to what he felt was exciting news about his work. She felt suddenly shocked by the revelation of his selfishness.

As Byron "had to" work more on nights and weekends, Carrie felt increasingly abandoned. Empty and depressed, she stopped doing housework. Her doctor said she was depressed, and offered antidepressants, but Carrie felt Byron could solve the problem just by returning to his old buoyancy with her.

Byron wanted this, but he was hurt by her withdrawal and too proud to beg for her attention. He felt out of control himself and drew into an angry shell for protection. He wanted Carrie to come find him but he couldn't ask her. Like a hurt child, he now threw occasional temper tantrums, which Carrie found terrifying. Increasingly neglectful of his own chores and responsibilities to her, Byron appeared as a bad child in need of reproach. And so she began treating him like one, placating and mollifying.

In Contraction, they took on reversed roles. Byron was no dashing Romeo, but a temperamental child; Carrie was no waiflike Juliet, but a Mommy. Their interaction began looking more and more like their families. The character of this couple in Contraction rests on two feelings: (1) their mutual sense of abandonment, which brings up old hunger and hurt; and (2) their persistent conviction that it's *Byron's* feelings and behavior that should structure their relationship—in this case his fall from grandiloquent hero to needy little child, which forces Carrie to shift her own role. The flip side of their Expansive Contract now emerged to dominate them.

A couple's character is thus reorganized and modified in their very first pass through Contraction. Carrie and Byron's focus remained on Byron, but new themes became figural: for Carrie, abandonment, loneliness, maternal burden, and fear for her physical safety; for

Byron, neglect, isolation, vanishing self-control, and the loss of dignity. Together, they look like an angry, overburdened mother and a sullen, acting-out child. To an outsider, and even to their few friends, they hardly look like the same couple. But of course they are; and these "new" qualities will be integrated into their character as they move through the full cycle.

Couples in Contraction often question the reality of their first stage of Expansion. They wonder if it was an illusion. As they fall into old ruts, they come to believe that the Stage of Contraction must be the deeper reality. Some are defeated by this "realization." They break up or resignedly stay together. Others acknowledge that the holiday is over and the time for hard work has begun. This, after all, is one of the Cultural Narrative's messages: hard times follow good, good times follow hard, and handling the change is the test of a couple's true character.

Now the partners bring out the worst in each other, and the character of the couple appears based on the qualities they least value in themselves and each other. The darker sides of self and partner now seem huge and fantastical. Previously suppressed aspects of each partner's character push into expression. The partners see their mates as changing before their eyes. The loving partner is cloying, the kind partner weak; the steady mate has become pigheaded; the one who gave, selfish. In a crisis of identity, the partners scramble to recover their balance. They blame each other for causing and uncovering the newly apparent problems, but they also take these flaws to heart.

The effect of this new "reality" may vary. Having observed parents and friends, received advice, watched movies, read books, and sorted through their own experience, couples naturally expect some disappointment to follow the glorious days. If this falls within reasonable bounds—as defined by these personal and cultural narratives—they will struggle to integrate their new experience. If not, they will more likely disengage at this point and find "better" mates.

To cope with disappointment, couples reorganize and defend against the chaos, conflict, and loss. They create rules to contain the pain. They avoid, limit, and defuse their fights, stepping away from difficult subjects or learning to discuss them in less threatening ways. Like the Expansive Contract, these rules and expectations define what is acceptable and what is not.

Even as the Stage of Contraction settles in, its eventual passage is foreshadowed by brief mini-cycles, albeit within the umbrella of Contraction. Reflective pauses follow close on the heals of heated fights and, for a moment, couples feel the sober perspective of Resolution. Sharon begins to wonder if, in her need for safety, she hasn't chosen or created a man who is too prim and repressed. Byron begins to see that the nurturing Carrie and the controlling Carrie are one and the same person. These integrative and reflective moments lay the ground for the third stage in the formation of the couple's core character.

## Character and the Stage of Resolution

To enter Resolution, couples must resolve a basic conflict. For example, our original couple, Jonathan and Marie, marry, answering Marie's question about Jonathan's commitment to her. To do this, they bring to bear qualities that had not been prominent in the relationship to date: aspects of their character that help them negotiate, integrate, or deepen their experience in the two previous stages. Resolution summons traits such as a sense of accommodation and compromise, and the ability to maintain perspective.

Resolution brings more complexity into the relationship. Marie sees Jonathan's ambivalence, his desire to be close and his anxiety about her demands; he understands her "irrationality" as one of many aspects of her forthright and generally animated personality. The character of the couple as experienced in either Expansion or Contraction now feels incomplete.

For a third time, a couple in Resolution thinks that it has "arrived." But now, for the first time, the full range of its character has been expressed, for it contains elements of all three stages. Resolution punctuates the formation of a couple's core character.

Couples in Resolution are like beavers building a dam, all busy negotiating, hammering things out, solving or setting aside problems. Complainers have changed into cheerful activists, who swallow their pride in the name of Togetherness and Maturity. And yet, despite similarities, each couple has its own style, its own particular way of reaching harmony or solving puzzles.

Jonathan and Marie, for example, are most comfortable in Resolution, because they prefer themselves as *reasonable* people. They liken themselves to Tracy and Hepburn, whose ironic wit carried them past the thorniest dilemmas. Expansion seems a sweet prelude to them, almost as misguided as Contraction, now that they have come home.

Patti and Marshall find Resolution a mainly sobering *emotional* experience. They feel chastened, forgive each other, and feel cleansed. They care for each other and love the wounded, imperfect persons to whom they are wed for life. In spite of everything, they are "there" for each other, accepting, embracing.

Gerry and Sharon first moved into the Stage of Resolution after they both realized how lonely they had become in their parallel lives. They each had been making small guarded moves to establish more contact with each other, but these had been tentative and too subtle to be successful. Each of them was feeling cut off. Sharon at this time was going through a particularly difficult time at work. Gerry responded to her sense of desperation with a kind of sustained, careful consideration, which let her feel nurtured, but not controlled; and she recalled how good he had been during the earlier part of their relationship. She responded by being more available emotionally than she'd been for a while. Soon they were talking about their separate lives, and discovering how unhappy both of them had been with the long, drawn-out fight. Sharon again saw Gerry as "different" from other men, and Gerry felt redeemed.

The Stage of Resolution suits Gerry and Sharon to a tee. The pleasures of negotiation and the safety provided by its broader perspective satisfy them as much as any romantic moment in Expansion. In fact, they feel almost no distinction between those two stages. Just talking together, no matter what the subject, is soothing and close.

As a couple, Gerry and Sharon sacrifice exuberance and expressiveness in order to maintain safety and comfort. Through this, they hope to keep alive the feelings of comfort and cooperation that infused their Expansive Stage.

Carrie and Byron, on the other hand, feel like foreigners in Resolution. They hate to negotiate, and they never compromise well. They adopt such tactics only as a means to an end, and only briefly: it all seems too cool and distant to them.

Recall that in Contraction Byron had become something of an angry adolescent and Carrie a scolding mother. Byron needed Carrie's attention in order to keep on track with his many projects. Without her praise and support he felt himself drifting. Worse, he literally "burned" for sexual contact with her. And yet he didn't know how to talk to her about it. However he began, he felt, she tried to placate him and soothe things over, without ever stopping to understand what he was saying. Just the thought of her mollycoddling him again drove him into a rage. As for Carrie, she lived in constant terror of both his anger and his absence.

One evening Byron came home late, tired and preoccupied. He was so despondent, so isolated, so absorbed with his sense of failure and futility that he didn't even want to talk to Carrie. Watching him, she felt hopeless. It was clear that things were not going to work out for them. She sat silently at the kitchen table, afraid to say anything that might set him off. After he finished his supper, Byron went upstairs. Carrie cleaned up the kitchen, then climbed the stairs herself, went into their bedroom, and put on her flannel nightgown with the blue and yellow flowers on it; then she got into bed.

So it had it come to this, she thought: all their romantic love together, their dreams, their magic. It was more than she could take. When Byron came in, she was under the covers, the entire bed shaking with her sobs.

Taken aback, Byron sat down beside her. Quietly, not even touching her, he watched her cry; and her state seemed to echo and express what he was feeling himself. He felt engulfed by feelings—tender, profoundly sad, but more: a sense of *déjà vu*. The memory of a childhood scene flashed upon him: he was sitting on the bed beside his mother, watching her cry and moan, her head in her hands, her frail body shaking. He couldn't have been more than eight. His father's drunken shouting had reduced her to a frail ball, huddled on the bed. He remembered how frightened he'd been, how helpless he felt when she clutched his arm for support. He'd wanted to be able to help, to stop her tears, to make her smile. But he hadn't been able to.

Now it was happening all over again, and it was his fault. Tears filled his eyes; his sadness felt endless. Shaking with sobs, he reached over, draped his arm around Carrie, and hugged her. They lay that way for half an hour. Then she emerged from the covers and looked at him more tenderly than ever before, and they began to talk. Byron said he felt he was ruining the only good thing that had ever happened to him. Carrie told him she'd been afraid to talk, because he wasn't listening anymore. Byron said he'd been feeling unappreciated, but he desperately needed her support. Feeling close, loved, and forgiven, they made up.

They entered a new period, marked by a renewed sharing of their feelings. They began feeling more confident about themselves, more solid, courageous even—as if they were breaking new ground. Byron liked this new feeling of maturity: it felt like a wondrous new suit he could put on. So he struggled mightily to take fair, reasoned positions. Carrie felt transformed, and she poured out her appreciation. Their sex life returned. Both were thrilled. No sooner had the forays from Contraction catapulted them into reasoned Resolution than it ushered them into Expansion again. Byron organized a weekend in the country for them. Carrie made special dinners.

Resolution did not exactly fit Byron and Carrie. They greatly preferred the expansiveness, childlike closeness, play, passion, and sexuality of Expansion. This time (and throughout their lives together) Resolution served primarily as a staging ground so they could return to the Expansive phase of their relationship. The character that emerged in their stage of Resolution rested on a determination to be honest and fair, to stop blaming each other for their own fears of failure and abandonment. But this kind of separateness, this effort to take responsibility for themselves was very hard for them and, therefore, short-lived. As soon as they could, they would fuse their lives and destinies. Consequently their Resolutions were like narrow ridges between the broad verdant plains of Expansion on one side, and the treacherous rocky terrain of Contraction on the other.

The first time through, most couples' time in Resolution tends to be brief. (Sharon and Gerry are an exception.) Most couples are so relieved, so elated at the escape from their imprisonment in Contraction, that, like Byron and Carrie, they move rapidly into Expansion again.

Resolution is the most inclusive stage and, with future cycles, couples tend to spend more and more time in it. They feel they can be more of their fuller selves in this stage, and they believe they know themselves best in it. Despite this recognition, most younger couples hurry on by.

## The Importance of the Entire Cycle

We have seen that the first cycle sets the basis for a couple's character. It prefigures the way the couple will be in their subsequent happy times. It defines their characteristic fight. It provides the partners with their customary ways of resolving strife. The character of a couple does not reside in one stage alone, neither the stage in which they prefer to be nor the stage in which they spend most of their time; it is the sum of how they are in the entire three-stage cycle.

Carrie and Byron, for example, move through romantic highs, devastating lows, and brief moments of perspective. Patti and Marshall begin in romance and plummet painfully but come together in an almost reverential period of Resolution. Gerry and Sharon pass quickly through Expansion and Contraction to finally achieve their goals in Resolution. Marie and Jonathan initially seem to spend equal time and give equal weight to each of the three stages, moving from deep friendship through alienation and on to a satisfying partnership.

The first time through the cycle, couples tend to think that whatever stage they are in at the moment represents their real character. After several turns of the cycle, though, the couples begin sensing that how they are throughout the cycle, and especially how they are through several cycles, represents their character better than does any single stage.

Ecological theory contains a concept called co-evolution.[2] Herds of buffalo, for example, are said to co-evolve with the grasses of the plains, each having an inherited character of its own but each taking on its particular character in relation to the other. Streams co-evolve with nearby trees and grasses, as do communities of people and the environment in which they live. So it is with action and imagery in couples.

The character of the individual and the character of the couple co-evolve as well. They adapt to and change with each other. The process is generally stronger for younger people because they are less formed when they first meet. Unless individuals are extremely rigid, though, they all change as the couple develops. Any subsequent change in the partners threatens the couple's stability. If, for example, religious or work experience transforms one person, the other will have to adapt for the relationship to survive. The organization of the couple will also have to adapt to individual changes.

In a similar way, any changes in the couple threaten the individuals' stability. If, for example, one partner becomes physically disabled and the other has to work more outside of the house, their normal roles and routines will change. Then the individuals may have to change their ideas of who they are; internal changes follow external ones. Adaptation and accommodation are essential to maintain stability.

* * *

As couples move through the stages, their character increasingly becomes an independent and powerful force. One might say that they have woven it three times, once in each stage; they will further refine it with each additional cycle. Each stage brings new aspects of each partner into play, and reshapes old ones. Gradually the collective pattern exerts more and more influence over the partners, until it is hard to know where individual and couple character begin and end.

The weave of a couple's character shifts constantly, like a rough surface changing in the sunlight. With each new cycle, the partners measure each new Expansive experience against those of their previous times, against their remembrances of Contraction, and against their accumulated experience of Resolution. As the stages define and shape the couple's experience, the partners' sense of themselves, their character, evolves.

# 9

---

# INTERACTIONAL
# SEQUENCES

---

Couples reveal their character through the sequences of behavior they follow. These sequences are like character in motion, habitual patterns of interaction that become the couple's characteristic gestures or dances. They can be very simple—two- or three-step interactions—or they can be more complex. Some simple examples are: I ask you to do something with me, you refuse, I ask again. Or: you act distracted; I come over and talk; you happily respond.

Not surprisingly, sequences emerge during a couple's first three-stage cycle. They initially appear when the partners are in Expansion and then continue to organize the partners' interaction through the next two stages. Once a couple has settled into one or two major sequences, they tend to follow them over and over again, cycle after cycle.

Sequences condense the couple's inner images and past experiences, and help them express their feelings through action. *Variations of the same typical sequences structure a couple's experience in all three stages.* Over time the sequences become repetitive and fixed, and can be considered the characteristic patterns that define which aspects of our character are included in the couple's relationship and which are not.[1]

Couples form sequences with astounding speed. Some sequences fall into place almost instantly, as though each partner were a piece in a puzzle just waiting for its mate. Even in the relatively loose days of Expansion, spontaneous experimentation soon falls within the lines of the emerging patterns. Other sequences develop more gradually. Sequences create order from chaos; they turn into patterns that limit, define, and focus our experience. Because they are so predictable, we feel safer and more secure following them.

Here are some ways sequences emerge:

• He tries to tell her something important. She reacts negatively to his tone of voice. He quickly learns he has to use a different tone if he expects her to respond favorably.

• She wants to be more assertive. He welcomes this if it involves their families or friends, but he gets angry if she disagrees with him about money or sex. So she takes initiative around the former issues, but tends to pull back around the others.

• He asks her out; she accepts and suggests something to do; he tentatively suggests something else; she restates her first choice; he gives in. This sequence can be played out almost every time he initiates anything toward her. He may suggest that they go to a movie, make love, take a walk, discipline one of the children; she will first agree but modify his proposal; he may try to return to his first suggestion but upon her insistence, they play out hers.

As any particular sequence develops, a couple pours more and more of their feelings and images into it. In the third example above, for instance, he may become more and more tentative, anticipating that she will reject anything he says. He reads her counterproposals as a lack of respect for him. But she may simply want him to be clear and firm before agreeing with him. His tentativeness may irritate her, and her responses may become more and more decisive, almost "tough," by contrast. Really, though, she wants to prod him into being more assertive. Perhaps her own parents followed such a pattern whenever they discussed something important, and she thought it worked well. But her toughness make his worrying worse; when she speaks, the image of his controlling mother flickers subliminally in his mind, and he starts feeling hopeless and trapped.

## What Are Sequences?

A sequence is like a dance that shapes and structures the couple's interaction. Consider how partners make decisions—where to live, how to spend money, whose parents' house to visit on vacations. These may all be conducted within a single interactional pattern such as the following: she initiates a discussion; he puts her off; she persists; he puts her off again; she gets angry; he puts her off again; she gets upset; he consoles her. Now they can collaborate on making a decision.[2]

Couples follow their typical sequences in *every* stage. In Expansion, the patterns organize a couple's happier experience. In bad times, they reveal their more shadowy sides, defining the couple's characteristic fight, characteristic misunderstanding, and typical ways of blaming and attacking each other. In Resolution, these patterns manage to balance both positive and negative qualities.

Take, for example, a sequence built around one partner's teaching the other how to do things better. In Expansion, this pair may have begun in a burst of enthusiasm—an eager student who delights in finding a loving teacher. In Contraction, the couple may grumble bitterly—the student feels criticized and controlled, the teacher feels unappreciated. In Resolution, the same pattern may continue, but the partners each have a more equal voice in determining when to start or when to stop it.

The meanings couples attach to their sequences change, depending on the stage. Positive and negative meanings, favorable and unfavorable antecedents, cheery and gloomy images, good and bad feelings: all may be part of the same sequence—but in different stages. For example, if you initiate a certain sequence in Expansion, I might feel relieved and comforted; and if I follow along, you might feel supported and close—no matter what the content of our dance. But if you initate the same sequence in Contraction, I might feel bossed, not relieved; and instead of going along with you, I might push you away. Feeling rejected, you might then pull back angrily yourself. If you initiate the same sequence in the Stage of Resolution, my response will be different again. I may respond more measuredly, and we may negotiate some kind of middle-ground outcome. That will be how we handle this sequence in the third stage. We have these stage-specific experiences whenever we act out the sequence—no matter what its content.

Sequences take place automatically, but they are not unconscious and can be easily identified and brought to mind. Ask any partner: "When he does ——, what do you do?" or: "When she's in a —— mood, how do you respond?" or "How do you feel?" Their responses will be quick and decisive. Sometimes people might say, "It depends," meaning that they have two or more different responses, perhaps one positive and the other(s) negative. "Sometime," a person might say, "I'll ask him to do something and he is as helpful as can be, but more often he'll react as if I were trying to put him in chains." The first part of this response describes a sequence common to the Expansive Stage, while the second opens up its flip side common to Contraction.

Why do couples choose one particular set of sequences rather than others? The answer depends on the factors discussed in Chapter 4: the inner templates each partner follows, their previous relationships, and each partner's particular expectations for this relationship.

## How Sequences Get Started

Once a relationship starts, we try things out and observe how our partners respond. We notice what is acceptable to them, and what is not. We watch for what interests them, what makes them smile, and what makes them angry. We tell our stories, and shape our feelings and actions in accordance with their reactions—shading and excluding some bits, emphasizing others. Some of us push the boundaries of what is acceptable, behaving in ways that increasingly draw our partners' criticism—until they finally indicate that their limits have been reached, and we pull back. Others are more cautious and limit themselves; the couple's sequences then fall well within safe interactional boundaries. Over time, the partners' responses become routine.

Couples generally organize themselves around several sequences, although one such sequence may dominate at any particular time.[3] In Expansion, the different sequences mingle. In hard times, one powerful stereotyped sequence often structures the relationship. "No matter what I say," one woman says, "*he* says the opposite." "I can't do anything around here without her telling me it's wrong," her mate replies.

Each step in a sequence commands the next; the partners respond to each other automatically like the fifteenth rehearsal of a script. With time, the sequences fix the couple's character.

These sequences are concentrated versions of the images we bring to our relationship. A man who reacts to his wife's requests as if he were being chained might have grown up with very controlling parents. A woman who reacts jealously to her partner's male friendships may have grown up with brothers who excluded her. A partner who is thrilled to be lovingly instructed might have had neglectful parents, and feels grateful for any attention at all. My request and your response, my demand and your refusal—both are glued together.

Powerful feedback loops maintain these patterns and keep them going. Everything one partner does to present a positive or a negative image is bolstered by the other's response. After a while, we anticipate the consequences of not following our scruples, and we do not need our partner's actual response to keep us in line. The sequences are internalized and played out unconsciously.

Once a couple finds a sequence that fits their particular character and style, they will follow it, no matter what stage they are in. For this reason, *all sequences have a three-fold nature.* They have different significance in each of the three stages, depending on the different prevailing moods and themes. Not only do the sequences shift their significance according to the stage the couple is in, but—because the three stages affect individuals differently—we reveal different aspects of our personality in the sequence of each stage.

The rest of this chapter will consider two major aspects of sequences. First we will examine *general* ways in which couples play out the sequences in each of the three stages. Then we will identify four very common *particular* sequences couples follow, and track them across all three stages.

## Sequences in Expansion

In Expansion, patterns are more flexible. They bring out our better qualities and minimize less desirable ones. We experiment: today I "chase" and you play coy; tomorrow you have to chase me to win my trust. We abandon stereotypes and try out things normally outside our repertoire.

Jake and Sandra met when both volunteered for a Parents-Teachers Organization project. They each took community work seriously and found that they enjoyed working together side by side. But their pleasure went beyond that: they had so much fun being partners that they started collaborating in a number of other pursuits, and their relationship flowered. They never tire of discussing things, doing things, or planning the future together. They think they can take on any project so long as they are together. We consider them a "collaborative" couple.

Harry and Samantha had known each other as casual friends for some time, but they were first drawn to each other when he consoled her on the death of her mother. Harry had a quiet and strong manner, which she found reassuring. Her expression of grief touched him deeply; he felt she was expressing feelings for them both. They formed a relationship. Over the years, they return to images of his concern and her expressivity, repeatedly maneuvering each other into the same positions they had when first they met. This couple seems more "complementary" in type.

Other patterns gel quickly, if not all at once. When one particular encounter works well, the partners tend to follow its pattern. Experimenting is exciting, but it can be strange and risky. Fairly soon, we slow down and adopt one or two basic patterns. During Expansion these patterns feel comforting, and they enhance what we want to emphasize in ourselves and our partners. These general patterns develop into repetitive sequences that structure the relationship. One might look like this:

A man may roughly offer to help his partner with a chore. She finds his manner endearing but awkward, so she smiles and suggests a better way for him to do it. Appreciating her interest, he tries out her suggestion, and he actually *does* perform better. She is so pleased, she gives him a kiss, which he returns. This sequence may take place a hundred times over the course of a long relationship, absorbing all manner of content, from how to dress to how to make love.

## Sequences in Contraction

In Contraction, sequences grow rigid. Play, experimentation, and the sense of choice all yield to an angry stiffness. This is what we commonly think of as people's defenses or character armor. In Contraction, a couple's life becomes narrow and routine. The same partner almost always initiates talk or sexual contact, the other responds wearily, angrily, resignedly. One criticizes, the other fights back. Words like "always" and "never" dominate their vocabulary, and the partners become glum, sardonic, and moralistic.

The sequences of Expansion persist, but are turned upside-down. Now they carry punitive, not rewarding, messages. Power differences appear, freezing one partner into a helpless or reactive position, or creating a bitter struggle for the upper hand. Partners who pursue turn into nags; partners who move back become hermits.

Consider the two examples mentioned above. In Contraction the sequences may run as follows:

The partners who collaborate, Jake and Sandra, start feeling claustrophobic, because they not only live together but work together. But at the same time, they are so bound up in their togetherness that each feels threatened by any move their partner makes toward independence. If Sandra spends an evening with friends, Jake sulks, and this discourages her from going out very often. If Jake goes to too many ballgames with his friends, Sandra schedules a pile of household chores for him on his return; he understands and cuts back going to the games. In Contraction, their sequences reflect both their dissatisfaction with their togetherness and their anxiety about being autonomous.

In Contraction, Harry, who had seemed so strong and quiet when he consoled Samantha, seems dull and unimaginative. She pulls away from his touch, yearning for a partner with more verve. He finds her aloof and rejecting and withdraws into himself. This confirms her view that he is too passive, and she attacks him for it. He angrily defends himself, but feels like failure because he cannot satisfy the woman who had given his life meaning. She begins avoiding him more.

As in Expansion, the sequences that dominate Contraction are condensations of images we bring from earlier experience. A woman who persistently refuses her partner's sexual invitations may have had intrusive and domineering parents. A man who feels bitterly unrecognized may have envied his more successful, highly praised siblings. No matter what the particulars, partners in Contraction lock onto each other's harshest images about the world.

## Sequences in Resolution

In Resolution, sequences grow more flexible; the partners develop a sense of perspective and regain their capacity for compromise. They acknowledge and accept each other's limitations as well as the limitations of the relationship itself. In this spirit, patterns that had seemed oppressive now take on the protective reassurance of routine. Partners develop a sense of how long each can linger with sex; how much they can tease before the other gets angry; how long a quarrel can go on before it becomes serious.

Individuals in Resolution have a more complex, less automatic response to their partners. Concessions are made for the sake of the relationship or out of a sense of personal integrity. "I just didn't like myself when I reacted to her badly," said one man, "so I forced myself to be more responsive. And you know what—it felt better." Meanwhile his partner had decided to choose her moments better, to sense whether he was receptive or not, in a good or bad mood, before asking for something. Each made this change independently of the other and claimed credit for it, claims that only came out in the next phase of Contraction.

In Resolution, partners learn how to separate reasonable demands from impositions. She knows he wants her to spend less time with her mother and may do so—somewhat. He knows she wants him to help figure things out about the house, and he does so—somewhat. Sequences in Resolution help the couple settle down. Day-to-day life becomes possible again, and the partners are able to carry out the tasks and responsibilities without constant bickering.

Consider our two examples. In Resolution their pattern might look like this:

Sandra and Jake decide to work collaboratively together in some arenas, but separately (or with others) in others. This allows them a blend of support and freedom, togetherness and self-development, and makes them feel that their relationship can help them both grow as people.

Harry and Samantha also approach life in a more complex way. Samantha may appreciate Harry's concern, but at the same time may encourage his independence and ask him to leave her alone more of the time. He may appreciate her honesty and maintain a distance, coming closer only when she says she needs him. But he may also now tell her when he needs *her* support. In times of stress, they may take turns at caring for each other.

This process re-forms the partners' boundaries. Over time, couples establish an elaborate map of their open and closed territories, and identify ambiguous areas that remain to be explored.

## Common Sequences

Let us now present four sequences that are very common to relationships. They are not an all-inclusive list, but they are familiar
sequences with which most readers should be able to identify.

### 1. *Pulling a third party into the relationship*

One partner's pulling a third person or another interest into the
relationship creates a "triangle."[4] This is a natural thing that all couples do, but some couples especially do it to defuse the intensity of
some conflicts. They may go out only with other couples, never alone
together. They may only do things with the children. They may talk
about the children, the dog, our parents, but almost never about
themselves. They may have to "get high" as a necessary prelude to
any sexual or conversational intimacy.

Some partners deeply enjoy gaining access to and being accepted
by their new mate's family. This may become a major aspect of the
couple relationship for them, making up for the lack of a warm, supportive family of their own. Indeed, some people form relationships
with a partner's mother or father that are as intense as the one with
their partner. Some partners find that working together with each
other in a family business provides them with the constant companionship and involvement they crave.

Over time, the triangle may become habitual. The couple will
then have a hard time functioning *without* the third party, and it may
include the latter even when it is not entirely appropriate. The third
party knits the couple together and makes them feel closer.

Third parties rarely feel intrusive to such couples during Expansion. Rather, friends or activities widen their experience and bring
them together. He delights at the new friends he meets through her,
while she enjoys finally learning the intricacies of baseball. He feels
warmly embraced by her parents. She feels he has opened the world
of literature and classical music to her. In Expansion, third parties are
vehicles for common activity.

Here is how this process may begin: Imagine that the couple is
alone; tension builds. Perhaps they have some conflict, feel bored, or
are uneasy with their expected intimacy. One or both partners then
bring in the third party. They might call up another couple and
arrange to go out to a movie. Or, if they have children, one of them
might mention that their child is having problems at day care, and the

other will animatedly respond. They may then talk to the child, discuss the problem together, and then turn to a game of Chutes and Ladders. Now they have relieved their tension or boredom.

Here is another illustration. In recent times, "blended" families create instant triangles. Imagine a woman who is dating a divorced man. One afternoon, she accompanies him and his daughter to the park, and sits quietly by while he reads the girl a story. She finds herself entranced by his gentle care. Eagerly hoping for a family of her own, she chooses one for herself: both the man-as-father and the little girl who will become her stepchild. Later this couple may argue about the child's intruding into their private life, but early on they feel so complete as a threesome that they feel something missing when they are alone without her.

During Contraction, the couple's use of third parties to avoid conflict becomes more pronounced. Partners may return to siblings, friends, and parents; those with jobs may seem more married to their work than to their mates. Some parents focus so intensely on a child that they rarely turn to each other. Not only does this result in their losing their intimate ties to each other; they wind up detouring the resolution of their problems through the third party. One familiar example of this is the child who serves as a "go-between" or the child whose ultimate success is seen as one or both parents' main goal in life.

In Contraction, a partner is likely to say "You don't spend enough time with the children," instead of "You don't spend enough time with me." And problems build up without being discussed, because the couple handles their tension by bringing in the third party rather than by working things out.

"Dysfunctional triangles" fill the literature of family therapy: alcoholism and workaholism make partners distant; blended families turn bitter when the biological parent overidentifies with *his* children.

The familiar triangle sequence in stepfamilies fits many other families as well. Almost invariably, the stepparent and the spouse have a dialogue something like this:

HE: "It's nine o'clock and Johnny's still up. Are you going to let him get away with it?"
SHE: "Why are you always on his case?"
HE: "You said you'd set some limits on when he went to bed, so we could have some time together."

SHE: "But he's feeling lonely tonight, and I feel bad for him."

HE (feeling left out): "If you weren't so quick to coddle him, he wouldn't act so lonely. He's just trying to get your attention."

SHE (feeling more protective of Johnny as he becomes more critical): "How can you be so insensitive? He's just a child."

HE (feeling defeated): "If that's how you feel, then let him spend the whole night with you. I'm sleeping in the living room anyway ..."

After a while lengthy sequences like this become quite abbreviated. As soon as one person mentions the child, the whole painful script flashes before their eyes, and their anger and anxiety flare up immediately. The dialogue might become something like this:

SHE: "Why don't you take Johnny to a ballgame this weekend?"
HE: "He doesn't need another ballgame."
SHE: "Forget it, then."
HE: "Okay, I will."

On the other hand, most triangles perform a conservative function: they help maintain a safe distance for the partners. He may be a workaholic, and she, after years of trying to get him home more, may respond by getting closer to the children or to her mother. Or maybe she watches TV all the time, or starts spending every spare minute with her neighbor. This works for a while, but whenever the couple finds themselves alone they fight. (Ironically, this kind of fight may not be dangerous; it helps to reestablish their safe distance.)

If partners fought directly with each other—e.g., over how they feel the other was shutting them out—instead of over a third party, it might be more painful for them at first, but it might help them deal openly with what disturbs them. Such direct engagement generally draws couples closer. Triangulated couples, on the other hand, usually avoid the very kind of direct contact that might help them out.

In Resolution, the triangulated third party functions in more complex ways, helping the partners maintain both their closeness and their distance. For example, I may be a hard worker. When I need to get away and be on my own, I may use work as a focus. But you and I might have evolved a way of talking about my work that brings it *into* our relationship, so it represents less of a threat to you, and less of a total escape to me.

Resolution involves a letting go and restructuring. I may let our children go off to summer camp; you may work less; we may both drink less or go to fewer evening meetings. When we do, we may still not be ready for a great deal of intimate, one-on-one engagement. But we may do things together, include others—moderately—in our activities, be alone together for very defined periods of time, so that we can separate before getting too anxious. Resolution brings more perspective to this kind of behavior. We can more easily detach from the third party when necessary, and we are less compelled to repeat the patterns that drag us down.

## 2. *Turning your partner into someone else*

This sequence echoes the Pygmalion legend made popular in the musical *My Fair Lady*, in which Pygmalion, a sculptor and king of Cyprus, could not find a partner he liked. No real woman could rival the woman of his dreams. But he fell in love with his own statue of Aphrodite, and the strength of his love gave the statue life. This story is a metaphor for couples in which one partner falls in love with the other not for who she is—in fact, he may not like who she is—but for who she *might be* with his shaping influence.

Sequences aimed at changing one's partner aim at restoring the person one met during the Expansive Stage or else creating a new, improved model. A couple's Expansive Contract often contains a "reform clause": one or both partners want to improve, and they agree to do so with the other's help. While the Pygmalion contract may later turn sour—the effort to change the other then feels judgmental and controlling—during Expansion it usually feels helpful and enhancing.

Partners feel that their mate's (transformational) help will help them achieve their aims in life. They are pleased at the amount of love and attention they receive, and they feel much more important than ever before in their lives. Suddenly, they are on center stage. Thrilled at how the relationship has increased their resources, both helped and helper feel valued and empowered. In Expansion, sequences aimed at growth, change, and enhancement give the couple a tremendous sense of their potential. They feel they can actually transform each other, thus realizing their deepest hopes and dreams.

Women, for example, often agree to help men become more sensitive and expressive, to put their work in perspective, to dress better, to be more polished and worldly wise, to get along better with their families, to be closer to their children. Men often agree to help women deal more forthrightly with their colleagues, to stand up to their parents (and even their children), to dress better, and to worry less.

Here is another example: Sara comes home week after week with complaints about her critical boss. John listens patiently, soothing and comforting her bruised ego. She asks him for advice, and he advises her to stand up and be tough. One day she does this, and it is a success: her boss seems more respectful. She is immensely pleased with herself and with John, who—for his part—feels happy with her success. His consulting capital has increased, and Sara now treats him with more affection, and opens more areas of her life to him for his comments.

In Contraction, what began as helpful ends up feeling oppressive. Resentment and defiance spring up, and struggles for control ensue. Here is how trying to turn one's partner into someone else looks in Contraction:

A demand for change—be more stylish, be more expressive, spend more time with the children—is ignored. The demand is reiterated, perhaps rephrased, but resistance increases. This leads to a stalemate, the "cold war" of coupling.

A demand for change is refused and rejected. This leads to an even stronger demand for change, and an even stronger rejection. Soon, escalating sequences of demand and refusal develop, sometimes leading to explosive and violent scenes. In the most explosive form of this sequence, one finds an abusive man chasing a woman whose defiance so threatens his ego, that he wants to control her, even if it means hurting her, or an angry, verbally abusive woman pursuing a defensive, retreating man from room to room, until he turns and hits her.

The person being asked to change may be partly responsible himself for this request. He may even have invited his partner's help in the first place, asking her to push, cajole, or support him to change—even over his objections. But when she starts, he decides he does not really want it. He says she no longer feels supportive, but now seems judgmental and controlling instead. So he resists her. When he does, his partner feels betrayed; and, in fact, she has been. However unholy the original agreement might have been, it was mutual; and it was a core element in their Expansive Contract.

This sequence gets more complicated when our efforts to change each other actually succeed. This is because our efforts to change our partner often cover up our own difficulties with whatever trait we're trying to change. For example, we might push our partner to appear more fashionable in order to hide our insecurity about our own appearance. Or we might aggressively "teach" another to be a good sexual partner in order to cover our own anxieties about sex—for example, our difficulties with being receptive and letting down our guard versus our fear of being controlled.

As long as our partner resists our demand, our own insecurities can remain hidden. But if our partner *does* change—does dress better or talk more freely—we may become even more anxious, and instead of congratulating her become puzzlingly critical and withdrawn.

The question of *power* is at the core of many such struggles. My sense of competence may be invested in my ability to reform you, yours in your ability to focus on me. When you refuse my advice, I feel disempowered, and your power becomes defiant. Pygmalion calls the tune: the statue responds by choosing to dance or not. In Expansion, Pygmalion seemed supportive and helpful; but in Contraction he comes across as harsh and unaccepting, and his partner feels constantly criticized and put down. His message is, "You're *unacceptable* as you are," and she no longer likes it.

Eventually, most of us resent a partner's persistent efforts to change us. They just feel mean and tiresome. As our resentment builds, we refuse to change, even in ways we think are for our own good. As this pattern continues, our partner feels rejected and unappreciated, too. In the face of mutual rejection, we fight or we distance ourselves, yearning once again for a partner who will love us simply for who we are.

In Resolution, partners stop imposing their will on each other. The shift may begin when the one who has repeatedly tried to change his partner no longer feels such pressure to do so; he lets go, first out of frustration and, perhaps later, out of respect. (It may also begin with the model declaring her independence and the frustrated sculptor eventually conceding.)

In Resolution, Pygmalion begins to see his partner as separate from himself—an imperfect person, perhaps, but good enough. The partner who wanted to be changed may declare her independence: you'll have to love me as I am or not at all. Or, perhaps, she may find others to inspire and guide change—friends, self-help groups, or a therapist.

Sometimes the helper becomes the helped. Such reversal of roles may help to loosen the oppressive bond of Contraction. Often, however, because the basic pattern is maintained, such a couple will fall back into Contraction.

The essence of Resolution lies in its flexibility. I may encourage you to change, or you may ask me to help you change. In either case, you will let yourself be influenced by my taste or judgment, but you exercise more choice about the extent of my influence; and sometimes you refuse it. The pattern provides predictability—we both agree that I should help you change—but the many variations on pattern permit perspective and freedom.

### 3. Completing yourself with your partner

None of us is self-sufficient. We all need someone else to comfort us, enliven us, tone us down. Knowing this, we choose partners who "complete" us, who provide the qualities and talents we lack. The sequence involves a search for complementarity.

Here is a familiar example: A steady person who feels dull hooks up with someone expressive and spontaneous. In Expansion, your steadiness makes me feel secure and I am free to express myself. In a vicarious way, my spontaneity enlivens you and makes you feel more interesting. The steadier you are the more spontaneous I can be; the more spontaneous I am, the sturdier you are. In spiraling sequences, we play off each other like two sides of the same coin.

Here are some other examples:

- A private person who listens well connects with a very social person who likes to talk.
- A person who needs to feel attractive finds someone who appreciates beauty, which means her.
- A well-organized but slightly plodding person gets together with a freewheeling, disorganized person.

At first, in Expansion, we rejoice at finding in our partner what we feel we lack ourselves. Our mate adds to who we are, compensating for our limits and deficiencies. Complementarities emphasize our closeness, our fusion, our inability to do without each other. We have a sense of perfect fit. If we were incomplete before, now we are whole, brimming over with the exuberance and joy of having found our missing half. Amy Tan, in her novel *The Joy Luck Club,* describes the feeling like this:

> With imagined tragedy hovering over us, we became inseparable, two halves creating the whole: yin and yang. I was victim to his hero. I was always in danger and he was always rescuing me. I would fall and he would lift me up. It was exhilarating and draining. The emotional effect of saving and being saved was addicting to both of us. And that, as much as anything we ever did in bed, was how we made love to each other: conjoined where my weaknesses needed protection.[5]

During Contraction, the negative sides of our complementarities emerge. My sturdiness becomes plodding; your spontaneity becomes outrageous. The more plodding I become, the more I "drive" you to outrageous acts. Your expressiveness now seems hysterical; my stoicism, defensive and withholding. The more emotional you become, the more I hold things in; the more I withhold my feelings, the more you express yours. Eventually we believe that we *are* the roles we enact in these negative complementary positions.

In Contraction, complementary relationships restrict us and highlight our weaknesses. Whereas I was once glad that you spoke so expressively for us both, now I feel you preempting my efforts at self-expression. The articulateness I had previously admired now diminishes me. I might point out your verbosity; you may point out my dullness, and the fight is on.

Take another example: Whereas before I had felt enlivened by your enthusiasm, now I feel overwhelmed. You won't give me the chance to be myself. I withdraw; you come on stronger; the stronger you come on, the deeper I go into my shell. The more I withdraw, the more you feel abandoned, and so you scold me, but I only move further back. Before, I had felt safe in your presence, but now I feel under attack. Before, I felt safe in sexual surrender, but now I feel endangered.

In complementary relationships each of us depends as much on what we give as on what we receive. We may need to feel strong or weak, calm or frenzied, articulate or mysterious. When our partner tries to express *our* side of the equation, we feel threatened, and—directly or not—often punish him or her for it. We tell our inarticulate partner that his conversation at the party was game but awkward—perhaps a bit embarrassing, if the truth be known. We respond to our insecure partner's attempt at being assertive by criticizing her tone of voice.

Contraction freezes us within our roles, and we become more fully identified with them. If I am the strong one, the "Rock of Gibraltar," then I will not express my insecurities, because I think you will turn away from me if I do. Similarly, if your being assertive alienates me, you may try to hold it back, worrying that if you push me away, I might not be there for you if you happen to need me. The roles that once so perfectly completed us now imprison us within narrow confines.

In Resolution, we pull back from totally identifying with our complementary roles. You may be strong—but not always and not completely. I may be dependent—but sometimes I can be decisive and act independently. We may only discover these complexities when our partners are not available to play their assigned roles. You might be away on a trip, and I have to make a decision without you. You, previously the strong one, may have just lost your job, and you need me to take care of you.

In Resolution the positive and negative aspects of complementary relationships coexist—with an emphasis on the positive. Partners may lack a passionate sense of completion, but they return to the complementarity they had created in Expansion. I may be your rock and you my fire most of the time, but we now tolerate digressions. We also know that there is more to each of us than the pattern emphasizes. We find security in our roles, but feel free knowing that they are only roles.

#### 4. *Pursuing and distancing with each other*

One general sequence comes close to subsuming all the others: the dance of pursuit and distance.[6] This may be as close to a universal pattern as we find in today's couples. It begins when one member of the couple, usually (but not always) the man, withdraws from the intimacy of Expansion. It could be a little, it could be a lot. The meaning of this withdrawal depends partly on how he does it—for instance, he might withdraw angrily, guiltily, sweetly, or cautiously—and partly on how his partner interprets it. He might simply withdraw quietly, or he might say he "really needs some space"—a code word in our culture for "leave me alone." He might move angrily into himself. He might have an affair. Or he might build up several small withdrawals such as increasing attention to work, weariness upon return home, and so forth.

His partner's particular past colors her response. To the extent that she fears abandonment and rejection, for example, she may cast his withdrawal in a very sinister light. On the other hand, if she likes the private time his withdrawal makes possible, she may take longer to object—or may not object at all. If she has resolved never to chase a man again, for example, she may remain as still as she can, even though his increasing withdrawal makes her anxious.

*His* history colors his reaction to her reaction. If, for example, he has a history of intrusive people in his life—mothers, fathers, lovers, for example—he will cast her reaction in a sinister light. And so the dance spirals downward.

Through the media, the dance of pursuit and distance has become so familiar that it is an essential part of today's Cultural Narrative. Most couples pull further apart, we are told, after the happy days of early relationships. The portrait of "love-starved" women pursuing "withholding" men fits many people's experience. Even though men can also be "love-starved" and women also "withholding," the stereotype reflects a common reality. Women often want to talk more than their male partners. Men often feel trapped or cornered, and withdraw.

A woman caught in this situation feels betrayed and abandoned. Wondering why her partner cannot come through for her, she asks if it is something wrong with her. As her objections grow, he feels betrayed. No longer interested in being drawn out, he moves inward and becomes reclusive. The relationship reaches a painful stalemate.

Simultaneously, a similar but opposite dance often takes place around sexual issues, with the same "withdrawn" men pursuing the same "aggressive" women. In this dance, men feel abandoned, women invaded and controlled. In effect, the dance and its roles shape the partners' feelings more than their gender does, so the common notion that the dance of pursuit and distance is basically gender-driven is not really true.

During Expansion, when one partner pursues, the other often turns and responds. The distance between them moves like an accordion, and they can be free and happy together; later, the distance may open up again, but this is all right, too. The emotional space between partners is elastic, not fixed. Either can experience the pleasure of being warmly sought after, as well as the pleasure of being warmly received.

Contemporary couples pass through several phases of this dance. Following the traditional form, men still tend to initiate contact. Women, more aware of the emotional consequences of relationships, respond warily. Early on, though, women begin to share the initiative. It may start in little ways: "Let's go out with Carole and Sean," she suggests. Or, "What do you think about when we kiss?" Or, "Would you like to have Christmas dinner with my family?" Now it's the man who responds, generally positively—glad she's attentive and and taking care of their lives together—and sometimes negatively because he feels a little cornered. Her initiatives and his responses bring new aspects of their personalities into the relationship.

At this point, the dance is still flexible. Either partner can initiate; either can respond. Each sets limits without offending the other. Experimenting, the partners find a safe, stable distance between themselves. From here, they can either travel closer toward greater intimacy or further away toward more autonomy. By the fifth time she has checked a certain aggressive advance of his, for example, he gets the picture: to get close to her, he has to approach slowly.

Eventually the sequence becomes fixed, with women tending to initiate most verbal, and men most sexual, exchanges. During Expansion, men find this pursuit helpful, if sometimes uncomfortable. Most men do not easily express their fears or feelings. Women can let them off the hook by "knowing" what they think and expressing it for them.

Sequences in Contraction begin when he pulls away in a way that upsets her or when she moves in a way that he finds objectionable. Couples often argue endlessly about who is to blame for having started things off. "I only pull away because you constantly have something for me to do," he will insist. "I hate pursuing you," she will counter. "I only do it because you never do anything without my telling you and you never tell me about yourself without my pulling it out of you."

They need not argue about who begins the sequence; each does, often in anticipation of what the other will do: on the weekend, he anticipates that she will want to talk, and he pulls deep into his TV sports to ward her off; she knows that he will get deeply engrossed in the baseball game that afternoon, so she nervously tries to engage him in the morning.

In shorthand, the interactional sequence in Contraction goes as follows:

He withdraws a little.
She invites him to remain engaged.
He feels ambivalent but maintains his distance.
She is a little anxious, and her renewed invitation has an edge to it.
He withdraws further.
As he does, her fears about relationships start rising to the surface, even though she is trying to keep them down. She asks him to return.
Her request sounds demanding, needy, and "emotional." He becomes more suspicious. He "knows" she's demanding too much: she wants to swallow him up and control him. So he withdraws further, angrily and with open rejection.
The more he withdraws, the more she pursues. The more she pursues, the more he withdraws.

Couples play this sequence out around an infinite number of themes: a concern about the children; the desire to plan a vacation; the decision about which movie to attend; the suggestion that he pick up some groceries, clean up the kitchen, or share his feelings. No matter what she proposes, he feels trapped and finds a way to oppose her initiative.

All the other sequences we have described can be thought of as specific cases of this cultural archetype of pursuit and distance. For example, "Pygmalion" suggests a change, and his partner first complies, then defies him. In complementary couples, the anxious partner may always seek the support of the sturdy partner; in Contraction, he refuses to support her. The talkative partner seeks a listener; in Contraction, she has too much to do.

In this sequence, we externalize our problems by blaming our partners and seeing ourselves as their victims. The sequence also puts both partners in a double bind. For the woman it goes like this: If she pursues, she does not win because he still withdraws. If she does not pursue or express her opinion, she feels left alone, abandoned, and unable to resolve many important matters, such as when to have a child, how to deal with her relatives, or how to talk together in a "less threatening way." He will not pursue unless she appears desperate, which is demeaning; and then she has him to herself only on terms that make her feel self-defeating and despicable.

For the man it goes like this: If he withdraws, he does not win: he loses his partner. Even though she keeps pursuing him, she does it in more and more upsetting ways, often aggressively or fuming with accusations. In other words, his behavior brings about the reaction he most fears. But if he considers pursuing her, as she has asked, he feels as if he has been forced to comply with her wishes. He feels controlled.

After being in this position long enough, he begins to lose sight of his own wishes; and when she, in exasperation, responds to his distance with statements like "Well, what *do* you want?" he may seem stubborn and withholding, but often he doesn't really know and can't say. This is important. It is not that he *won't* say; it's that he *can't* say. In some primitive way, he feels she has taken his personality away; he must erect a wall to guard himself. But the more he guards himself, the less self he finds he has left to guard.

The most difficult problem to treat in the sexual life of couples arises when one partner loses sexual desire. This "dysfunction" is often a specific form of the dance of pursuit and distance. The more one person—often a man—approaches, the more his partner pulls back, and the less she is in touch with her own independent desire.

Eventually, in Contraction the pursuit-and-distance sequence becomes the central dynamic. It does not matter *what* they are discussing. It could be where to go out to dinner, "When can we talk?," "Why can't we make vacation plans?," or "We need to make decisions about the children." The interactional process absorbs every theme; the content in any discussion vanishes into the process itself. Only the pain of distance and control can be discussed, and only then in the same circular blaming way. There is no exit.

The partners' positions in this dynamic become identified with roles—"This is what he does every time"—and the roles become identified with character—"This is really who you are." The person we met in Expansion now seems a superficial representation, a fake, a manipulation, whereas the person encountered in *this* stage feels real, more like the bedrock of character. Partners uncover "precedents" for this character, and now we hear aspersions about families such as "Your mother or father is just like that," and "I suppose you can't help it, given your family." In Expansion individuals seemed like flowers rising out of their families' bounty, or heroes triumphant over their families' failings. Now they seem like lowly creatures, predetermined to express their families' worst.

Not surprisingly, the "character" that emerges is often stereotyped, especially by gender. Stereotypical roles—"women who love too much," closed-off men—disappoint and infuriate both partners. However, when men remain "soft" and communicative during Contraction, they are often accused of being whiny—of not being "men" and of not providing the strength and support the woman needs. When women remain independent and forthright, men often accuse them of being uncaring, aggressive, controlling—in short, not feminine. It's a "no win" situation.

The character consolidated by the dance of pursuit and distance becomes harder to escape. Some couples yield to it. Others, trying to prove that they could still be the loving person they were in Expansion if they only had the right partner, now turn to affairs. They compulsively reenact the Expansive Stage with new people. While an affair might help one partner remain in the Expansive Stage (with a lover), it condemns the couple to Contraction, because it drains off the energy and discontent that might push them beyond it.

In Resolution, the futility of pursuit and distance becomes clear to couples, and they seek alternatives. She resolves not to pursue him; he resolves not to react. She promises to be more patient—if he lets her know when he *will* be available. He promises to hang in when discussion gets intense—if she will stop reacting to him so angrily. Generally, these alternatives work only briefly, leaving many couples discouraged; but sometimes they click. After all, it feels good to them to be patient, to hang in, to break out of their imprisoning roles and sequence.

These forays away from the sequence of pursuit and distance lend it complexity. Now the partners have a little more flexibility about initiating, responding, and reacting. The pursuer will still retain much of the initiative, but perhaps will say affectionately and with humor: "I know this is a bad time to bring this up, but ..." Or, "You probably think I want something, and you're right: but it's you—so can that be all bad?" He is less fixed in response: sometimes he remembers how good it felt to be pursued, can see how hard she is working not to intrude or control, and actually responds warmly to her. He might respond ambivalently, but more reasonably or with self-deprecating humor. He might say, "This is a bad time, but tomorrow evening would be fine." Or, "I'm afraid I can't deal with that for at least three months, but I'll write it in the calendar and I'll bring it up then." In other words, he achieves both distance and connection. The distance created is close to what is acceptable for both partners—perhaps a little too distant for one and a little too close for the other, but tolerable to both.

So far, we have seen how a couple's character is formed in its first cycle through the three stages, and we have examined some of the most common sequences of couple interaction that extend across all three stages. Now we must turn to a more longitudinal question: what happens to couples over time. As they move through the years, they continue to cycle through the same three stages; but they do not keep going through the same endless circle. Rather, they move forward through time like a spiral, a corkscrew, moving through the same three stages again and again, but never seeming to be in the same place twice. As a couple continues to pass through life, its cycles take on a somewhat different tone. We consider this aspect of couple life in the following chapter, which examines how couples' subsequent cycles shape and modify their character over time.

# 10

---

# THE COUPLE'S
# CHARACTER OVER TIME

---

Unlike individuals, couples do not encounter stage after stage of new development as they grow older. They continue to cycle in spiral fashion through the same three stages. These cycles mold and reinforce their character.

A couple's first few cycles are tremendously important, because they bring *new* information into the relationship. The partners share feelings they never shared before, tell stories they never told before, realize wishes they never understood before. After the first few cycles, however, the amount of new information churned up in any new cycle is likely to decline, and the couple's patterns and sequences become fairly fixed. Couples then pass through the stages with a ritualistic sameness. Their experience in each stage becomes less dramatic, more like a general state of being.

Once they have adopted their typical sequences, couples establish a "Home Base" in one stage and spend most of their time there. They move out of Home Base, via forays or cycles, into one or both of the other two stages, and then return.

All couples take their own path through life. There is no blueprint for the "right way" to follow. Over time, each couple develops a richness and complexity, which express the flowering of its own particular character. After many turns of the wheel, a couple's character resembles a facc: as much as it seems changed by the years, it is also

175

more deeply etched in its own form. We might not have predicted this ironic twinkle or that particular pattern of wrinkles, but, once we see the face, all its features fit our recollection of the face of youth.

## Jonathan and Marie

Jonathan and Marie tend to see themselves as mature, psychologically sophisticated people, and they yearn to be in the Stage of Resolution. But, although they behave as rationally as they can, they cannot resolve all their problems this way, and over the years they have struggled mightily. During the first part of their life together, they managed to spend most of their time in Resolution. Later, though, things shifted, and their Home Base became Contraction.

Because Jonathan and Marie are so invested in their image as reasonable people, they tend to put off decisions that might bring out conflicts. Thus they procrastinated on the decision to marry, to have a child, and later, to move to Philadelphia when Marie received a job offer there. To bring these decisions to a head, Marie, who gets frustrated first, brings on a crisis. She threatens to or actually does leave. She ran off to her parents' house, for example, when they could not decide to marry; and she told Jonathan she was prepared to take the children and leave him to move to Philadelphia alone if she had to. These crises bring to a head the long-simmering themes that characterize their relationship: Jonathan's fear of being controlled, Marie's fear of being ignored.

Only by this move does Marie reestablish her dignity and power. Her threat frightens Jonathan, who apologizes, affirms his love for her, and then urges her to return. This permits Marie to let down her guard and cry, and Jonathan can then once again feel important. Taking her in his arms restores his own dignity and power, and they both experience a brief period of closeness that reminds them of their early days. They laugh and joke and once again see themselves as Tracy and Hepburn.

These moments pass too quickly. A little fight, precipitated by Jonathan's ignoring her or by Marie's ordering him about, lets them down hard. Eventually, they learn various strategies for climbing out of the depths, and toward the more reasonable plains of Resolution. But these do not always work, and they remain vulnerable to the pull of Contraction. When they fall in, it seems harder and harder to escape.

## Home Base

After their first few cycles, couples who go through life together tend to dwell mainly in one stage, their Home Base. Whether they cycle frequently or infrequently, this stage becomes their home, and it is from here that they leave to make changes. Home Base, with its familiar feelings, sequences, and themes, powerfully influences a couple's character, for it structures how the partners experience themselves most of the time. Home Base is virtually always in Resolution or Contraction, since few if any couples can remain for long in the excitement and vulnerability that characterize the Stage of Expansion.*

Home Base serves as a staging ground for forays, mini-cycles, and full cycles. Naturally, the quality of a couple's cycles differs according to which stage it leaves from and returns to. Suppose, for example, a couple resides primarily in Contraction. Their cycles begin with a move into Resolution, then move into Expansion, and ultimately return to Contraction. These couples may eagerly anticipate change, work to achieve it, and feel relieved when it comes. But since their cycles usually end in disappointment, their experience is mixed. They live with a sense of defeat, always fearing that their solutions will not last.

Couples who reside in Resolution have a different experience. They may be torn between resisting change—it is good enough where they are, and by tackling a thorny problem they might get stuck in Contraction—or risk it for even greater gains in Expansion. Their cycles either begin in excitement and move fairly rapidly into a painful period of Contraction, or else they move directly into Contraction. These couples then usually end up back in Resolution for the next long period of time. Even though they may resist change,

---

*Some couples may seem to be constantly cheery; they are always happy—at least to the outside observer—and they may appear attentive to each other for months on end. Such behavior may indeed mean this couple has made Expansion their Home Base, and this is more likely to be the case in a couple's first few years together; but their behavior is more likely a reflection of how happy they feel in their Home Base of Resolution.

they fear it less than those who reside in Contraction, because they can expect to land on their feet once it is over.

Home Base generally represents the couple's social identity, too. After a few cycles, friends and acquaintances increasingly relate to the couple on these terms, and even families eventually fall into line. The character we express in our Home Base may actually represent only a small part of our individual repertoire, but it most defines who we are in the couple relationship, the person our partner sees as our essential self. The more our partners and others relate to us as our persona in our Home Base, the more we feel constrained to act that way.

Sometimes we object to this. Feeling boxed in, we want to get away, to be our *old* selves, our *fuller* selves, both at work and with friends. This is why we seek out buddies and confidants. We value our confidants to the extent that they know our fuller selves. This is why affairs, which begin in expansiveness, can feel redeeming: they open us to parts of ourselves that we have generally placed under wraps.

Two types of conflicts commonly arise around Home Base. First, many couples find themselves in a Home Base they do not like, and yearn for another. They may continue like this for many years either until they change successfully (a couple's Home Base *may* change: see below) or until they eventually accept the Home Base they have. Or, of course, they may divorce.

A second type of conflict comes when the partners each prefer *different* Home Bases and disagree over where they'd rather be. Consider Stan and Nancy. Nancy would rather be in a reasonable state of Resolution most of the time, so she can carry on her work, raise her children, and take charge of her life. But Stan pines for Expansive experience, and constantly pulls her toward passion and fun. So the two of them struggle, each tugging the other toward their own preferred stage.

Such couples usually dwell in Contraction until they strike a deal. One then accepts the other's choice, even though this establishes an inherent tension (or sadness) in the relationship. They might try moving between the two preferred stages as best they can: in this scenario their relationship passes through more frequent cycles; no single Home Base holds and defines them, and their relationship can become very tumultuous.

In the case of Stan and Nancy, this might mean that Stan will agree to work hard at his job and at all the family domestic chores most of the year. In exchange for this, Nancy will agree to free herself for romantic vacations and for summers in which the usual household tasks do not take priority. Such a balance may work. But if Stan becomes more impatient, and starts demanding more and more "fun time," he may insist on taking trips or having wild parties on weekends. Nancy will then rebel, and the ensuing fight will land them in the midst of a deep period of Contraction.

If these couples cannot strike a deal, they will continue to wrangle. Such a situation is a strong invitation for one or both of them to look for some other partner with whom they can live more comfortably. Thus she might look for a more easygoing, reasonable man who enjoys the daily things of life; he might start an affair.

A couple's Home Base may change over the years. At first, a couple may live in Resolution most of the time; later on, if things worsen, in Contraction; or the reverse may be true. When Home Base shifts, couples may feel transformed. If this shift is from Resolution to Contraction, they may be alarmed, and perhaps raise questions of divorce. If it is into Resolution, it may feel like a triumph or a miracle.

With the shift, the other stages continue, and full cycles recur; but the change is like having gone through an *identity crisis*, and the partners must get used to what feels like new selves. As they pass through their old Home Base, they often expect to linger, to get stuck again, to restabilize their relationship within its old terms. When they move past that point and settle again—and again—in their new Home Base, they come to believe that the change is real. This makes them renegotiate old positions, including those in their social network. The renegotiations, in turn, reinforce the primacy of the new Home Base.

## Resources Outside the Home Base

Often, reaching impasses, we realize that we have grown stale. We find ourselves responding to new situations with old, clichéd solutions. At such times, we need an infusion of new information—new emotional experience or a new perspective on our situation. The more we dig into Home Base and believe it is our true character, the more resistant we grow to anything that challenges us. To change, we have to leave our Home Base and get information from the other two stages. This can be done in several ways: (a) through small forays into another stage and back, (b) through a brief mini-cycle through all three stages, or (c) through a full adaptive cycle. In times of crisis, we are often impelled to move anywhere rather than staying where we are. Through our move, we can experience new or unfamiliar aspects of ourselves, which are resources we may need in order to change.

The third option, a full cycle through all three stages again, can take us on a journey which may last months, even years. But when the problem blocking us is sufficiently severe and destabilizing, we will need that time. This is how we find ourselves launched into cycle after cycle over the course of our lives.

The most obvious resource for couples whose Home Base is Contraction is the problem-solving capacity of the Stage of Resolution. Throughout their lives together, partners struggle to tap into its cool perspective and spirit of compromise in order to cope with their difficulties.

The need for couples to leave a Home Base in Resolution may be less obvious. Take, for example, a couple whose partners are always reasonable. As time goes on, they have less and less emotional access to the primitive stuff of Expansion or Contraction. Despite their comfortable routine, though, life invariably brings them setbacks that disrupt their patterns and make them stumble. Not well-prepared for problems with deep emotional resonance, they are thrown off balance and thrust into a new cycle.

Imagine that one partner has been diagnosed with multiple sclerosis. Both are filled with sadness and dread. What will this mean for them? How will they have to change their own lives in order to meet their responsibilities? They try to talk reasonably about it, looking at the changes that may lie ahead. But for a while they do not express many feelings. They try to handle the problem in their own style, maintaining perspective and a "stiff upper lip," but the longer the discussion goes on the more lonely and separate they feel. If they continue, their "adaptation" to the illness will include a painful, alienating distance.

These partners may need to cry, alone and together. They may need to rage in ways that do not fit into Resolution. They need to express their fear, their sense of helplessness, and their relief at still having each other. Their intimacy will return only if they do this; otherwise their reasonableness will become dry and empty. And so they move out of their Home Base for a period of time.

* * *

Many difficulties in life cannot be resolved without access to more emotionally charged experience. It is a task like Aeneas' descent into the Underworld in a time of crisis. The partners need deeper contact with their past, with the more repressed aspects of their character, and with each other. By activating the cycle and revisiting the other two stages, they can revive old images, reexperience long-buried feelings, and allow new patterns and images to surge forth.

This is especially true regarding the experience contained in Contraction. Some people must fight openly—that is, pass again through Contraction—before they can negotiate with each other. The unacknowledged wounds and unexpressed rage of couples who intellectually, for example, may block their ability to negotiate in good faith. First they have to let their feelings out; then they can decide where to go from there. Passing through Contraction as part of a new cycle gives us access to our "shadow," our less rational selves. In Contraction, we can reencounter our pain and rage, touch again our memories of being hurt and vulnerable. Recapturing these raw feelings lets us experience the fullness of who we are, and we bring this revitalized understanding into our relationship. Seen this way, the Stage of Contraction is a treasure trove for couples in times of change.

Expansion, of course, with its warm passions and fond hopes, is also a resource for couples who have grown tired and depleted. Without the feel of ourselves in Expansion, we may find it hard to climb out from the depths of Contraction. Good fights may make negotiating possible, but not without play and intimacy in between. The journey from Contraction to Resolution often leads back through Expansion: first comes difficulty, then—with catharsis—intimacy, and, finally, as good faith is built up, the possibility of a solution.

The yearning for Expansive experience can sometimes itself pull couples out of Contraction and Resolution, thus activating a full cycle. Many couples, for example, are ambivalent about Resolution: they prefer its safety but long for the delight and closeness of Expansion. So they often abandon their safety—say on vacations—even knowing, because it has happened before, that Contraction will follow on the heels of their pleasure.

Couples in Contraction may intensify their difficulties in order to momentarily leap over Resolution into Expansiveness, knowing reconciliation and a renewed sense of mutual respect often follows a big fight. They are willing to pay the price.

Crisis, by setting couples off on a new cycle that brings them in touch with their own untapped riches, thus presents them with opportunities for growth.

## Ritualistic Mini-cycles

Couples go through two general kinds of cycles over their lifetimes. The first is a *ritualistic* mini-cycle, which acts to reinforce and preserve their usual patterns. The second is a longer, full *adaptive* cycle, which helps them adjust to and incorporate change while maintaining their basic identity.

Mini-cycles bring the couple away from Home Base and back in a fairly short period of time. They may take only a few hours—sometimes even minutes—but they confirm the couple's usual sequences. A mini-cycle may begin with a fight in the morning, a period of several hours apart, which lends a sense of perspective, and an actual resolution that same evening. The resolution may lead to a half hour of romantic sentiment, a moment of Expansion that settles back into the matter-of-fact attitude of Resolution.

Mini-cycles may also begin with moments of expansiveness or a new perspective. A couple in Resolution may go out to dinner to celebrate one partner's promotion. The other brings flowers and orders champagne, and they find themselves feeling momentarily close and special. But they cannot sustain that feeling. The intimacy makes them nervous, and they get into a fight on the way home about nothing in particular. They get over it, even see the fight for what it is, but the expansive moment is past, replaced by the perspective of Resolution.

The emotional field for mini-cycles falls across a broad spectrum. It may be intense, featuring tremendous fights, powerful catharses; or it may be mild, with small inconsequential quarrels, polite apologies, and small triumphs.

The mini-cycles come to have a *ritualistic* quality. Their point seems to be time and again to wrestle the couple's discomfort into manageable form. As with most rituals, they take place regularly and frequently. They vary little, and little new is learned. Such mini-cycles bring no real adaptation, no deeper understanding of why the couple fights, no integration, for example, of the fighting's historical roots. But each time the couple goes through them, the partners revisit each stage which went into the formation of their character. They remind themselves of who they are, in a sense, by revisiting the stages that have made them that way. The rearticulation of their character through these mini-cycles lends continuity and stabililty to their relationship.

Byron and Carrie, for example, go through many mini-cycles in the course of their relationship. Because they each crave reassurance and support, their feelings are easily hurt, and they slide quickly from feeling good to feeling resentful, abandoned, hurt, and gloomy. Almost any change causes them to spin into a mini-cycle.

When Carrie got pregnant, they were both elated. But soon afterwards, Byron worried that a new baby would mean the end of his special relationship with Carrie, and he became moody and distant. Carrie took this as a sign that he did not care for her, and that he was not really happy at her being pregnant. So she became unhappy and worried herself. Now the two of them were aloof and distant, each hurting, each tense and worried. Recognizing this and feeling guilty, Byron decided to make a celebration. So he got flowers and a reservation at a fancy restaurant, and took Carrie out on the town. The new attention made Carrie feel appreciated once again, and the warmth of her response again made Byron feel loved and special. In the course of a day and a half, they had moved through one of their characteristic mini-cycles. The themes of the mini-cycle were not new. Instead, they were the couple's usual themes, and the mini-cycle acted to reinforce the themes by which they lived.

Carrie and Byron go through similar mini-cycles whenever one of them has hurt feelings. This happened when Carrie got hurt because Byron took an extra day on a business trip, when Byron felt abandoned because Carrie wanted to spend all day Saturday with a cousin who was in town for a brief visit, when Carrie felt Byron less interested than she wanted him to be in their daughter's first birthday party, and so on. Mini-cycles reinforce a couple's relationship patterns.

## Adaptive Cycles

One fact about couples holds true in both directions. New situations throw couples off stride. And, in order to adapt to being off stride, couples must move into new situations, with new information and resources.

In general, couples have two ways of dealing with new information, new experience: either *integrate* it into their relationship or *cordon* it off. If they cannot find new resources or deal adequately with new information, couples will be unable to adapt. Then, unable to maintain their stability, they will slide more deeply into Contraction.

In order to adapt to some disruptive events, many couples must *depart* from their Home Base and move into another stage. Such transitions generally begin a full cycle; by the time the couple has journeyed through all three stages again, they will have found a way of handling their new situation.

All sorts of situational and developmental crises can stimulate adaptive cycles—a move, a new job, a new child, the death of a parent, the onset of menopause. So can a psychological or life-stage crisis in one or both partners. Concessions made early in relationships often prove disruptive later on. Think of one partner's conversion to the other's religion, or of one partner's reaction to a form of sexual behavior that at first seemed all right but which now feels out of character. Or consider one partner's agreement not to have children for a while, which may conflict directly with his or her identity as a future parent.

An internal crisis usually begins as one partner's sole concern, but it then spreads to the relationship. My midlife affair, for instance, may have begun with questions and doubts about myself, but it quickly becomes a crisis of commitment between us. Your memory of a childhood trauma may torment you inwardly at first; but when you experience my angry statements as "just like" your father's abusive behavior, our relationship is put on center stage. Internal crises have a knack for pointing out whatever weaknesses exist in a relationship. Then we must find a way to resolve the problem, a process that may first move us into an intense experience of Contraction, and then, through a negotiated settlement, into Resolution.

Internal crises often emerge through personal reflection and the desire to better one's situation: a woman's wish to be more assertive and to achieve equality; a man's desire for greater authenticity or expressiveness. Often these internal crises are aided or precipitated by others—friends, siblings, colleagues who get us thinking through their example or active agitation.

Crisis brings disruption and disequilibrium. Our ordinary ideas and patterns do not seem to work: a long walk no longer brings a sense of perspective; the usual attempt to "talk through" problems fails. Couples who depend on faith and stamina to endure or outlast problems sometimes encounter problems that won't go away, or that pass their threshold of tolerance. Think, for example, about a partner's defiant affair or recurrent substance abuse.

When we cannot resolve our problems within our Home Base, we search elsewhere for new information and new solutions. I may spend more time with my friends or family, but this may alienate me further from you. You may pull more deeply into yourself, hoping to avoid our problems, or you may start reading popular psychology articles or see a therapist. Moving outside our usual realms of thought, feeling, and action usually pulls us even further off balance. New information makes us think; we remember things about ourselves, and come to a new understanding of our situation. Crisis brings both danger and opportunity. We move into an adaptive cycle which, unlike the ritualistic cycles, requires us to integrate new information. The changes we undergo will become part of our couple's character.

Consider Gerry and Sharon. This couple, as you will recall, is concerned with being equal and rational, safe and in control, and both partners are intent on forbidding any abuse of power in their relationship. We presented their first cycle in Chapter 8. What happens to them as time goes on?

The next cycle they entered was triggered by the awareness that they were developing some significant differences in terms of their work. Because his was a small, owner-operated catering business, Gerry had to spend a good deal of extra time at his work during holiday times and weekends. Sharon, as a middle manager in a larger corporation, had a simpler schedule. She also had many more benefits "built in" to her job. Over time, Sharon found herself resenting the extra time Gerry was spending on his work; it began to feel like an imposition to her. She felt that since he was his own boss, he could structure his time better and arrange to be with her more, share more equally (as they had originally planned) in the shopping and housework, and so on. But Gerry felt this showed how little Sharon understood the nature of his work. He was in a field where his clients were in control, not himself. He was dismayed and irritated by what he felt was her insensitivity to his schedule.

The more irritated Gerry became, the more anxious Sharon

became. Again, the image of the dangerously angry male surged up in her mind. She withdrew to protect herself, and for a time they were again in Contraction, on parallel tracks, each feeling misunderstood and unloved.

They took months in this cycle to resolve this dilemma. Finally, Gerry initiated a reasonable period of "serious talking," and they began sharing their feelings again. Once again moving into the Stage of Resolution they loved so well, they drew up a new schedule for themselves, planned a vacation, and forgave each other.

This was one adaptive cycle for them.

Things then went well until Sharon got a promotion. It meant she had to spend more time at her work—not so much at her office, but doing more preparation and homework in the evenings. She had gotten a considerable raise in salary for her job, but she felt increasingly unsupported again at home. There was more housework than they could both manage. They were both too busy. And Sharon was wondering about having children. But how could she imagine having a child, when her leaving work would cost them such a huge part of their income?

When she raised these concerns with Gerry, he reacted as though she were criticizing him instead of consulting in their normal manner. He pulled into himself, and she couldn't coax him out. Eventually she gave up, and they fell into that cool formality that characterizes their stay in Contraction. During this period, Gerry was also having trouble with some important customers, and he felt he just couldn't please everyone. It reminded him of his boyhood when, no matter what he tried, he could never really help his mother or, as he came to see it, "I could never do enough." Eventually he shared this insight with Sharon, and they moved into the Stage of Resolution.

In this adaptive cycle, Resolution brought them new information and resources:

They shared their problem with other family members, and received some advice they had never heard before.

They spent several weekends talking quietly with each other about how they felt about money and about having children.

They made a few changes in their schedule: (a) they agreed they could afford to have someone clean their apartment once every two weeks; (b) they set up both a retirement and a college tuition savings plan for the child they anticipated having; (c) Gerry agreed to look for one or two partners, both to help him expand his business and to give him more free time.

Adaptive cycles, by shaping and deepening the couple's characteristic sequences, help them handle new situations. As the couple integrates new information, adding new resources to its repertoire, its character becomes richer, fuller, and more complex.

## Folding in New Information

Transitions from stage to stage and from one cycle to the next are dynamic moments in couples' lives. While adaptive cycles are stimulated by disruptive experience, cycles themselves are disruptive and tend to jar the couple loose. They elicit new feelings and imagery that the individuals had kept hidden. Further cycles thus replenish and reorganize the couple's store of information. This in itself can be refreshing and can open up the possibility of resolving old problems.

In the first full cycle, each transition brought forth an astonishing amount of new information and experience. A couple's next few cycles continue to generate new material that they weave into their lives together. The partners rub up against each other's depressions and elations, fears and fulfillments. They observe how reasonable and unreasonable, how defensive or open the other can be. With each cycle, they learn more about their individual and collective styles.

As the couple adapts, their character appears fixed and full. It is not. New patterns will emerge in response to life's dramatic events. New themes will surface as individuals grow bolder or more desperate, reveal more about themselves, or recognize important memories from their past.

Relationships organize only *part* of our individual character, and thus large parts of our individual repertoire lie dormant, ever ready to be tapped by each adaptive cycle. Later crises may bring them into the open. When these traits—our courage, cowardice, unexpected resourcefulness, or maddening passivity—emerge, they may become permanent, even central aspects of the relationship.

Suppose, for example, that a woman comes in contact with a hitherto repressed memory of incest. She may have been the "pursuer" in her relationship, always initiating activities, contact, and discussions. But now, depressed, she may withdraw from her mate. The couple's essential sequence becomes reorganized. It is *he* who eventually, and unsuccessfully, pursues, while *she*, ever more defensive, puts him off. Her previously repressed rage may emerge and focus on him.

He may become more patient with her if they are a "complementary" couple, or he may match her increasing rage, and they will escalate into dangerous waters if they are a "symmetrical" couple.

While they are dealing with this new information, they may stay mainly in Contraction; but during the brief time in Expansion they may become affectionate, perhaps even "childlike" in an effort to mute the terror of incest. Thus, even at this time of great change and revelation, they will bring out new material—here, their childlike dependency—and thus enrich the possibilities of future Expansive Stages. The new information will transform their experience of Resolution as well. Its distance provides a welcome relief from the intense pain. Such a couple's perspective in Resolution might take the form of recognizing that they have a long journey ahead and need to be patient and understanding with each other.

## Adapting by Narrowing

Couples can also adapt to new information by narrowing their lives and pushing discordant experience aside.

Over the years, for example, some couples assign a smaller place to sex in their lives. The Cultural Narrative goes along with this, by proclaiming that sexual excitement fades with familiarity. More often, couples control their sexual activity because it threatens one or both of the partners: one or both partners are threatened by their lack of satisfaction, their inability to talk about this to their partner, or their partner's particular sexual habits or tastes.

Suppose that a woman wants a break from sexual activity after the birth of a child, and the man, feeling that he ought not and cannot wait, winds up feeling angry, rejected, and deprived. The couple fights; what had been a mutual pleasure becomes a source of tension. Sex becomes "his thing," not hers, and they have a difficult time recovering.

Such a fight might precipitate a new adaptive cycle—as described in the preceding section—whose outcome is a renewed, perhaps enhanced sex life together. If they took this path, the couple would be catapulted into Contraction where they might reexperience both her fear of doing things to please others and his fear of being cut off emotionally. This may be just what they needed to feel in order to get beyond their struggle. Understanding themselves more deeply, they could be more accepting: She could say "No" without his hearing it as a personal rejection. His acceptance could lead her toward more willing participation in their sexual life. His confession that he becomes lonely without physical contact might help them expand their repertoire beyond largely genitally-oriented sex, and toward greater warmth and affection. In this way, information opened up by the move through Contraction as part of an adaptive cycle can become integrated into a couple's new Resolution.

But a couple might also handle such a fight simply by pulling back and limiting their shared activity. They might rationalize this by telling each other—sometimes explicitly but often not—that they are now in a new stage of life. For example, more like co-parents than a romantic couple.

Couples may resolve conflicts over control by doing less together. They may decide to deal with one partner's difficult parents by limiting contact with them. They may resolve differences around disciplining children by assigning the task to one of them and making the other more distant and less available.

Some couples close down quickly; they may remain closed down forever, or suddenly snap open when one partner, "waking up" to an unexpressed part of herself, demands change or release. Some couples incorporate more and more experience, until they reach some kind of "limit." After that, they seem frozen, rigid, and noncompliant; they stop taking in or processing any new information, and remain a rehash of their past selves. Other couples slowly contract, like yesterday's balloon, until they appear—both to themselves and others—as a mere shadow of their past potential.

Such a cordoning-off process is neither foolproof nor forever. Couples may resolve not to discuss their parents, but when someone's mother gets sick, the topic becomes unavoidable. A couple may successfully limit sexual contact, until a particularly hot movie or a few drinks loosen one or both partners' boundaries, and they wander into the forbidden zone. Neither the partners' inner lives nor the external world in which they move obediently follows their decisions about what should and should not go on in their life together. Despite their temporary capacity to cordon off threatening areas, couples' boundaries can always fall, and the potential for change and transition is ever present.

## The Influence of Outsiders

Off balance, people seek a helping hand[1] and reach out to bring new ideas and people into their relationship.

In the same spirit, we read self-help books and speak to friends, ministers, strangers, and psychotherapists to find a cure for what is wrong or an anchor in the storm. Every adaptive cycle presents the possibility that some important outsider will enter the lives of couples.

The Cultural Narrative is another "outsider" that invariably appears in times of crisis. We often try to adjust our behavior in relation to its directives and norms.

Imagine a young couple putting their six-month-old child into day care so the wife can return to work. Both sets of in-laws immediately launch critiques. "Why have a child," they say, "if you're not going to take care of her?" At first the couple unites against this intrusion. But as the days go on, each finds that same critical voice within. "Why, indeed, should they have a child if someone's not home to care for her?" But who should stay at home? Neither of them wants to; that's why they chose day care in the first place.

They now slide into Contraction, blaming each other for the fall. "It wasn't *my* idea to have a baby in the first place," says one. "But why can't **you** work less?" the other retorts. They question gender roles, examine how they differ from the parents' model. Finally, after much discussion between them and with friends, they decide that it would be better for their child if they were both fulfilled in their work. The decision brings them back into the Stage of Resolution. The new resolution is less automatic than their original solution. It includes the guilt they felt about failing their parents' expectations and the triumph of self-acceptance in the light of that failure. By wrestling with the Cultural Narrative, their parents' narrative, and their own narrative about what it means to bring a child into their family, they have changed and become more deeply themselves.

## The Rhythm and Shape of Cycles

The lives of couples differ widely, and it is difficult to make generalizations about the shape and contour of their later cycles. We can predict that they will indeed continue to spiral through the stages, but we cannot say when or how or for how long at a stretch.

Couples' later cycles differ in a number of features, and the particular features any couple develops become defining aspects of their character. Consider, for example, such aspects of couples' cycles as their rhythm, style, scope, duration, depth, and richness.

One of the most defining qualities of couples' character is the *rhythm* of their cycles. Some couples move smoothly and regularly from stage to stage. Others move in jerky, unpredictable leaps. The relation of one cycle to the next also has a rhythm. Some couples move regularly from cycle to cycle like clockwork. Others have no such pattern and seem to move more randomly. Some couples' cycles lengthen over time; others become shorter.

Jonathan and Marie, for example, move gradually from Expansion into Contraction, but their move from Contraction to Resolution is one great, convulsive leap. From there, they ease into Expansion. This rhythm remains intact throughout their relationship; but, over time, they spent increasing amounts of time in Resolution.

Other couples seem always to be in crisis. They move constantly through the full cycle in radical, dramatic leaps. Each move into Contraction is catastrophic and raises the question of divorce. Each move into Resolution is a moment of spiritual enlightenment. These moments introduce periods of joy and celebration, as though the couple had found a second chance in life. Patti and Marshall are like this.

Couples like Byron and Carrie are completely absorbed in whatever stage they are in and always appear surprised when they move. Even after twenty years, Contraction so takes them over that they cannot imagine escaping it short of divorce. But when they enter Expansion, they feel relatively untainted by the trials of Contraction or by any perspective of Resolution. It is as though they live each stage in a different valley, each separated by high mountains, with almost no communications between the valleys.

The rhythm of the cycles stems, first of all, from the general movement of stages. Is it regular or irregular, long or quick, heavy or light? Which stage dominates? With Byron and Carrie, for instance, the stages seem to have little relation to one another; each is a world unto itself. This is an *exclusive* view of the relationship between the stages.

Gerry and Sharon's rational relationship continually works the first two stages into Resolution. Always trying to balance good and bad, they seek the complex answer and negotiate their differences. They have few boundaries between the stages of their cycles, and tend to *blend* all the stages into one.

Other couples, seeing the stages as *harmonious*, give the stages a more equal relationship. They are satisfied to move from one set of feelings to another and experience the three stages taken all together as a "richness" of life.

Still other couples feel the stages as *complementary*: they are deliriously happy *now* because they were openly miserable *then*. These couples often feel their gains depend on their capacity to be open and honest about conflicts, and their best times always seem to follow fights.

The *styles* by which couples navigate the cycles reveal their character, too. Some couples move boldly from stage to stage with a lot of energy, while others seem timid and listless. Some are confident; others fearful. Some leap and plunge, others move cautiously. Some couples' partners move together, others' always tug at each other.

Let us mention a few more aspects about couples' later cycles. Consider their *scope*. Some couples' cycles embrace large amounts of passionately charged material. Other couples move timidly through a carefully edited landscape (as in traditional courtship days). Some move through cycles of great intensity, alternating between dramatic highs and profound lows, while others keep in the mid-ground, excluding information and experience that threatens their equanimity.

Consider the *duration* of cycles. Some couples spend distinct, carefully patterned amounts of time in each stage; others' time varies. Some couples move quickly; others linger. Some take long, sweeping cycles that extend over years; others may enter a new cycle every six or seven months.

Consider the *depth* or *richness* of cycles. Some couples' cycles become less intense over time, gradually "dragging out" and diminishing in impact. Other couples seem to maintain their capacity for intensity, and it bursts forth in times of crisis, no matter how long they have been together. This seems to be linked to how much material couples can integrate as they move through time—how much they remember, how much they include in the stories they tell. Some couples seem to forget even their most recent preceding stage; others carry almost all their history with them.

## The Question of Difference

Many cycles seem set off by questions of difference. Differences between partners create an almost electric potential that can spark their initial attraction, but also galvanize subsequent conflict. Since any two partners have different perspectives, tension between them is inevitable. Many couples try to organize themselves around their differences—they resolve them, avoid them, or simply try to live in spite of them. This becomes part of their character as well.

Organization around difference changes from stage to stage. In Expansion, differences enhance and enrich couples; in Contraction, they narrow and constrict them; in Resolution, differences provide a basis for negotiation and compromise. When couples in Expansion or Resolution encounter a major difference that they *cannot* resolve, the experience may catapult them out of these stages and into Contraction. There they will remain until they find a resolution, either through compromise and concession or by cordoning off enough of its toxic effects so their compatibility can break through.

Consider a difference that is first celebrated in Expansion, but becomes troublesome later on. One partner has entered the relationship with a wide network of friends, which she is intent on preserving. At first, the new people seem like a gift, a wonderful "find" for her partner; he delights in meeting them. But as time goes on, her friends weary him. He notices how often she takes time away from him to see them. She brings them into their apartment, even when he wants his privacy; her friends prevent his having intimate time with her. He may start to wonder if she deliberately wants it that way. As they move into Contraction, he feels constricted by what he sees as her *in*attention to him, and contrasts it with how outgoing, effusive, and open she manages to be with her friends.

For her part, she wonders why he is so niggling and withdrawing. Doesn't he like her friends? To her, that's like not liking ... her! She has brought these people into their life together, and now he acts as if he can't stand them. She resents his surliness, his lack of enthusiasm, his disparaging looks and comments.

Later, as the couple reaches Resolution, they may strike a deal. She will keep up her friendships; he will try to be kinder to them and even to make new friends himself, and she will agree to spend more "together time" with him, especially when he says he needs her. This cycle will be repeated over and over. In Expansion, her friends will enrich and enliven the couple. In Contraction, they will be a source of contention. And in Resolution, they will be a focus for negotiation.

Ideally, as we move through life, we develop a better sense of who we are. But the contradiction between our sense of self and our role in the couple can create problems. Characteristically, one partner moves toward greater independence, and the other—unwilling to make "changes" in the status quo—begrudgingly responds. The balance between independence and togetherness is continually fine-tuned.

Take the example of two high school sweethearts who fell in love when they were seventeen. As they advance through life, their sense of identity changes. They separate from their parents, become parents themselves, take on the adult role in society, jobs, friendships. They adjust to each other's growth. If, after raising three children, the wife then wants to return to school to pursue a career, the husband will have to see her differently.

As we change, we challenge our partners to see us in new ways. If they refuse, we face a dilemma. Feeling pressure to go back to "the old ways," the partner who is changing will become more and more resentful. The other will wonder why things are not okay left the way they were.

Many couples' disputes arise from their growing in different ways at different times. For example, I need more intimacy; you want more independence, so conflict develops. Or, early in our life together, you may pull me closer to our growing family, but I may prefer moving more deeply into my career world; later, tired and disillusioned with my career, I may move closer to the family, just when you, finally freed from the children, are eager to start a career of your own. Similarly, one partner, at forty-five, may feel completely done with the raising of young children, while his second wife—with no children of her own—may desperately want to be a mother. Different developmental pulls can create tremendous tension.

As a couple continues through the years, each partner needs room in which to grow, even if this means the other is not invited, cannot or does not wish to go along. Both partners need permission to change from what they were before. Partners can be "out of sync" with each other, but they can still give permission for the other to be where they have to be. They can still accept a degree of growth and individuation from their partner, without feeling forced to change themselves. In most successful couples, partners have the capacity to tolerate each other's change without taking it as a personal affront.

Because the cycle consists of three stages, I can experience you in at least three ways: Expanded, Contracted, and in Resolution. Because these different ways are so unlike one another, it often feels as if you are a composite of three different people, wearing three different costumes, and following three different credos—and indeed this may be closer to the truth than I wish to admit.

- What I want from you may change. When I want "space," I want you to step back and give it lovingly. When I want succor, I want you to move closer and give without limit or obligation. In exchange, I promise to do the same.
- Where I had asked for love and protection, now I may ask for the suspension of that protection, so that I can find my way myself.
- Where I had asked for understanding, now I may ask for challenge and confrontation.
- Where I had asked for criticism and conflict, now I may ask for quiet calm and a space in which I can heal.
- Where I had asked for guidance and direction, now I may ask you simply to "be there" to back me up.

Such requests can destabilize the rhythms and patterns a couple has spent years building up. But if they are not attended to, the very basis on which the couple has come together may dissolve in bitter recrimination.

This is why each couple is unique. Middle-aged couples who have been together for fifteen or more years, for example, are different from middle-aged couples who have just gotten together. A couple composed of an older twice-married man and a never-married woman are different from a couple of the same age, both of whose partners have been married once. A couple in their twenties will be quite different in another ten years. Further, individual development and couple development must be seen in dialectic relationship. When our partners are able to "keep up" with all our changes and support us in spite of our shifts and reversals, we are profoundly appreciative; when they cannot, we may become disillusioned, angry, and bitter.

"Why *can't* he encourage me, just this once!" we say. Or, "Why can't she just *trust* me!" If one partner changes beyond what the other can tolerate, the relationship is likely to end.

We weave all these issues around difference into our character as a couple.

## Couple Development Through the Cycles

We began this chapter by saying that couples' character, formed through the first turn of the cycle, is honed and deepened with each subsequent cycle. We do not wish to give a wrong impression here. Couples do not necessarily get wiser and better, broader and deeper, and increasingly more flexible with each passing year. Couples increasingly become themselves.

According to our Cultural Narrative, couples should aim toward a Home Base in Resolution, which would let them encompass more experience, negotiate without going through constant challenge, and accept difference without fear and alienation. Couples who dwell in Resolution tend to keep their repertoire more open and alive. Time together breeds loyalty, trust, and acceptance, and paves the way to deeper friendship or passion.

Still there are couples who would rather abandon this cool world for hot moments in Expansion's sun. They live more volatile lives, which are as fulfilling for them as are those of the more quiet ones who dwell primarily in Resolution.

Even couples who are essentially satisfied with their lives contract with as much regularity and necessity as they expand. We are no more interested in prescribing Resolution for everyone than we are in genetic engineering that would eliminate facial wrinkles. We prefer to celebrate the profound originality of each couple, expanding and contracting in their own way, and journeying through life with the character they have established and defined.

# 11

---

# How Couples Change

---

When couples move smoothly through the three stages and through successive cycles, couples' lives seem as simple as the progression of the seasons. Life's ordinary experience seems to keep their wheels moving. We often take this kind of change for granted: couples grow and develop, responding to the different events they experience.

Another kind of change, however, cannot be taken for granted. This happens when couples feel stuck in Contraction and cannot get out. At this point, they do not care what stage their Home Base is in, nor how many times they have come unstuck before. All they know is that things are bad, and they want to change. All their efforts fail, and the partners become more and more dismayed. How to change at *these* times is the main question couples agonize over, and is the focus of this chapter.

Let's begin with the broad outline of how and why couples move from one stage to the next. Their "natural" movement actually depends on the ever-present conflict between new experience and the partners' desire for stability.

In the early days of a relationship, the character of one stage pulls us off balance and creates the need for the next. However exhilarating it may be, Expansion stretches us beyond our ordinary activities, capacities, and feelings; eventually we feel *too* open and too committed, worry that we have promised too much, and feel out of control and off balance. To compensate, we contract. This is why we rarely sustain Expansion for very long.

Each couple finds a way of making this transition. Jonathan and Marie, for instance, become uneasy being so close with each other, so disengaged from their work—so they pull away into their separate worlds. Both feel relieved at being involved again in part of their lives that makes them most secure. Their relief is so tangible that they hardly notice having gone too far.

Contraction begins as an attempt to regain our balance, to return to the routines and ways of knowing ourselves that made up our lives before the relationship began. But as we pull in, we invariably over-shoot the mark, go beyond our "normal" selves again, and swing into the pinched world of Contraction. This experience is not just painful; it distorts and stretches us as much as Expansion did. Again, we scramble to regain our equilibrium, wishing for a return to Expansion or to some as yet undefined state. We insist we are *more* as individuals and as a couple than we now feel, but something other than what we remember from Expansion. As we push to restore the balance of things, we perceive glimmerings of what might be a better resolution, fragments of what will become Resolution. The overshift into Contraction sets up our subsequent move into Resolution.

Again, each couple develops characteristic ways to move from Contraction into Resolution. Jonathan and Marie drift further apart until Marie cannot tolerate the distance any longer and precipitates a crisis by leaving or threatening to leave. Her move usually jolts Jonathan to his senses and gets the two of them talking in the more considered cadences of Resolution.

When we reach Resolution, we often try to settle in. If this is our Home Base, we may indeed linger for a while. Sometimes we stay until new problems arise, and then begin moving back toward Contraction. Sometimes we are so relieved by reaching Resolution that we move into a stage of Expansion. Whatever the case, each subsequent Stage of Expansion inevitably yields to Contraction, each move into Contraction inevitably requires another move to Resolution ... and so the process goes. Whatever our Home Base, new experiences, new and old yearnings continue to throw us off balance. We are constantly pulled toward Expansion and away from it, toward Contraction and away from it, toward Resolution and away from it.

We virtually never remain in Resolution. Its capacity to resolve conflict does not extend far enough. The challenge of new experience knocks us out of equilibrium. Powerful positive experiences like the birth of a child or the purchase of a home thrust us into Expansion. Painful and threatening experiences—illness, or a setback at work— drop us into Contraction. My wanting to change some aspect of my life upsets you. An experience with your parents throws you into a tailspin; and, when I try to reassure you, you act as though I am trying to divert your attention and you spurn my help. Confused and hurt, I draw back, abandoning you in your time of need ... and we are catapulted out of Resolution.

## Stability and Adaptation

Couples seem to experience several different kinds of change. One kind seems "natural" and easy, like simply growing, or like the progression of the seasons. Another kind may be voluntary, as when couples decide to change in order to improve their lives. Most of the time, however, it seems that *couples change because they want to remain stable.* How can this paradox be true?

The answer comes when we realize that the effort to remain stable requires constant change, and that every change requires new efforts to remain stable. Every living system aims toward balance and continuity.[1] We sweat in order to maintain a steady internal temperature. We rest when we are tired and exercise when we feel sluggish. We change our self-image to fit our new activities, and we change activities to fit our evolving self-image. Like a tightrope walker,[2] we make constant adjustments to maintain our equilibrium. Every new situation throws us off balance and requires us to adjust until we feel stable again.

Being in a couple makes this process even more complex. If our partner changes—gets a better job, becomes more assertive—we have to adjust. If we do not, the relationship will swing out of kilter. So we make the small (or not-so-small) changes we need to make in order to keep the relationship on an even keel. We try to keep things stable, and not overshoot the mark.

If you get a job with longer hours, for example, I try to shift my schedule so I can take on more of the domestic work. If I have to go out of town to see a sick relative, you "fill in." If the change is prolonged, small adjustments may pile up, tilting us toward a different self-image or different feelings toward each other. Generally speaking, if our relationship is to remain stable, your changes must balance the changes I make and vice versa.

The tension between new situations and our need for stability always pushes us off balance. In disequilibrium, our old ways of thinking and doing no longer work, but we have not yet found new ways that do.[3] Momentarily at sea, we struggle to regain our balance. The effort changes us and often moves us into a new stage.

*Systems in disequilibrium are vulnerable to change.* Disappointment disrupts the mood and patterns of Expansion and eventually forms the basis for new patterns in Contraction. The calm stance of Resolution seems preposterous after one discovers a partner's affair; and, after a momentary confusion, we return to Contraction. But Contraction can also be disrupted, as by a sudden windfall or a professional success. Whenever this happens, new ideas can pierce our defenses, presenting us with more optimistic ways to see our relationship, and thus providing us with a route out of difficulty.

Off balance, we grab desperately at new ways of saving ourselves, much as we would clutch at a lifeboat in a rough sea. Sometimes these lifeboats are positive, as when an insight into our partner's character permits us to become more compassionate and less judgmental, thus keeping our relationship alive. But the lifeboats can also have a negative impact. One partner may feel relieved by renewing his religious conviction, but this change may disrupt the relationship as a whole.

Movement is a constant feature of couples' lives. Some comes from the small adjustments discussed above. Some comes from the crises that accompany major challenges of life, such as:

• Individual developmental milestones, like graduating from a training program, reaching midlife, or retiring;
• Family developmental crises, like marriage, the birth of a child, a child's entering or leaving school, the empty nest, or taking on responsibilities for one's parent;
• Situational crises, like the loss of a job or a promotion to a much better job, the onset of a major illness, a child's school troubles, an affair, or major sexual difficulties;
• Deliberate efforts to change, like a woman's becoming more assertive, a man's deciding to become more active in his household, or one partner's decision to change careers or take on a program of self-improvement;

- The tendency to overadapt to new situations, as when some couples completely shift roles in response to one partner's illness.

Crises build on one another. A midlife crisis may include an extramarital affair. Substance abuse may accompany disappointment in a partner's availability. When several crises converge, a couple's life can be highly vulnerable to change.

If I, for example, have been thinking that we should stop depending on each other for everything, then an act of disloyalty on your part may be just the blow that convinces me to stake my separate ground. Later, even if I forgive you, I may insist that we depend less on each other and do more with our separate friends. The pain I feel makes me determined, and eventually you accept my greater independence, thus completing the reorganization of our relationship.

## Tension Between Individual and Relationship

Tension between individual partners and the couple is one of the most important sources of disequilibrium. Not only do we adapt our behavior and attitudes to maintain our relationships but we try to maneuver our relationships in order to maintain our internal stability: to keep our feelings within a safe range; to sustain a recognizable and acceptable self-image. Our internal stability depends on how we love, defend, rationalize and comfort ourselves. This is not so easy when we are in such close proximity to our partners, whose ways of dealing with us provides constant feedback about our character and continually jostle our emotional stability. So we carefully monitor our partners' behavior and feedback and try to manipulate it to get the right results.

If we worry that we are selfish, for example, we may try to get our partners to help us cover up by praising our generosity even when, in our own mind, we continue our general course of selfishness. Take, for example, the husband who works all the time, and did so before there were children. When his wife urges him to spend more time with the children, he indignantly says that he already puts himself out *for them*. She is supposed to agree, to reinforce his imagery of self-sacrifice. If a partner refuses to support our desired self-image and we still seek relief from self-doubt, then we might resort to move anywhere from bullying—"You have some nerve after all I've given to you"—to withdrawing from the situation so that our partners' perceptions of our flaws are not so penetrating.

Much of the distance between partners is established in the service of protecting our good self-images and keeping out threatening statements, requests, and demands: "Tell me what you're feeling," or "Why can't you earn more money?" or "Why don't you want to make love to me?" The distance might become stable but it might also threaten one of the partners, who feels it as rejecting not protecting. The rejected partner might push for engagement, which further threatens the distancing partner, who fears that his partner is trying to take him over. On the other hand, he believes it is reasonable to ask after his feelings, and he would be humiliated to say that his partner is taking him over. He distances further, telling himself that he is generous to do so; this way he preserves his dignity and stops himself from attacking her character. This increased distance threatens her more, now evoking images of childhood abandonment, feelings which she thought she had put behind her. To combat this defeat, she stops pursuing him and attacks his character: he is callous and afraid of intimacy. He counters: she is empty by herself and needs him too much.

In this way, a series of adjustments, each calculated to stabilize the interior environment of an individual partner, leads to an action that threatens the other. A downward spiral is created in the relationship which reels into a state of considerable disequilibrium—because of the partner's individual efforts to achieve equilibrium. In such a state, the couple is vulnerable to change.

## Forays

Exactly how do couples move from stage to stage? Remember from the previous chapter that, once couples arrive at a Home Base, they may move out in several ways. They may take brief mini-cycles which return them quickly to their Home Base, thus reinforcing their usual patterns. Or they may set off on a more lengthy adaptive cycle. Sometimes they may shift suddenly and dramatically, as when they move from Expansion into Contraction following a traumatic event.

More frequently, though, couples move by venturing bit by bit toward another stage until, crossing a threshold, they find themselves within it. We call such movements *forays*.

A foray is a move by which the couple experiences one stage while still residing primarily in another. For example, during periods of Expansion, couples have fights, and partners have doubts about the relationship. They may feel a foreboding of hard times ahead, but their relationship is not dominated by either the doubts or the fights. These fights are forays into Contraction. The couple will make up afterwards, reconfirming their love and togetherness and maintaining their hold on Expansion.

In Contraction, the couple may periodically break their mood of alienation and conflict, as when a vacation reminds them of earlier good times. A child's graduation may momentarily bring them together. A particularly virulent fight might so frighten them that they pull back from the edge. During these moments, the couple may sense the light at the end of the tunnel. These are forays into Resolution.

The Stage of Resolution is often interrupted by fights reminiscent of Contraction, as well as by expansive moments filled with promise of exciting times ahead. But these different moods do not take over. When the more sober mood of partnership, negotiation, and perspective reasserts its sway, both good and bad moments are seen as forays.

When forays accumulate, we may finally move into another stage. At first this happens tentatively, but gradually we start spending more and more time in the *new* stage. As we do, we can either develop new patterns that form a basis for the new stage or we can again take up patterns that characterized our previous stays in the new stage.

At some point we cross a threshold. The cumulative effect of these forays rises like an incoming tide. One moment we are in one stage; the next we have passed into another. It feels as though it has happened all at once. Even though forays have been accumulating for some time, there is a moment during which we move into the next stage.

Patti and Marshall, for example, remained in their first stage of Expansion for about two years, from the time they met until after they got married. During this time, they had many arguments, some of them serious; on several occasions they wondered if they really belonged with each other. These arguments, misgivings, and self-doubts all occurred, however, *within* a context of generally upbeat feelings about their relationship. These arguments were their forays into Contraction. Resolving them time and again, Patti and Marshall remained in Expansion. But after their marriage, as their problems increased, the balance tipped. The forays into Contraction now involved bitter feelings about the other, deep misgivings, sore pride. Arguments over Simon's behavior, sex, and money led to harsh mutual criticism, which the usual apologies could not easily wash away. These forays were bridges through which the couple moved into their first stage of Contraction.

## Forays as Revelations

We often experience forays as surprises, discoveries; sometimes so unexpected as to be shocking. One moment, everything seems bleak; then a simple shift of mood, thought, or context transforms the dreadful situation into something we can handle. Or, just as we are cruising along through life, thinking everything is fine, doubts suddenly seem to materialize on all sides, and we find ourselves fighting for our own survival.

Sometimes the revelation is about each other: a discovery of vulnerability where malice had been assumed; a discovery of strength where weakness had been attributed; an emergence of sweetness where bitterness had ruled.

Sometimes these revelations are about ourselves:

- I don't fall apart in the face of your anger, and this makes both of us less afraid.
- My loneliness is so deep that I yearn for you, in spite of myself, in spite of how much I think I want to be away from you.
- I never believed I could keep my distance for so long, and I'm not sure when—or even, if—I want to be close again.

Sometimes the revelations are about the relationship:

- I'm amazed that our relationship can survive all of our fighting. I was sure that you would divorce me or I would go into the world's longest-lasting cocoon. I actually feel better for having survived the fights. That's the surprising thing. I guess we surpassed my expectations and I'm proud of us.
- I thought I was stronger, that I would let your criticism roll off my back by now. I've worked so hard to be less sensitive. But I can't; I can't make myself feel good about you.

Forays take many forms. We may come to a compromise about relatives, in-laws, or bedtime hours. After a fight, we may feel so beaten down that it seems silly to fight and, for a moment, we accept each other. A particularly special event, like the graduation of a child or a partner's job promotion, might temporarily unite couples. We might say too much in an ugly fight and have to move away from each other for a while. All these forms disrupt the powerful sequences that organize us in one particular stage, thus opening up the possibility of moving into another stage.

Here is a foray in the life of Jonathan and Marie. First, let us look at one of their typical sequences in Contraction.

Marie reminds Jonathan to pick Beth up from the day care center that evening; Jonathan reacts as he has so often before.

"I know that. You don't have to *remind* me all the time."

"I don't remind you all the time, so don't get all huffy about it," she retorts.

"I wouldn't get huffy if you didn't treat me like an idiot. It's amazing that I manage my life at all when you're not around ..."

At this point, they are off and running. Eventually the dust settles, and they ease back together, but without any resolution or further discussion of what might have really caused the fight. Exchanges like this are painful, and the frequent repetition of almost identical sequences is dispiriting.

Now the foray: One day, Marie, who is feeling weary and drained, starts out with a similar reminder. For some reason, Jonathan notices how tired she looks and does not react so defensively. Perhaps her voice actually sounds more like a request than a command. In any case, he simply says, "Sure."

Marie almost misses his reply and is about to argue, but she stops within a split second, does a double-take, and sits down. Tears come to her eyes, so palpable is her sense of relief. As he observes her, Jonathan feels a flush of sympathy, and they smile at each other. Although nothing is said, they knew something tender and different has taken place, and they are grateful for it. This may be the first unguarded moment they have had with each other for weeks. Its impact may only last an hour, perhaps a day or two, but it reminds them of the many good feelings they have for each other.

If this were an isolated event, it would probably not have much impact on them. But if it is one of many such events, the forays will accumulate, pass a *threshold,* and help bring them out of Contraction and into Resolution.

## The Move from Contraction into Resolution

The change that occupies our attention more than any other is the shift from Contraction to Resolution. This is the change that psychotherapy and most self-help books focus on. In our view, this change is never permanent, but always part of an ongoing cycle; people in long relationships make it many times.

How do couples escape from Contraction? How do the forays accumulate and pass over the threshold that takes them into Resolution?

In the first cycle or two, Contraction may be so disturbing, so raw and unstable, that it creates the conditions for its own demise. In this state "young" couples may escape into Resolution with relative ease. They may be angry and frightened—but they are still close. Often, they have cathartic fights that are followed by relief, repentance, and resolutions to be nicer and kinder to each other forever. Resolution is incredibly brief, and the couple moves rapidly back into Expansion.

However, over time couples develop a second, more stable form of Contraction. This rests on the defensive patterns they build up to take the edge off their rage and disappointment. They try to escape, but their problems feel chronic and immovable. They make daily resolutions: be calmer, more understanding; stand up for themselves without attacking their partners; be more helpful, less critical. They have "important" talks with their partners, enlist the aid of friends, consult psychotherapists. But they rarely succeed; and when they do, the causes of their success seem mysterious.

Why do we fail and why do we succeed when we try to change our troubled relationships? The key ingredient is disequilibrium. The very state we try to avoid facilitates our changing. If our patterns in Contraction are rigid and stable, our efforts to change will almost always fail. When our patterns are looser, destabilized, our efforts are more likely to succeed. Crisis loosens the interactional sequences that organize our lives, thus permitting us to have access to other feelings, other moods, other memories—say, the way we had felt about each other during Expansion.

*Disequilibrium opens the doors to new information.* This may consist of what we see in others, what we learn from outsiders, or what we sense inside ourselves. During crisis, our internal and external forms of organization loosen up; memories, feelings, and thoughts bubble up and give our situation a new cast. We more easily reach out for help, toward ideas or people who can provide security. The latter includes everything from an intervention by a therapist to a phrase in a self-help book to a sense of spiritual revival.

Disequilibrium drives couples forward. Without it, couples would languish and grow rigid. Because we fear change and confusion, though, we often resist the catalytic agent of our own development. This is a mistake. If a tightrope walker is leaning to one side, but refuses to acknowledge it and make an adjustment, he or she will fall. Many couples are in a similar situation: leaning to one side, about to take a tumble—as when they hold desperately to the spent promises of an earlier Expansion or dwell exclusively in the distortions of Contraction. On the other hand, the capacity to see times of disequilibrium as occasions for learning, even if it means having to struggle with painful feelings, is the sign of a more hopeful couple.

Perhaps it might be better to call disequilibrium a *condition* for change, which facilitates our own efforts to make things better.

Here is an example. Imagine that you have been trying to get me to open up in our relationship. I resist, because I feel coerced—it feels like my opening up would be for your sake, not mine; and yet I do want to tell you what's on my mind, for in my own way I am as lonely as you are. So we share the goal of talking more openly with each other, but our stable pursuit-and-distance sequence works against us.

Then, one day, my father is diagnosed with cancer. I have been very close to him, and the news is devastating to me. I can hardly think about anything else, and find myself constantly close to tears. You are kind and sympathetic, and now I begin to talk—first about my father and then about everything I have kept bottled up. In fact, I cannot stop talking. As I talk, I realize how much I love you, and my love for you mingles with the love I have for my father, so that I love you even more. Soon I grow curious about you, as though learning about you is a way to learn more about myself. I ask you about your response to my grief, and you respond. You ask me questions and I respond. We share a great sadness, and are close in a way that had escaped us before.

What happened? My father's illness was a "crisis" that opened me up emotionally, letting me break away from the patterns of Contraction. This helped us as a couple do what we could not do before.

Here is another example. In Contraction, you are convinced that I want to change you. You take this as a sign that I do not love you. I do love you, and we both vow to stop the pattern that feels so critical; and yet each time you do something that annoys me, I keep on responding—not by telling you how upset I am, but by criticizing you. Your efforts to stand up for yourself fail because your self-confidence isn't very high, and you half-think that I am right. You cry; this disarms me, and I comfort you. Temporarily, you feel cared for; and I, having gained the high ground again, feel consoled. Still, we remain in an unequal power relationship, and stay in Contraction.

At some point you begin to work outside the home. This gives you both an independent income and a work community that nurtures you. In time, this new arrangement pushes us into disequilibrium. My confidence is threatened because I don't feel as much control over you. You don't seem to need me so much. Now I pursue you, feeling weak. You wonder if you want me. Now you are free from my critical influence, but you are not sure what to do about my new vulnerability. Everything seems up in the air. We don't know how to act around each other: who cooks and who cleans; how to look at each other; whether to be affectionate or make love. We are like strangers.

During this time, we have many small reconciliations. At times I feel better and can affirm your new self-confidence; at times you are sympathetic to my fears. We feel like adults together then; we talk, listen to our favorite records, renegotiate the household chores that had fallen into disarray when you went to work. This is a foray, and it doesn't last. I might feel down one day and react critically to your independent stance; you rapidly reestablish your distance, and we are back in crisis.

With each foray, however, we lay a groundwork for moving into Resolution. We advance and fall back, advance and fall back again. Perhaps I start to see that, although you are more independent, you will not leave me. I begin to behave less distantly, less critically, and eventually you notice. You cautiously respond, and I answer in kind. Soon we are spending more and more time as partners. It feels a little businesslike to me, but I like it better than our angry struggles for control. Gradually we cross the threshold and move from Contraction into Resolution.

*Let's summarize this.* Couples in difficulty try to change. We may try to change for ages, but our forays from Contraction into Resolution develop momentum only when they come in a period of disequilibrium. When we are off balance, we have to deal with each other outside our usual sequences and stereotypes. Then we act, feel, and think differently about ourselves and our relationship. With new information, interaction is less automatic. We can come together in unfamiliar ways, and have to deal with each other differently. Each new settlement is a foray, and as the forays accumulate, we cross the threshold which brings us into Resolution.

## Distance and Differentiation

The move from Contraction into Resolution resembles the separation-individuation crises described in the literature of individual development.[4] The partners move from dependency on each other toward greater autonomy. This can be seen as a movement toward greater differentiation in the couple itself. Such a movement takes place in fits and starts: one day, the partners are dealing with each other in calm, "individuated," rational ways; the next, they are engulfed in angry conflict.

Expansion is intense, close, encompassing. It gives us a chance to pour forth our feelings of dependency, nurturing, and fusion. The initial movement into Contraction is a balancing reaction, a natural response to define and reestablish our individual boundaries. But this effort threatens our partners, who start opposing us. As a result, this phase of Contraction can be filled with angry, intense struggles in which we are as fused as in the intimacy of Expansion.

Eventually, in Contraction, we build emotional walls to protect our vulnerabilities. We stop sharing our tender thoughts, hide our feelings, and seek comfort in children, friends, and work. We write off our hopes for our partners. Instead of autonomy, we create distance; in fact, the road to autonomy in relationships often passes through angry distance.

In order to establish our distance, we emphasize how *different* we are from our partners. The second, more settled phase of Contraction is filled with differentiating statements like these:

"Why can't you see things my way for once?"

"You don't understand me anymore; I wonder if you ever have."

"I am *not* like you."

"Leave me alone, for once!"

Distance eventually creates safety and perspective, and we can see our partners less defensively. From there, angry, differentiating statements may take on more neutral meanings. The exasperated statement "I'm damned if I understand you!" can sound truly perplexed: "I really *don't* understand you. You really *are* different from me. Your actions must mean something besides what I thought."

More neutral statements begin to build up. As they do, we feel our separateness: our partner is neither who we thought nor who we wish them to be. We can no longer define them solely by their characteristics in Expansion—how they please and enhance us—or by their capacity to deprive and hurt us in Contraction. They are fuller than either stereotype. And we are different from them.

This process throws us off balance. Autonomy alternately feels safe and frightening. We are liberated from the antagonistic views of Contraction, but we are alone. We want to be with someone; we want to be engaged, comforted, and protected. We may even rush back into close relationship with our partners, which for a moment feels wonderful.

But our newfound autonomy is fragile. We are wary. We watch for signs of falling back into Contraction; our very vigilance is like a self-fulfilling prophecy. We fall back, rapidly reestablishing our distance, oscillating between the safe distance of late Contraction and the controlled engagement of early Resolution. Each forward movement is a foray, each backward movement a return.

Sometimes the forays build momentum and come to define the relationship. Then the couple establishes itself in Resolution. Sometimes the forays lack sufficient momentum and the couple falls back into Contraction for a protracted period of time.

When the forays are weak or the hold of Contraction is particularly strong, only a prolonged period of disequilibrium can open the way for forays to gain strength. This happens when greater distance and differentiation exhaust the couple's usual interactional sequences. The partner who relentlessly pursues, for example, finally feels too humiliated by her role and declares that she will find meaning and comfort elsewhere. This may leave her partner stunned, the relationship in disequilibrium.

A person who has dedicated himself to improving his partner may tire of her defiance and pull into himself, robbing the relationship of its modus vivendi, while his partner flounders with no one to defy, but no idea of what to do independently. The partners grow distant, more off balance. In such a state, they might oscillate wildly. In a single day, they might both feel extremely close and think of divorce. They might go for weeks at a time convinced that nothing good will ever come of their relationship, and then for weeks they might feel that they have finally made it together.

How do some couples like this seemingly leap into the Stage of Resolution? Sometimes a swing, a foray into Resolution, is so powerful that it pulls them completely into its domain. They swing far enough to have time to talk, time to build up credibility with each other. Then, when they start swinging back toward Contraction, they have the confidence to stop the swing and work out their differences instead.

More often the leap is a little more prosaic. We feel compelled to make a choice. We say the time has come to "face the music," or "deal with the reality of our situation." In crisis we may emerge from our defensive positions and deal with each other like tired warriors, trying to make the best deal possible. As simply as possible, we say, "This is who I am. This will have to do."

## A Brief Summary of What Works

In times of difficulty, couples will first fall back on the patterns that usually help them resolve other tough situations. If these do not work, they may need to do something, anything, that can get them a little distance, a bit of perspective. From this more distant place, less engaged in the struggle, they may be able to appreciate whatever is new and different in their relationship. They may then see ways in which they and their partner have *already* changed.

At this point, one partner may try something unexpected: an unconditional, friendly gesture; an act that departs from the usual patterns, thus freeing the other from the predictable response. This may be a kind deed, an apology, an invitation to talk things out. It departs from the usual "contingent" statements: "I'll change if you will." The noncontingent move says, "Here I stand. I'm taking this vacation (this new job, this attitude), but I love you, and I'll stand by you—no matter what." Such a move breaks the uneasy balance of bargained conditions. If one partner changes all by himself, the other simply has to adjust. The new perspective that emerges may serve as a foray into Resolution.

## Complexity and Curiosity

We never completely consolidate our shift into Resolution. But we can lengthen our stays there and increase our ability to escape Contraction. This comes about when we begin appreciating complexity.

Your distance, for example, may once have seemed hostile; now I see that sometimes you withdraw when you are anxious, and I may find a note of quiet acceptance in your solitude. This different explanation of your distance comforts me much more than what I assumed was your rejection during our darker days. For your part, you might sense that you have grown dependent on my pursuit. Perhaps you sense this when I occasionally refuse to seek you out, or when I am gone and you miss me. Even as you pull away, you want me to want you. My pursuit becomes more textured in your eyes: you see threads of love and vitality mixing with my neediness and wish to control—which were all you previously saw.

It does not matter where complexity begins. Each softening of the pattern leads to variations that bring out new qualities. Qualities of Expansion resurface. You may once have loved how my feistiness pierced your lonely shell; now, more wary, you enjoy how it touches you slightly, pressing a bit, but not penetrating. You may once have seemed a gallant anchor in the storm of my life; now I find you a bit stolid but still reassuring.

The capacity to see complexity, to hold apparently contradictory ideas at the same time, is essential to Resolution. As we grow, we learn to better tolerate ambiguity.

We revise our narratives to emphasize complexity and underline how time has changed our perceptions: "At first, I could only see her virtues," one partner might say. "Then, only her faults. But now I see both, and it seems all right. We know each other now; we know what to expect." The individual and couple narratives now consolidate, validating the movement from fusion to autonomy. The need to reconstruct each other progresses to the acceptance of limitations.

## Sometimes It Does Not Work

Some couples, however, do not increasingly appreciate complexity; nor do they move into Resolution. By the time these couples have journeyed through several cycles, Contraction means long periods of unshakable alienation. No effort to get out of Contraction seems to work. Cynical and worn out, they have already stopped trying to remodel their partners. Instead, they dig even more deeply into their defensive positions: "I'm just staying with you because I don't believe in divorce ... don't want to hurt the children ... am afraid to be alone." The rigidity of these positions can be so great that only a great crisis will now shake them. Only a transformational experience will redeem them. This is the story of the following chapter, "Turning Points and Transformations."

Such a desperate situation happened with Jonathan and Marie, during their life in Philadelphia in the 1980s.

Recall that Marie had been offered a job she desperately wanted. Jonathan resisted. Marie became angry and finally said she would move in spite of and without him if she had to. In the face of her fury, Jonathan relented. But their time in the new city seemed to be an increasing disaster.

The resolution of their dilemmas proved superficial, and they remained alienated. Jonathan, fuming with resentment, adopted a "wait and see" attitude. But as he "waited," one problem after the next assailed the couple.

They had trouble finding a home; squeezed by the pressures of time, they settled for one that neither of them really liked. Then, a few months after they arrived, Jonathan lost his job. Thrown off course, doubting his abilities ("I think I've peaked out; from here it's all downhill"), he floundered and became increasingly morose. He went through a number of job interviews and finally found another position, but it was not with a firm he liked. He was tempted to handle his insecurity by moving into another affair, but he resisted.

Marie, still angry with Jonathan for making such a fuss about moving, seemed preoccupied with her own job. After all, she was doing well. She felt furious that Jonathan had lost his. "Just when things are finally going well," she said, "why do you have to create more problems?" She maintained a wary distance and would not make up. Jonathan, who also felt isolated in the new city, responded by pulling back even further, refusing to apologize, and refusing even to talk except for discussing daily decisions about the house and kids.

Their pattern had shifted. Now it was Jonathan, not Marie, who felt abandoned. As a result, their usual ways of resolving difficulties were inoperative. Marie did not threaten to leave. Jonathan did not apologize. When he finally did, Marie seemed uninterested. Because he felt so down on himself, the effort to bring her closer felt humiliating, so he could not sustain it. He could not even accept an occasional sympathetic response from her. The minute she drew close, he scornfully withdrew. Each felt too compromised as individuals to compromise with each other.

They hoped "something would happen" that would make things magically better. But it did not. Instead, things got worse. Their middle child, Andrew, became listless and pale, and was found to be ill with a kidney disease that required months of treatment. Jonathan's father seemed to be developing Alzheimer's disease. Instead of bringing them together, this news drove them into their own separate grief; neither of them could console the other.

Their state of Contraction deepened. It seemed they were holding on together only for the sake of the children, and because they feared divorce.

Shortly after this, several things happened all close together: Marie found a lump in one breast, and became frightened about cancer. Even though the lump was benign, she was very shaken, and furious at what she took as Jonathan's lack of support. Jonathan had to deal with his father's stroke, and he returned to New York for a couple of weeks. When he returned he was even more depressed and withdrawn.

Marie moved into a separate bedroom. She did not know what to do. The marriage had always improved in the past, but she was at her wits' end. She was even more successful at her work, but she felt emotionally isolated from everyone. Distraught, she began an affair with an older European doctor, who was visiting her department for three months. But then—sensing that this was not the right answer for her—she broke it off. Jonathan's response was to pull away even more strongly. He was angry, filled with self-pity, and depressed.

The two of them struggled time and again to regain their balance, but nothing they tried could pull their relationship together. They could not get back on an even keel. Instead, resentment, blame, guilt, and despair drove them further and further apart. Drifting in opposite directions, more and more hopeless, they became deeply alienated from each other. Still living together, they barely spoke. Both appeared to be going their separate ways.

Their usual patterns had broken down, and Jonathan and Marie seemed unable to change. They were unable either to end the relationship or to revitalize it.

# 12

---

# TRANSFORMATIONAL
# EXPERIENCE

---

At least once in their lives, many if not most couples move into a place of great difficulty. No matter how hard they try to change, no matter how understanding they want to be, they remain stuck in an unremitting state of Contraction. All their usual ways of solving problems break down, and they founder on the edge of dissolution. They have moved far beyond the familiar thresholds of Contraction and have entered a dark wilderness from which there seems no exit.

At such times, only two options seem possible: resignation and disengagement from each other, or divorce.

Indeed, this is a point at which many couples separate. Partners, faced with the choice, often resign themselves to unsatisfying relationships. They prefer to try to endure, to contain their bitter disappointment and dull their pain. They may do this "for the children," or out of religious principles, or because they fear the unknown more than their familiar suffering, or out of inertia. They often try to find fulfillment elsewhere—with children, friends, work, and hobbies. Some turn to alcohol or drugs; others begin affairs. Eventually some of these disengaged couples find a way to renew their relationship; but usually even they seem ready to return to their fortresses at the least provocation.

There is yet another option for couples. This is the experience of transformation. It is not a voluntary choice, and it only appears in the lives of a small number of couples; but no experience couples go through is more dramatic than this. This is a moment when, after having been mired in a bleak, unending state of Contraction, the partners actually manage to break away from the depths of despair and *transform* their relationship.[1]

## A Transformational Experience

A transformational experience changes us in a fundamental way. It becomes a great divide, appearing as a moment of great clarity and insight from which everything that happened earlier either seems inadequate or appears as part of some preparation for our new intimacy.[2] Such a moment changes the way we view ourselves and our situation. In this instant, the confusion and pain of our life lift, and we see a great truth that liberates us from all that had oppressed us before.

Transformations are characterized by an initial period of chaos, confusion, and despair. The experience itself comes suddenly, as an unexpected burst of clarity. Afterwards, we feel redeemed. We can reclaim ourselves and others—even the parts we had rejected before—for we see things in a new light and from a new perspective. Feelings of joy and elation, and a sense of calm and wisdom follow, and there is a great sense of relief. Afterwards, our priorities seem reordered and we focus on the essentials, while discarding what now seems unimportant.

Paradoxically, the crisis created when a couple contemplates separation and divorce may open the way to a transformational experience that will bring the partners a depth of intimacy they had not known before. A transformation is different from the adaptive measures that ordinarily move a couple from Contraction to Resolution. Its change feels total, magical, as though the couple has swiftly been lifted out of a dark dungeon and into the light of day.

At some level, transformations are familiar to everyone. We have all had moments when we feel terrible and then, instantly, and for some unknown reason, feel wonderful. Sometimes we are caught on the horns of a dilemma, frustrated and feeling defeated. Then, inexplicably, we wake up one morning feeling fine and in full possession of what now seems the obvious solution to the dilemma.

The transformation of couples works in the same way. No one

can completely prepare for transformational change. We work for years to understand ourselves, to grow more independent, to have more access to our feelings, to gain compassion for others—in short, to put ourselves in position where we can change. And yet, even then, effort alone will not do the trick.

Transformational change comes when we least expect it, when we are not trying to achieve it. It comes when we are in crisis, off balance, out of control, and not entirely rational. Only then, on the verge of giving up, and when we least suspect it, does all that we have worked for suddenly come together—all at once and without any conscious effort.

Such an experience is not part of our Cultural Narrative. The Cultural Narrative of long-term relationships suggests that, eventually, couples will work things out; they will become staid and stable, seem a bit funny and perhaps whimsical to their children and friends, and become fond of each other, like the couple in *On Golden Pond*. The Cultural Narrative also has a place for couples who wind up becoming "intimate enemies," always grumbling and complaining. But it does not have a place for couples who manage to turn things around so mightily that their relationship is reborn.

Transformation leads through considerable pain and the active possibility of divorce, and even as we approach it, we generally pull back into resignation or leap forward into divorce. Both of these options feel easier than the prolonged uncertainty that precedes transformations. As a result, the latter seem reserved for those few couples who have great enough stamina, courage, and faith—and good fortune.

A transformational experience is like a journey to the wilderness and back. This journey brings the death of the old and a rebirth into the new. The relationship is reborn as we change, as we view our partners in a new light, and as our ways of being together change. This chapter is about those fortunate couples whose journey, we hope, will enlighten the journeys of all couples, no matter which particular path they take.

## A Journey to the Brink of Despair

At first, the journey that ultimately results in a transformational experience looks no different from any other journey that seems to be drifting helplessly toward divorce. But those who will be transformed have invested a great deal of themselves in their relationship, and do not take the possibility of divorce lightly.

There is a point on the journey where all the strategizing and blaming, all the anxiety and anger, fail. The partners feel bitterly disappointed; this disappointment becomes the dominant, inescapable theme of their relationship. They acknowledge to themselves that their hopes and expectations have not and in all likelihood *will* not be met. They acknowledge the extent of their disappointment.

I might admit to myself, for instance, that I will always feel judged by you, that you will never be an enthusiastic parent with me, or join me in religious observance, or like my friends, and that our sex life is simply a failure.

We may share our disappointment with our partners, but we do this not to draw a response; we say it out of grief to relieve the tightness inside. We begin to give up on each other and on our idealized image of relationships. We feel sad and resigned to our fate. So we stop the manipulations by which we had hoped to transform our partners: we stop trying so hard to bring them closer, to reform them, to punish them for their wrongdoings.

At this point couples are not ready to let go completely. The partners hold on, through resentment and through fear of divorce, of the unknown, of being alone and unprotected. These fears resonate with the wounds of past losses.

Divorce means separation from the person in whom we have invested more of ourselves than anyone since our parents. We cannot imagine breaking loose without leaving broken strands of ourselves embedded in them.

But the drift toward divorce may feel unstoppable. Talk to people who divorce, and you will hear the imagery of death in their language: "Something has died in me," they say, or, "I feel like I'll die if he leaves." These statements are uttered sincerely, and they conceal a deep truth. Our ways of relating to each other and, momentarily, to ourselves *must* die before we can be open to each other in new ways. In our era, where we look for so much in our relationships, the annihilation of a relationship often serves as a vessel for its death and rebirth.

## Disengagement and Giving Up

A couple's disillusionment may be deeper when it comes after great hopes and promise. Remember, some couples experience the promises of Expansion with much more intensity than others; these couples are often far more disappointed by experiencing the repeated falls into Contraction. Already worn down, fragile and bitter, these couples are ripe for an even bigger fall. They can be blown over by any wind. It could be a failure at work, a parent's death, the onset of illness, a child's bad school report. Even good experiences in other arenas of life can push them over the edge because they highlight the failure of the relationship. For these couples, the sense of disappointment deepens and moves toward disillusionment. Despair and desperation follow. We have tried everything and nothing has helped; we are tired of trying. Trying is frustrating, humiliating, and exhausting.

At this point, we feel like victims of a cruel fate, powerless to save ourselves or the relationship. Everything we try fails, and our efforts come flying back in our faces like a cold wind. We grow hopeless and no longer care.

Disillusionment leads to giving up and giving up leads to disengagement, to holding ourselves apart. It provides a separation, a disjunction—similar to what happens to the gears of a car when the clutch is permanently depressed. But it also forces us to take responsibility for our own lives. Finally we have to admit that our partners will not or cannot come through for us; we have to take care of ourselves.

Giving up breaks down the couple's key interactional sequences. We lose the motivation to pursue our partners, for example, and they, in turn, barely respond to our initiatives. Arguments become brief and lifeless. Since so much of the life of struggling couples revolves around their efforts to change each other, stopping such efforts leaves them with little to do with each other. Giving up creates a void. We grow passive with each other. This makes us strangely innocent and receptive to new information.

Some new information comes from inside us: as we shed our habitual behavioral constraints, old images and old feelings come forth; we recall nightmares, fears of being lost, yearnings for a good parent, our desire to be loved. We are not defended. Without the need to prove our points or defend ourselves from our partners, we observe that they are different from the stereotyped view we had built up about them.

When we do engage each other during this period, it feels in a way like being with someone new—still alienating but arousing genuine curiosity. In addition to their flaws, we are aware of the good we had originally seen in them. We can see the attraction and promise that had been so compelling before. This is not just nostalgia; it results from no longer having to defend ourselves and justify our hurt and angry feelings.

Some information comes from the outside: friends and relatives come forth and speak their minds about the relationship:

"He was such a sour person."

"She really was trying but you couldn't see it."

Even though we are each likely to have changed over time, in our conflict we have held to rigid images of each other which lag behind the present reality. Our change may have been *outside* our relationship. (After divorce, people commonly note that their partners seem suddenly to have changed dramatically, often in the ways they had requested. Such statements tend to be rueful: "I worked so damned hard on him and I never knew it was having an effect. Now some other woman is going to get the benefit!")

Following disengagement, then, our experience of each other combines an acknowledgment of the old with a recognition of something new. It thus creates the potential for a new relationship. We can see our partner as someone separate from what we have imagined. When this happens, it can be a shocking, shaking discovery: we see how truly alone we are, how alien our partner is, how little our presumed similarities are. We see that our bond to each other is very tenuous, and we are close to leaving.

Disengagement also helps set us free. We may not be particularly happy with this newfound freedom, but it is a great relief to stop trying so hard, and it can be fascinating to look around with new eyes.

## Into the Wilderness and Beyond

Some disengaged couples do not divorce. They may put the decision off or resolve to do so at some later date—after a child reaches a certain age or when a partner finishes a graduate program and can support himself financially. In any case, they remain together in loose alliance. This is a time of great confusion. Those who still live with their partners generally continue to share household tasks, child-related activities, financial decisions, and even a social life with friends and relatives. As they carry on, life feels unreal, as if they are acting in a play.

All of our ordinary assumptions and impulses are called into question. In this state of uncertainty, we waver about the decision to divorce. One moment we feel certain, purposeful:

"I've got to get out of this relationship if I'm going to survive."

"I am resolved to build a better life than this one."

The next minute, we feel totally crazy and wonder just what we think we are doing. For a while it seems clear that we have to break free in order to find peace or to find a better self than we have encountered in the relationship. But, at some point, we may stop believing in our goals and simply feel lost. At this point we have entered an emotional wilderness.

As with mythological heroes of old, the journey into this wilderness will test our strength, our courage, our resourcefulness, and our devotion. We worry that we cannot tolerate the loneliness, and wonder why we had to get away so from our partner. We see how dependent we had grown, and experience the simple loss of our partner's presence as an amputation—even if it is only to be in a room together, arguing. What do we do in the morning and the evening when we are alone? How do we prepare for work, read the newspaper, decide on a vacation? There is no one to bear witness.

Often, our partner is so nearby, a room or a phone call away, that the temptation to compromise and prematurely come in from the wilderness is enormous. Such premature compromise means falling back into a relationship knowing that nothing basic has changed and that the dissatisfaction that led to this point will soon return. Almost as soon as we are tempted to yield to what seems like security, we know that it will not be secure at all. It feels like selling ourselves short.

Some refuse to compromise because the time in the wilderness has great meaning in itself. Many of us need to feel that we can live alone if we have to, without a relationship, that we can live without the deal that we had made in our original Expansive Contract. We need to know if we can make our own social contacts, provide our own security, love ourselves, value ourselves, care for ourselves, or care for our children by ourselves.

Perhaps, we discover, we need to feel strong enough never again to place ourselves in a demeaning position with a partner. So we learn to survive the loneliness and to do the small and large things for which we had depended on our partners. Others have to be alone long enough to feel how much we do depend on our partners, even though we have spent a lifetime denying any such needs. And we acknowledge how much we miss them. It may be that we have to let go of the idea that our partner must change—get a better job, lose weight, become more communicative—before we can feel good. Some must learn to be more assertive, some more passive.

This time in the wilderness is good precisely because we are alone, we have time to contemplate, and we must take full responsibility for our feelings and actions. Where before we blamed our partner for our problems, now we struggle to see how it is not primarily our partner's fault that we suffer. It is mostly our own. We must come to terms with ourselves. This is what the wilderness means.

## The Moment of Clarity

For what seems like an eternity, we may waver between divorce and hanging on, between feeling determined and feeling victimized, between seeking truths and giving in to despair. Then, just when it seems we are most tempted to give up, we experience a moment of clarity. As we let go of our need to imprison our partners in the cramped, distorted view we had built of them, we suddenly *see* them as they are.

We see the whole person. We see the person we had fallen in love with, their beauty and sweetness, their playfulness, and their sadness. We see the partner we had come to fear, cool and withholding, aggressive and needy, bullying and angry. We see the calm, reasonable person we had come to depend on and to negotiate with. For a moment, we hold the full changing cycle in a single glance.

These moments of discovery sometimes feel like the fruit of sustained effort. Sometimes they appear as a blinding realization or a spiritual awakening. A sense of redemption often follows such awakenings. Couples regain themselves and their relationship, have a chance to undo the wrongs they have done, and, by forgiving each other, reconnect with their partner and recover their self-respect.

Transformational experience takes us beyond the confusion into a state of innocence. Giving up, we surrender to an unknown fate; we become passive, curious, open, without preconception. We have stopped struggling and feel calm, as in the still air after a storm. We return to the innocence we experienced during the first days of the

Expansive Stage. By joining this to the knowledge we have gained in the cycles of Expansion, Contraction, and Resolution, we feel whole again.

In this state of innocence, we are more easily moved. Our hearts open to our partners, and we feel reconnected. We can now see differences as differences, not signs of malice. Our incompleteness, our inadequacy, and that of our partners, arise because we are human. We understand that our partners cannot complete us or satisfy our every need: that is a truth of life. Simultaneously, we accept our difference and our connection, our limits and our potential. In this way, we redeem both ourselves and our relationship.

## Both an Individual and a Couple Experience

Going into the wilderness is both an individual and a couple experience. Clearly, the confusion, the fears, the discoveries—the thoughts and feelings—are individual. Frequently, one partner is more adrift than the other, and the transformation may begin with a personal revelation that is not initially a "couple experience." Still, even if one partner takes this journey alone, the relationship can be transformed. When one partner moves beyond the usual sequences, images, and patterns, both will have to change. The old rules do not apply, and they will confront each other in new and unexpected ways.

To be sure, partners rarely achieve these states of clarity simultaneously. Often, though, when one makes such a breakthrough, the other will respond. If their timing is truly off, if they are desperately out of sync, then it is true: the partners may never come together. This might be the case if one is very much ready to renew the relationship and the other is still absorbed in his or her own private journey. And even when both achieve a kind of individual enlightenment, there is no guarantee that they will choose each other.

Simultaneity of feeling is not essential in order for a relationship to be transformed. The main requirement is that both partners are vulnerable, open to change. Both partners have experienced loss, fear, and confusion. When one or both move into the place of calm and connectedness, a chain of new experiences can begin.

We convey our feelings to our undefended partner in immediate, powerful ways. We say how frightened and hurt we have been, how we depended on each other and then felt let down; and our words have a palpable impact. We finally talk openly to each other. No one has to defend against innuendos.

This is not a painless period. We each say things that hurt, but the pain feels simple and healing. When I say that I just couldn't live up to your expectations of me, we both know it is so. We both know how hard my failure is to take and how hard it is to admit it. When you say you felt abandoned the way a child feels abandoned by her father, we weep together, both for your loneliness and for the way I betrayed us both. We describe our experience and ask only that the other bear witness.

Our experience in the wilderness has changed us. In our unguarded states we see and acknowledge our partners' changes. Bearing witness to the latter's hard-won gains is an affirming experience, much like our early time in Expansion. But this moment is less giddy than those earlier days. Exhausted and quiet, we appreciate the beauty of that other person with whom we have shared such a harrowing time. We are survivors together.

We bear witness to what we have valued all along. We spend more time together, talking candidly, as though for the first time. We learn again who this person, our partner, is; we listen compassionately to his or her story, and it is told without blame.

Here, it is easier to forgive past cruelties. And as we forgive our partners, we forgive ourselves. As we forgive each other and acknowledge the independent yet closely woven stories of our lives, we feel profoundly connected. When we share that feeling, it is like a ritual, a marriage; only this time we understand the meaning of marriage and choose it, still.

In our times, marriage has a voluntary cast. Two people meet, like, and, perhaps, love each other, and decide to stay together. This means that they can also leave each other and many do. It is not that people generally choose divorce lightly; that is rare. But they do believe that they can choose to stay or, if life together becomes unbearable, they can leave; and holding tight to this option remains a comfort as a last line of self-defense.

After transformational experiences all this changes. The choice we make no longer seems like a choice. We feel so deeply intertwined that it feels more like a recognition of the reality of our bond than a matter of choosing someone or something. We are joined the way people of the same family feel joined—beyond choice, absolutely, no longer contingent on the quality of the relationship.

Joseph Campbell puts it this way: "Marriage is a relationship. When you make the sacrifice in marriage, you're sacrificing not to each other but to unity in the relationship." You are "no longer this one alone; your identity is in a relationship. Marriage is not a simple love affair, it's an ordeal, and the ordeal is the sacrifice of the ego to a relationship in which two have become one."[3]

## The Cycle Is Unbroken

Transformations mark new beginnings and powerful connections but they do not transport us to Paradise. We are likely to rest more securely in ourselves and our relationships, but eventually we will get back to disagreements and distrust. We may still get frightened when we get too close for too long or stray too far from each other. We will share joys but also further disappointments. We will continue to cycle through the three stages. We may have a new Home Base—Resolution. But the Home Base is not an end point; the relationship remains dynamic.

It is likely, however, that we will have a different experience of the disagreements, the disappointments, the joys—the entire range of our feelings—as we cycle from stage to stage. Now we assume the continuity of the relationship and wonder primarily about the form it will take.

## Jonathan and Marie

Jonathan and Marie had a transformational experience like this two years ago, which finally brought them out of the depths of despair into which they had sunk during their years in Philadelphia, and from which it had seemed there was no escape.

The reader will recall from the last chapter that a series of difficult events had assailed Jonathan, Marie, and their family since their arrival in Philadelphia. Their arrival itself had come at the end of a huge fight over moving in the first place. A few months after they arrived, Jonathan lost his job, floundered, and became depressed. Tempted though he was to handle his pain by moving into another affair, he resisted. But he remained depressed. Marie seemed totally preoccupied with her own job, and Jonathan took her distance as proof of her contempt and disdain for him.

Then, in rapid succession, the family endured a series of major crises. Their middle child Andrew got seriously ill with a kidney disease. Marie found a lump in one breast, and even though it was benign, she was very shaken up by the event, and by what she took as Jonathan's lack of support. Jonathan's father became ill, and Jonathan had to go back to New York for a few weeks. When he returned he was even more desperately withdrawn. Marie, although ever more successful at work, felt isolated. Distraught, she began an affair with a friend, and then—sensing that it was not the answer she sought—broke it off. Jonathan's response was to pull away even more strongly.

During this time the two of them struggled again and again to regain their balance, but nothing they tried could pull their relationship together. They could not get back on an even keel. Instead, resentment, blame, guilt, and despair drove them further and further apart. Drifting in opposite directions, more and more hopeless, they became deeply alienated from each other. Still living together, they barely spoke. Both were going their separate ways.

Both of them acknowledged that their marriage was—for all practical purposes—over. Privately, they began thinking what they would do if and when they divorced. They even voiced the possibility aloud to friends and, once, to each other. "Look what we've done to our children," they said, tormentedly. At last they were staring at the impossible: their marriage, which had endured all this time, would probably end in failure and divorce.

Let us look at how each of them was handling this.

Jonathan, deeply depressed, felt like a failure. His career had bottomed out, and he was filled with feelings of failure and self-contempt. He felt he had failed to develop himself as a person, too—both as a parent and a mate. Although he was deeply hurt by Marie's affair, he agreed that it was "fair play," and felt she was somehow "entitled" to have her own affair. After all, he had done the same thing years ago when *she* had been vulnerable. He felt he deserved the cold treatment he was getting, but it hurt too much and he felt he could not live with it much longer. He thought about leaving his family, getting a divorce, going back to Boston or New York. His father was ill with Alzheimer's Disease. His mother was miserable. He felt called upon to take on his family obligations: at least there he might be able to succeed. But the thought of leaving his children kept him from acting on any of these impulses.

The children had deeply affected Jonathan over the past few years. In dealing with his depression, Jonathan had turned more and more to them—especially to Andrew. The new job he'd found was less demanding, less glamorous than his earlier ones, and he had much more time to be at home. In fact, he was home more than ever: he was home more than Marie. He had begun fixing the children's meals, playing games, watching TV, taking them on walks or on shopping trips.

Marie was in a quandry. She felt alienated from her family and herself. She was incredibly busy, and yet she no longer knew what she wanted. Her plan to be a physician had succeeded and brilliantly— but not in the ways she had imagined. Busier than she had ever wanted to be, she felt isolated both in her teaching department and in the hospital; she had few close friends, and she felt disconnected from herself.

Now she was beset by vague flashes of emotion—anger, embarrassment, anxiety—as well as by physical symptoms that she thought might be early signs of menopause. She had been shaken by the workup of her breast lump; she began to worry about her own mortality. Looking around, she felt guilty at having less time for her children than she wanted; and, after what had happened with Andrew, she felt increasingly anxious about their health and well-being. When she saw how gloomy Jonathan looked, and how little she could or even wanted to help him, she felt like a failure in her marriage. She knew that Jonathan had many problems of his own, but she also felt she had let him down.

For the first time in her life, Marie began wondering deeply about her own inner feelings. She realized she had been moving so fast, she had gotten out of touch with herself. It struck her that she had never fully grieved for the loss of the father she had so loved. And she was aware of feeling guilty about the four hundred miles between her and her mother, at a time when her mother was getting older and more helpless. In spite of her success in the professional world, Marie felt like a failure, an emotional cripple.

She began to have deeply conflicting feelings, alternately attacking herself for her selfishness and ambition, for the affair with Nat, for having abandoned her mother ... and hopefully wondering what it would be like to divorce Jonathan and be on her own once again.

Both of them were lost in their own particular wilderness; helpless, detached, and unhappy, each was considering divorce. They saw their relationship as having come to naught, and each felt like a failure.

As Jonathan spent more and more time with the children, he grew less attached to his own work, and some new things began happening to him. He began enjoying himself more and more with the kids. He felt less critical of Marie, of the kids, and of himself; and, gradually, he began to act less selfishly. Instead of acting like the Crown Prince around whom everything had to revolve, he now felt lucky to have his children, to have a job, to have a house. And he began letting go of his driving ambition. He loved his kids tremendously, and he felt a simple, unconditional acceptance from them toward him. It seemed to open him up. As he let go, he accepted himself more, and he felt greater acceptance for Marie, in spite of all her frailties. His father's illness made him realize how short life really was, and he wondered what was so important to fight about. Regretful, he felt he had ruined his marriage by his own pushing and shoving, his lack of compromise, his arrogance and selfishness. Slowly, Jonathan began making small, helpful, considerate gestures around the house. He didn't help himself first at the table. When Marie seemed tired, he asked if there was anything he could do. Quietly, so slowly that neither he nor Marie realized anything was happening, he began changing in subtle ways.

As this change took place, Marie was thinking about divorce, maybe marrying someone else, maybe not; but in any case feeling lonely for the rest of her life. Was the next step to get a lawyer? In this frame of mind, Marie found herself absentmindedly appreciating the small considerations Jonathan was showing her. She responded without even thinking about it. But Jonathan noticed her response as different, and wondered what was going on.

Over a few weeks, Marie noticed Jonathan with the children, and saw how much he loved them, and they him. She noticed his sadness: he had aged, and seemed dignified in his sadness. No longer peevish and arrogant, he seemed to have matured; and in this maturity, he became attractive to her. But he seemed so far away, so unapproachable. She felt Jonathan's concern about helping a client in his work, felt his concern for his father, and she realized—in a moment of clarity—that he was no longer the same person he had been before. He was no longer critical and demanding. He had pulled away and left her free. And now she freely felt a desire to be close to him again.

In this moment, Marie felt herself let go of her own hardness and anger. So what if Jonathan had made mistakes? She had made them, too, she freely admitted. So what if he had hurt her (Marie could hardly believe she was thinking this). She had hurt him, too. Now she felt an unequivocal, unconditional love rise within her. Success at work was important, but it could not bring her in touch with her inner self. It could not make her happy. Slowly, she let her guard down. She relaxed, and nothing bad happened. No one even seemed to notice. She began acting kindly, and Jonathan responded with kindness toward her.

One evening they were home together, exhausted. Each of them was feeling a newfound calm: the absence of selfishness, the lack of demands, the end of blame. They fixed each other a drink and sat on the couch together.

"Do you still love me?" Marie said.

"Yes. Actually I do," Jonathan answered.

"I love you, too," she said.

It was nothing more dramatic than that, and yet it was the most dramatic exchange they had ever had together. They both looked at each other, and felt transformed, released, forgiven, reborn.

Over the next several weeks, their experience of letting go expanded and deepened. They felt their new perspective building. It was as if their relationship had been resurrected on the ashes of its own imminent demise.

This transformation led Marie and Jonathan back into a fairly long period of Resolution, which was followed by a new phase of Expansion. Since then, their experience has stayed with them as a living presence. To be sure, they still fight. They still move into periods of Contraction. But when they do, they do not revisit Contraction's bitter depths as they had so many times before. Not since their moment of clarity. They now have something stronger to fall back on and pull them out when they need it. They have a sense of deep love and acceptance for each other, which helps them through the bad times that come up.

Jonathan and Marie have found a new starting point, a new place of resolve, a new Home Base. Their cycles now begin from a place in Resolution, and they no longer reside mainly in Contraction. This has been the force of their transformational experience.

# 13

---

# Applications

---

If this book has done its job, you should be better oriented to the predictable cycles of intimate relationships. You know that every relationship has its ups and downs, and that, lacking perspective, couples often become impatient and worry that bad periods will last forever. When we resolve a problem and feel better, we cling to our solutions and good feelings. But, with the exception of divorce, none of these periods are final. And even difficult relationships cycle through periods of Expansion and Resolution. The repetition of cycles is a reality we must learn to expect and live with.

The cyclical perspective runs against the prevailing linear view, which suggests that with hard work and the development of interpersonal skills we can continually improve our lives. But life is more than a skill to be learned. It holds too many natural crises and obstacles for steady improvement to hold its ground. Children come and go; partners begin and end jobs. Many events are beyond our control. We have personal problems—depressions and anxieties; we eat and drink addictively; we worry. Each of these difficulties can push our relationship into a Stage of Contraction, which means we must struggle over and over to achieve Resolution and moments of expansiveness.

People accept the seasons of the year, the passage of day and night, yet they tend to fight the notion that relationships move through cycles. How differently we would feel about relationships if we simply accepted the fact that bad times are inescapable.

232

# Recognition: Constructing a Self-Portrait

We hope you recognize yourself in our discussion, finding in it the general outlines of your experience, while having room for your own idiosyncrasies. In order to sharpen your understanding of this new perspective, let us suggest that you construct a self-portrait of you in your couple—past or present—guided by the following questions:

1) Remembering the experience of expansiveness and the sense of promise that filled the early days of your relationship, how did you and your partner feel special, open, and able? How exhilarated did you feel, how free of the negative patterns of past relationships? As a woman, did you feel both assertive and feminine? As a man, both masculine and receptive?

2) What was the original "deal" you and your partner made together—your Expansive Contract? For example:

• One would provide stability, the other would provide adventure.

• You would be best friends in a hostile world, supporting each other even when others doubted you.

3) Describe how you and your partner began to pull back into yourselves. Who did it first? Who most? Who felt most abandoned? Who asked for room?

4) What did you tell yourself in order to explain this painful change in your relationship? Did the explanation make it more or less painful? For example: "I deserve this" or "I suppose we have to go through this kind of period."

5) What patterns of conflict and alienation emerged during this Stage of Contraction? For example,

• You approached, and he distanced; you felt invalidated or abandoned, and he felt controlled or invaded; you looked angry and demanding, and he looked unfeeling and withdrawn.

• He was so critical that you felt he must want someone else, so you became depressed and lackadaisical around the house. The more critical he got, the sadder you got; or, the sadder you got, the more critical he got.

6) What did you do and tell yourself to make this pattern more tolerable? Did you convince yourself that things would somehow get better? Did you search for others who appreciated you? Did you set to work to make things better? Did you:

- Distance yourself in the face of your partner's rejection?
- Try and try to please in the face of criticism?
- Hang in but turn off?

7) How did you resolve the struggles and deal with your disappointment about the loss of the Expansive Contract? Did you:

- Learn to minimize the negative effects of the dance of pursuit and distance, or did you learn to share the initiation of contact and become more responsive when the other initiated?
- Insist on being yourself until your partner backed off his criticism?
- Learn to stand in and learn to negotiate?
- Accept some limitations on the relationship: on what your partner had to give; on what you might do or feel; on what might happen between you?

8) Did the resolution(s) generally

- Trade greater limitations for peace: a decision to avoid certain topics or activities?
- Resolve conflicts through compromise: you can take the job you want if we live near my parents?
- Seem even more complete, so that you felt different about each other?

9) How did you feel about yourselves after entering the Stage of Resolution? Did the resolution bring relief, freedom, vibrancy, renewed intimacy? Did it emphasize limitation or a sense of being somewhat compromised? Did it just feel solid and secure? Did it feel like parts of all of these? What is the truest meaning of Resolution for you?

10) What is your preferred stage? Which is your partner's? If they are different, how do you deal with the difference?

11) Which is your Home Base? How much do you stay there? Has it shifted in the course of your relationship? Have you spent several years or even decades first in one stage and then in another?

12) Can you identify a mini-cycle when you leave your Home Base and return within an hour, a day, even a week? You begin in Contraction, for example, have a moment of calm, clear conversation, which is such a relief that you feel momentarily elated, but fight almost immediately and settle back into Contraction—with nothing particularly learned or gained, or lost, for that matter.

13) What patterns and sequences do you think you and your

partner follow through your three-stage cycle? How has this changed over the years?

14) Can you identify two or more full cycles? The first would begin with Expansion and move through Contraction and Resolution. Eventually your cycles begin in Home Base—usually Resolution or Contraction—and cycle back to it, but in their course they integrate new experience into the relationship. What might this be for you?

15) What makes you move from stage to stage, from cycle to cycle? Is it something that knocks you off balance, something that represents a difference, something *beyond* the two of you as partners?

16) Do your cycles have a rhythm? Do you move in great, dramatic leaps, either thrilled with each other or totally infuriated and turned off, or do you move in smooth, almost imperceptible transitions?

17) Do you cycle often or do you stay mostly in your Home Base, rarely venturing out?

If you answered these questions, you will have a fairly complete and complex picture of your relationship. Its purpose is no more and no less than to understand yourself better. If your partner has also completed the questionnaire, you may find it interesting to compare the responses, and then, if you wish, to try to reconcile the differences. The responses that do not match will highlight areas of struggle for you. Correspondences may point out areas where you are closer than you knew. Try to be curious, to ask questions before you argue. The process may be difficult, but it should prove immensely rewarding.

## Dealing with Disappointment: Four Suggestions

Disappointment and betrayal seem inherent in relationships, for our partners can never provide all the companionship, romance, sex, or encouragement we dream about. This is especially true in contemporary America.

We spend enormous amounts of time and energy trying to avoid disappointment. This effort distorts our lives, just as an earnest adaptation to physical injury can distort our bodies. To avoid pain in one foot, for instance, we lean so heavily on the other that we develop a limp; the limp pulls our back out of shape, creating pain that interrupts our sleep, and so forth. So it is with disappointment. To avoid it, we deny truths about ourselves and our partners. We hold ourselves emotionally rigid. We lean heavily on some aspects of ourselves but exclude others; we avoid risky subjects and activities. This leads to an "interactive limp"—for example, no sex because it is an area of potential conflict, no disagreement because it may lead to distance.

A better question is not how to avoid disappointment but how to cope with it. To cope, we must be clear-eyed, using all the emotional and intellectual resources at our disposal. We must believe we can get past our problems—not once but many times.

Each cycle is a journey in which we encounter parts of ourselves and of our relationship that have remained relatively dormant during our stay at our Home Base. We discover yearnings and passions that had been buried, anger that had been controlled, memories that had been repressed. But however inevitable and enriching these journeys are, they frighten us. Their disequilibrium makes us anxious, and we fear the unknown. What then is the most productive approach to take in such upsetting times? We here present four simple suggestions the reader might find helpful.

1) *Let yourself relax.* To some extent the cycle is simply going to run its course, especially if its rhythms have been pretty well established over the years. If you think about it, much of the terrain should be familiar. Instead of frantically leaping into motion to help or to hide when problems settle in, quiet yourself long enough to become a good observer. Watch what your partner does when you approach or don't approach. Watch what happens when you stop criticizing—even justifiably. Watch what happens when you both are at your worst—is it constant, or are there frequent little oases and frequent efforts to improve things which are simply not noted, joined, and amplified?

2) *Be curious instead of judgmental or fearful.* As you observe the aspects of your partner that you have found most upsetting, ask yourself whether they are necessarily bad, especially if you don't react to them. Is a person's desire to be alone really so rejecting, a person's desire to talk really intrusive, demanding, controlling? Is a partner's touch always insensitive? What happens if you don't fight back? Don't justify? What happens if, upon hearing a complaint, you simply say, "You're right"?

To be curious is to step outside of the powerful sequences that primarily organize the life of couples in the Stage of Contraction. When you step outside the sequence, you free yourself from it. When you step outside long enough, despite your partner's efforts to bring you back, the relationship will invariably move into the next stage, Resolution. Try it. It may be counterintuitive but the refusal to protect yourself is disarming to partners.

3) *Make friends with Contraction.* This is possible if you treat Contraction like a challenging old friend—or relative—who has caused you great difficulty but is filled with useful information about your life. Imagine interviewing a parent who had hurt you badly when you were a child. For years you keep your distance but eventually you want to know more about the story of your life; and the only way to find out is to reacquaint yourself with this feared or hated parent. After a series of interviews and with time to think about them, you don't exactly adore the parent, but a fondness, a sense of having shared a common history, emerges and becomes more important. You even look forward to meetings despite the fact that he or she will continue, in some measure, to hurt your feelings.

Another way to look at Contraction is as an upsetting dream. Dreams are interesting because they are windows into our unconscious; they tell us about the deeper layers of feelings and images that inform our daily lives. Processing dreams enriches our lives, often providing keys to problems that elude our rational efforts. As with dreams, we can say when Contraction looms: "Oh, good, I've been meaning to get a look at you. I don't feel as sure of what I'm doing—even though I've been feeling good—without listening to your voice."

If you welcome Contraction, you will not even be able to hold onto it. It will move you and fascinate you, but move by like a fast-flowing river.

4) *Affirm complexity.* We have defined character in a complex way: the regular passage through three stages. This means that all three stages are equal partners, and it would be wrong to subordinate one to another, or to call one false and the other real, one enduring and the other ephemeral.

Complexity feels more true to life. Our view makes us less concerned with "getting it right" than with appreciating the richness of each cycle, each move through the stages. We are less focused on the search for happiness (Expansion) or maturity (Resolution) than we are on sincere engagement (between partners and within ourselves) throughout the cycle. We are not interested in fault-finding. Within this view, there is more room to be ourselves—that is, to be our many selves. There is room to grow and to regress, to be changeable and idiosyncratic.

## Implications for Psychotherapy: A New Therapy of Cycles and Complexity

Psychotherapy may be seen as the restoration of complexity. This restoration is immensely aided by a cyclical view of couple development and character. By the time most couples come to therapy, they have poured themselves into narrow vessels and look like caricatures of themselves. A sullen and withdrawn man appears with an angry, demanding woman—little else shows through the adopted roles. A needy and depressed woman comes in with a vigorous and concerned man—"Nothing's wrong that a little exercise and sex won't cure," he says—and that's the extent of their initial presentation.

The therapist's job is to release the couple from their imprisoning caricatures. This is accomplished by disrupting the sequences that organize the couple's life. When sequences are disrupted, the couple is thrown momentarily off balance, and new qualities or characteristics may emerge.

A therapist might, for instance, insist that the distancing partner decide what he wants in a particular situation and pursue it with his partner. She might block the efforts of a Pygmalion-like man to change his partner: "Suppose your wife were to remain how she is, forever, that she is unchangeable. How would you deal with her then? And how would you respond to him [this said to the wife] if he simply stopped criticizing—forever?"

By disrupting sequences, therapists challenge couples to find new ways of being. At first, this creates confusion. Then the adaptive process begins: the couple begins to move through its cyclic journey. They resolve the dilemmas posed by the therapist, sometimes superficially, sometimes deeply, thus moving into Resolution. Since they have generally been stuck in Contraction for a long time, this is cause for celebration, and they move rapidly into a brief period of Expansion.

But their hold on the new organization is tenuous; they fall back into Contraction. Now the therapist again helps to disrupt the sequence, perhaps this time helping to bring out qualities that had been precluded by the partners' caricatured roles. The couple again moves into Resolution, then Expansion: being seen as more than an imprisoning stereotype feels liberating, exhilarating.

Still, they cannot sustain the mood of either Resolution or Expansion, and they fall again into Contraction. Again the therapist helps to disrupt, perhaps enabling them to fight openly about an important difference, perhaps enabling them to come together more intimately than they are accustomed to.

Maybe by the third or fourth disruption, the couple can sustain a new organization in Resolution. Both therapist and couple will be tempted to say good-bye—they have achieved their goals. But eventually the couple will again move back into Contraction; they will wonder then if anything they learned really helped, if any of the changes were real. This is a crucial moment in therapy. As the couple's work unravels, the therapist may also feel disheartened.

The therapist with the cyclical view knows better. Her job is to help the couple keep moving through the cycles. She helps the couple see that Contraction is neither truer nor deeper than Resolution or Expansion, but that it is an important aspect of their character. They can avoid Contraction only by becoming rigid and unadaptive. The therapist helps the couple stay longer in Expansion, because they realize that Expansion also reflects much of who they are and is neither self-delusion nor necessarily setting themselves up for a (bad) fall. And, of course, the therapist helps the couple enjoy the safety and perspective of Resolution, but without getting so attached to it that they shut out the other two stages.

For most couples, one stage is less developed than the others. For example, some couples move constantly between romantic moments and angry fights, but know little about compromise, negotiation, or the discussion of differences. Others alternate between Resolution's calm conversations and Contraction's silent alienation, but know little about Expansion's exuberance and intimacy. The development of one stage may require a fuller development of the others as well. One task of therapy, therefore, is to help expand the couple's experience of their underdeveloped stage.

Couples will continue to cycle. Their capacity to accept themselves in the fullness of the cycles is a far better measure of well-being than any rigid adherence to the codes of Resolution, which seem to be the accepted standards of adulthood in our "therapeutic culture."

## Questions and Answers

All theory is like a flashlight. If it is any good, it lights up the places where you direct its beacon. We would like to illustrate the usefulness of our theory of couple development by clarifying questions that have arisen from participants in seminars and workshops where we have presented this material.

Q: Why don't you talk more about children in this book?

A: We agonized over this question for a long time. No factor divides the experience of couples more than whether they have children or not. And nothing affects the lives of couples with children more than their kids. Couples with young children usually sleep less and, especially if they both work, are more stressed than other couples. They have less time for themselves, fewer intimate moments, less time to let fights play out—so their fights often go underground.

Children's developmental markers have deep impacts on the lives of their parents: when the first child goes off to school; when one or more children enter adolescence; when the first and last child leaves home. All these markers influence couples, both directly and indirectly: when children leave, we relive our own departures from home and reexperience our feelings of loss; or, trying to do better than our parents, we try to heal ourselves by reworking our own childhood through the ways we treat our children.

This is just the tip of the iceberg: we could write an entire book on the ways that children influence couples or on the reciprocal relationship of parents and children. But that has been done many times over. It is called family systems theory.

The distinction between couples with and without children is not simple. Many couples without children spend a lot of time considering whether they want children or not. And couples who want children but who cannot easily have them—this includes same-sex couples as well as couples with an infertility problem—often launch into lengthy, costly, and emotionally wrenching attempts to bring them into their lives. These attempts—infertility workups, artificial insemination, in-vitro attempts at becoming pregnant, efforts at adoption—sometimes succeed and sometimes do not. Still other couples make a decision—sometimes unequally shared—*not* to have children.

In writing this book, we wanted to develop a theory that would have the broadest possible applicability. We wanted to avoid a prescriptive theory of stages—i.e., that having children is the *normal* way for couples to go. We wanted couples both with and without children to be able to relate their experiences to the book. So we decided to focus on experience between partners and to deemphasize the influence of children—much as we deemphasized the specific influence of work, religion, and community.

Q: Can it happen that *one* partner is in one stage and the *other* in another? I'm thinking of a couple where the woman seems very happy with her life, but her husband is always complaining.

A: Individuals may differ from each other but couples are a collective entity who are in one stage or another. There are many couples in which one member is usually in a much better place than the other. These are "complementary" couples. But the complementary relationship moves through the three stages.

When they meet, for example, the unhappy person gains a caretaker, the caretaker gets to nurture someone, and, together, they feel enhanced; they each have an outlet for their yearnings. Later the caretaker may feel stuck in the role and dole large doses of punishment with each helpful effort; the unhappy partner may come to believe that it is his partner's good fortune or "phony" good mood that keeps him down and punish his partner by making himself harder and harder to help. In Resolution, they may work out a deal whereby help is measured out in moderate doses, with some even crossing the complementary line to the helper, and punishment is kept to a minimum. This may be such a relief that the next time the unhappy person comes for help, the happy person lavishes care, making the unhappy person feel fuller, more complete—and so the cycle begins again.

Stages have to do with the mood and organization of the relationship, not the internal state of partners. Hence, paradoxically, a relatively unhappy person can participate in a Stage of Expansion and Promise, and a relatively happy person can participate in a stage of Contraction and Betrayal.

Q: Your theory seems to work when partners are similar, when they tend to be in the same place at the same time. But what happens when they are very different. What, for example, do you have to say about "mixed marriages?"

A: In one sense, every marriage is a "mixed marriage." One

partner is older, the other younger. One comes from one ethnic or cultural group, the other from a different one. The partners in every couple bring tremendous diversity into their relationship.

For some people of mixed religion or mixed culture, however, conflict seems to arise constantly. Relatives sometimes have a way of fanning this. But the conflict cannot be blamed on relatives, for the partners themselves may hold very different attitudes and expectations, and the question of *loyalty* to one's traditions and the issue of each partner's own *cultural identity* may be crucial.

The partners of a "mixed marriage" may spend a good deal of time defining the character of their couple around how they deal with the difference. Will they celebrate two holidays in December, or one—which one?—or none? Will they try to bring his black relatives together with her white family, or will they spend time separately with the two? Or will they withdraw from both? Couples organized around a major difference identified as "mixed" will often find themselves moving—slipping into a new stage or starting a new cycle—in relation to shifts in how this difference affects them. The death of a parent, a period of relative financial well-being, the birth of a child, and so on can all trigger profound family and personal conflicts inherent in that major difference.

In such cases, a healthy mutual respect for each other's traditions seems the best guide. Partners whose relationship bridges ethnic or cultural worlds will need to face their differences honestly. Their capacity to revel in the differences in Expansion, and to negotiate and compromise in Resolution, will determine their longevity.

Q: Do some couples only have two stages, at least after the first few cycles?

A: This is a question that comes up often. People recognize that they are alternating between Resolution and Contraction but feel that they no longer experience anything like the expansiveness of the first stage. Others say that they alternate between Expansion and Contraction, going "up and down like a yo-yo" or "like a roller coaster," but never find a way to talk with each other in the reasonable way of Resolution.

We are a little uncertain on this point. At the least, Expansion in the first group and Resolution in the second seem very brief and very underdeveloped. On reflection, we do think that all three stages persist in every couple, that at least the potential—and dormant organization—for the underdeveloped stage is always there, ready to find expression. We have seen couples dulled by years in Contraction, with only brief forays in Resolution, suddenly burst forth into an expansive phase. This might happen after they have been shaken by an explicit discussion of divorce or after an unexpected joy (a child born to a long infertile couple). And we have seen couples whose capacity for Resolution has been almost nonexistent begin to have reasonable conversations—sometimes with the help of therapy, sometimes with common entry into a Twelve-Step program or a religious community.

Q: Does this mean that we can develop underdeveloped stages?

A: Yes. In fact, one way to conceive of therapy is the development of the underdeveloped stage. For some couples, for example, the fear of fighting keeps their relationship very muted, yet they openly regret the absence of passionate sex. By enabling them to find the courage to fight—that is, to dare to remain in Contraction for more than a moment—we often increase their capacity for authentic sexual engagement.

Other couples need to learn how to talk: to listen to one another, to take responsibility for one's own part in a struggle, to compromise. Learning to talk and compromise tends to provide the stability that lets them take chances with each other, thus enhancing both the Stage of Resolution and the Stage of Contraction.

Some couples are at home in Contraction and Resolution but look at the Expansion as a foreign country. Still, they yearn to sail to its faraway shores. Sometimes, in "growth-oriented" therapy, we provide the encouragement for the partners to step outside of their conservative skins—together, at the same time—and to slowly build a synergistic process. He might talk about a sad childhood incident that he had kept to himself for years; she might respond with a touch, a hug, where before she had only listened; he might cry and she console. Later the roles may be reversed. Then, for a time, they may feel very tender, very close, both young and old at the same time— together with so much more of themselves.

With the development of the underdeveloped stage, the whole cycle changes. How? We leave it to you to imagine for yourself what would happen to your whole relationship if the least developed stage become much better developed. But this leads to another general question.

Q: Can the pattern of a couple's cycles change over time? Or are you saying that once they get into a pattern their course is somehow fixed and determined?

A: The most consistent fact about couples is their capacity for change. At the same time, couples tend to follow the routines and patterns the partners have evolved together. Having said this, though, the answer to the question is, yes. The pattern of a couple's cycles can and does change all the time.

For example, a couple that had been moving regularly through three-stage cycles may suddenly enter a period of unexpected and repeated setbacks. They may stagger under the blows, slide into Contraction, and then—with great effort—climb out into a period of Resolution, only to be hit with another crisis. After several crises of this sort, they may find themselves unable to try to get out of Contraction. Defeat and failure seem to bind them, but they cannot get away. Consider a couple whose happy marriage founders in a period of infertility. Finally she becomes pregnant ... then miscarries. The partners try to be supportive, but blame each other all the same. Suppose he then begins to drink and loses his job. They apply for adoption, but—just as they are on the verge of getting their child—the birth mother changes her mind, and they are left staring at a marvelously furnished but empty baby's room. A parade of events like this can stop the pattern of a couple's cycling, and mire them in one stage or another. They can become stuck.

Q: Do stages get longer and longer as a couple moves on in life?

A: It may happen that way, but not necessarily. Most couples spend longer and longer periods of time in their Home Base as they get older; and it is more likely than not that the Home Base will become Resolution after a long marriage and after the individual partners are older. But couples are always capable of moving into a new stage and disrupting their rhythm. Depending on the issues they have in their own lives and on the events that they meet, they may move more slowly or more rapidly through the three stages. It is hard to predict with any certainty.

Q: What does your theory have to say about couples who resign themselves to bad marriages?

A: Resignation to an unfulfilling marriage may be a constantly bitter and emotionally unsettling experience for one or both partners, or it may be easier, more acceptable, and, eventually, more settled. When bitter, it is like a Cold War, periodically flaring up in fights and threats of separation and divorce. With each fight, the couple's original pain reemerges: separation seems both frightening and a desirable solution, a way to escape. The thought of divorce is a constant companion to severely troubled couples.

The resigned couples who become settled manage to find ways of enduring the difficulty. Their resignation moves toward disengagement. They pull back from each other and from the promise their marriage once held. Some can hold this position indefinitely. Others may find separate ways to heal their wounds and restore some of the confidence that had been damaged by their struggles. Eventually some of these disengaged couples may find a way to renew their relationship, although they are always ready to return to their distant fortresses at the least provocation.

Q: What happens to a couple after a divorce? Don't the partners still have *some* kind of relationship with each other? What does your theory say about that?

A: Couples can continue going through cycles even after divorce. Especially when children are involved, partners can move into a new period of Expansion, stumble into yet another period of chilly Contraction, and emerge into a period of Resolution.

Consider, for example, parents whose divorce was bitter and nasty. They slowly emerge from Contraction into a new state of Resolution—organized by the divorce agreement, whose rules now regulate their behavior. After a period of time, they may feel that the divorce was "for the best," and both partners begin to get along in their separate lives. Soon, although the bitter feelings persist, they find themselves able to pick up the kids without rancorous scenes; and they are able to communicate about the daily or weekly details of their children's lives with a new sense of pleasure. They can talk, but not be hurt. A modest Expansive Stage opens up.

Sooner or later, though, an argument may burst the bubble. One partner's delay in bringing the kids to the other's house, just before a long vacation trip, say, or on the eve of a major holiday, may infuriate the latter and lead to a horrible battle. Now the partners revisit the worst scenes of their time together. They are again convinced that "nothing has changed." They congratulate themselves in having divorced, but swear that they will from now on have *nothing* to do with each other. This period of Contraction continues until some other shift in needs, events, or relationships may manage to lift them past it—say, one child's graduation from school, or birthday party, or sudden injury, brings both parents together again, similarly concerned, or similarly touched.

Divorce is a *point* in a couple's relationship. It may be a decisive endpoint. It may be an inflection point, ushering in a new kind of relationship, that still follows many of the basic lines of their lifelong pattern. When divorced partners continue their relationship for years on end, the relationship follows the cycles described in the preceding chapters.

Q: What about blended families? What particular problems will they have, and how does it fit your theory of cycles?

A: With the divorce and remarriage rates so high, blended families are a very important contemporary phenomenon. A couple will split, and instead of two partners, there may soon be four ... or even more: Billy and Susie split. Billy meets Gwen, who used to be with Steven. Susie meets Hal, who used to be with Nan. The next year, in order to arrange a simple "family" Thanksgiving dinner, Billy, Susie, Gwen, Steven, Hal, and Nan must all talk to one another (and to their parents and their other children). This is the tip of the iceberg of the blended family.

Being part of a blended family *demands* a complex perspective. The matrix in which one lives is marvelously interwoven. Many different people's needs, desires, agendas, contracts, broken promises, past hurts, family loyalties, and recurrent disappointments are all entwined together. Every simple decision seems like a U.N. resolution.

The most complex aspect of blended families is that many different cycles are all going on at the same time, intersecting each other and causing unimaginable difficulties as an everyday matter of course. The cycles of the first married pair intersect those of the second married pair. When one set of ex-marrieds is going through a severe time of Contraction, it will affect everyone else who has to negotiate with them for time or care. When one set of currently marrieds is going through an expansive period, they may seem almost intolerably happy to their former spouses, triggering off any number of uncooperative maneuvers. We advise the partners in a blended family to identify their own stages and cycles and perhaps observe those of the others with whom their lives are involved.

Q: Will someone go through the same kind of cycles in a second, third, or subsequent relationship?

A: No. The cycles we go through as couples depend on the mix of both partners. First of all, we change over time, so that we ourselves are never the same in two subsequent relationships. Furthermore, if our partners differ, our present couple can never be exactly the same. This explains the well-known observation that a person can be happy and carefree in one relationship, the "rock of stability" in another, but an earnest partner in the third.

Q: If I read you right, your "Transformations" chapter seems like an argument *for* a couple's staying together and *against* their splitting up. Isn't this a somewhat moralistic stance?

A: We're not saying that all couples or any particular kind of couple ought to stay together. Couples split for good reason. Maintaining a relationship is like navigating a branching river: some make it through a series of forks; others do not. The chapter on "Transformations" was meant to describe the experience of those relatively few couples who manage to turn things around, who snatch victory from the jaws of defeat. It's not a prescription for other couples to follow. But it is true that we admire these couples.

Q: I'm thinking about a couple that has been together a long time, and has gone through a lot of different experiences together. How do the partners manage to balance the changes each individual partner goes through, which may seem at times to threaten the couple's stability?

A: That's a wonderful question. People in couples are constantly changing, and their relationship is constantly changing, too. The art of balancing their experience together, so that neither of them bears the burden of underwriting the other's individual "growth," is the secret that keeps a couple alive. We have dealt with some of the issues involved in this question in our chapters on Resolution and Transformation.

If the partners genuinely love and respect each other, each will try to make allowances for what the other really needs. At the same time, they won't do things that hurt their partners. Usually, one partner feels a pressure for change, and that pressure creates a new crisis. If they can resolve the crisis with their usual methods of compromise, negotiation, and balancing off, that's how they'll handle it. But if the crisis is too different—say, if the wife has decided to go back to graduate school and pursue a career, and the husband doesn't think they can afford this—they will have to explore new ground. They will haul out new issues of entitlement, commitment, and mutual sacrifice. They may arrange for one partner to pursue his or her career for several years, and then encourage the other. They may move apart for a while, each exploring what it might mean to live a little *less* closely to the other, and then come back together to renegotiate a conjoint plan.

If the request puts a tremendous strain on the couple—say, if one partner decides he or she wants to have an affair—the couple will have to fall all the way back to their original contract together. They may then want to renegotiate this contract, either openly or tacitly. Or they may find that they simply can't renegotiate it, and they will acknowledge having reached a turning point of great import. Something will then have to give.

Q: How do you look at the issues involved when one partner's development seems at odds with his or her involvement in their couple?

A: Both the couple and its individual partners are always growing and developing. Every couple has to deal with how these two different entities affect each other. Balancing the partners' growth against the growth of the couple involves considering (1) each partner's stage of individual development, and the challenges he or she is facing in life; (2) the stage of development the couple has reached over time, and the particular challenges the partners are facing together; (3) the relationship between these two; and (4) the relationship between the challenges a couple is facing and the couple's place in their three-stage cycle, including its resting place.

This leads back to the question of difference in the couple. Couples need to build both a sense of connectedness and a belief that both partners can grow through the relationship. Enduring couples are more likely to accept and tolerate differences in each other's wants and needs.

Partners sometimes reach times in their lives when they need more time alone, or more time with others, or more time for their work or projects. They are not acting to sabotage or undermine the couple, only to redefine their place in it, for the current period. It is important to try to understand this, and to adapt and adjust to the changes one's mate is making.

## Philosophical Valediction

Broadly speaking, a couple's move through the three-stage cycles can be seen from two perspectives: The first emphasizes conflict, movement, and change; the second, harmony, stability, and inclusion.

According to the first perspective, couples are really quite different in each of their three stages. Each stage finds the partners feeling differently, behaving differently, and following different images and rhythms. In addition, the couple seems different every time it makes a transition back to some stage in which it has been before. It doesn't just "go back" to that stage: it "moves ahead" to revisit it. Each immersion, each transition, is an entry into a new time and place, a new context, a new phase of relationship, a new reality. Following this view, couples are constantly on the move, ever seeking new territory, ever discovering new aspects of themselves, both singly and together.

The difference between the two partners is a force that continually drives them forward. Tension keeps waxing and waning between the individual partners (the "ones") and the couple (the "two"). Differences between the partners, changes in their social context or in their developmental course, all constantly act to destabilize the couple. Their effort to solve contradictions and reequilibrate leads them from stage to stage, ever seeking new solutions. Difference thus gives the couple life, feeling, pain, accomplishment, history.

According to this perspective, the "one" and the "two" tumble over each other like the ends of a rotating dumbbell, as the couple moves through time together.

According to the second perspective, the couple takes its identity from its core imagery, its core conflicts and core patterns. All three stages blend into its basic character and unitary identity. Over time, differences diminish: they are subsumed into the couple's overall life. The process is like making a stew: the diverse ingredients gradually blend with one another, creating a new entity, neither dominated by any particular ingredient nor readily betraying its constituents.

The second perspective seeks out the unity, the harmony in things, in relationships, in ourselves. In a sense, all three stages are me, all three stages are you, all three stages are us. Even though everything constantly changes, the basic themes and images are the same, through all the shifting oscillations and rhythms. The complexity of our relationship is no longer confusing but is seen as its very nature: the particular complexity of our life together. Our acceptance of the tensions—between stages, between your preferred stage and mine, between you and me—stabilizes us and creates our character.

Of these perspectives can both be combined—for at times we emphasize the *difference* in our relationship, and at times we emphasize the stability. Cycles are not timeless, and the stages do change over time. We may continually reenter the same stream—but never at the same spot.

The endless flux between self and other, separateness and connection, despair and fulfillment, plays itself out in several contexts; in our time, one of the most central contexts is within the framework of the couple. Being part of a couple permits each one of us to participate in life's mythic struggles. The struggle is formidable, the obstacles fierce, but some couples manage to make it through. Some make it through for a few months, others for a few years; and some manage to hold together, through all the twists and turnings of the road, for several decades and even a lifetime. Those couples who manage to endure the years of turmoil and uncertainty strike us as truly heroic.

# REFERENCES

## PREFACE

1. Christopher Lasch, *The Culture of Narcissism: American Life in an Age of Diminishing Expectations* (New York: W.W. Norton, 1978).

2. Robert N. Bellah, Richard Madsen, William Sullivan, Ann Swidler, and Steven Tipton, *Habits of the Heart* (Berkeley: University of California Press, 1985).

3. The prototype of this book for our own generation was *Childhood and Society,* by Erik Erikson (New York: W.W. Norton, 1950).

4. Daniel L. Levinson, *The Seasons of a Man's Life* (New York: Knopf, 1978).

5. Gail Sheehy, *Passages: Predictable Crises of Adult Life* (New York: Bantam Books, 1976).

6. Carol Gilligan (*In a Different Voice: Psychological Theory and Women's Development* [Cambridge: Harvard University Press, 1982]), for example, took Lawrence Kohlberg (*Collected Papers on Moral Development and Moral Education* [Cambridge: Moral Education Research Foundation, Harvard University, 1973]) to task because his theory of moral development emphasizes and values the development typical of men more than that of women. Because of this emphasis on male qualities, such as making decisions free from

one's social context, few women—but many men—appear to reach moral maturity.

## CHAPTER 2

1. See the discussion on romantic love in Annette Lawson's *Adultery: An Analysis of Love and Betrayal* (New York: Basic Books, 1988). Also see Joseph Bedier's *Tristan and Isolde,* translated by Hilaire Belloc and Paul Rosenfeld (New York: Vintage Books, 1965); Denis de Rougemont's *Love in the Western World* (Princeton: Princeton University Press, 1983 [1939]); and George Duby's *The Knight, the Lady, and the Priest: The Making of Modern Marriage in Mediaeval France* (London: Allen Lane, 1984). Consider also the discussion in Ethel Spector Person's *Dreams of Love and Fateful Encounters: The Power of Romantic Passion* (New York: W.W. Norton, 1988).

2. See de Rougemont, op. cit.; also see Robert C. Solomon, *About Love* (New York: Simon and Schuster, 1988).

3. See Denis de Rougement, op. cit.

4. Consider the rash of motion pictures on this theme, from *Kramer vs. Kramer* to *The War of the Roses.*

5. There are demographical analyses of the lives of couples by Oliver Bjorksten and Thomas J. Stewart in "Contemporary Trends in American Marriage," pp. 3–59, in Carol C. Nadelson and Derek C. Polonsky, eds., *Marriage and Divorce: a Contemporary Perspective* (New York: Guilford, 1984). Also see Philip Blumstein and Pepper Schwartz, *American Couples: Money, Work, Sex* (New York: William Morrow, 1983).

6. For those interested in reading about the history of the American (or Western) couple and family, we suggest John Demos, "Myths and Realities in the History of American Family Life," in Henry Grunebaum and Jacob Christ, eds., *Contemporary Marriage: Structure, Dynamics, and Therapy* (Boston: Little, Brown, 1976), pp. 9–32. Also see Demos, *Past, Present and Personal: the Family and the Life Course in American History* (New York: Oxford University Press, 1986); Ellen Rothman, *Hands and Hearts: A History of Courtship in America* (New York: Basic Books, 1984); and Edward Shorter, *The Making of the Modern Family* (New York: Basic Books, 1975).

7. See Barbara Ehrenreich, Elizabeth Hess, and Gloria Jacobs,

*Remaking Love: the Feminization of Sex* (Garden City, N.Y.: Anchor/Doubleday, 1986). See also Annette Lawson, op. cit., and Francesca Cancian, *Love in America: Gender and Self-Development* (Cambridge: Cambridge University Press, 1987).

8. There are many new books—such as Harriet Lerner's *The Dance of Anger* (New York, Harper and Row, 1985); Lilian Rubin's *Intimate Strangers: Men and Women Together* (New York: Harper and Row, 1983); and Deborah Tannen's *You Just Don't Understand: Women and Men in Conversation* (New York: William Morrow, 1990)—which offer explanations for the difficulty of intimate relationships between women and men.

9. See Ellen K. Rothman, op. cit.

10. Readers interested in family systems theory may find the following books helpful in learning about the basic tenets of the field: *Foundations of Family Therapy,* by Lynn Hoffman (New York: Basic Books, 1981); *Families and Family Therapy,* by Salvador Minuchin (Cambridge: Harvard University Press, 1974); *Change,* by Paul Watzlawick, John Weakland, and Richard Fisch (New York: W.W. Norton, 1974); *The Aesthetics of Change,* by Bradford P. Keeney (New York: Guilford Press, 1983); *The Family Interpreted,* by Deborah Anna Luepnitz (New York: Basic Books, 1988); *Family Therapy: Full-Length Case Studies,* edited by Peggy Papp (New York: Gardner Press, 1977); *The Family's Construction of Reality,* by David Reiss (Cambridge: Harvard University Press, 1981).

11. Erich Fromm's *The Art of Loving* (New York: Harper and Row, 1955) may be the first of a long line of books espousing this point of view, which has become as much a commonplace in therapeutic circles as it is in *Cosmopolitan, Redbook,* and *Glamour.*

## CHAPTER 3

1. The cultural narrative is a notion comparable to *Zeitgeist.* We have chosen to talk of it as a narrative because the social, economic, and cultural factors that give rise to the spirit of the times are crystallized in, and expressed through, stories. It is through images and stories that these broad influences are brought to individuals. Since we wanted a concept that bridged the gap between large social forces and individual consciousness, we chose the term "cultural narrative."

More thinkers than we can name have influenced the idea of a cultural narrative, from Hegel and Nietzsche in the philosophical tradition to F. O. Matthiesson, Randolph Bourne, and Van Wyck Brooks in the tradition of American letters. Barry Dym described the concept of "inventing" history in an unpublished doctoral dissertation, *The Chaos of a New Freedom* (Harvard University, 1972).

2. Among the most influential of the feminist writings are Nancy Chodorow's *The Reproduction of Mothering: Psychoanalysis and the Sociology of Gender* (Berkeley: University of California Press, 1978); Dorothy Dinnerstein's *The Mermaid and the Minotaur: Sexual Arrangements and Human Malaise* (New York: Harper and Row, 1976); Carol Gilligan's *In a Different Voice: Psychological Theory and Women's Development* (Cambridge: Harvard University Press, 1982); and Jean Baker Miller's *Toward a New Psychology of Women* (Boston: Beacon Press, 1976). See also: *Making a Difference: Psychology and the Construction of Gender,* by Rachel Hare-Mustin and Jeanne Marecek, eds. (New Haven: Yale University Press, 1990); *The Family Interpreted: Feminist Theory in Clinical Practice,* by Deborah Anna Luepnitz (New York: Basic Books, 1988); *The Invisible Web: Gender Patterns in Family Relationships,* edited by Marianne Walters, Betty Carter, Peggy Papp, and Olga Silverstein (New York: Guilford Press, 1988); and *Women's Growth in Connection: Writings from the Stone Center,* by Judith V. Jordan, Alexandra G. Kaplan, Jean Baker Miller, Irene P. Stiver, and Janet L. Surrey (New York: Guilford Press, 1991).

3. See *Women's Ways of Knowing: The Development of Self, Voice, and Mind,* by Mary Field Belenky, Blythe McVicker Clinchy, Nancy Rule Goldberger, and Jill Mattuch Tarule (New York: Basic Books, 1986).

## CHAPTER 4

1. This chapter borrows liberally from object relations theory. The borrowing is general; we follow no one school or theorist but have naturally learned a great deal from D. W. Winnicott (see *Playing and Reality* [London: Tavistock Publications, 1971]); W. R. D. Fairbairn (see *An Object Relations Theory of Personality* [New York: Basic Books, 1954]); Harry Guntrip (*Psychoanalytic Theory, Therapy and the Self* [New York: Basic Books, 1971]); Karen Horney (see *New Ways in Psychoanalysis* [New York: W.W. Norton, 1939]); Otto

Kernberg (see *Object Relations Theory and Clinical Practice* [New York: Jason Aronson, 1976]).

We do not subscribe to all of the ideas of the object relations theorists and, in particular, we depart from the pathological emphasis of concepts like "identifications" and "introjects." We are actually closer to Piaget's cognitive psychology—in particular, to the idea that children "internalize" templates or "schema" from the external world, including schema of new situations to which they have "accommodated" (see Jean Piaget, *The Child's Construction of Reality* [London: Routledge Paul and Kegan, 1955]).

2. Here we are again borrowing from the object relations theorists and, in particular, from the ideas of projective identification. For readers interested in further exploring these ideas, see Henry V. Dicks's *Marital Tensions: Clinical Studies Towards a Psychological Theory of Interaction* (London: Routledge and Kegan Paul, 1967). The best contemporary work is probably Thomas H. Ogden's *Projective Identification: Psychotherapeutic Technique* (New York: Jason Aronson, 1982). An excellent popular explanation of projective identification is provided by Maggie Scarf's *Intimate Partners: Patterns in Love and Marriage* (New York: Random House, 1987).

3. "Splitting" is an important concept in object relations theory. Here we use it much as Thomas Ogden, op cit., does.

4. See Fritz S. Perls, *Ego, Hunger and Aggression* (New York: Random House, 1969; first published in 1947 by Allen & Unwin, London).

## CHAPTER 5

1. The distinction between symmetrical and complementary systems was originally drawn by Gregory Bateson in his anthropological monograph, *Naven* (Palo Alto: Stanford University Press, 1958). Bateson amplified this in *Steps to an Ecology of Mind* (New York: Ballantine Books, 1972). It was then adopted by many family systems therapists, beginning with P. Watzlawick, D. Jackson, and J. Beavin in their now classic *Pragmatics of Human Communication* (New York: W.W. Norton, 1967).

2. Consider, for example, the views expressed in Robert J. Sternberg and Michael L. Barnes, eds., *The Psychology of Love* (New Haven: Yale University Press, 1988); or the general tenor of the

essays in Willard Gaylin and Ethel Person, eds., *Passionate Attachments: Thinking About Love* (New York: Free Press, 1988). Maggie Scarf's adherence to object relations theory in her work, op. cit., can also be understood to pathologize the experience of the Expansive Stage.

3. These terms originate with Carl G. Jung. See his "Anima and Animus," in *Aspects of the Feminine* (Princeton: Princeton University Press, 1982, pp. 77–100).

4. Virginia Woolf's *Orlando* (New York: Harcourt Brace Jovanovich, no year given; original, 1928) expresses some of this delightful quality.

5. This is an idea long held by historians commenting on their own craft. The first to articulate the idea of inventing history in its most radical form was probably Van Wyck Brooks in his essay "A Usable Past," in *Three Essays on America* (New York: Knopf, 1934).

The notion has grown in psychoanalytic circles and in the realm of recent literary theory. See, for example, Donald P. Spence's *Narrative Truth and Historical Truth* (New York: W.W. Norton, 1982), and *The Freudian Metaphor: Toward Paradigm Change in Psychoanalysis* (New York: W.W. Norton, 1987). See also Roy Schafer's *The Analytic Attitude* (New York: Basic Books, 1983). See also Carolyn G. Heilbrun, op. cit.

6. Clifford Sager pioneered the idea of implicit marital contracts. See *Marriage Contracts and Couple Therapy: Hidden Forces in Intimate Relationships* (New York: Brunner/Mazel, 1976).

## CHAPTER 6

1. Theodore Roethke, "In a Dark Time," in *The Collected Poems of Theodore Roethke* (New York: Anchor/Doubleday, 1975), p. 231.

## CHAPTER 8

1. *Webster's Third New International Dictionary,* Unabridged (Springfield, Mass.; G. and C. Merriam, 1981), p. 376.

2. See Gregory Bateson, op. cit.

## CHAPTER 9

1. For those who want to read further about sequences, we suggest Jay Haley's *Problem-Solving Therapy* (New York: Harper and Row, 1976); Salvadore Minuchin's *Families and Family Therapy* (Cambridge: Harvard University Press, 1974); Lynn Hoffman's "Enmeshment and the Too Richly Cross-Joined System," *Family Process,* 14 (1975), 457–68; and Barry Dym's "Eating Disorders and the Family: a Model for Intervention," in *Theory and Treatment of Anorexia Nervosa and Bulimia: Biomedical, Sociocultural and Psychological Perspectives,* Steven Wiley Emmett, ed. (New York: Brunner/Mazel, 1985).

2. David Kantor and Will Lehr's *Inside the Family* (San Francisco: Jossey-Bass, 1975) was one of the first works describing the positions people play in family sequences. According to them, family members act as mover, opposer, follower, or bystander, and these roles in their family's interactional sequences become part of their family identity.

3. Sequences vary in the length of time they span and the ground they encompass. Many, for instance, take place within minutes; others play out over days and weeks, and still others may evolve slowly, over months and even years. See Bruenlein, op. cit., and Dym, op. cit.

4. Triangles—and the process of triangulating—have been discussed extensively in the family therapy literature. See Murray Bowen, *Family Therapy in Clinical Practice* (New York: Jason Aronson, 1978); Minuchin, op. cit.; and Haley, op. cit. It is also a well-developed concept in social psychology. See T. Caplow, *Two Against One: Coalitions in Triads* (Englewood Cliffs, N.J.: Prentice-Hall, 1968).

5. Amy Tan, *The Joy Luck Club* (New York: G. P. Putnam's Sons, 1989), p. 12.

6. The archetypal dance of pursuit and distance has become a commonplace of the family therapy literature; the idea's origins are difficult to trace. For example, Phoebe Prosky's unpublished article "Some Thoughts on Family Life from the Field of Family Therapy" approached this idea. David Kantor talked about such an idea when he spoke of "psychopolitics"; see *Inside the Family* (San Francisco: Jossey-Bass, 1975). Barry Dym wrote an unpublished paper in 1973 called "The Struggle for Power: a Paradigm for Contemporary Couples"; like Phoebe Prosky's article, it was circulated quite a bit. David

C. Treadway's "Learning Their Dance, Changing Some Steps," in *Casebook of Marital Therapy,* Alan Gurman, ed. (New York: Guilford, 1985), is an excellent and relatively recent incarnation of the idea as applied to couples dealing with alcohol abuse. Furthermore, psychodynamic and feminist writers have offered comparable versions of this idea. In other words, it is common property by now.

## CHAPTER 10

1. Gregory Bateson talks about systems in disequilibrium in which the process of change "feeds on the random." In other words, systems that are off balance may be influenced by all kinds of random and otherwise peripheral forces because these systems are so vulnerable to change. See *Mind and Nature: A Necessary Unity* (New York: E.P. Dutton, 1979), pp. 47–48.

## CHAPTER 11

1. This is a basic tenet of general systems theory, first elaborated by Ludwig von Bertalanffy in *General Systems Theory* (New York: George Braziller, 1968).

2. Bradford P. Keeney offers this tightrope-walker metaphor in his excellent discussion of cybernetic theory, *Aesthetics of Change* (New York: Guilford Press, 1983).

3. Oscillation between states of equilibrium and disequilibrium has been described by many scientists. Family therapists particularly draw from Ilya Prigogine, "Structure, Dissipation and Life," in *Theoretical Physics and Biology* (Amsterdam: North-Holland Publishing Co., 1969). The influence of the disequilibrium theorists is most accessible in Lynn Hoffman, op. cit.

4. The family theorist who pioneered and proselytized notions of differentiation was Murray Bowen, op. cit., but the idea is common among psychodynamic writers. They tend to chart the development of children in terms of successive separation/individuation crises in which the child gradually establishes an autonomous personality, separate from its mother (parent). A good place to start in this literature is Margaret S. Mahler, Fred Pine, and Anni Bergman, *The Psychological Birth of the Human Infant: Symbiosis and Individuation* (New

York: Basic Books, 1975). For a more popular version, see Louise J. Kaplan's *Oneness and Separateness: From Infant to Individual* (New York: Simon and Schuster, 1978).

## CHAPTER 12

1. In 1990 Barry Dym asked a faculty group at the Family Institute of Cambridge, "Why do some couples come back from long periods of alienation, separation, and contemplation of divorce?" The resulting discussion was both enlightening and helpful in confirming the notions in this chapter. Participants at that meeting included Carol Becker, Laura Chasin, Richard Chasin, Donna Healey, Jeffrey Kerr, Lee Manoogian, Caroline Marvin, Thomasine McFarlin, Terry Real, Sallyann Roth, Carter Umbarger, Charles Verge, and Kathy Weingarten.

2. See Joseph Campbell, *The Hero with a Thousand Faces* (New York: Pantheon, 1979). Campbell lays out the common ground of the heroic journeys and spiritual quests from many of the world's traditional cultures. This section loosely follows the stages Campbell describes.

3. Joseph Campbell, *The Power of Myth* (New York: Doubleday, 1988), p. 6.

# INDEX